J. OSWALD

SANDERS

THREE SPIRITUAL CLASSICS IN ONE VOLUME

Spiritual Leadership

Spiritual Maturity

Spiritual Discipleship

MOODY PUBLISHERS

CHICAGO

ISBN: 978-0-8024-3412-8

Originally delivered by fleets of horse-drawn wagons, the affordable paperbacks from D. L. Moody's publishing house resourced the church and served everyday people. Now, after more than 125 years of publishing and ministry, Moody Publishers' mission remains the same—even if our delivery systems have changed a bit. For more information on other books (and resources) created from a biblical perspective, go to www.moodypublishers.com or write to:

Moody Publishers
820 N. LaSalle Boulevard
Chicago, IL 60610

1 3 5 7 9 10 8 6 4 2

Printed in China

CONTENTS

Spiritual Leadership

Spiritual Maturity

Spiritual Discipleship

Spiritual Leadership

PRINCIPLES OF EXCELLENCE
FOR EVERY BELIEVER

J. OSWALD SANDERS

Preface

This book had grown out of two series of messages delivered to the leaders of Overseas Missionary Fellowship at conferences in Singapore in 1964 and 1966. It was then suggested that these messages could be amplified and shared with a wider public. The author has acceded to this request.

The principles of leadership in both the temporal and spiritual realms are presented and illustrated in these pages from both Scripture and the lives of eminent men and women of God. Not every reader will have access to many of the biographies from which these illustrations are drawn, and this has encouraged the author to include pertinent incidents from the lives of persons whose leadership has been more than unusually successful. Whenever possible, sources are indicated. In the case of Scripture references, that translation has been used that appeared to the author to be most accurate and expressive.

The material has been presented in a form that is calculated to be of help even to younger Christians in whose hearts the Holy Spirit is working to create a holy ambition to place all their power at the disposal of the Redeemer. If there is something, too, that will rekindle aspirations and crystallize a fresh purpose in the hearts of those further along the road of leadership, the aim of the book will be realized.

J. Oswald Sanders

CHAPTER 1

An Honorable Ambition

To aspire to leadership is an honourable ambition.
1 TIMOTHY 3:1 NEB

Should you then seek great things for yourself?
Seek them not.
JEREMIAH 45:5

Most Christians have reservations about aspiring to leadership. They are unsure about whether it is truly right for a person to want to be a leader. After all, is it not better for the position to seek out the person rather than the person to seek out the position? Has not ambition caused the downfall of numerous otherwise great leaders in the church, people who fell victim to "the last infirmity of noble minds"? Shakespeare expressed a profound truth when his character Wolsey said to the great English general:

Cromwell, I charge thee, fling away ambitions,
By that sin fell the angels; how can a man then,
The image of his Maker, hope to profit by't?

No doubt, Christians must resist a certain kind of ambition and rid it from their lives. But we must also acknowledge other ambitions as noble, worthy, and honorable. The two verses at the beginning of this chapter provide a warning—and an encouragement—for sorting out the difference. When our ambition carries out a burning desire to be effective in the service of God—to realize God's highest potential for our lives—we can keep both of these verses in mind and hold them in healthy tension.

Part of that tension is the difference between Paul's situation and ours. We may understand his statement (1 Timothy 3:1, above) in terms of the prestige and respect given to Christian leaders today. But such was far from Paul's mind. In his day, a bishop faced great danger and worrisome responsibility. Rewards for the work of leading the church were hardship, contempt, rejection, and even death. The leader was first to draw fire in persecution, first in line to suffer.

Seen in this light, Paul's encouragement does not seem so open to misuse by people merely seeking status in the church. Phonies would have little heart for such a difficult assignment. Under the dangerous circumstances that prevailed in the first century, even stouthearted Christians needed encouragement and incentive to lead. And so Paul called leadership an "honorable ambition."

We ought never to forget that the same situation faces Christians today in certain parts of the world. Leaders of the church in China suffered most at the hands of Communists. The leader of the Little Flock in Nepal suffered years in prison after church members had been released. In many troubled areas today, spiritual leadership is no task for those who seek stable benefits and upscale working conditions. It remains true that any form of spiritual warfare will inevitably single out leaders who by their role present obvious targets.

Paul urges us to the work of leading within the church, the most important work in the world. When our motives are right, this work pays eternal dividends. In Paul's day, only a deep love for Christ and genuine concern for the church could motivate people to lead. But in many cultures today where Christian leadership carries prestige and privilege, people aspire to leadership for reasons quite unworthy and self-seeking. Holy ambition has always been surrounded by distortions.

And so we find the ancient prophet Jeremiah giving his servant Baruch some very wise and simple counsel: "Are you seeking great things for yourself? Don't do it!" (Jeremiah 45:5 NLT). Jeremiah was not condemning all ambition as sinful, but he was pointing to selfish motivation that makes ambition wrong—"great things for yourself." Desiring to excel is not a sin. It is motivation that determines ambition's character. Our Lord never taught against the urge to high achievement, but He did expose and condemn unworthy motivation.

All Christians are called to develop God-given talents, to make the most of their lives, and to develop to the fullest their God-given gifts and capabilities. But Jesus taught that ambition that centers on the self is wrong. Speaking to young ministers about to be ordained, the great missionary leader Bishop Stephen Neill said: "I am inclined to think that ambition in any ordinary sense of the term is nearly always sinful in ordinary men. I am certain that in the Christian it is always sinful, and that it is most inexcusable of all in the ordained minister."[1]

Ambition which centers on the glory of God and welfare of the church is a mighty force for good.

The word *ambition* comes from a Latin word meaning "campaigning for promotion." The phrase suggests a variety of elements: social visibility and approval, popularity, peer recognition, the exercise of authority over others. Ambitious people, in this sense, enjoy the power that comes with money, prestige, and authority. Jesus had no time for such ego-driven ambitions. The true spiritual leader will never "campaign for promotion."

To His "ambitious" disciples Jesus announced a new standard of greatness: "You know that those who are regarded as rulers of the Gentiles lord it over them, and their high officials exercise authority over them. Not so with you. Instead, whoever wants to become great among you must be your servant, and whoever wants to be first must be slave of all" (Mark 10:42–44). We will consider this amazing statement at length in a later chapter. Here at the outset of this study of spiritual leadership, we will simply highlight Jesus' master principle: True greatness, true leadership, is found in giving yourself in service to others, not in coaxing or inducing others to serve you. True service is never without cost. Often it comes with a bitter cup of challenges and a painful baptism of suffering. For genuine godly leadership weighs carefully Jesus' question: "Can you drink the cup I drink or be baptized with the baptism I am baptized with?" (Mark 10:38b). The real spiritual leader is focused on the service he and she can render to God and other people, not on the residuals and perks of high office or holy title. We must aim to put more into life than we take out.

"One of the outstanding ironies of history is the utter disregard of ranks and titles in the final judgments men pass on each other," said Samuel Brengle, the great Salvation Army revival preacher. "The final estimate of men shows that history cares not an iota for the rank or title a man has borne, or the office he has held, but only the quality of his deeds and the character of his mind and heart."[2]

"Let it once be fixed that a man's ambition is to fit into God's plan for him, and he has a North Star ever in sight to guide him steadily over any sea, however shoreless it seems," wrote S. D. Gordon in one of his well-known devotional books. "He has a compass that points true in the thickest fog and fiercest storm, and regardless of magnetic rocks."

The great leader Count Nikolaus von Zinzendorf (1700–1760) was tempted by rank and riches; indeed, he is most widely known by the title of honor noted here. But his attitude toward ambition was summed up in one simple statement: "I have one passion: it is He, He alone." Zinzendorf turned from self-seeking to become the founder and leader of the Moravian Church. His followers learned from their leader and circled the world with his passion. Before missionary work was popular or well-organized, the Moravians established overseas churches that had three times as many members as did their churches back home—a most unusual accomplishment. Indeed, one of every ninety-two Moravians left home to serve as a missionary.

Because we children of Adam want to become great,
He became small.

Because we will not stoop,
He humbled Himself.
Because we want to rule,
He came to serve.

CHAPTER 2

The Search for Leaders

No one from the east or the west
or from the desert can exalt a man.
But it is God who judges:
He brings one down, he exalts another.
PSALM 75:6–7

Give me a man of God—one man,
One mighty prophet of the Lord,
And I will give you peace on earth,
Bought with a prayer and not a sword.
GEORGE LIDDELL[1]

Real leaders are in short supply. Constantly people and groups search for them. A question echoes in every corner of the church—“Who will lead?” Throughout the Bible, God searches for leaders too.

“The Lord has sought out a man after his own heart and appointed him leader of his people” (1 Samuel 13:14).

“Go up and down the streets of Jerusalem, look around and consider, search through her squares. If you can find one person who deals honestly and seeks the truth, I will forgive this city” (Jeremiah 5:1).

"I looked for a man among them who would build up the wall" (Ezekiel 22:30).

The Bible shows us that when God does find a person who is ready to lead, to commit to full discipleship, and take on responsibility for others, that person is used to the limit. Such leaders still have shortcomings and flaws, but despite those limitations, they serve God as spiritual leaders. Such were Moses, Gideon, and David. And in the history of the church, Martin Luther, John Wesley, Adoniram Judson, William Carey, and many others.

To be a leader in the church has always required strength and faith beyond the merely average. Why is our need for leaders so great, and candidates for leadership so few? Every generation faces the stringent demands of spiritual leadership, and most unfortunately turn away. But God welcomes the few who come forward to serve.

"The church is painfully in need of leaders," lamented the English Methodist preacher William Sangster. "I wait to hear a voice and no voice comes. I would rather listen than speak—but there is no clarion voice to listen to."[2]

If the world is to hear the church's voice today, leaders are needed who are authoritative, spiritual, and sacrificial. Authoritative, because people desire reliable leaders who know where they are going and are confident of getting there. Spiritual, because without a strong relationship to God, even the most attractive and competent person cannot lead people to God. Sacrificial, because this trait follows the model of Jesus, who gave Himself for the whole world and who calls us to follow in His steps.

Churches grow in every way when they are guided by

strong, spiritual leaders with the touch of the supernatural radiating in their service. The church sinks into confusion and malaise without such leadership. Today those who preach with majesty and spiritual power are few, and the booming voice of the church has become a pathetic whisper. Leaders today—those who are truly spiritual—must take to heart their responsibility to pass on the torch to younger people as a first-line duty.

Many people regard leaders as naturally gifted with intellect, personal forcefulness, and enthusiasm. Such qualities certainly enhance leadership potential, but they do not define the spiritual leader. True leaders must be willing to suffer for the sake of objectives great enough to demand their wholehearted obedience. Spiritual leaders are not elected, appointed, or created by synods or churchly assemblies. God alone makes them. One does not become a spiritual leader by merely filling an office, taking course work in the subject, or resolving in one's own will to do this task. A person must qualify to be a spiritual leader.

Often truly authoritative leadership falls on someone who years earlier dedicated themselves to practice the discipline of seeking first the kingdom of God. Then, as that person matures, God confers a leadership role, and the Spirit of God goes to work through him. When God's searching eye finds a person qualified to lead, God anoints that person with the Holy Spirit and calls him or her to a special ministry (Acts 9:17; 22:21).

Samuel Brengle, a gifted leader who served for many years in the Salvation Army, outlined the road to spiritual authority and leadership:

> It is not won by promotion, but by many prayers and tears. It is attained by confession of sin, and much heart-searching and humbling before God; by self-surrender, a courageous sacrifice of every idol, a bold uncomplaining embrace of the cross, and by eternally looking unto Jesus crucified. It is not gained by seeking great things for ourselves, but like Paul, by counting those things that are gain to us as loss for Christ. This is a great price, but it must be paid by the leader whose power is recognized and felt in heaven, on earth, and in hell.[3]

God wants to show such people how strong He really is (2 Chronicles 16:9). But not all who aspire to leadership are willing to pay such a high personal price. Yet there is no compromise here: in the secret reaches of the heart, this price is paid, before any public office or honor. Our Lord made clear to James and John that high position in the kingdom of God is reserved for those whose hearts—even the secret places where no one else probes—are qualified. God's sovereign searching of our hearts, and then His call to leadership, are awesome to behold. And they make a person very humble.

One last thing must be said, a kind of warning. If those who hold influence over others fail to lead toward the spiritual uplands, then surely the path to the lowlands will be well worn. People travel together; no one lives detached and alone. We dare not take lightly God's call to leadership in our lives.

CHAPTER 3

The Master's Master Principle

Whoever wants to become great among you must be your servant, and whoever wants to be first must be slave of all.

MARK 10:43–44

Given the importance of competent leaders in the church—and in business and government too—we might expect that the Bible would use the term more often. In fact, the King James Bible (on which many of my generation have been nurtured) uses *leader* only six times. Much more frequently, the role is called *servant*. We do not read about "Moses, my leader," but "Moses, my servant." And this is exactly what Christ taught.[1]

Jesus was a revolutionary, not in the guerrilla warfare sense but in His teaching on leadership. He overturned an existing order. In the world's ears, the term *servant* spoke everywhere of low prestige, low respect, low honor. Most people were not attracted to such a low-value role. When Jesus used the term, however, it was a synonym for greatness. And that was a revolutionary idea. It still is!

Christ taught that the kingdom of God was a community where each member served the others. He defined His ultimate purpose using that term:

"For even the Son of Man did not come to be served, but to serve, and to give his life as a ransom for many" (Mark 10:45). Paul wrote in the same vein: "Serve one another in love" (Galatians 5:13). Our loving service should spread also to the needy world around us. But in most churches, a few people carry the load.

Jesus knew that the idea of leader as "loving servant of all" would not appeal to most people. Securing our own creature comforts is a much more common mission. But "servant" is His requirement for those who want to lead in His kingdom.

The sharp contrast between our common ideas about leadership and the revolution Jesus announced is nowhere clearer than in the Gospel of Mark 10:42–44: "You know that those who are regarded as rulers of the Gentiles lord it over them, and their high officials exercise authority over them. Not so with you. Instead, whoever wants to become great among you must be your servant, and whoever wants to be the first must be slave of all."

This was such a revolutionary idea that even those closest to Jesus, the disciples James and John, used their ambitious mother in a scheme to secure top positions in the coming kingdom before the other ten received their due. These two disciples took very seriously Jesus' promise about sitting on glorious thrones and judging the tribes of Israel (Matthew 19:28), but they misunderstood how to get there.

Despite their friendship, Jesus did not give an inch to their campaign for office. "You don't know what you are asking," was His reply (Matthew 20:22). James and John wanted the glory, but not the cup of shame; the crown, but not the cross; the role of master, but not servant. Jesus used this occasion to teach two principles of leadership that the church must never forget.

> ***The sovereignty principle of spiritual leadership.***
> "To sit at my right or left is not for me to grant. These places belong to those for whom they have been prepared" (Mark 10:40).

A more common response might have been: Honor and rank are for those who have prepared themselves for them, and worked very hard to get them. But here we see the fundamental difference in Jesus' teaching and our human ideas. God assigns places of spiritual ministry and leadership in His sovereign will. The New Living Translation makes the point of verse 40 very clear: "God has prepared those places for the one he has chosen."

Effective spiritual leadership does not come as a result of theological training or seminary degree, as important as education is. Jesus told His disciples, "You did not choose me, but I chose you and appointed you" (John 15:16). The sovereign selection of God gives great confidence to Christian workers. We can truly say, "I am here neither by selection of an individual nor election of a group but by the almighty appointment of God."

The suffering principle of spiritual leadership. "Can you drink the cup I drink and be baptized with the baptism I am baptized with?" (Mark 10:38).

No hedging here. No dodging the hard realities. Jesus simply and honestly set forth the cost of serving in His kingdom. The task was magnificent and difficult; men and women leading in that task must have eyes wide open, and hearts willing to follow the Master all the way.

To the Lord's probing question, the disciples responded glibly, "We are able." What tragic lack of perspective! But Jesus knew what lay ahead. They would indeed drink the cup and know the baptism. They would fail miserably and be restored gloriously. Eventually, James would be executed, and John would finish his days in isolated confinement.

If the disciples figured to learn about leadership on the fast track and with appropriate perks and bonuses, Jesus soon disillusioned them. What a shock it was to discover that greatness comes through servanthood, and leadership through becoming a slave of all.

Only once in all the recorded words of Jesus did our Lord announce that He had provided an "example" for the disciples, and that was when He washed their feet (John 13:15). Only once in the rest of the New Testament does a writer offer an "example" (1 Peter 2:21), and that is an example of suffering. Serving and suffering are paired in the teaching and life of our Lord. One does not come without the other. And what servant is greater than the Lord?

THE SPIRIT OF SERVANTHOOD

Jesus' teaching on servanthood and suffering was not intended merely to inspire good behavior. Jesus wanted to impart the spirit of servanthood, the sense of personal commitment and identity that He expressed when He said, "I am among you as one who serves." Mere acts of service could be performed with motives far from spiritual.

In Isaiah 42, we read about the attitudes and inner motives that the coming Messiah would demonstrate as the ideal servant of the Lord. Where Israel failed to live up to this ideal, the Messiah would succeed. And the principles of His life would be a pattern for ours.

Dependence. "Here is my servant, whom I uphold" (Isaiah 42:1). This verse speaks of the coming Messiah. Jesus fulfilled the prophecy by emptying Himself of divine prerogative ("made himself nothing," Philippians 2:7). He surrendered the privileges of His God-nature and became dependent on His heavenly Father. He became in all ways like a human being. What a staggering paradox. As we become "empty" of self and dependent on God, the Holy Spirit will use us.

Approval. "My chosen one in whom I delight" (Isaiah 42:1). God took great delight in His servant Jesus. On at least two occasions, God declared that delight audibly (Matthew 3:17; 17:5). And that delight was reciprocal. In another Old Testament reference to the coming Messiah, the Son testifies, "I delight to do thy will, O my God" (Psalm 40:8 KJV).

Modesty. "He will not shout or cry out, or raise his voice in the streets" (Isaiah 42:2). Neither strident nor flamboyant, God's servant conducts a ministry that appears almost self-effacing. What a contrast to the arrogant self-advertising of so many hypesters today, both in and out of the church.

On this very point the devil tempted Jesus, urging Him to attempt a headline-grabbing leap from the rooftop of the temple (Matthew 4:5). But Jesus did not seek headlines and did not fall to the plot.

So quiet and unobtrusive is the great Servant's work that many today doubt His very existence. Jesus exemplifies the description of God found later in Isaiah: "Truly you are a God who hides himself" (Isaiah 45:15). This quality seems to be shared among all the host of heaven. Even the picture given to us of the cherubim—God's angel servants—use four of their six wings to conceal their faces and feet. They too are content with hidden service (Isaiah 6:2).

Empathy. "A bruised reed he will not break, and a smoldering wick he will not snuff out" (Isaiah 42:3). The Lord's servant is sympathetic with the weak, mercifully understanding toward those who err. How often do people who fail wear the treadmarks of fellow pilgrims? But the ideal Servant does not trample on the weak and failing. He mends bruises and fans the weak spirit into a flame. Those who follow in His steps will never walk over people.

Many of us, even Christian workers, see a person whose life is a wreck and "pass by on the other side." We seek a ministry more rewarding and worthy of our talents than bearing up the frail side of humanity. But from God's point of view, it is noble work to reclaim the world's downtrodden people. When we find some of those the world calls "the least" and seek to meet their needs, Christ tells us we can think of them as Him (Matthew 25:45).

How dimly Peter's own wick burned in the garden and the judgment hall, but what a blaze on the day of Pentecost! God's ideal Servant made that miserable man's life a brilliant flame.

Optimism. "He will not falter or be discouraged till he establishes justice on earth" (Isaiah 42:4). Pessimism and leadership are at opposite ends of life's attitudes. Hope and optimism are essential qualities for the servant of God who battles with the powers of darkness over the souls of men and women. God's ideal Servant is optimistic until every part of God's work is done.

Anointing. "I will put my Spirit on him" (Isaiah 42:1). None of these leadership qualities—dependence, approval, modesty, empathy, or optimism—are sufficient for the task. Without the touch of the supernatural, these qualities are dry as dust. And so the Holy Spirit comes to rest upon and dwell in the ideal Servant. "You know . . . how God anointed Jesus of Nazareth with the Holy Spirit and power, and how he went around doing good" (Acts 10:37–38). Jesus' ministry began when the Spirit descended at His baptism, and then how the Servant began to shake the world!

Are we greater than our Lord? Can we do effective ministry without the Spirit of God working through us at every step? God offers us the same anointing. May we follow close to the great Servant, and receive the Spirit who shows us more of the Master.

CHAPTER 4

Natural and Spiritual Leadership

When I came to you . . . my message and my preaching were not with wise and persuasive words, but with a demonstration of the Spirit's power.

1 CORINTHIANS 2:1, 4

Leadership is influence, the ability of one person to influence others to follow his or her lead. Famous leaders have always known this.

The great military leader Bernard Montgomery spoke of leadership in these terms: "Leadership is the capacity and will to rally men and women to a common purpose, and the character which inspires confidence."[1] An outstanding example of this statement was Sir Winston Churchill, leader of Britain during World War II.

Fleet Admiral Nimitz said: "Leadership may be defined as that quality that inspires sufficient confidence in subordinates as to be willing to accept his views and carry out his commands."

General Charles Gordon once asked Li Hung Chang, a leader in China, two questions: "What is leadership? And how is humanity divided?" Li Hung replied: "There are only three kinds of people—those who are immovable, those who are movable, and those who move them!" Leaders move others.

John R. Mott, a world leader in student ministries, believed that "a leader is a man who knows the road, who can keep ahead, and who pulls others after him."[2]

P. T. Chandapilla, an Indian student leader, defined Christian leadership as a vocation that blends both human and divine qualities in a harmony of ministry by God and His people for the blessing of others.[3]

President Harry S. Truman (1945–1953) said cogently: "A leader is a person who has the ability to get others to do what they don't want to do, and like it."

Spiritual leadership blends natural and spiritual qualities. Yet even the natural qualities are supernatural gifts, since all good things come from God. Take personality, for instance. Montgomery said that "the degree of influence will depend on the personality, the 'incandescence' of which the leader is capable, the flame which burns within, the magnetism which will draw the hearts of others toward him."[4] Both natural and spiritual qualities reach their greatest effectiveness when employed in the service of God and for His glory.

Yet spiritual leadership transcends the power of personality and all other natural gifts. The personality of the spiritual leader influences others because it is penetrated, saturated, and empowered by the Holy Spirit. As the leader gives control of his life to the Spirit, the Spirit's power flows through him to others.

Spiritual leadership requires superior spiritual power, which can never be generated by the self. There is no such thing as a self-made spiritual leader. A true leader influences others spiritually only because the Spirit works in and through him to a greater degree than in those he leads.

We can lead others only as far along the road as we ourselves have traveled. Merely pointing the way is not enough. If we are not walking, then no one can be following, and we are not leading anyone.

At a large meeting of mission leaders in China, the discussion turned to leadership and its qualifications. The debate was vigorous. But through it all, one person sat quietly listening. Then the chair asked if D. E. Hoste, general director of China Inland Mission, had an opinion. The auditorium became still.

With a twinkle in his eye, Hoste said in his high-pitched voice: "It occurs to me that perhaps the best test of whether one is qualified to lead, is to find out whether anyone is following."[5]

BORN OR MADE?

Are leaders born or made? Surely, both. On the one hand, leadership is an "elusive and electric quality" that comes directly from God. On the other, leadership skills are distributed widely among every community, and should be cultivated and developed. Often our skills lie dormant until a crisis arises.

Some people become leaders by opportunity and timing. A crisis comes, no one better qualified steps forward, and a leader is born. But closer investigation usually reveals that the selection was less fortuitous and more the result of hidden training that made the person fit for leadership.

Joseph is a perfect example (Genesis 37–45). He became prime minister of Egypt through circumstances that most people would call "lucky stars." In fact his promotion was the outcome of thirteen years of rigorous, hidden training under the hand of God.

When we contrast natural and spiritual leadership, we see just how different they are.

NATURAL	SPIRITUAL
Self-confident	Confident in God
Knows men	Also knows God
Makes own decisions	Seeks God's will
Ambitious	Humble
Creates methods	Follows God's example
Enjoys command	Delights in obeying God
Seeks personal reward	Loves God and others
Independent	Depends on God

People without natural leadership skills do not become great leaders at the moment of conversion. Yet a review of the history of the church reveals that the Holy Spirit sometimes releases gifts and qualities that were dormant beforehand. When that happens, a leader is born. A. W. Tozer wrote:

> A true and safe leader is likely to be one who has no desire to lead, but is forced into a position by the inward leading of the Holy Spirit and the press of circumstances. . . . There was hardly a great leader from Paul to the present day but was drafted by the Holy Spirit for the task, and commissioned by the Lord to

> fill a position he had little heart for. . . . The man who is ambitious to lead is disqualified. . . . the true leader will have no desire to lord it over God's heritage, but will be humble, gentle, self-sacrificing and altogether ready to follow when the Spirit chooses another to lead.[6]

Sangster's biography includes a private manuscript written when the English preacher and scholar felt a growing conviction to take more of a leadership role in the Methodist church.

> This is the will of God for me. I did not choose it. I sought to escape it. But it has come. Something else has come, too. A sense of certainty that God does not want me only for a preacher. He wants me also for a leader. I feel a commissioning to work under God for the revival of this branch of His Church (Methodist)—careless of my own reputation; indifferent to the comments of older and jealous men. I am thirty-six. If I am to serve God in this way, I must no longer shrink from the task—but do it. I have examined my heart for ambition. I am certain it is not there. I hate the criticism I shall evoke and the painful chatter of people. Obscurity, quiet browsing among books, and the service of simple people is my taste—but by the will of God, this is my task, God help me.
>
> Bewildered and unbelieving, I hear the voice of God say to me: "I want to sound the note through you." O God, did ever an apostle shrink from his task more? I dare not say "no" but, like Jonah, I would fain run away.[7]

Once Saint Francis of Assisi was confronted by a brother who asked him repeatedly, "Why you? Why you?"

Francis responded, in today's terms, "Why me *what*?"

"Why does everyone want to see you? Hear you? Obey you? You are not all so handsome, nor learned, nor from a noble family. Yet the world seems to want to follow you," the brother said.

Then Francis raised his eyes to heaven, knelt in praise to God, and turned to his interrogator:

> You want to know? It is because the eyes of the Most High have willed it so. He continually watches the good and the wicked, and as His most holy eyes have not found among sinners any smaller man, nor any more insufficient and sinful, therefore He has chosen me to accomplish the marvelous work which God hath undertaken; He chose me because He could find none more worthless, and He wished to confound the nobility and grandeur, the strength, the beauty and the learning of this world.[8]

Montgomery outlined seven qualities necessary for a military leader, each appropriate to spiritual warfare: the leader must 1) avoid getting swamped in detail; 2) not be petty; 3) not be pompous; 4) know how to select people to fit the task; 5) trust others to do a job without the leader's meddling; 6) be capable of clear decisions; 7) inspire confidence.[9]

John Mott spent time with students, and his tests emphasized youthful leadership development. One should inquire of a potential leader whether he or she 1) does little things well; 2) has learned to focus on priorities; 3) uses leisure well; 4) has intensity; 5) knows how to exploit momentum; 6) is growing; 7) overcomes discouragement and "impossible" situations; and 8) understands his or her weaknesses.[10]

A single life has immense possibilities for good or ill. We leave an indelible impact on people who come within our influence, even when we are not aware of it. Dr. John Geddie went to Aneityum (a Polynesian island) in 1848 and worked there for twenty-four years. Written in his memory are these words:

> When he landed, in 1848, there were no Christians.
> When he left, in 1872, there were no heathen.[11]

When the burning zeal of the early church began to draw converts at an extraordinary rate, the Holy Spirit taught a wonderful lesson on leadership. The church had too few leaders to care for all the needs, especially among the poor and the widows. Another echelon of leaders was needed. "Brothers, choose seven men from among you who are known to be full of the Spirit and wisdom. We will turn this responsibility over to them" (Acts 6:3).

These new leaders were first and foremost to be full of the Spirit. Spirituality is not easy to define, but you can tell when it is present. It is the fragrance of the garden of the Lord, the power to change the atmosphere around you, the influence that makes Christ real to others.

If deacons are required to be full of the Spirit, should those who preach and teach the Word of God be any less? Spiritual goals can be achieved only by spiritual people who use spiritual methods. How our churches and mission agencies would change if leaders were Spirit-filled! The secular mind and heart, however gifted and personally charming, has no place in the leadership of the church.

John Mott captured well the heart of spiritual leadership:

> Leadership in the sense of rendering maximum service; leadership in the sense of the largest unselfishness; in the sense of full-hearted absorption in the greatest work of the world: building up the kingdom of our Lord Jesus Christ.[12]

CHAPTER 5

Can You Become a Leader?

Send some men to explore the land of Canaan. . . .
From each ancestral tribe send one of its leaders.
NUMBERS 13:2

When Jesus selected leaders, He ignored every popular idea of His day (and ours) about what kind of person could fit the role. Jesus' band of disciples started out untrained and without influence—a motley group for world change.

Any campaign for change today would have a star-studded cast of directors and advisers. In Jesus' group, where was the prominent statesman, the financier, the athlete, professor, or acclaimed clergy? Instead, Jesus looked for a humbler sort of person, unspoiled by the sophistication of His day.

Jesus chose from the ranks of workers, not professional clergy. When Hudson Taylor did the same thing, selecting mostly lay men and women for his missionary team to China, the religious world was shocked. Today that is a widely recognized, though not always approved, procedure.

Jesus chose people with little education, but they soon displayed remarkable flair. He saw in them something no one else did, and under His skillful hand they emerged as leaders who would shock the world. To their latent talents were added fervent devotion and fierce loyalty, honed in the school of failure and fatigue.

Natural leadership qualities are important. Too often these skills lie dormant and undiscovered. If we look carefully, we should be able to detect leadership potential. And if we have it, we should train it and use it for Christ's work. Here are some ways to investigate your potential:

- How do you identify and deal with bad habits? To lead others, you must master your appetites.
- How well do you maintain self-control when things go wrong? The leader who loses control under adversity forfeits respect and influence. A leader must be calm in crisis and resilient in disappointment.
- To what degree do you think independently? A leader must use the best ideas of others to make decisions. A leader cannot wait for others to make up his or her mind.
- How well can you handle criticism? When have you profited from it? The humble person can learn from petty criticism, even malicious criticism.
- Can you turn disappointment into creative new opportunity? What three actions could you take facing any disappointment?
- Do you readily gain the cooperation of others and win their respect and confidence? Genuine leadership doesn't have to manipulate or pressure others.
- Can you exert discipline without making a power play? Are your corrections or rebukes clear without being destructive? True leadership is an internal

quality of the spirit and needs no show of external force.

- In what situations have you been a peacemaker? A leader must be able to reconcile with opponents and make peace where arguments have created hostility.
- Do people trust you with difficult and delicate matters? Your answer should include examples.
- Can you induce people to do happily some legitimate thing that they would not normally wish to do? Leaders know how to make others feel valued.
- Can you accept opposition to your viewpoint or decision without taking offense? Leaders always face opposition.
- Can you make and keep friends? Your circle of loyal friends is an index of your leadership potential.
- Do you depend on the praise of others to keep you going? Can you hold steady in the face of disapproval and even temporary loss of confidence?
- Are you at ease in the presence of strangers? Do you get nervous in the office of your superior? A leader knows how to exercise and accept authority.
- Are people who report to you generally at ease?

A leader should be sympathetic and friendly.

- Are you interested in people? All types? All races? No prejudice?
- Are you tactful? Can you anticipate how your words will affect a person? Genuine leaders think before speaking.

- Is your will strong and steady? Leaders cannot vacillate, cannot drift with the wind. Leaders know there's a difference between conviction and stubbornness.
- Can you forgive? Or do you nurse resentments and harbor ill-feelings toward those who have injured you?
- Are you reasonably optimistic? Pessimism and leadership do not mix. Leaders are positively visionary.
- Have you identified a master passion such as that of Paul, who said, "This *one thing* I do!" Such singleness of motive will focus your energies and powers on the desired objective. Leaders need a strong focus.
- How do you respond to new responsibility?

How we handle relationships tells a lot about our potential for leadership. R. E. Thompson suggests these tests:

- Do other people's failures annoy or challenge you?
- Do you "use" people, or cultivate people?
- Do you direct people, or develop people?
- Do you criticize or encourage?
- Do you shun or seek the person with a special need or problem?[1]

These self-examinations mean little unless we act to correct our deficits and fill in the gaps of our training. Perhaps the final test of leadership potential is whether you "sit" on the results of such an analysis or do something about it. Why not take some of the points of weakness and failure you just identified or are already aware of and, in cooperation with the Holy Spirit, who is the Spirit of discipline, go into intentional character training. Concentrate on strengthening those areas of weakness and correcting faults.

Desirable qualities were present in all their fullness in the character of our Lord. Each Christian should make it his constant prayer that Christlikeness might more rapidly be incorporated into his or her own personality.

Adding leadership potential to our lives usually requires that we shake off negative elements that hold us back. If we are overly sensitive when criticized and rush to defend ourselves, that must go. If we make excuses for failure and try to blame others or circumstances, that must go. If we are intolerant or inflexible, so that creative people around us feel hemmed in, that must go.

If we are disturbed by anything short of perfection in ourselves and others, that must go. The perfectionist sets goals beyond his reach, then sinks into false guilt when he falls short. Our world is imperfect, and we cannot expect the impossible. Setting modest, realistic goals will help a perfectionist move through a problem without discouragement.

If you cannot keep a secret, do not try to lead. If you cannot yield a point when someone else's ideas are better, save yourself the frustration of failed leadership. If you want to maintain an image of infallibility, find something else to do besides leading people.

CHAPTER 6

Insights on Leadership from Paul

Now the overseer must be above reproach, the husband of but one wife, temperate, self-controlled, respectable, hospitable, able to teach, not given to drunkenness, not violent but gentle, not quarrelsome, not a lover of money. He must manage his own family well and see that his children obey him with proper respect. . . . He must not be a recent convert, or he may become conceited. . . . He must also have a good reputation with outsiders.

1 TIMOTHY 3:2–7

An architect friend once said to me as we looked at a building he had just completed, "It's humbling to see your own ideas suddenly standing as brick, mortar, and paint!" The comment reminded me of how much clearer are spiritual principles when we see them lived out in people instead of merely stating them in the abstract. Paul embodied principles of leadership that he also described in his letters. He certainly thought the life of individual believers and churches ought to resemble a solid foundation on Christ (see 1 Corinthians 3:9–17). Looking at Paul's life, we can see leadership all the more clearly.

The reputation of a great leader grows with the years. Surely Paul's moral and spiritual greatness is all the more evident the more he is studied and analyzed. A. W. Tozer called him the world's most successful Christian. It is sheer irony and miracle that God would select one of the most aggressive opponents of the early Christian movement and make him into its most outstanding leader.

Paul was uniquely equipped for the major role to which God called him. A present-day parallel to this amazing man would be someone who could speak in Chinese in Beijing, quoting Confucius and Mencius; write cogent theology and teach it at Oxford; and defend his cause using flawless Russian before the Soviet Academy of Sciences. By whatever comparison, Paul was certainly one of the most versatile leaders the church has known.

His versatility is apparent in the ease with which he adapted to various audiences. Paul could address statesmen and soldiers, adults and children, kings and royal officials. He was at ease in debate with philosophers, theologians, and pagan idol worshippers.

Paul had a brilliant grasp of the Old Testament. He studied under the influential rabbi Gamaliel, and as a student Paul was second to none. His own testimony records: "I was advancing in Judaism beyond many Jews of my own age and was extremely zealous for the traditions of my fathers" (Galatians 1:14).

A natural leader by any measure, Paul became a great spiritual leader when his heart and mind were captured by Jesus Christ.

Paul had boundless, Christ-centered ambition. His supreme love for Christ coupled with the obligation to share Christ's message were his powerful lifetime motives (Romans 1:14; 2 Corinthians 5:14). His authentic missionary passion helped him leap over all cultural and racial barriers. All people were his concern. A person's wealth or poverty, status or intellect had no bearing on Paul's concern for him.

In addition to his own schooling and experiences, Paul enjoyed the illumination and inspiration of the Holy Spirit. Qualities of leadership Paul taught are as relevant now as during the first century AD. We dare not toss them off as antiquated or carelessly regard them as mere options.

The selection from 1 Timothy quoted at the head of this chapter spells out qualifications for spiritual leadership. Let us look at it again, and consider its parts.

SOCIAL QUALIFICATIONS

With respect to relationships within the church, the leader is to be above reproach. Detractors should not have a rung to stand on. If a charge is proffered against him, it fails because his life affords no grounds for reproach or indictment of wrongdoing. His adversary finds no opening for a smear campaign, rumor mongering, or gossip.

With respect to relationships outside the church, the spiritual leader is to enjoy a good reputation. An elder known to the author was a businessman who often took preaching appointments on the Lord's Day. His employees used to say that they could tell when he had been preaching on Sunday because of his ill temper on Monday. Those outside the church can see plainly when our lives fall short of our testimony. We cannot hope to lead people to Christ by living an example of such contradiction.

Outsiders will criticize; nonetheless they respect the high ideals of Christian character. When a Christian leader full of high ideals lives a holy and joyful life in front of unbelievers, they often want to cultivate a similar experience. The character of the elder should command the respect of the unbeliever, inspire his confidence, and arouse his aspiration. Example is much more potent than precept.

MORAL QUALIFICATIONS

Moral principles common to the Christian life are under constant, subtle attack, and none more so than sexual faithfulness. The Christian leader must be blameless on this vital and often unpopular point. Faithfulness to one marriage partner is the biblical norm. The spiritual leader should be a man of unchallengeable morality.

The spiritual leader must be temperate, not addicted to alcohol. To be drunk is to show a disorderly personal life. Drunkenness is a disgrace anywhere, and much more so when it captures a Christian. A leader cannot allow a secret indulgence that would undermine public witness.

MENTAL QUALIFICATIONS

A leader must be prudent, a person with sound judgment. This principle describes "the well-balanced state of mind resulting from habitual self-restraint"—the inner character that comes from daily self-discipline. Jeremy Taylor called this quality "reason's girdle and passion's bridle."[1] The ancient

Greeks, who valued this quality, described it as a disciplined mind not swayed by sudden impulse or flying to extremes. For example, courage to the Greeks was the "golden mean" between rashness and timidity; purity was the mean between prudery and immorality. In a similar way, the Christian leader who possesses a sound mind has control of every part of his personality, habits, and passions.

As to behavior, the leader must be respectable. A well-ordered life is the fruit of a well-ordered mind. The life of the leader should reflect the beauty and orderliness of God.

Then the leader must be ready and able to teach. In a leader, watch for this desire, this spark. It creates opportunities to help others understand the meaning of spiritual life. The leader feels the joy of the Spirit and wants others to know God as well. Moreover, the leader's responsibility for teaching those under him should be supported by a blameless life.

Teaching is hard work, and doing it well takes time, preparation, study, and prayer. Samuel Brengle lamented:

> Oh, for teachers among us; leaders who know how to read hearts and apply truth to the needs of the people, as a good physician reads patients and applies remedies to their ills. There are soul-sicknesses open and obscure, acute and chronic, superficial and deep-seated that the truth in Jesus will heal.[2]

John Wesley had these gifts. He never indulged in a cheap disparagement of the intellect and was always trying to promote knowledge of the Scriptures and spiritual renewal among the people. He was intellectually gifted and possessed an impressive command of English literature. An eminent preacher declared that he knew of no sermons that gave greater evidence of an intimate knowledge of classical and general literature than those of Wesley. Yet he was widely known as a person "of one Book." That kind of breadth, focused on the Scriptures, is a high example of the consecrated intellect of the spiritual leader.

PERSONALITY QUALIFICATIONS

If you would rather pick a fight than solve a problem, do not consider leading the church. The Christian leader must be genial and gentle, not a lover of controversy. R. C. Trench says that the leader should be one who corrects and "redresses the injustices of justice." Aristotle taught that the leader should be one who "remembers good rather than evil, the good one has received rather than the good one has done." The leader must be actively considerate, not merely passive and certainly not withdrawn but irenic in disposition, always seeking a peaceful solution, and able to diffuse an explosive situation.

Then the leader must show hospitality. This ministry should never be seen as an irksome imposition but rather as one that offers the privilege of service. *The Shepherd of Hermas*, a widely used book written in the second century AD, mentions that a bishop "must be hospitable, a man who gladly and at all times welcomes into his house the servants of God."

When Paul wrote his letter to Timothy, inns were few, dirty, and known for their immoral atmosphere. Visiting Christians depended on open doors of hospitality. A friend of the author, a person with a rather large portfolio of business and church responsibilities, kept an "open home" policy for visitors and the underprivileged on each Lord's Day. It was a practice that enriched his life and blessed others, and demonstrated this important quality of spiritual leadership.

Covetousness and its twin, the love of money, disqualify a person for leadership. Financial reward cannot enter a leader's mind in the exercise of ministry. The leader must be as willing to accept an appointment with a lower remuneration as one with a higher.

Before going to Madeley, John Fletcher was told by his benefactor, Mr. Hill, that he could have a position in Dunham in Cheshire, where "the parish is small, the duty light, and the income good." Moreover it was "in fine sporting country!"

"Alas, sir," replied Fletcher, "Dunham will not suit me. There is too much money and too little labor."

"A pity to decline such a living," said Hill. "Would you like Madeley?"

"That, sir, would be the very place for me." And in that church the man who cared nothing for money had a remarkable ministry, still being felt in this generation.[3]

DOMESTIC QUALIFICATIONS

The Christian leader who is married must demonstrate the ability to "manage his own family well and see that his children obey him with proper respect" (1 Timothy 3:4). We cannot accept the picture of a stern, unsmiling patriarch, immune to laughter and impervious to emotion. But Paul urges a well-ordered home where mutual respect and supportive harmony are the keynotes. Failure to keep home in order has kept many ministers and missionaries from their fullest potential.

To reach this goal, a spouse must fully share the leader's spiritual aspirations and be willing to join in the necessary sacrifices. Many a gifted leader has been lost to high office and spiritual effectiveness because of an uncooperative spouse. Without a benevolent and happy discipline in one's home, can a Christian worker be expected to manage a ministry? Can hospitality be offered if children carry on without restraint? Can a ministry to other families be effective if one's own family is in disarray?

While a leader cares for church and mission, he must not neglect the family, which is his primary and personal responsibility. The discharge of one duty in God's kingdom does not excuse us from another. There is time for every legitimate duty. Paul implies that a person's ability to lead at home is a strong indicator of his readiness to lead in ministry.

MATURITY

Spiritual maturity is indispensable to good leadership. A novice or new convert should not be pushed into leadership. A plant needs time to take root and come to maturity, and the process cannot be hurried. The seedling must take root downward before it can bear fruit upward. J. A. Bengel says that novices usually have "an abundance of verdure (vegetation)" and are "not yet pruned by the cross." In 1 Timothy 3:10, referring to qualifications for deacons, Paul urges, "They must first be tested."

The church in Ephesus was a decade old when Timothy became its pastor. This church had in it a galaxy of gifted teachers, so there were many men of mature experience in it; hence Paul's insistence that the new minister be mature—not as old as the others but as spiritually rooted and fruitful. Paul did not insist on maturity as a qualification to lead the newly established church at Crete (Titus 1:5–9), where mature members were not yet present. In the early stages of building a church, we cannot insist on maturity, but every care must be taken that those developing the work be stable in character, spiritual in outlook, and not ambitious for position.

Paul warns that a person not ready for leadership, and thrust into the role, "may become conceited and fall under the same judgment as the devil" (1 Timothy 3:6). A new convert does not yet possess the spiritual stability essential to leading people wisely. It is unwise to give key positions too early even to those who demonstrate promising talent, lest status spoil them. The story of the church and its mission is filled with examples of failed leaders who were appointed too soon. A novice suddenly placed in authority over others faces the danger of inflated ego. Instead, the promising convert should be given a widening opportunity to serve at humbler and less prominent tasks that will develop both natural and spiritual gifts. He should not be advanced too fast, lest he become puffed up. Neither should he be repressed, lest he become discouraged.

Paul did not appoint elders in every place on his first missionary journey. He sometimes waited until a later visit when questions about spiritual development had been clarified by time and experience (Acts 14:23). Timothy was converted during Paul's first journey, but not ordained until the second journey.[4]

"It is the mark of a grown-up man, as compared with a callow youth, that he finds his center of gravity wherever he happens to be at the moment, and however much he longs for the object of his desire, it cannot prevent him from staying at his post and doing his duty," wrote Dietrich Bonhoeffer. That is just what a new convert finds difficult to do. Steadfastness is a characteristic that accompanies a growing maturity and stability.

Maturity is shown in a magnanimous spirit and broad vision.Paul's encounter with Christ transformed him from a narrow-minded bigot into a full-hearted leader. The indwelling Christ enlarged his passion for others, broadened his view of the world, and deepened his convictions. But even in Paul's case, these changes took time.

The importance of the above requirements for leadership in the Christian church are recognized even in secular circles. The pagan Onosander described the ideal field commander: "He must be prudently self-controlled, sober, frugal, enduring in toil, intelligent, without love of money, neither young nor old, if possible the father of a family, able to speak competently, and of good reputation."[5]

If the world demands such standards of its leaders, the church of the living God should select its leaders with even greater care.

CHAPTER 7

Insights on Leadership from Peter

To the elders among you, I appeal as a fellow elder, a witness to Christ's sufferings and one who will also share in the glory to be revealed: Be shepherds of God's flock that is under your care, serving as overseers—not because you must, but because you are willing, as God wants you to be; not greedy for money, but eager to serve; not lording it over those entrusted to you, but being examples to the flock. And when the Chief Shepherd appears, you will receive the crown of glory that will never fade away. Young men, in the same way be submissive to those who are older. All of you, clothe yourselves with humility toward one another, because, "God opposes the proud, but gives grace to the humble." Humble yourselves, therefore, under God's mighty hand, that he may lift you up in due time. Cast all your anxiety on him because he cares for you.

1 PETER 5:1–7

Peter was the natural leader of the apostolic band. What Peter did, the others did; where he went, the others went. His mistakes, which sprang from his impetuous personality, were many, but his influence and leadership were without equal. We do well to ponder the advice of Peter's mature years to spiritual leaders of every generation.

See that your "flock of God" is properly fed and cared for, Peter urges (1 Peter 5:2). Such is a shepherd's primary responsibility. In these words we can hear the resonance of Peter's never-to-be-forgotten interview with Jesus after his failure, the conversation that restored him and assured him of Jesus' continuing love and care (John 21:15–22). Likewise, these "strangers in the world" (1 Peter 1:1) about whom Peter was writing were themselves passing through deep trials. Peter could feel for them and with them, and he wrote his letter to elders with that in mind.

Peter does not approach his readers from above, as a virtuoso apostle. Rather, he takes the position of fellow elder, alongside the others, bearing similar burdens. He also writes as a witness to the sufferings of Christ, one whose heart has been humbled by failure, broken and conquered by Calvary's love. He is a leader who looks across at others but not down. A shepherd's work requires a shepherd's heart.

First, Peter deals with a leader's motivation. The spiritual leader is to approach the work willingly, not by coercion. Leaders of the church in Peter's day faced challenges that would daunt the stoutest heart, yet Peter urges that they not faint or retreat from them. Nor should leaders serve from a sense of mere duty but because of love. The work of pastoring and helping new believers is to be done "as God wants," not directed by personal preferences or desires. Barclay captures the spirit of Peter's plea:

> Peter says to the leaders, "Shepherd your people like God." Our whole attitude to the people we serve must be the attitude of God. What a vision opens out! What an ideal! It is our task to show people the forbearance of God, the forgiveness of God, the seeking love of God, the limitless service of God.[1]

When God calls us, we cannot refuse from a sense of inadequacy. Nobody is worthy of such trust. When Moses tried that excuse, God became angry (Exodus 4:14). Let us not pass the buck of leadership because we think ourselves incapable.

The spiritual leader cannot have money in his eyes when service beckons. Do not work as one "greedy for money," Peter warns (1 Peter 5:2). Perhaps Peter had in mind Judas, whose passion for money led to his fall. Leaders will be called upon to formulate policy, to set budgets and decide priorities, to deal with property. None of that can be done well if personal gain looms as a background motive.

Paul Rees suggests that the greed Peter warns against extends beyond money to fame and prestige, which are sometimes a more insidious temptation. Whether for fame or fortune, avarice cannot coexist with leadership in the church.[2]

"I am not sure which of the two occupies the lower sphere, he who hungers for money or he who thirsts for applause," wrote J. H. Jowett. "A preacher may dress and smooth his message to court the public cheers, and laborers in other spheres may bid for prominence, for imposing print, for grateful recognition. All this unfits us for our task. It destroys perception of the needs and perils of the sheep."[3]

The Christian leader must not be dictatorial. "Not lording it over those entrusted to you" (1 Peter 5:3). A domineering manner, an unbridled ambition, an offensive strut, a tyrant's talk—no attitude could be less fit for one who claims to be a servant of the Son of God.

A leader must be a worthy example for the people. "But being examples to the flock" (1 Peter 5:3). These words remind us of Paul's advice to Timothy: "But set an example for the believers in speech, in life, in love, in faith and in purity" (1 Timothy 4:12). Peter teaches that elders need the shepherd spirit. Should elders ever forget whose flock they lead, Peter reminds them that it is God's. Jesus is the Chief Shepherd; we are assistants and associates working under His authority.

If done "as God wants," then leadership will surely include intercessory prayer. The saintly Bishop Azariah of India once remarked to Bishop Stephen Neill that he found time to pray daily, by name, for every leader in his extensive diocese. Little wonder that during his thirty years of eldering there, the diocese tripled its membership and greatly increased in spiritual effectiveness.[4]

The leader must be clothed "with humility" (1 Peter 5:5). The verb refers to a slave's tying on a white apron, which gives this verse an added note of meaning. Was Peter recalling the sad night when he refused to take the towel and wash his master's feet? Would pride keep other leaders from joyful service? Pride ever lurks at the heels of power, but God will not encourage proud men in His service. Rather, He will oppose and obstruct them. But to the undershepherd who is humble and lowly in heart, God will add power and grace to the work. In verse 5, Peter urged leaders to act humbly in relating to others. But in verse 6 he challenges leaders to react humbly to the discipline of God. "Therefore humbly submit to God's strong hand" is Charles B. Williams's rendering.

Peter concludes this section of teaching with a mention of heavenly reward: "When the Chief Shepherd appears, you will receive the crown of glory that will never fade away" (1 Peter 5:4). An athlete's crown would wither; even a king's crown would rust. But no such loss comes to the Christian servant who has chosen treasures in heaven to comforts on earth.

Are we alone in the leader's role? Do we work in solitude? Not at all, Peter announces. Rather, our frustrations and worries are shared with God, who offers relief and reprieve. "Cast all your anxiety on him because he cares for you" (1 Peter 5:7). The Christian leader need not fear that care of the flock of God will be too heavy a burden. By God's invitation, the leader can transfer the weight of spiritual burdens onto shoulders bigger, stronger, broader, and durable. God cares for you. Let worries go!

CHAPTER 8

Essential Qualities of Leadership

Now the overseer must be above reproach, the husband of but one wife, temperate, self-controlled, respectable, hospitable, able to teach, not given to drunkenness, not violent but gentle, not quarrelsome, not a lover of money. He must manage his own family well and see that his children obey him with proper respect. (If anyone does not know how to manage his own family, how can he take care of God's church?) He must not be a recent convert, or he may become conceited and fall under the same judgment as the devil. He must also have a good reputation with outsiders, so that he will not fall into disgrace and into the devil's trap.

1 TIMOTHY 3:2–7

Jesus trained His disciples superbly for their future roles. He taught by example and by precept; His teaching was done "on the road." Jesus did not ask the Twelve to sit down and take notes in a formal classroom. Jesus' classrooms were the highways of life; His principles and values came across in the midst of daily experience. Jesus placed disciples into internships (Luke 10:17–24) that enabled them to learn through failure and success (Mark 9:14–29). He delegated authority and responsibility to them as they were able to bear it. Jesus' wonderful teaching in John 13–16 was their graduation address.

God prepares leaders with a specific place and task in mind. Training methods are adapted to the mission, and natural and spiritual gifts are given with clear purpose. An example is Paul, who never could have accomplished so much without directed training and divine endowment.

Similarly, God prepared Adoniram Judson to become a missionary pioneer in Burma by giving to this remarkable leader qualities necessary for launching the gospel in the Indian subcontinent—self-reliance balanced by humility, energy restrained by prudence, self-forgetfulness, courage, and a passion for souls.

Martin Luther has been described as a man easy to approach, without personal vanity, and so plain in his tastes that people wondered how he could find any pleasure with so little money. He had common sense, a playful humor, eager laughter, sincerity, and honesty. Add to those qualities his courage, conviction, and passion for Christ. It is no wonder that he inspired loyalty in others that had the strength of steel.[1]

Professor G. Warneck described Hudson Taylor, the missionary pioneer to China: "A man full of faith and the Holy Ghost, of entire surrender to God and His call, of great self-denial, heartfelt compassion, rare poser in prayer, marvelous organizing faculty, indefatigable perseverance, and of astounding influence with men, and withal of child-like simplicity himself."[2]

God gave these leaders gifts and talents that fit the mission to which they were called. What raised these men above their fellows was the degree to which they developed those gifts through devotion and discipline.

DISCIPLINE

Without this essential quality, all other gifts remain as dwarfs: they cannot grow. So discipline appears first on our list. Before we can conquer the world, we must first conquer the self.

A leader is a person who has learned to obey a discipline imposed from without, and has then taken on a more rigorous discipline from within. Those who rebel against authority and scorn self-discipline—who shirk the rigors and turn from the sacrifices—do not qualify to lead. Many who drop out of ministry are sufficiently gifted, but have large areas of life floating free from the Holy Spirit's control. Lazy and disorganized people never rise to true leadership.

Many who aspire to leadership fail because they have never learned to follow. They are like boys playing war in the street, but all is quiet. When you ask, "Is there a truce?" they respond, "No, we are all generals. No one will obey the command to charge."

Donald Barnhouse noted with interest that the average age of the 40,000 people listed in *Who's Who in America*—the people who run the country—was under twenty-eight. Discipline in early life, which is ready to make sacrifices in order to gain adequate preparation for life tasks, paves the way for high achievement.[3]

A great statesman made a speech that turned the tide of

national affairs. "May I ask how long you spent preparing that speech?" asked an admirer.

"All my life," he replied.

The young man of leadership caliber will work while others waste time, study while others snooze, pray while others daydream. Slothful habits are overcome, whether in thought, deed, or dress. The emerging leader eats right, stands tall, and prepares himself to wage spiritual warfare. He will without reluctance undertake the unpleasant task that others avoid or the hidden duty that others evade because it wins no public applause. As the Spirit fills his life, he learns not to shrink from difficult situations or retreat from hard-edged people. He will kindly and courageously administer rebuke when that is called for, or he will exercise the necessary discipline when the interests of the Lord's work demand it. He will not procrastinate, but will prefer to dispatch with the hardest tasks first. His persistent prayer will be:

God, harden me against myself,
The coward with pathetic voice
Who craves for ease and rest and joy.
Myself, arch-traitor to myself,
My hollowest friend,
My deadliest foe,
My clog, whatever road I go.[4]

Few men were more faithful and courageous in giving loving rebuke or speaking frankly to people than Fred Mitchell, British director of the China Inland Mission and chairman of the English Keswick Convention. Sensitive and affectionate, he did not turn from the unpleasant interview. He always spoke in love, after much prayer. But his words did not always fall on receptive ears. He confided how much he had suffered when his faithfulness to God's work led to the loss of a friend. As he reached older age, Fred spent even more time praying before speaking. Often when he needed to deal with a matter of discipline, he would write a letter, then keep it for several days. Sometimes, on rereading it, he was assured it was right to send it, so it would be mailed. Sometimes he destroyed the draft and wrote another.[5]

When the founder of the World Dominion Movement, Thomas Cochrane, was interviewed for the mission field, he faced this question: "To what position of the field do you feel specially called?" He answered, "I only know I should wish it to be the hardest you could offer me"—the reply of a disciplined person.

Lytton Strachey described Florence Nightingale:

> It was not by gentle sweetness and womanly self-abnegation that she brought order out of chaos in the Scutari hospitals, that from her own resources she had clothed the British Army, that she had spread her dominion over the serried and reluctant powers of the official world; it was by strict method, by stern discipline, by rigid attention to detail, by ceaseless labor, by the fixed determination of an indomitable will. Beneath her cool and calm demeanor, there lurked fierce and passionate fires.[6]

Samuel Chadwick, the great Methodist preacher and principal of Cliff College, made an immense impact on his generation. He rose at six each morning and took a cold bath, summer and winter. His study light was seldom out before two in the morning. That rigorous lifestyle was the outward expression of his intense inner discipline.[7]

Throughout his life, George Whitefield rose at four in the morning and retired each night at ten. When that hour struck, he would rise from his seat, no matter who his visitors or what the conversation, and say good-naturedly to his friends, "Come, gentlemen, it is time for all good folks to be at home."[8]

> Barclay Buxton of Japan would urge Christians to lead disciplined lives whether they were in business or evangelistic work. This included disciplined Bible study and prayer, tithing, use of time, keeping healthy with proper diet, sleep, and exercise. It included the rigor of disciplined fellowship among Christians who differed from each other in many ways.[9]

These glimpses of personal biography illustrate the meaning of an unknown poet:

The heights by great men reached and kept
Were not attained by sudden flight;
But they, while their companions slept,
Were toiling upward in the night.

If a leader shows strong discipline, others will see it and cooperate with the expectations placed on them. At this point, leadership by example is crucial.

There is another element in discipline that receives too little attention. We must be willing to receive from others as well as give to others. Some sacrificial souls delight in sacrificing themselves, but refuse reciprocal gestures. They do not want to feel obligated to those they are serving. But real leadership recognizes the value of the gestures of others. To neglect receiving kindness and help is to isolate oneself, to rob others of opportunity, and to deprive oneself of sustenance. Our example in this is the ultimate Servant Jesus, who came to serve but graciously accepted the service of others—people like His hosts Mary and Martha, the use of the colt He rode into Jerusalem, and others.

Bishop Westcott admitted at the end of his life to one great mistake. He had always helped others, but just as rigorously he had resisted others serving him. As a result, his life had an empty spot where sweet friendship and human care might have been.[10]

VISION

Those who have most powerfully and permanently influenced their generation have been "seers"—people who have seen more and farther than others—persons of faith, for faith is vision. Moses, one of the great leaders of all history, "endured, as seeing him who is invisible" (KJV). His faith imparted vision. Elisha's servant saw the obvious menace of the encircling army, but Elisha saw the vast invisible hosts of heaven. His faith imparted vision.

Powhatten James wrote:

> The man of God must have insight into things spiritual. He must be able to see the mountains filled with the horses and chariots of fire; he must be able to interpret that which is written by the finger of God upon the walls of conscience; he must be able to translate the signs of the times into terms of their spiritual meaning: he must be able to draw aside, now and then, the curtain of things material and let mortals glimpse the spiritual glories which crown the mercy seat of God. The man of God must declare the pattern that was shown him on the mount; he must utter the vision granted to him upon the isle of revelation. . . . None of these things can he do without spiritual insight.[11]

Charles Cowman, founder of the Oriental Missionary Society, was "a man of vision. Throughout his life he seemed to see what the crowd did not see, and to see wider and fuller than many of his own day. He was man of far horizons."[12]

Vision involves foresight as well as insight. President McKinley's reputation for greatness rested in part on his ability to put an ear to the ground and listen for things coming. He turned his listening into vision; he saw what lay ahead. A leader must be able to see the end results of the policies and methods he or she advocates. Responsible leadership always looks ahead to see how policies will affect future generations.

The great missionary pioneers were people of vision. Carey saw the whole globe while fellow preachers limited the world to their parish borders. Henry Martyn saw India, Persia, and Arabia—the Muslim world—while the church at home squabbled over petty theological disagreements. People said of A. B. Simpson: "His lifework seemed to be to push on alone, where his fellows had seen nothing to explore."

A senior colleague once told Douglas Thornton of Egypt: "Thornton, you are different from anyone else I know. You are always looking at the end of things. Most people, myself included, find it better to do the next thing." Thornton's answer: "I find that the constant inspiration gained by looking at the goal is the chief thing that helps me to persevere."[13] An ideal, a vision, was absolutely necessary to him. He could not work without it. And that explained the largeness of his views and the magnitude of his schemes.

Eyes that look are common; eyes that see are rare. The Pharisees looked at Peter and saw only an unschooled fisherman—not worth a second look. Jesus saw in Peter a prophet and preacher, saint and leader who would help turn the world upside down.

Vision involves optimism and hope. The pessimist sees difficulty in every opportunity. The optimist sees opportunity in every difficulty. The pessimist tends to hold back people of vision from pushing ahead. Caution has its role to play. We all live in a real world of limitation and inertia. Cautious Christians draw valuable lessons from history and tradition, but are in danger of being chained to the past. The person who sees the difficulties so clearly that he does not discern the possibilities cannot inspire a vision in others.

Browning described the courageous optimist:

One who has never turned his back,
But marched breast-forward,

Never doubting clouds would break,
Never dreamed, though right were worsted,
Wrong would triumph.

Vision leads to venture, and history is on the side of venturesome faith. The person of vision takes fresh steps of faith across gullies and chasms, not "playing safe" but neither taking foolish risks. Concerning Archbishop Mowll it is written:

> It was a mark of his greatness that he was never behind his age, or too far ahead. He was up at the front, and far enough in advance to lead the march. He was always catching sight of new horizons. He still had a receptive mind for new ideas at an age when many were inclined to let things take their course.[14]

Leaders take lessons from the past, but never sacrifice the future for the sake of mere continuity. People of vision gauge decisions on the future; the story of the past cannot be rewritten.

A vision without a task makes a visionary.
A task without a vision is drudgery.
A vision with a task makes a missionary.[15]

WISDOM

"Wisdom is the faculty of making the use of knowledge, a combination of discernment, judgment, sagacity, and similar powers. . . . In Scripture, right judgment concerning spiritual and moral truth" (Webster).

If knowledge is the accumulation of facts and intelligence the development of reason, wisdom is heavenly discernment. It is insight into the heart of things. Wisdom involves knowing God and the subtleties of the human heart. More than knowledge, it is the right application of knowledge in moral and spiritual matters, in handling dilemmas, in negotiating complex relationships. "Wisdom is nine-tenths a matter of being wise in time," said Theodore Roosevelt. Most of us are "too often wise after the event."[16]

Wisdom gives a leader balance and helps to avoid eccentricity and extravagance. If knowledge comes by study, wisdom comes by Holy Spirit filling. Then a leader can apply knowledge correctly. "Full of . . . wisdom" is one of the requirements for even subordinate leaders in the early church (Acts 6:3).

Knowledge and wisdom, far from being one,
Have ofttimes no connection. Knowledge dwells
In heads replete with thoughts of other men:
Wisdom, in minds attentive to their own.
Knowledge is proud that he has learned so much,
Wisdom is humble, that he knows no more.
—Author Unknown

D. E. Hoste knew the importance of wisdom for leaders:

When a person in authority demands obedience of another, irrespective of the latter's reason and conscience, this is tyranny. On the other hand, when, by the exercise of tact and sympathy, prayer, spiritual power and

> sound wisdom, one is able to influence and enlighten another, so that a life course is changed, that is spiritual leadership.[17]

Paul's prayer for the Christians at Colosse should always be on our lips: That "God . . . fill you with the knowledge of his will through all spiritual wisdom and understanding" (Colossians 1:9).

DECISION

When all the facts are in, swift and clear decision is another mark of a true leader. A visionary may see, but a leader must decide. An impulsive person may be quick to declare a preference, but a leader must weigh evidence and make his decision on sound premises.

Once sure of the will of God, a spiritual leader springs into action, without regard to consequences. Pursuing the goal, the leader never looks back or calculates escape strategies if plans turn sour. Nor does a true leader cast blame for failure on subordinates.

Abraham showed swift and clear decisiveness during the crisis in Canaan and the rescue of Lot (Genesis 14). In his relations with his nephew, Abraham showed both the active and passive sides of spirituality. In his unselfish yielding of his right to the choice of pasturelands (Genesis 13), Abraham displayed the passive graces of godliness. But when Lot was captured during a battle at Sodom, Abraham took immediate action. With great bravery he pursued the enemy and gained a victory over superior numbers. This is true faith.

Moses became the leader of Israel when he abandoned Egypt's power and privilege and identified with the Hebrew slaves and their suffering (Hebrews 11:24–27). These were momentous decisions. This is true faith.

Paul's first question after his dramatic conversion was "What shall I do, Lord?" (Acts 22:10). Without hesitation Paul acted on his new knowledge of Christ's deity. To be granted light was to follow it. To see duty was to do it.

The catalog of saints in Hebrews 11 is a study of vision and decision. They saw the vision, counted the cost, made their decisions, and went into action. The same sequence is evident in the lives of great missionary leaders. Carey saw the vision in Kettering and made his decision for India, though the difficulties of getting there loomed as high as heaven itself. Livingstone saw the vision in Dumbarton, made his decision, overcame all obstacles, and proceeded to Africa.[18] Circumstances cannot frustrate such people, or difficulties deter them.

The spiritual leader will not procrastinate when faced with a decision, nor vacillate after making it. A sincere but faulty decision is better than weak-willed "trial balloons" or indecisive overtures. To postpone decision is really to decide for the status quo. In most decisions the key element is not so much knowing what to do but in living with the results.

Charles Cowman had the reputation of being a man of purpose. His eyes were fixed on one great object. With him, a vision was the first step in an action plan. The moment he sensed a possibility, he was uneasy until achievement was underway.

A young man beginning his work with the Coast Guard was called with his crew to try a desperate rescue in a great storm. Frightened, rain and wind pounding his face, the man cried to his captain, "We will never get back!" The captain replied, "We don't have to come back, but we must go out."

COURAGE

Leaders require courage of the highest order—always moral courage and often physical courage as well. Courage is that quality of mind that enables people to encounter danger or difficulty firmly, without fear or discouragement.

Paul admitted to knowing fear, but it never stopped him. "I came to you in weakness and fear, and with much trembling," he reported in 1 Corinthians 2:3, but the verb is *came*. He did not stay home out of fear for the journey. In 2 Corinthians 7:5, Paul confesses "conflicts on the outside, fears within." He did not court danger but never let it keep him from the Master's work.

Martin Luther was among the most fearless men who ever lived.[19] When he set out on his journey to Worms to face the questions and the controversies his teaching had created, he said, "You can expect from me everything save fear or recantation. I shall not flee, much less recant." His friends warned of the dangers; some begged him not to go. But Luther would not hear of it. "Not go to Worms!" he said. "I shall go to Worms though there were as many devils as tiles on the roofs."[20]

When Luther appeared there before the court of Emperor Charles V, he was shown a stack of his writings and called upon to recant. Luther replied, "Unless I can be instructed and convinced with evidence from the Holy Scriptures or with open, clear, and distinct grounds of reasoning, then I cannot and will not recant, because it is neither safe nor wise to act against conscience."

Then he likely added: "Here I stand. I can do no other. God help me! Amen."

A few days before his death, Luther recalled that day. "I was afraid of nothing: God can make one so desperately bold."

Not everyone is courageous by nature. Some people are more naturally timid than Luther. But whether we are bold or reticent, God calls leaders to be of good courage and not to capitulate to fear. Such a call to courage would be rather pointless if nobody feared anything. Because fear is a real part of life, God gives us the Holy Spirit, who fills us with power. But we must let that power do its work, and not fear.

Consider these two contrasting statements: "The doors [were] locked for fear of the Jews" (John 20:19), and, "When they saw the courage of Peter and John" (Acts 4:13). These statements describe the same disciples, and the same opposition. The difference is time. What happened between the first and the second? The Holy Spirit did "not give a spirit of timidity, but a spirit of power" (2 Timothy 1:7).

Courageous leaders face unpleasant and even devastating situations with equanimity, then act firmly to bring good from trouble, even if their action is unpopular. Leadership always faces natural human inertia and opposition. But courage follows through with a task until it is done.

People expect leaders to be calm and courageous during a crisis. While others lose their heads, leaders stay the course. Leaders strengthen followers in the middle of discouraging setbacks and shattering reverses.

Facing the ruthless armies of Sennacherib, Hezekiah

made his military preparations and then set about strengthening the morale of his people. "Be strong and courageous," he told them. "Do not be afraid or discouraged because of the king of Assyria and the vast army with him. . . . With him is only the arm of flesh, but with us is the LORD our God to help us and to fight our battles." And then the Scriptures report that "the people gained confidence from what Hezekiah the king of Judah said" (2 Chronicles 32:7–8). Here is leadership, active and strong.

HUMILITY

Humility is also a hallmark of the spiritual leader. Christ told His disciples to turn away from the pompous attitudes of the oriental despots, and instead take on the lowly bearing of the servant (Matthew 20:25–27). As in ancient days, so today humility is least admired in political and business circles. But no bother! The spiritual leader will choose the hidden path of sacrificial service and approval of the Lord over the flamboyant self-advertising of the world.

We often regard John the Baptist as great because of his burning eloquence and blistering denunciation of the evils of his day. His words pierced and exposed the hearts of many a petty ruler. But his real greatness was revealed in one infinitely wise affirmation: "He must increase, but I must decrease" (John 3:30 KJV). Here John's spiritual stature rings clear and strong.

A leader's humility should grow with the passing of years, like other attitudes and qualities. Notice Paul's advance in the grace of humility. Early in his ministry, he acknowledged: "I am the least of the apostles and do not even deserve to be called an apostle" (1 Corinthians 15:9). Later he volunteered: "I am less than the least of all God's people" (Ephesians 3:8). Toward the end of his life, he spoke of the mercies of Christ and his own sense of place: "Christ Jesus came into the world to save sinners—of whom I am the worst" (1 Timothy 1:15).

William Law writes in his devotional classic *Serious Call*:

> Let every day be a day of humility; condescend to all the weaknesses and infirmities of your fellow-creature, cover their frailties, love their excellencies, encourage their virtues, relieve their wants, rejoice in their prosperities, compassionate over their distress, receive their friendship, overlook the unkindness, forgive their malice, be a servant of servants, and condescend to do the lowliest offices of the lowest of mankind.[21]

On one occasion when Samuel Brengle was introduced as "the great Doctor Brengle," he noted in his diary:

> If I appear great in their eyes, the Lord is most graciously helping me to see how absolutely nothing I am without Him, and helping me to keep little in my own eyes. He does use me. But I am so concerned that He uses me and that it is not of me the work is done. The axe cannot boast of the trees it has cut down. It could do nothing but for the woodsman. He made it, he sharpened it, and he used it. The moment he throws it aside; it becomes only old iron. O that I may never lose sight of this.[22]

The spiritual leader of today is the one who gladly worked as an assistant and associate, humbly helping another achieve great things. Robert Morrison of China wrote: "The great fault in our missions is that no one likes to be second."[23]

INTEGRITY AND SINCERITY

Paul spoke of his failures and successes with an openness few of us are prepared to copy. Even before his conversion he served God sincerely (2 Timothy 1:3) and with great personal integrity. Later he wrote: "In Christ we speak before God with sincerity" (2 Corinthians 2:17).

These two qualities of leadership were part of God's law for the Israelites (Deuteronomy 18:13). God wants His people to show a transparent character, open and innocent of guile.

A prominent businessman once replied to a question: "If I had to name the one most important quality of a top manager, I would say, personal integrity." Surely the spiritual leader must be sincere in promise, faithful in discharge of duty, upright in finances, loyal in service, and honest in speech.

CHAPTER 9

More Essential Qualities of Leadership

Deacons, likewise, are to be men worthy of respect, sincere, not indulging in much wine, and not pursuing dishonest gain. They must keep hold of the deep truths of the faith with a clear conscience. They must first be tested; and then if there is nothing against them, let them serve as deacons.

1 TIMOTHY 3:8–10

HUMOR

Our sense of humor is a gift from God that should be controlled as well as cultivated. Clean, wholesome humor will relax tension and relieve difficult situations. Leaders can use it to displace tension with a sense of the normal.

Samuel Johnson advised that people should spend part of each day laughing. Archbishop Whately, the great apologist, wrote: "We ought not only to cultivate the cornfield of the mind but the pleasure grounds also." Agnes Strickland claimed that "next to virtue, the fun in this world is what we can least spare."[1]

Criticized for including humor in a sermon, Charles Spurgeon, eye twinkling, said: "If only you knew how much I hold back, you would commend me." Later writing on the subject, he said: "There are things in these sermons that may produce smiles, but what of them? The preacher is not quite sure about a smile being a sin, and at any rate he thinks it less a crime to cause a momentary laughter than a half-hour of profound slumber."

Helmut Thielecke wrote:

> Should we not see that lines of laughter about the eyes are just as much marks of faith as are the lines of care and seriousness? Is it only earnestness that is baptized? Is laughter pagan? . . . A church is in a bad way when it banishes laughter from the sanctuary and leaves it to the cabaret, the nightclub and the toastmasters.[2]

Humor is a great asset and an invaluable lubricant in missionary life. Indeed it is a most serious deficiency if a missionary lacks a sense of humor. A Swede was urged by friends to give up the idea of returning to India as a missionary because it was so hot there. "Man," he was urged, "it is 120 degrees in the shade!"

"Vell," said the Swede in noble contempt, "ve don't always have to stay in the shade, do ve?"

A. E. Norrish, a missionary to India, testified:

> I have never met leadership without a sense of humor; this ability to stand outside oneself and one's circumstances, to see things in perspective and laugh. It is a

> great safety value! You will never lead others far without the joy of the Lord and its concomitant, a sense of humor.[3]

Douglas Thornton was often more amusing than he tried to be. He had a delightful way of mixing up two kindred proverbs or idioms. Once he told his companions that he always had two strings up his sleeve. They then asked him if he also had another card to his bow. Such exchanges enliven heavy committee meetings and create wholesome laughter.

After a half century of ministry, F. J. Hallett claimed that in the actual work of a parish, the most successful leader is the one who possesses a keen sense of humor combined with a clear sense of God's grace. The humor lends pungency, originality, and eloquence to sermons.

Of one great preacher it was said that he used humor as a condiment and a stimulant. At times, paroxysms of laughter would rock his audience—never about sacred matters. Following the joke, he would quickly swing to the sublime. His humor never fell into frivolity.

A good test of the appropriateness of a joke is whether the humor controls us or we control it. About Kenneth Strachan, general director of the Latin American Mission, it was said: "He had a keen sense of humor, but he had a sense of the fitness of things. He knew the place for a joke and his humor was controlled."[4]

ANGER

Can this be right? An angry leader? Indeed, Jesus had this quality, and when we use it rightly, we follow Him. In Mark

3:5, Jesus "looked around at them in anger." The Pharisees had just given Him a stubborn, silent answer to a question, so He gave them an equally silent rebuke.

Holy anger has its roots in genuine love. Both are part of the nature of God. Jesus' love for the man with the withered hand aroused His anger against those who would deny him healing. Jesus' love for God's house made Him angry at the sellers and buyers who had turned the temple into a "den of robbers" (Matthew 21:13). Yet in both these cases and others, it was ultimately Jesus' love for those doing wrong that caused Him to be angry with them. His anger got their attention!

Great leaders—people who turn the tide and change the direction of events—have been angry at injustice and abuse that dishonors God and enslaves the weak. William Wilberforce moved heaven and earth to emancipate slaves in England and eliminate the slave trade—and he was angry!

F. W. Robertson described his sense of anger on one special occasion: "My blood was at the moment running fire, and I remembered that once in my life I had felt a terrible might; I knew and rejoiced to know that I was inflicting the sentence of a coward's and a liar's hell."[5] Martin Luther claimed that he "never did anything well until his wrath was excited, and then he could do anything well."

But holy anger is open to abuse. Many who feel it allow anger to become their downfall. It can all too easily become a preferred response even when other responses would be more effective. Bishop Butler teaches six conditions that make anger sinful:

- When, to favor a resentment or feud, we imagine an injury done to us
- When an injury done to us becomes, in our minds, greater than it really is
- When, without real injury, we feel resentment on account of pain or inconvenience
- When indignation rises too high, and overwhelms our ability to restrain
- When we gratify resentments by causing pain or harm out of revenge
- When we are so perplexed and angry at sin in our own lives that we readily project anger at the sin we find in others[6]

Paul argues for holy anger when he repeats the advice of Psalm 4:4: "In your anger do not sin" (Ephesians 4:26). This anger is not selfish and does not center on the pain you currently feel. To be free of sin such anger must be zealous for truth and purity, with the glory of God its chief objective.

Thou to wax fierce
In the cause of the Lord!
Anger and zeal
And the joy of the brave,
Who bade thee to feel,
Sin's slave?
—Author Unknown

PATIENCE

Spiritual leaders need a healthy endowment of patience. Chrysostom called patience the queen of virtues. Often we think of patience in passive terms, as if the patient person is utterly submissive and half asleep. But this version of patience needs a biblical corrective. Barclay teaches from 2 Peter 1:6 (where the King James Version uses the term *patience*):

> The word never means the spirit which sits with folded hands and simply bears things. It is victorious endurance . . . Christian steadfastness, the brave and courageous acceptance of everything life can do to us, and the transmuting of even the worst into another step on the upward way. It is the courageous and triumphant ability to bear things, which enables a man to pass breaking point and not to break, and always to greet the unseen with a cheer.[7]

Patience meets its most difficult test in personal relationships. Paul lost his patience dealing with John Mark. Hudson Taylor once confessed: "My greatest temptation is to lose my temper over the slackness and inefficiency so disappointing in those on whom I depend. It is no use to lose my temper—only kindness. But oh, it is such a trial."[8]

Many leaders can identify with Taylor's struggle. But in the face of doubting Thomas, the unstable Peter, and traitorous Judas, how marvelous was the patience of our Lord!

A leader shows patience by not running too far ahead of his followers and thus discouraging them. While keeping ahead, he stays near enough for them to keep him in sight and hear his call forward. He is not so strong that he cannot show strengthening sympathy for the weakness of his fellow travelers. "We who are strong ought to bear with the failings of the weak," Paul wrote in Romans 15:1.

The person who is impatient with weakness will be ineffective in his leadership. The evidence of our strength lies not in the distance that separates us from other runners but in our closure with them, our slower pace for their sakes, our helping them pick it up and cross the line.

Ernest Gordon described his father, A. J. Gordon, with these words: "Criticism and opposition he endured without recrimination."[9]

When we lead by persuasion rather than command, patience is essential. Leaders rightly cultivate the art of persuasion that allows maximum individual decision making and ownership of a plan. Often, a leader's plan of action must wait for collegial support—ever patient—until the team is ready. D. E. Hoste remembered a great leader:

> I shall never forget the impression made upon me by Hudson Taylor in connection with these affairs. Again and again he was obliged either to greatly modify or lay aside projects which were sound and helpful but met with determined opposition. . . . Later, in answer to patient continuance in prayer, many of [these] projects were [put into] effect.[10]

FRIENDSHIP

You can measure leaders by the number and quality of their friends. Judged by that measuring rod, Paul had a genius for friendship. He was essentially a gregarious man. His relationship with Timothy was a model of friendship between generations; Paul and Luke are a model between contemporaries.

A. B. Simpson earned this sterling tribute: "The crowning glory of his leadership was that he was a friend of man. He loved the man next to him and he loved mankind."[11] David's leadership sprang from his genius at gathering around him men of renown who were ready to die for him. So fully did he capture their affection and allegiance that a casual wish was to them a command (2 Samuel 23:15). They were prepared to die for him, because they knew David was fully ready to die for them.

The apostle Paul similarly had loyal friends. "No man in the New Testament made fiercer enemies than Paul, but few men in the world had better friends. They clustered around him so thickly that we are apt to lose their personality in their devotion."[12] Yes, Paul led his friends into all sorts of risks for Christ's sake, but they followed him cheerfully, confident of his love for them. Paul's letters glow with warm appreciation and personal affection for his fellows.

Leaders must draw the best out of people, and friendship does that far better than prolonged argument or mere logic. John R. Mott counseled leaders to "rule by the heart. When reasons and arguments fail, fall back on the heart-genuine friendship."

Robert A. Jaffrey played a major role in opening Vietnam to the gospel. He did so largely because of this quality that all great leaders share. "Nothing can take the place of affection. . . . Intellect will not do. Bible knowledge is not enough." Jaffrey loved people for their own sakes. He was happy in the presence of human beings, whatever their race and color.[13]

Few Christian leaders enjoy the reputation won by Charles Spurgeon, the greatest British preacher of the late nineteenth century. His biographer wrote that "he exercised an absolute authority, not because of sheer willfulness, though he was a willful man, but because of his acknowledged worth. Men bowed to his authority because it was authority backed by united wisdom and affection."

One greater than Spurgeon or David or Paul ruled His followers by friendship and affection. Of Him it was written, "Having loved his own who were in the world, he now showed them the full extent of his love" (John 13:1). Indeed, Peter confessed with broken heart in response to Jesus' enduring affection, "Lord, you know all things; you know that I love you" (John 21:17).

TACT AND DIPLOMACY

The root meaning of *tact* has to do with touching. The tactile sense is the ability to feel through touch. Concerning relationships, tact is the ability to deal with people sensitively, to avoid giving offense, to have a "feel" for the proper words or responses to a delicate situation.

Diplomacy is the ability to manage delicate situations, especially involving people from different cultures, and certainly from differing opinions.

Leaders need to be able to reconcile opposing viewpoints without giving offense or compromising principle. A leader should be able to project into the life and heart and mind of another, then setting aside personal preferences, deal with the other in a fashion that fits the other best. These skills can be learned and developed.

A leader needs the ability to negotiate differences in a way that recognizes mutual rights and intelligence and yet leads to a harmonious solution. Fundamental to this skill is understanding how people feel, how people react.

Joshua used wonderful tact when he divided the Promised Land among the tribes of Israel. A wrong move would have splintered an already wobbly nation. Joshua had to be both forthright and fair. His tact beamed brightly again when the tribes of Reuben and Gad built their own altar, and thus nearly created a civil war. Joshua had wisdom learned in the school of God. His close walk with God gave him the diplomacy to steer a course away from needless bloodshed and toward national healing.

William Carey was unconsciously a diplomat. One of his fellow workers testified: "He has attained the happy art of ruling and overruling others without asserting his authority, or others feeling their subjection—and all is done without the least appearance of design on his part."[14]

INSPIRATIONAL POWER

The power of inspiring others to service and sacrifice will mark God's leader. Such a leader is like a light for others around. Charles Cowman worked hard, but he also possessed the ability to get others to work hard. His zeal and drive—and inspiration—were infectious.[15]

Pastor Hsi was one of the truly great leaders of his time in China. He too possessed this power to an extraordinary degree. A friend commented on Hsi's inspiring presence: "His power was remarkable. Without any effort, apparently, he seemed to sway everybody. Instinctively people followed and trusted him. He had great power of initiative and enterprise. You could not be with him without gaining a wholly new ideal of Christian life and service."[16]

Nehemiah had this quality. The people in Jerusalem were utterly disheartened and dispirited when he arrived. In no time he built them into an effective team of workers. Such were his powers that before long we read, "The people had a mind to work" (Nehemiah 4:6 KJV).

General Mark Clark, addressing a class of trainees, said of Winston Churchill: "I doubt if any man in history has ever made such grim utterances, yet given his people such a sense of strength, exuberance, even of cheerfulness."[17]

When France fell to the German armies and Britain was left alone in the fight, the British cabinet met in their chambers with a sense of deep gloom. When Churchill entered, he looked around at the disconsolate ministers, then said, "Gentlemen, I find this rather inspiring." Small wonder that he was able to galvanize a nation into effective counterattack.

EXECUTIVE ABILITY

However spiritual a leader may be, he cannot translate vision into action without executive ability. It is true that subtle dangers lie in organization, for if it is overzealous it can become an unsatisfactory substitute for the working of the Holy Spirit. But lack of method and failure to organize have spelled doom for many promising ministries.

The King James Version translates Isaiah 30:18: "The Lord is a God of judgment." Here the word *judgment* means method, order, system, or law. So God is methodic and orderly. And God requires of His managers and stewards that "all things be done decently and in order." Bible commentator Sir George Smith writes: "It is a great truth that the Almighty and All-merciful is the All-methodical too. No religion is complete in its creed, or healthy in its influence, which does not insist equally on all these."[18]

Our duty is to reflect the orderliness of God in all we do for Him. Evangelism is not a matter of organizing people into the kingdom, but neither is evangelistic work justified in ignoring careful planning. We depend on the Spirit leading converts to salvation, but we also plan and act on our plans for the sake of the gospel's reach.

John Wesley had a genius for organization that is still evident in the church he founded. Because he was such a gifted executive, his movement was unshaken when death deprived it of his presence and guidance. His judgment of others, his skill in deploying them to the mission's best advantage, and to win their loyal submission amounted to genius and spared the movement from disasters that others experienced.[19]

THE THERAPY OF LISTENING

To get at the root of problems, a leader must develop into a skillful listener. Too many strong personalities are compulsive talkers. "He won't listen to me," complains a missionary. "He gives the answer before I have had a chance to state the problem."

To many people, sympathetic listening is inefficient—merely waiting until someone else can state a point. But genuine listening seeks to understand another without prejudgment. A problem is often half-solved when it is clearly stated. One missionary casualty moaned: "If only he had listened to me. I needed someone to share a problem."

Leaders who want to show sensitivity should listen often and long, and talk short and seldom. Many so-called leaders are too busy to listen. True leaders know that time spent listening is well invested.

A would-be politician approached Justice Oliver Wendell Holmes for advice on how to get elected. Holmes replied: "To be able to listen to others in a sympathetic and understanding manner, is perhaps the most effective mechanism in the world for getting along with people, and tying up their friendship for good."[20]

THE ART OF LETTER WRITING

Any position of leadership involves a considerable amount of correspondence, and letters are self-revealing. Take Paul for example. We know more about his moral integrity, intellectual honesty, and spiritual life from his letters than from any other source. When a difficult situation required his attention, he dipped his pen in tears, not acid. "For I wrote you out of great distress and anguish of heart" (2 Corinthians 2:4).

After his strong letter to the erring Corinthians, Paul's tender heart led him to wonder if he had been too severe. "Even if I caused you sorrow by my letter, I do not regret it.

Though I did regret it—I see that my letter hurt you, but only for a little while—yet now I am happy . . . because your sorrow led you to repentance" (2 Corinthians 7:8–9). The point of his letter was not to win an argument, but to settle a spiritual problem and produce maturity among the Christians there.

Paul's letters are filled with encouragement, were gracious in compliment, and rich in sympathy. Those who received them were always enriched (Philippians 1:27–30). But that did not restrain him from being faithful in correcting faults. "Have I now become your enemy by telling you the truth? . . . how I wish I could be with you now and change my tone, because I am perplexed about you!" (Galatians 4:16, 20).

Clear language is important in our letters, but more important is the right spirit. For all their usefulness, letters have significant limitations as a medium of communication. They cannot smile when they are saying something difficult, and therefore additional care should be taken to see that they are warm in tone.

Letter writing formed an important part in Paul's program of instruction and follow-up. So it was for George Whitefield. It was said of him that after preaching to large crowds, he would work late into the night writing letters of encouragement to new converts.

CHAPTER 10

Above All Else

Choose seven men from among you who are known to be full of the Spirit and wisdom. . . . They chose Stephen, a man full of faith and of the Holy Spirit.
ACTS 6:3, 5

Spiritual leadership requires Spirit-filled people. Other qualities are important; to be Spirit-filled is indispensable.

The book of Acts is the story of people who established the church and led the missionary enterprise. We cannot fail to note that even the office of deacon required people "full of the Holy Spirit." These officers were to be known for integrity and judgment, but preeminently for their spirituality. A person can have a brilliant mind and possess artful administrative skill. But without spirituality he is incapable of giving truly spiritual leadership.

Behind all the busyness of the apostles was the executive activity of the Spirit. As supreme administrator of the church and chief strategist of the missionary enterprise, He was everywhere present. The Spirit did not delegate authority into secular or carnal hands, even when a particular job has no direct spiritual teaching involved; all workers must be Spirit-led and filled. Likewise today, selection of kingdom leaders must not be influenced by worldly wisdom, wealth, or status. The prime consideration is spirituality. When a church or missions organization follows a different set of criteria, it essentially removes the Spirit from leadership. As a consequence, the Spirit is grieved and quenched, and the result is spiritual dearth and death for that effort.

Selecting leaders apart from spiritual qualifications leads always to unspiritual administration. A. T. Pierson compared such a situation to a large corporation that wants to oust its CEO. Slowly, in the board and among the directors and vice presidents, people subtly oppose the chief's methods and spirit. They quietly undermine his measures, obstruct his plans, thwart his policies. Where the chief once enjoyed cooperation and support, he meets inertia and indifference until at last he resigns from sheer inability to carry out policy.[1] In the same way, appointing leaders with a secular or materialistic outlook prevents the Holy Spirit from making spiritual progress in that place.

The Holy Spirit does not take control of anyone against his or her will. When people who lack spiritual fitness are elected to leadership positions, He quietly withdraws and leaves them to implement their own policies according to their own standards, but without His aid. The inevitable result is an unspiritual administration.

The church at Jerusalem listened to the apostles' instructions and selected seven men who possessed the one necessary qualification. As a result of their Spirit-filled work, the church was blessed: the men selected to distribute food and earthly care were soon seen as the Spirit's agents in dispensing heavenly blessings. Stephen became the first martyr for Christ, and his death played a large role in the conversion of

Paul. Philip became an evangelist and was used by the Spirit to lead the great revival in Samaria. Leaders who are faithful in the exercise of their gifts prepare the way for promotion to greater responsibilities and usefulness.

The book of Acts clearly demonstrates that leaders who significantly influenced the Christian movement were Spirit-filled. It is reported of Him who commanded His disciples to tarry in Jerusalem until they were endued with power from on high that He Himself was "anointed . . . with the Holy Spirit and power" (10:38). Those 120 in the upper room were all filled with the Spirit (2:4). Peter was filled with the Spirit when he addressed the Sanhedrin (4:8). Stephen, filled with the Spirit, bore witness to Christ and died a radiant martyr (6:3; 7:55). In the Spirit's fullness Paul began and completed his unique ministry (9:17; 13:9). Paul's missionary companion Barnabas was filled with the Spirit (11:24). We would be strangely blind not to see this obvious requirement for spiritual leadership.

These early leaders of the church were sensitive to the leading of the Spirit. Because they had surrendered their own wills to the Spirit's control, they were delighted to obey His promptings and guidance. Philip left the revival in Samaria to go to the desert, but what a convert he found there (8:29)! The Spirit helped Peter to overcome his bias and meet with Cornelius, which led to blessings for the Gentile world (10:19; 11:12). The Spirit called Paul and Barnabas as first missionaries of the church (13:1–4). Throughout his busy life, Paul obeyed the Spirit's restraints and constraints (16:6–7; 19:21; 20:22). The leaders of the church at Jerusalem submitted to the Spirit. "It seemed good to the Holy Spirit and to us" was how the council articulated their judgments (15:28).

The Spirit intervened to bring the gospel to the Gentiles. The Spirit's great purpose is missions. Should that not be ours too?

Just now as I write, the Spirit is moving among Asian churches, giving them a new missionary vision and passion. Japanese churches have sent missionaries from Taiwan to Brazil. While the number of North American and European missionaries remains static, the heavenly Strategist is awakening the Asian church to her missionary obligations. Recently, more than three thousand Third World Christians have obeyed the call of God to missions.

Paul counseled leaders in the church at Ephesus on how to understand their office. "Keep watch over yourselves and all the flock of which the Holy Spirit has made you overseers" (Acts 20:28). Those leaders did not hold office by apostolic selection or popular election but by divine appointment. They were accountable not only to the church but also to the Holy Spirit. What a sense of assurance and responsibility, what a spiritual authority this teaching brought them, and brings to us!

Without the filling of the Holy Spirit at Pentecost, how could the apostles have faced the superhuman task ahead? They needed supernatural power for their truceless warfare against the devil and hell (Luke 24:29; Ephesians 6:10–18).

To be filled with the Spirit means simply that the Christian voluntarily surrenders life and will to the Spirit. Through faith, the believer's personality is permeated, mastered, and controlled by the Spirit. The meaning of *filled* is not to "pour into a passive container" but to "take possession of the mind." That's the meaning found in Luke 5:26: "They were filled with awe." When we invite the Spirit to fill us, the Spirit's power grips our lives with this kind of strength and passion.

To be filled with the Spirit is to be controlled by the Spirit. The Christian leader's mind, emotions, will, and physical strength all become available for the Spirit to guide and use. Under the Spirit's control, natural gifts of leadership are lifted to their highest power, sanctified for holy purpose. Through the work of the now ungrieved and unhindered Spirit, all the fruits of the Spirit start to grow in the leader's life. His witness is more winsome, service more steady, and testimony more powerful. All real Christian service is but the expression of Spirit power through believers yielded to Him (John 7:37–39).

If we pretend to be filled, or hold back on our willingness to let the Spirit control us, we create the kind of trouble A. W. Tozer warns against:

> No one whose senses have been exercised to know good or evil can but grieve over the sight of zealous souls seeking to be filled with the Holy Spirit while they are living in a state of moral carelessness and borderline sin. Whoever would be indwelt by the Spirit must judge his life for any hidden iniquities. He must expel from his heart everything that is out of accord with the character of God as revealed by the Holy Scriptures. . . . There can be no tolerance of evil, no laughing off the things that God hates.[2]

The filling of the Spirit is essential for spiritual leadership. And each believer has as much of the Spirit's presence as he or she will ever need. Our task is to remain yielded to Him.

SPIRITUAL GIFTS

Christians everywhere have undiscovered and unused spiritual gifts. The leader must help bring those gifts into the service of the kingdom, to develop them, to marshal their power. Spirituality alone does not make a leader; natural gifts and those given by God must be there too.

In our warfare against evil, we need the supernatural equipment God has provided in the spiritual gifts given to the church. To be used effectively, those gifts must be enriched by spiritual grace.

Often, though not always, the Holy Spirit imparts gifts that naturally fit the character and personality of the Christian leader. And the Spirit raises those gifts to a new level of effectiveness. Samuel Chadwick, the noted Methodist preacher, said that when he was filled with the Spirit, he did not receive a new brain but a new mentality; not a new tongue but new speaking effectiveness; not a new language but a new Bible. Chadwick's natural qualities were given a new vitality, a new energy.

The coming of spiritual gifts in the life of the Christian does not eliminate natural gifts but enhances and stimulates them. New birth in Christ does not change natural qualities but brings them in line with holy purpose; when they are placed under the control of the Holy Spirit, they are raised to new effectiveness. Hidden abilities are often released.

The one called by God to spiritual leadership can be confident that the Holy Spirit has given him or her all necessary gifts for the service at hand.

CHAPTER 11

Prayer and Leadership

I urge, then, first of all, that requests, prayers, intercession and thanksgiving be made for everyone. . . .

1 TIMOTHY 2:1

The spiritual leader should outpace the rest of the church, above all, in prayer. And yet the most advanced leader is conscious of the possibility of endless development in his prayer life. Nor does he ever feel that he has "already attained" (KJV). Dean C. J. Vaughan once said: "If I wished to humble anyone, I should question him about his prayers. I know nothing to compare with this topic for its sorrowful self-confessions."

Prayer is the most ancient, most universal, and most intensive expression of the religious instinct. It includes the simplest speech of infant lips, and the sublime entreaties of older age. All reach the Majesty on high. Prayer is indeed the Christian's vital breath and native air.

But, strange paradox, most of us find it hard to pray. We do not naturally delight in drawing near to God. We sometimes pay lip service to the delight and power of prayer. We call it indispensable; we know the Scriptures call for it. Yet we often fail to pray.

Let us take encouragement from the lives of saintly leaders who overcame this natural reluctance and became mighty in prayer. Of Samuel Chadwick it was said:

> He was essentially a man of prayer. Every morning he would be astir shortly after six o'clock, and he kept a little room which was his private sanctum for his quiet hour before breakfast. He was mighty in public prayer because he was constant in private devotion. . . . When he prayed he expected God to do something. "I wish I had prayed more," he wrote toward the end of his life, "even if I had worked less; and from the bottom of my heart I wish I had prayed better."[1]

"When I go to prayer," confessed an eminent Christian, "I find my heart so loath to go to God, and when it is with Him, so loath to stay." Then he pointed to the need for self-discipline. "When you feel most indisposed to pray, yield not to it," he counseled, "but strive and endeavor to pray, even when you think you cannot."

Mastering the art of prayer, like anything else, takes time. The time we give it will be a true measure of its importance to us. We always find the time for important things. The most common excuse for little time spent in prayer is the list of "to-dos" that crowd our day—all our many duties. To Martin Luther, an extra load of duties was reason enough to pray more, not less. Hear his plans for the next day's work: "Work, work from early till late. In fact I have so much to do that I shall spend the first three hours in prayer."

If Luther was busy, and prayed, so can we.

Try to explain exactly how prayer works and you will quickly run against some very difficult puzzles. But people who are skeptical of prayer's validity and power are usually those who do not practice it seriously or fail to obey when God reveals His will. We cannot learn about prayer except by praying. No philosophy has ever taught a soul to pray. The intellectual problems associated with prayer are met in the joy of answered prayer and closer fellowship with God.

The Christian leader who seeks an example to follow does well to turn to the life of Jesus Himself. Our belief in the necessity of prayer comes from observing His life. Surely if anyone could have sustained life without prayer, it would be the very Son of God Himself. If prayer is silly or unnecessary, Jesus would not have wasted His time at it. But wait! Prayer was the dominant feature of His life and a recurring part of His teaching. Prayer kept His moral vision sharp and clear. Prayer gave Him courage to endure the perfect but painful will of His Father. Prayer paved the way for transfiguration. To Jesus, prayer was not a hasty add-on, but a joyous necessity.

> In Luke 5:16 we have a general statement which throws a vivid light on the daily practice of the Lord. "And He withdrew Himself in the deserts and prayed." It is not of one occasion but of many that the evangelist speaks in this place. It was our Lord's habit to seek retirement for prayer. When He withdrew Himself from men, He was accustomed to press far into the uninhabited country—He was in the deserts. The surprise of the onlookers lay

> in this, that one so mighty, so richly endowed with spiritual power, should find it necessary for Himself to repair to the source of strength, that there He might refresh His weary spirit. To us, the wonder is still greater, that He, the prince of Life, the Eternal word, the Only-begotten of the Father, should prostrate Himself in meekness before the throne of God, making entreaty for grace to help in time of need.[2]

Christ spent full nights in prayer (Luke 6:12). He often rose before dawn to have unbroken communion with His Father (Mark 1:35). The great crises of His life and ministry began with periods of special prayer, as in Luke 5:16: "Jesus often withdrew to lonely places and prayed"—a statement that indicates a regular habit. By word and example He instructed His disciples on the importance of solitude in prayer (Mark 6:46, following the feeding of the five thousand; Luke 9:28, preceding the Transfiguration). To the person on whom devolves the responsibility for selecting personnel for specific spiritual responsibilities, the example of the Lord's spending the night in prayer before making His choice of apostles (Luke 6:12) is luminous.

Both our Lord and His bond slave Paul made clear that true prayer is not dreamy reverie. "All vital praying makes a drain on a man's vitality. True intercession is a sacrifice, a bleeding sacrifice," wrote J. H. Jowett. Jesus performed miracles without a sign of outward strain, but "he offered up prayers and petitions with loud cries and tears" (Hebrews 5:7).

Sometimes our prayers are pale and weak compared to those of Paul or Epaphras. "Epaphras . . . is always wrestling in prayer for you," wrote Paul in Colossians 4:12. And to the same group: "I want you to know how much I am struggling for you" (Colossians 2:1). The Greek word used for "struggle" here is the root for our words *agony* and *agonize*. It is used to describe a person struggling at work until utterly weary (Colossians 1:29) or competing in the arena for an athletic prize (1 Corinthians 9:25). It describes a soldier battling for his life (1 Timothy 6:12), or a man struggling to deliver his friends from danger (John 18:36). True prayer is a strenuous spiritual exercise that demands the utmost mental discipline and concentration.

We are encouraged to note that Paul, probably the greatest human champion of prayer, confessed, "We do not know what we ought to pray for." And then he hastened to add, "The Spirit himself intercedes for us with groans that words cannot express. And he who searches our hearts knows the mind of the Spirit, because the Spirit intercedes for the saints in accordance with God's will" (Romans 8:26–27). The Spirit joins us in prayer and pours His supplications into our own.

PRAY IN THE SPIRIT

All Christians need more teaching in the art of prayer, and the Holy Spirit is the master teacher. The Spirit's help in prayer is mentioned in the Bible more frequently than any other help He gives us. All true praying comes from the Spirit's activity in our souls. Both Paul and Jude teach that effective prayer is "praying in the Spirit." That phrase means that we pray along the same lines, about the same things, in the same name, as the Holy Spirit. True prayer rises in the spirit of the Christian from the Spirit who indwells us.

To pray in the Spirit is important for two reasons. First, we are to pray in the realm of the Spirit, for the Holy Spirit is the sphere and atmosphere of the Christian's life. In this we often fail. Much praying is physical rather than spiritual, in the realm of the mind alone, the product of our own thinking and not of the Spirit's teaching. But real prayer is deeper. It uses the body, requires the cooperation of the mind, and moves in the supernatural realm of the Spirit. Such praying transacts its business in the heavenly realm.

Second, we are to pray in the power and energy of the Spirit. "Give yourselves wholly to prayer and entreaty; pray on every occasion in the power of the Spirit" (Ephesians 6:18 NEB). For its superhuman task, prayer demands more than human power. We have the Spirit of power as well as the Spirit of prayer. All the human energy of heart, mind, and will can achieve great human results, but praying in the Holy Spirit releases supernatural resources.

The Spirit delights to help us pray. In each of our three chief handicaps, we can count on the Spirit's help. Sometimes we are kept from prayer by sin in our heart. As we grow in trust and submission, the Holy Spirit leads us to the blood of Christ, which cleanses every stain.

Sometimes the ignorance of our minds hinders our prayers. But the Spirit knows the mind of God and shares that knowledge with us as we wait and listen. The Spirit does this by giving us a clear conviction that a particular prayer request is part of God's will for us, or not.

Sometimes we are earthbound because of the infirmity of the body. We get sick, we feel ill, we are weak. The Spirit will quicken our bodies and enable us to rise above weaknesses, even those imposed by sultry tropical climates.

Then, as if these three conditions were not enough, the spiritual leader must oppose Satan in prayer. Satan will try to depress, to create doubt and discouragement, to keep a leader from communion with God. In the Holy Spirit, we have a heavenly ally against this supernatural foe.

Spiritual leaders should know the experience of praying in the Spirit as part of their daily walk. Do we ever try to live independently of the Spirit? Do we fail to see full answers to prayer? We can read all day about prayer, and experience little of its power, and so stunt our service.

The Bible often explains prayer as spiritual warfare. "For our struggle is . . . against the rulers, against the authorities, against the powers of this dark world and against the spiritual forces of evil in the heavenly realms" (Ephesians 6:12). In this struggle phase of prayer, three personalities are engaged. Between God and the devil stands the Christian at prayer. Though weak alone, the Christian plays a strategic role in the struggle between the dragon and the Lamb. The praying Christian wields no personal power, but power nonetheless delegated by the victorious Christ to whom that faithful believer is united by faith. Faith is like a reticulating system through which the victory won on Calvary reaches the devil's captives and delivers them from darkness into light.

Jesus was not so much concerned over wicked people and their deeds as with the forces of evil that caused those people to sin. Behind Peter's denial and Judas's betrayal was the sinister hand of Satan. "Get thee behind me, Satan," was the Lord's response to Peter's presumptuous rebuke

(KJV). All around us are people bound in sin, captives to the devil. Our prayers should ascend not only for them but against Satan who holds them as his prize. Satan must be compelled to relax his grip, and this can only be achieved by Christ's victory on the cross.

As Jesus dealt with sin's cause rather than effect, so the spiritual leader should adopt the same method in prayer. And the leader must know how to help those under his charge who are also involved in that same spiritual warfare.

In a telling illustration, Jesus compared Satan to a strong man, fully armed. Before anyone can enter such a man's house and set captives free, the man must first be bound. Only then can a rescue succeed (Matthew 12:29). What could it mean to "tie up the strong man" except to neutralize his might through the overcoming power of Christ who came "to destroy [nullify, render inoperative] the works of the devil" (NLT)? And how can that happen except by the prayer of faith that lays hold of the victory of Calvary and claims it for the problem at hand? We cannot hope to effect a rescue from Satan's den without first disarming the adversary. God makes available His divine authority through prayer, and we can confidently claim it. Jesus promised His disciples: "I have given you authority . . . to overcome all the power of the enemy" (Luke 10:19).

The spiritual leader will be alert to the most effective way to influence people. Hudson Taylor is well known for his expression, "It is possible to move men, through God, by prayer alone." During his missionary career he demonstrated the truth of his claim a thousand times.

PRACTICE

It is one thing to believe such power is available in prayer, but another thing to practice it. People are difficult to move; it is much easier to pray for things or provisions than to deal with the stubbornness of the human heart. But in just these intricate situations, the leader must use God's power to move human hearts in the direction he believes to be the will of God. Through prayer the leader has the key to that complicated lock.

It is the supreme dignity and glory of the human creature to be able to say yes or no to God. Humans have been given free will. But this poses a problem. If by prayer we can influence the conduct of others, does such power encroach on free will? Will God temper one person's freedom to answer another person's prayer? It seems difficult to imagine. And yet, if prayers cannot influence the course of events, why pray?

The first point to make is that God is consistent with Himself always. God does not contradict Himself. When God promises to answer prayer, the answer will come—always in a manner consistent with divine nature, for "he cannot disown himself" (2 Timothy 2:13). No word or action from God will contradict any other word or action of God.

The second point in resolving these questions is that prayer is a divine ordinance. God has commanded prayer, and we can be confident that as we meet revealed conditions for prayer, answers will be granted. God sees no contradiction between human free will and divine response to prayer. When God commands us to pray "for kings and those in authority," there is implied power to influence the course of men and events. If not, why pray? Our obligation to pray stands above any dilemma concerning the effects of prayer.

Third, we can know the will of God concerning the prayer we raise. Our capacity to know God's will is the basis for all prayers of faith. God can speak to us clearly through our mind and heart. The Bible instructs us directly concerning the will of God on all matters of principle. In our hearts the Holy Spirit ministers to instruct us in the will of God (Romans 8:26–27). As we patiently seek the will of God concerning our petition, the Spirit will impress our minds and convince our hearts. Such God-given conviction leads us beyond the prayer of hope to the prayer of faith.

When God lays a burden on our hearts and thus keeps us praying, He obviously intends to grant the answer. George Mueller was asked if he really believed that two men would be converted, men for whom Mueller had prayed for over fifty years. Mueller replied: "Do you think God would have kept me praying all these years if He did not intend to save them?" In fact, both men were converted, one shortly after Mueller's death.[3]

In prayer we deal directly with God and only in a secondary sense other people. The goal of prayer is the ear of God. Prayer moves others through God's influence on them. It is not our prayer that moves people, but the God to whom we pray.

Prayer moves the arm
That moves the world
To bring deliverance down.
—Author Unknown

To move people, the leader must be able to move God, for God has made it clear that He moves people in response to prayer. If a scheming Jacob was given "power with God and with men," then surely any leader who follows God's prayer principles can enjoy the same power (Genesis 32:28 KJV).

Prevailing prayer that moves people is the outcome of a right relationship with God. The Bible is very clear on the reasons why prayers go unanswered, and every reason centers on the believer's relationship with God. God will not cooperate with prayers of mere self-interest, or prayers that come from impure motives. The Christian who clings to sin closes the ear of God. Least of all will God tolerate unbelief, the chief of sins. "Anyone who comes to him must believe" (Hebrews 11:6). In all our prayers the paramount motive is the glory of God.

Great leaders of the Bible were great at prayer. "They were not leaders because of brilliancy of thought, because they were exhaustless in resources, because of their magnificent culture or native endowment, but because, by the power of prayer, they could command the power of God."[4]

CHAPTER 12

The Leader and Time

Make the best use of your time. . . .
EPHESIANS 5:16 PHILLIPS

The quality of a person's leadership will be in part measured by time: its use and its passage. The character and career of a young person depends on how he or she spends spare time. We cannot regulate school or office hours—those are determined for us—but we can say what we will do before and after those commitments. The way we employ the surplus hours, after provision has been made for work, meals, and sleep, will determine if we develop into mediocre or powerful people. Leisure is a glorious opportunity and a subtle danger. A discretionary hour can be wisely invested or foolishly wasted. Each moment of the day is a gift from God that deserves care, for by any measure, our time is short and the work is great.

Minutes and hours wisely used translate into an abundant life. On one occasion when Michelangelo was pressing himself to finish a work on deadline, someone warned him, "This may cost your life!" He replied, "What else is life for?"

Hours and days will surely pass, but we can direct them purposefully and productively. Philosopher William James affirmed that the best use of one's life is to spend it for something that will outlast it. Life's value is not its duration but its donation—not how long we live but how fully and how well.[1]

Time is precious, but we squander it thoughtlessly. Moses knew time was valuable and prayed to be taught to measure it by days, not by years (Psalm 90:12). If we are careful about days, the years will take care of themselves.

A leader will seldom say, "I don't have the time." Such an excuse is usually the refuge of a small-minded and inefficient person. Each of us has the time to do the whole will of God for our lives. J. H. Jowett said:

> I think one of the cant phrases of our day is the familiar one by which we express our permanent want of time. We repeat it so often that by the very repetition we have deceived ourselves into believing it. It is never the supremely busy men who have no time. So compact and systematic is the regulation of their day that whenever you make a demand on them, they seem to find additional corners to offer for unselfish service. I confess as a minister, that the men to whom I most hopefully look for additional service are the busiest men.[2]

Our problem is not too little time but making better use of the time we have. Each of us has as much time as anyone else. The president of the United States has the same twenty-four hours as we. Others may surpass our abilities, influence, or money, but no one has more time.

As in the parable of the pounds ("minas" in the NIV; Luke 19:12–27), where each servant was given the same amount of money, we each have been given the same amount of time. But few of us use it so wisely as to produce a tenfold return. The parable recognizes different abilities; the servant with less capacity but equal faithfulness received the same reward. We are not responsible for our endowments or natural abilities, but we are responsible for the strategic use of time.

When Paul urged the Ephesians to "redeem" the time (see 5:16 KJV), he was treating time like purchasing power. We exchange time in the market of life for certain occupations and activities that may be worthy or not, productive or not. Another translation renders the verse "Buy up the opportunities," for time is opportunity. Herein lies the importance of a carefully planned life: "If we progress in the economy of time, we are learning to live. If we fail here, we fail everywhere."

Time lost can never be retrieved. Time cannot be hoarded, only spent well. These lines were found engraved on a sundial:

The shadow of my finger cast
Divides the future from the past;
Before it stands the unborn hour
In darkness and beyond thy power;
Behind its unreturning line
The vanished hour, no longer thine;
One hour alone is in thy hands,
The now on which the shadow stands.
—*Author Unknown*

In the face of this sobering reality, the leader must carefully select priorities. He or she must thoughtfully weigh the value of different opportunities and responsibilities. The leader cannot spend time on secondary matters while essential obligations scream for attention. A day needs careful planning. The person who wants to excel must select and reject, then concentrate on the most important items.

It is often helpful to keep records of how each hour in a given week is spent, and then look at the record in the light of scriptural priorities. The results may be shocking. Often the record shows that we have much more time available for Christian service than we imagine.

Suppose that we allot ourselves a generous eight hours a day for sleep (and few need more than that), three hours for meals and conversation, ten hours for work and travel. Still we have thirty-five hours each week to fill. What happens to them? How are they invested? A person's entire contribution to the kingdom of God may turn on how those hours are used. Certainly those hours determine whether life is commonplace or extraordinary.

The intrepid missionary Mary Slessor was the daughter of a drunkard. At age eleven she began working in a factory in Dundee, and there spent her days from six in the morning until six at night. Yet that grueling regimen did not prevent her from educating herself for a notable career.[3]

David Livingstone, at age ten, worked in a cotton mill in Dumbarton fourteen hours a day. Surely he had excuses for not studying, for not redeeming the little leisure left to him. But he learned Latin and could read Horace and

Virgil at age sixteen. At age twenty-seven, he had finished a program in both medicine and theology.

Similar examples are so numerous that we have little ground today to plead insufficient time for achieving something worthwhile in life.

Our Lord sets the perfect example of strategic use of time. He moved through life with measured steps, never hurried, though always surrounded by demands and crowds. When a person approached Him for help, Jesus gave the impression that He had no more important concern than the needs of His visitor.

The secret of Jesus' serenity lay in His assurance that He was working according to the Father's plan for His life—a plan that embraced every hour and made provision for every need. Through communion in prayer with His Father, Jesus received each day both the words He would say and the works He would do. "The words I say to you are not just my own. Rather, it is the Father, living in me, who is doing his work" (John 14:10).

Jesus' greatest concern was to fulfill the work committed to Him within the allotted hours. He was conscious of a divine timing in His life (John 7:6; 12:23, 27; 13:1; 17:1). Even to His beloved mother He said, "My time has not yet come" (John 2:4). Responding to Mary and Martha's distress, Jesus declined to change His schedule by two days (John 11:1–6). When He reviewed His life at its close, He said: "I have brought you glory on earth by completing the work you gave me to do" (John 17:4). Jesus completed His life's work without any part spoiled by undue haste or half done through lack of time. His twenty-four hours a day was sufficient to complete the whole will of God.

Jesus told His disciples: "Are there not twelve hours in the day?" (KJV). J. Stuart Holden saw in our Lord's words both the shortness of time and the sufficiency of time. There were indeed twelve hours in the day, but in fact there were fully twelve hours in the day.[4]

Conscious of time, Jesus spent His time doing things that mattered. No time was wasted on things not vital. The strength of moral character is conserved by refusing the unimportant.

No trifling in this life of mine;
Not this the path the blessed Master trod;
But every hour and power employed
Always and all for God.
—Author Unknown

How interesting that the Gospel accounts contain no hint of any interruption ever disturbing the serenity of the Son of God. Few things are more likely to produce tension in a busy life than unexpected interruptions. Yet to Jesus there were no such things. "Unexpected" events were always foreseen in the Father's planning, and Jesus was therefore undisturbed by them. True, at times there was hardly time to eat, but time was always sufficient to accomplish all the Father's will.

Often the pressure a spiritual leader feels comes from assuming tasks that God has not assigned; for such tasks the leader cannot expect God to supply the extra strength required.

One busy man told me how he mastered the problem of interruptions. "Up to some years ago," he testified, "I was always annoyed by them, which was really a form of selfishness on my part. People used to walk in and say, 'Well, I just had two hours to kill here in between trains, and I thought I would come and see you.' That used to bother me. Then the Lord convinced me that He sends people our way. He sent Philip to the Ethiopian eunuch. He sent Barnabas to see Saul. The same applies today. God sends people our way.

"So when someone comes in, I say, 'The Lord must have brought you here. Let us find out why He sent you. Let us have prayer.' Well this does two things. The interview takes on new importance because God is in it. And it generally shortens the interview. If a visitor knows you are looking for reasons why God should have brought him, and there are none apparent, the visit becomes pleasant but brief.

"So now I take interruptions as from the Lord. They belong in my schedule, because the schedule is God's to arrange at His pleasure."

Paul affirms that God has a plan for every life. We have been "created in Christ Jesus to do good works, which God prepared in advance for us to do" (Ephesians 2:10). Through daily prayer, the leader discovers the details of that plan and arranges work accordingly. Each half hour should carry its load of usefulness.

John Wesley and F. B. Meyer, men who influenced the world for Christ, divided their days into five-minute periods, then tried to make each one count. All of us could benefit by similar discipline. For example, much reading can be done during otherwise wasted minutes.

Meyer's biographer tells how he would redeem the time:

> If he had a long railway journey before him, he would settle himself in his corner of the railway carriage, open his dispatch case which was fitted as a sort of stationery cabinet, and set to work on some abstruse article, quite oblivious of his surroundings. Often at protracted conventions, and even in committee meetings, when the proceeding did not demand his undivided attention, he would unobtrusively open his case and proceed to answer letters.[5]

Another miser with time was W. E. Sangster. His son writes of him:

> Time was never wasted. The difference between one minute and two was of considerable consequence to him. He would appear from his study. "My boy, you're not doing anything. I have exactly twenty-two minutes. We'll go for a walk. We can walk right around the common in that time." He then hurtled out of the house at tremendous speed and I normally had to run to catch up. He would then discourse on current affairs (five minutes), Surrey's prospects in the country championship (two minutes), the necessity for revival (five minutes), the reality of the Loch Ness monster (two minutes), and the sanctity of William Romaine (three minutes). By that time we would be home again.[6]

A leader needs a balanced approach to time lest it become his bondage and downfall. Without a grip on time, the leader works under unnecessary strain. Even when the leader has done the utmost to fulfill daily obligations, vast areas of work always remain. Every call for help is not necessarily a call from God, for it is impossible to respond to every need. If the leader sincerely plans his day in prayer, then executes the plan with all energy and eagerness, that is enough. A leader is responsible only for what lies within the range of control. The rest he should trust to our loving and competent heavenly Father.

Procrastination, the thief of time, is one of the devil's most potent weapons for defrauding us of eternal heritage. The habit of "putting off" is fatal to spiritual leadership. Its power resides in our natural reluctance to come to grips with important decisions. Making decisions, and acting on them, always requires moral energy. But the passing of time never makes action easier, quite the opposite. Most decisions are more difficult a day later, and you may also lose an advantage by such delay. The nettle will never be easier to grasp than now.

"Do it now" is a motto that led many people to worldly success, and it is equally relevant in spiritual matters. A helpful method for overcoming procrastination is to carefully set deadlines, and never miss or postpone even one.

A lifelong reader was asked by friends, "How do you get time for it?" He replied, "I don't get time for it; I take time."[7]

CHAPTER 13

The Leader and Reading

When you come, bring . . . my scrolls,
especially the parchments.
2 TIMOTHY 4:13

Reading maketh a full man; speaking, a ready man;
writing, an exact man.
BACON

Paul's counsel to Timothy, "Give heed to reading" (1 Timothy 4:13 ASV), surely referred to the public reading of the Old Testament. But Paul's advice is appropriate for other areas of reading as well. Paul's books—the ones he wanted Timothy to bring along—were probably works of Jewish history, explanations of the Law and prophets, and perhaps some of the heathen poets Paul quoted in his sermons and lectures. A student to the end, Paul wanted to spend time in study.

During his imprisonment and shortly before his martyrdom in 1536, William Tyndale wrote to the governor-in-chief, asking that some goods be sent him:

> A warmer cap, a candle, a piece of cloth to patch my leggings. . . . But above all, I beseech and entreat your

> clemency to be urgent with the Procureur that he may kindly permit me to have my Hebrew Bible, Hebrew grammar and Hebrew Dictionary, that I many spend time with that in study.[1]

Both Paul and Tyndale devoted last days on earth to the study of the parchments. Spiritual leaders of every generation will have a consuming passion to know the Word of God through diligent study and the illumination of the Holy Spirit. But in this chapter our special interest is a leader's supplementary reading.

The leader who intends to grow spiritually and intellectually will be reading constantly. Lawyers must read steadily to keep up on case law. Doctors must read to stay current in the ever-changing world of health care. So the spiritual leader must master God's Word and its principles, and know as well the minds of those who look to the leader for guidance. To do so, the leader must have an active life of reading.

These days, the practice of reading spiritual classics is on the wane. We have more leisure today than ever before in history, but many people claim to have no time for reading. A spiritual leader cannot use that excuse.

John Wesley had a passion for reading, and he did so mostly on horseback. Often he rode a horse fifty and sometimes ninety miles in a day. His habit was to ride with a volume of science or history or medicine propped in the pommel of his saddle, and thus he consumed thousands of books. Besides his Greek New Testament, three great books took possession of Wesley's mind and heart during his Oxford days: *Imitation of Christ*, *Holy Living and Dying*, and

The Serious Call. These three were his spiritual guides. Wesley told the younger ministers of the Methodist societies to read or get out of the ministry!

Leaders should determine to spend a minimum of half an hour a day reading books that feed the soul and stimulate the mind. In a perceptive series on "The Use and Abuse of Books," A. W. Tozer said:

> Why does today's Christian find the reading of great books always beyond him? Certainly intellectual powers do not wane from one generation to another. We are as smart as our father, and any thought they could entertain we can entertain if we are sufficiently interested to make the effort. The major cause of the decline in the quality of current Christian literature is not intellectual but spiritual. To enjoy a great religious book requires a degree of consecration to God and detachment from the world that few modern Christians have. The early Christian Fathers, the Mystics, the Puritans, are not hard to understand, but they inhabit the highlands where the air is crisp and rarefied, and none but the God-enamored can come. . . . One reason why people are unable to understand great Christian classics is that they are trying to understand without any intention of obeying them.[2]

WHY READ?

"Read to refill the wells of inspiration," was the advice of Harold Ockenga, who took a suitcase of books on his honeymoon![3]

Bacon's famous rule for reading: "Read not to contradict or confute, nor to believe and take for granted, nor to find talk and discourse, but to weigh and consider. Some books are to be tested, others to be swallowed, and some few to be chewed and digested."[4] Indeed, if we read merely to stock our head with ideas, to feel superior to others, or to appear learned, then our reading is useless and vain.

The spiritual leader should choose books for their spiritual benefit. Some authors challenge heart and conscience and point us toward the highest; they spark our impulse to service and lead us to God.

Spiritual leaders should also read for intellectual growth. This will require books that test wits, provide fresh ideas, challenge assumptions, and probe complexities.

The leader should read to cultivate his preaching and writing style. For that, we need to read those masters who instruct us in the art of incisive and compelling speech. Tozer recommended John Bunyan for simplicity, Joseph Addison for clarity and elegance, John Milton for nobility and consistent elevation of thought, Charles Dickens for sprightliness, and Francis Bacon for dignity.

The leader should read, too, to acquire new information, to keep current with the time, to be well informed in his or her own field of expertise.

The leader should read to have fellowship with great minds. Through books we hold communion with the greatest spiritual leaders of the ages.

A good book has great power. In *Curiosities of Literature*, Benjamin Disraeli gives a number of instances where a person has been magnificently influenced by a solitary book. As I have read the biographies of great Christians, time and again one book has brought their lives to crisis and produced a revolution of ministry. That book is Charles G. Finney's *Lectures on Revivals of Religion*.[5]

WHAT TO READ

If a man is known by the company he keeps, so also his character is reflected in the books he reads. A leader's reading is the outward expression of his inner aspirations. The vast number of titles pouring from presses today makes discriminating choice essential. We can afford to read only the best, only that which invigorates our mission. Our reading should be regulated by who we are and what we intend to accomplish.

An old author whose pen name was Cladius Clear said that a reader could divide his books as he would people. A few were "lovers," and those books would go with him into exile. Others are "friends." Most books are "acquaintances," works with which he was on nodding terms.

Matthew Arnold thought that the best of literature was bound within five hundred book covers. Daniel Webster preferred to master a few books rather than read widely. To them he would appeal for genuine knowledge of the human heart, its aspirations and tragedies, hopes and disappointments. Indiscriminate reading serves no one well. Hobbes, the English philosopher, once said, "If I had read as many books as other people, I would know as little."

Samuel Brengle said this about poetry:

> I like the poets whose writings reveal great moral character and passion—such as Tennyson and some

> of Browning. The works of others have light, but I prefer flame to light. Shakespeare? A mind as clear as a sunbeam—but passionless, light without heat. Shelley? Keats? There's a sense in which they were perfect poets, but they don't move me. Beautiful—but wordmongers. There's an infinite difference between the beauty of holiness and the holiness of beauty. One leads to the highest, loftiest, most Godlike character; the other often—too often—leads to an orgy of sensation.[6]

Sir W. Robertson Nicoll, for many years editor of *British Weekly*, found biography the most attractive form of general reading because biography transmits personality. To read the lives of great and consecrated men and women is to kindle one's own heart toward God. Imagine how the missions movement has been inspired by the biographies of William Carey, Adoniram Judson, Hudson Taylor, Charles Studd, or Albert Simpson.[7]

Joseph W. Kemp, widely known for his preaching and teaching, always kept a good biography on hand. Ransome W. Cooper wrote:

> The reading of good biography forms an important part of a Christian's education. It provides him with numberless illustrations for use in his own service. He learns to assess the true worth of character, to glimpse a work goal for his own life, to decide how best to attain it, what self-denial is needed to curb unworthy aspirations; and all the time he learns how God breaks into the dedicated life to bring about his own purposes.

A leader should neither be content with easy books nor satisfied with reading only in his specialty. Muriel Ormrod counseled:

> It is better that we should always tackle something a bit beyond us. We should always aim to read something different—not only the writers with whom we agree, but those with whom we are ready to do battle. And let us not condemn them out of hand because they do not agree with us; their point of view challenges us to examine the truth and to test their views against Scripture. And let us not comment on nor criticize writers of whom we have heard only second-hand, or third-hand, without troubling to read their works for ourselves. . . . Don't be afraid of new ideas—and don't be carried away with them either.[8]

The leader should immerse himself in books that equip him for higher service and leadership in the kingdom of God.

> *A little learning is a dangerous thing;*
> *Drink deep, or taste not the Pierian Spring;*
> *There shallow draughts intoxicate the brain,*
> *And drinking largely sobers us again.*
> *—Alexander Pope*

HOW TO READ

By reading we learn. By meditating on the themes of our reading, we pluck the fruit from the tree of books and add nourishment to our minds and our ministries. Unless our reading includes serious thinking, it is wasted time.

When Robert Southey, the poet, was telling a Quaker lady how he learned Portuguese grammar while he washed, and French literature while he dressed, and science while he took breakfast, and so on, filling his day utterly, she said quietly, "And when does thee think?" We can read without thinking, but such reading has not profit for us. Spurgeon counseled his students:

> Master those books you have. Read them thoroughly. Bathe in them until they saturate you. Read and reread them, masticate and digest them. Let them go into your very self. Peruse a good book several times and make notes and analyses of it. A student will find that his mental constitution is more affected by one book thoroughly mastered than by twenty books he has merely skimmed. Little learning and much pride comes of hasty reading. Some men are disabled from thinking by their putting meditation away for the sake of much reading. In reading let your motto be "much, not many."[9]

Use the following proven strategies for making your reading worthwhile and profitable:

- What you intend to quickly forget, spend little time reading. The habit of reading and forgetting only builds the habit of forgetting other important matters.
- Use the same discrimination in choosing books as in choosing friends.

- Read with pencil and notebook in hand. Unless your memory is unusually retentive, much gained from reading is lost in a day. Develop a system of note taking. It will greatly help the memory.
- Have a "commonplace book," as they are called—a book to record what is striking, interesting, and worthy of second thought. In that way you will build a treasure trove of material for future use.
- Verify historical, scientific, and other data.
- Pass no word until its meaning is known. Keep a dictionary at hand.
- Vary your reading to keep your mind out of a rut. Variety is as refreshing to the mind as it is to the body.
- Correlate your reading—history with poetry, biography with historical novel. For example, when reading the history of the American Civil War, take up also the biography of Lincoln or Grant and the poetry of Whitman.

Canon Yates advised that every good book needs three readings. The first should be rapid and continuous, to give your mind an overview and to associate the book's material with your previous knowledge. The second reading should be careful and paced. Take notes and think. Then after an interval of time, a third reading should be like the first. Write a brief analysis of the book on the inside back cover. Thus will the book make a solid imprint on your memory.

A Scottish minister in Lumsden town had collected seventeen thousand volumes that he browsed with great delight. But his son said later, "Though he spent much time and pains on his sermons, he did not cut a channel between them and his reading."[10]

Beware the danger of the Lumsden syndrome. A book is a channel for the flow of ideas between one mind and another. The Lumsden preacher may have had the benefit of books for his own spiritual life, but the people in his church apparently never felt the influence of his reading. Leaders should always cut a channel between reading and speaking and writing, so that others derive benefit, pleasure, and inspiration.

A country minister in Australia known to this writer was a great book lover. Early in his ministry he determined to develop a biblically and theologically literate congregation. He helped his people learn to love books and led them into progressively deeper and weightier spiritual literature. The result is that a number of farmers in that district have significant libraries and thoughtful faith.

More ministers should try to lead in this way, guiding the church toward intelligent reading and larger, more committed, more resilient faith.

CHAPTER 14

Improving Leadership

If you are a leader, exert yourself to lead.
ROMANS 12:8 NEB

Every Christian is obliged to be the best for God. Like any other worthwhile activity, if leadership can be improved, we should seek to improve it. In so doing, we prepare ourselves for higher service that may be just around the next corner, though unseen at the present.

Not every Christian is called to major leadership in the church, but every Christian is a leader, for we all influence others. All of us should strive to improve our leadership skills.

The first steps toward improvement involve recognizing weaknesses, making corrections, and cultivating strengths. Many reasons explain why church leadership is less than the best, and some of the following considerations may apply to you.

- Perhaps we lack a clearly defined goal that will stretch us, challenge faith, and unify life's activities.
- Perhaps our faith is timid, and we hesitate to take risks for the kingdom.
- Do we show the zeal of salvation in Christ, or is our demeanor morbid and sad? Enthusiastic leaders generate enthusiastic followers.

- We may be reluctant to grasp the nettle of a difficult situation and deal courageously with it. Or we may procrastinate, hoping that problems will vanish with time. The mediocre leader postpones difficult decisions, conversations, and letters. Delay solves nothing, and usually makes problems worse.
- Perhaps we sacrifice depth for breadth, and spreading ourselves thin, achieve only superficial results.

EXERT YOURSELF TO LEAD

Romans 12:1 issues this imperative to leaders: "Offer your bodies as living sacrifices, holy and pleasing to God." The Greek aorist tense of the verb "offer" (which signifies a one-time act that is finished and done) is followed by thirty-six present-tense verbs (continuous action) that specify what should happen once we obey and offer. Two of those results are especially noteworthy here.

First, "exert yourself to lead" (Romans 12:8 NEB). Barclay translates this phrase, "If called upon to supply leadership, do it with zeal." Here is the summons to dive wholeheartedly into leadership, to serve with energy, to leave no room for sloth. Are we doing it?

Does your leadership show the intensity typical of Jesus? When the disciples saw the Master ablaze with righteous anger at the desecration of His Father's temple, they remembered the writings: "Zeal for your house will consume me" (John 2:17). So strong was Jesus' zeal that His friends thought He had abandoned common sense (Mark 3:21) and enemies charged Him with having a demon (John 7:20). Do people ever use "zeal" and your name in the same sentence?

Similar intensity marked Paul at every stage of his life. Wrote Adolph Deissman: "The lightning of the Damascus road found plenty of flammable material in the soul of the young persecutor. We see the flames shoot up, and we feel the glow then kindled lost none of its brightness in Paul the aged." We should strive for such continuing intensity as we grow older. Age tends to turn a flame into embers—the fire needs fresh fuel always.

Before his conversion, Paul's zeal drove him to terrible cruelty against the early Christians, such that he mourned over it later. That same zeal, cleansed and redirected by the Holy Spirit, carried into his new life in Christ and led to amazing achievements for the very church he once tried to destroy.

Full of the Spirit, Paul's mind was aflame with the truth of God and his heart glowed with God's love. At the center of his life was passion for the glory of God. No wonder people followed Paul. He exerted himself to lead. He did it with intensity and zeal. And the spirit of his life was contagious to those around him.

KEPT AT BOILING POINT

Our second present-tense verb in Romans 12 comes from verse 11: "Never be lacking in zeal, but keep your spiritual fervor, serving the Lord." Harrington Lees translates this verse: "Not slothful in business, kept at boiling point by the Holy Spirit, doing bondservice for the master."

This verse points to the dynamic behind consistent, zealous service: "Kept at boiling point by the Holy Spirit." For most people in leadership, boiling points come easily on special occasions. Most leaders know times of great spiritual excitement, of the burning heart, of special nearness to God, and more than ordinary fruitfulness in service, but the problem is staying there! Verse 11 holds out the alluring possibility of living "aglow with the Spirit" (RSV). We need not go off boil if the Spirit is the great central furnace of our lives.

Bunyan's Christian discovered this secret while visiting the Interpreter's house. He could not understand how the flames kept leaping higher while someone poured water on them. Then he saw another toward the rear pouring on the oil.[1]

In His great sermon on prayer, Jesus promised that the Holy Spirit would be given if only we ask. "If you then, though you are evil, know how to give good gifts to your children, how much more will your Father in heaven give the Holy Spirit to those who ask him!" (Luke 11:13). When we trust Christ for salvation, this promise is fulfilled in us, for Paul teaches that "if anyone does not have the Spirit of Christ, he does not belong to Christ" (Romans 8:9).

IMPROVING LEADERSHIP

Hudson Taylor, founder of the China Inland Mission, was a simple yet astute man. He had the gift of saying tremendously significant things in a deceptively simple way. In a letter dated 1879 to the secretary of the mission, Taylor said:

> The all-important thing to do is to
> 1. Improve the character of the work
> 2. Deepen the piety, devotion and success of the workers
> 3. Remove stones of stumbling, if possible

4. Oil the wheels where they stick
5. Amend whatever is defective
6. Supplement, as far as may be, what is lacking

Such simple advice reveals insight into a leader's responsibility. Let's expand and apply. The leader must care for:

Administration—To improve the character of the work. The leader must discover which departments are functioning below standards and remedy the defect. This may involve new job descriptions, or establishing new reporting procedures and other lines of communication.

Spiritual tone—To deepen the piety, devotion, and success of the worker. The tone of the church or mission will be a reflection of its leaders. Water rises to the level of its source. The spiritual health of the leadership group should be a primary concern among higher echelon leadership. Job satisfaction is also important. If leaders show their colleagues methods to improve success, their sense of fulfillment will be reflected in an improvement in the quality of their work.

Group morale—To remove stones of stumbling. Friction among a team should be minimized. When problems are neglected, morale drops and performance decreases. If the problem has a remedy, it should be put into place at once. If the problem is a person, the delinquent should be dealt with as soon as the facts are clear, and let the chips fall. Of course the problem or person should be treated with consideration and love, but the work of God cannot be sacrificed for the sake of keeping peace.

Personal relationships—To oil the wheels where they stick. Warm relationships among team members are vital.

Some workers prefer to administer; others want to love people. Only the latter are leaders. In handling people, the oil can filled with love is much more effective than the acid bottle filled with cold directives.

Problem solving—To amend what is defective. One of the chief duties of leaders is to solve tough problems within the organization. Creating problems is easy; solving them is difficult. The leader must face the problem realistically, and follow through until the solution is reached.

Creative planning—To supplement what is lacking. Criticizing plans is easier than creating them. The leader must see the goal clearly, plan imaginatively, and employ tactics that lead to success. In this department there is always a short supply of people ready and qualified to perform.

One more matter for improving leadership potential: resist the idea of "leadership from the rear." True leadership is always out front—never from the rear or the sidelines. It was leadership from the rear that led Israel back into the wilderness.

Many churches and organizations are in a stalemate because leaders have submitted to a kind of blackmail from the rear. No dissident or reactionary element should be allowed to determine group policy against the consensus of the spiritual leaders.

CHAPTER 15

The Cost of Leadership

Can you drink the cup I drink or be baptized with the baptism I am baptized with?
MARK 10:38

To aspire to leadership in God's kingdom requires us to be willing to pay a price higher than others are willing to pay. The toll of true leadership is heavy, and the more effective the leadership, the greater the cost.

Quinton Hogg, founder of the London Polytechnic Institute, devoted a fortune to the enterprise. Asked how much it had cost to build the great institution, Hogg replied, "Not very much, simply one man's life blood."[1]

That is the price of every great achievement, and it is not paid in a lump sum. Achievement is bought on the time-payment plan, with a new installment required each day. The drain on resources is continuous, and when payments cease, leadership wanes. Our Lord taught that we could not save ourselves in the task of offering salvation to others. When Jesus said, "For whoever wants to save his life will lose it, but whoever loses his life for me will find it" (Matthew 16:25), part of what He meant has to do with hoarding personal resources in the vain hope that they will preserve us.

Samuel Brengle wrote:

> Spiritual power is the outpouring of spiritual life, and like all life, from that of the moss and lichen on the wall to that of the archangel before the throne, it is from God. Therefore those who aspire to leadership may pay the price, and seek it from God.[2]

SELF-SACRIFICE

This part of the cost must be paid daily. A cross stands in the path of spiritual leadership, and the leader must take it up. "Jesus Christ laid down his life for us. And we ought to lay down our lives for our brothers" (1 John 3:16). To the degree the cross of Christ is across our shoulders and over our backs, so the resurrection life of Christ is manifest through us. No cross, no leadership. Paul declared, "I die every day" (1 Corinthians 15:31a).

"Whoever wants to be first must be slave of all. For even the Son of Man did not come to be served, but to serve, and to give his life as a ransom for many" (Mark 10:44–45). Each of the heroes of faith in Hebrews 11 was called to sacrifice as part of his or her service. Those who lead the church are marked by a willingness to give up personal preferences, to surrender legitimate and natural desires for the sake of God. Bruce Barton quotes a sign at a service station: "We will crawl under your car oftener and get ourselves dirtier than any of our competition."[3] That is the kind of service the Christian seeks to give.

Samuel Zwemer remarked that the only thing Jesus took pains to show after His resurrection were His scars.[4] On the Emmaus road His disciples recognized neither Him nor His message. Not until Jesus broke the bread and they possibly saw the scars did they know the person for who He was. When Jesus stood among His demoralized band in the upper room after the resurrection, He showed them both "his hands and [his] side."

Scars are the authenticating marks of faithful discipleship and true spiritual leadership. It was said of one leader, "He belonged to that class of early martyrs whose passionate soul made an early holocaust of the physical man."[5] Nothing moves people more than the print of the nails and the mark of the spear. Those marks are tests of sincerity that none can challenge, as Paul knew well. "Let no one cause me trouble," he wrote, "for I bear on my body the marks of Jesus" (Galatians 6:17).

Hast thou no scar?
No hidden scar on foot, or side, or hand?
I hear thee sung as mighty in the land,
I hear them hail the bright ascendant star:
Hast thou no scar?
Hast thou no wound?
Yet, I was wounded by the archers, spent.
Leaned me against the tree to die, and rent
By ravening beasts that compassed me, I swooned:
Hast thou no wound?
No wound? No scar?
Yes, as the master shall the servant be,

And pierced are the feet that follow Me;
But thine are whole. Can he have followed far
Who has no wound? No scar?
—*Amy Carmichael*[6]

Paul described himself and his burden this way:

On every hand hard-pressed am I—yet not crushed!
In desperate plight am I—yet not in despair!
Close followed by pursuers—yet not abandoned by Him!
Beaten to earth—yet never destroyed!
Evermore bearing about in my body
The imminence of such a death as Jesus died,
So that the life, too, of Jesus might be shown forth
In this body of mine
Always, always while I yet live
Am I being handed over to death's doom
For Jesus' sake!
So that in this mortal flesh of mine, may be
Shown forth also
The very life of Jesus
2 Corinthians 4:8–11 (A. S. Way)

LONELINESS

Nietzsche believed that life always gets harder toward the summit—the cold gets colder, the wind stronger, the burden of responsibilities heavier.[7]

Because the leader must always be ahead of his followers, he lives with a particular loneliness. Though he may be friendly, there are areas of life where he must walk alone. Though he may seek counsel and support from others, decisions come back to the leader alone. Dixon Hoste felt the loneliness when Hudson Taylor retired and placed the leadership of China Inland Mission on his shoulders. Said Hoste after the appointment: "And now I have no one, no one but God!" There he stood on the mount with his God.

We naturally enjoy and need the company of others, and want to share with others the heavy burden of responsibility and care. It is sometimes heartbreaking to make decisions that affect the lives of beloved fellow workers—and to make them alone. Moses paid the price for his leadership—alone on the mountain, alone on the plain, misunderstood and criticized.

The Old Testament prophets were lonely men. Enoch walked alone in a decadent society as he preached judgment. His compensation was the presence of God. Jonah was alone in vast Nineveh, a heathen city of a million souls. The loneliest preacher today is the person who has been entrusted with a prophetic message ahead of the times, a message that cuts across the temper of the age.

Gregarious Paul was a lonely man, misunderstood by friends, misrepresented by enemies, deserted by converts. How poignant are his words to Timothy: "You know that everyone in the province of Asia has deserted me" (2 Timothy 1:15).

"Most of the world's greatest souls have been lonely," wrote A. W. Tozer. "Loneliness seems to be the price a saint must pay for his saintliness." The leader must be a person who, while welcoming the friendship and support of all who offer it, has sufficient inner resources to stand alone—even in the face of stiff opposition to have "no one but God."

On without cheer of sister or of daughter,
Yes, without stay of father or of son,
Lone on the land, and homeless on the water,
Pass I in patience till my work be done
—F. W. H. Meyers

FATIGUE

"The world is run by tired men." Perhaps an overstatement, but there is a grain of reality here. The demands of leadership wear down the most robust person. But Christians know where to find renewal. "Therefore . . . do not lose heart. Though outwardly we are wasting away, yet inwardly we are being renewed day by day" (2 Corinthians 4:16). Even Jesus grew weary in ministry and had to rest (John 4:6). Jesus felt depleted in power, inner resources tapped, when the needy woman touched His clothing (Mark 5:30). No lasting good can be accomplished without this expenditure of nervous energy and personal power.

The spirit of the welfare state does not produce leaders. If a Christian is not willing to rise early and work late, to expend greater effort in diligent study and faithful work, that person will not change a generation. Fatigue is the price of leadership. Mediocrity is the result of never getting tired.

To the secretary of the Church Missionary Society, Douglas Thornton wrote:

> But I am weary! I have only written because I am too weary to be working now, and too tired to sleep. . . . I am getting prematurely old, they tell me, and doctors do not give me long to live unless the strain is eased a

> bit. My wife is wearier than I am. She needs complete rest a while. . . . Oh, that the church at home but realized one half of the opportunities of today! Will no one hear the call? Please do your best to help us.[8]

Here were tired missionary leaders grasping the swiftly passing opportunities of their day.

CRITICISM

"There is nothing else that so kills the efficiency, capability and initiative of a leader as destructive criticism. . . . It tends to hamper and undercut the efficiency of man's thinking process. It chips away at his self-respect and undermines his confidence in his ability to cope with his responsibilities."[9]

No leader lives a day without criticism, and humility will never be more on trial than when criticism comes.

In a letter to a young minister, Fred Mitchell once wrote:

> I am glad to know that you are taking any blessing there may be found in the criticism brought against you by _________, in which case even his bitter attack will yield sweetness. It does not matter what happens to us, but our reaction to what happens to us is vital. You must expect more criticism, for this comes with responsibility. It causes us to walk humbly with God, and to take such action as God desires.[10]

Samuel Brengle, noted for his sense of holiness, felt the heat of caustic criticism. Instead of rushing to defend himself, he replied: "From my heart I thank you for your rebuke. I think I deserved it. Will you, my friend, remember me in prayer?" When another critic attacked his spiritual life, Brengle replied: "I thank you for your criticism of my life. It set me to self-examination and heart-searching and prayer, which always leads me into a deeper sense of my utter dependence on Jesus for holiness of heart, and into sweeter fellowship with Him."[11]

With such a response, criticism is turned from a curse into a blessing, from a liability into an asset.

Paul sought the favor of God, not of people. His hard work was not to please those around him (Galatians 1:10). Nor was Paul terribly disturbed by criticism. "I care very little if I am judged by you or by any human court; . . . It is the Lord who judges me" (1 Corinthians 4:3–4). Paul could afford to take lightly the comments and criticism of others, for his heart was owned by God (Colossians 3:22).

But link indifference to human opinion with a weak spiritual life, and the formula is disaster. The same independence from human opinion can be a valuable asset to the person whose life goal is the glory of God. Paul's ear was tuned to the voice of God, and human voices were faint by comparison. He was fearless of human judgment, because he was conscious of standing before a higher tribunal (2 Corinthians 8:21).

REJECTION

The leader who follows high spiritual standards may find himself following his Master on the pathway of rejection, for "he came unto his own and his own received him not."

J. Gregory Mantle tells of a minister whose congregation refused to accept his message. The minister wanted to lead his people into green pastures and beside still waters, but they were unwilling. The ungodly habits of his choir brought things to a head, and the minister invited the choir to resign. That the choir did, and it also persuaded the congregation to remain silent during the singing on the following Sunday. The minister sang alone.

Finally at wit's end, God spoke to him. On a park bench, he saw a piece of torn newspaper, which he picked up to read these words: "No man is ever fully accepted until he has, first of all, been utterly rejected." The minister needed nothing more. He had been utterly rejected for Christ's sake, and his recognition of the fact was the start of a fruitful ministry. Rejected by people, he had been accepted by God.

When A. B. Simpson resigned a pastorate, he learned the meaning of "destitute, despised, forsaken." He surrendered a comfortable salary, a position as senior pastor in a great American city, and all claim to denominational help for his yet untried work. He had no following, no organization, no resources, a large family to support, and everyone close to him was predicting failure. He often said that he looked down upon the stone in the street for the sympathy denied him by friends he treasured.

"The rugged path of utter rejection was trodden without complaint, and with rejoicing. He knew that though he . . . was going through fire and water, it was the divinely appointed way to the wealthy place."[12] To such a place Simpson was led. At his death he had established five schools for the training of missionaries, hundreds of missionaries in sixteen lands, and many churches in the United States and Canada that exerted a spiritual influence beyond their numbers.

"Often the crowd does not recognize a leader until he has gone, and then they build a monument for him with the stone they threw at him in life."[13]

PRESSURE AND PERPLEXITY

We naively think that the more we grow as Christians, the easier it will be to discern the will of God. But the opposite is often the case. God treats the mature leader as a mature adult, leaving more and more to his or her spiritual discernment and giving fewer bits of tangible guidance than in earlier years. The resulting perplexity adds inevitably to a leader's pressure.

D. E. Hoste said to a friend:

> The pressure! It goes on from stage to stage, it changes in every period of your life. . . . Hudson Taylor said how in his younger days, things came so clearly, so quickly to him. "But," he said, "now as I have gone on, and God has used me more and more, I seem often to be like a man going along in a fog. I do not know what to do."[14]

But when the time came to act, God always responded to His servant's trust.

COST TO OTHERS

People close to a leader pay a price too. Sometimes a heavier price. Fred Mitchell wrote to his children when he accepted the invitation to become British director of China Inland Mission:

> I have had many a sorrow of heart, and it still remains one of my chief regrets that I have not been able to give myself to mother and you children more. The harvest is great and the labourers few, which means that there have been many calls upon me. I do not justify my negligence, but any sacrifice made by you for our dear Lord Jesus' sake has not been unrewarded.[15]

It takes a leader to embark on a dangerous venture. It takes a leader to build for the kingdom. That's why Jesus' words were so passionate: count the cost; take up the cross (see Luke 14:25–33).

CHAPTER 16

Responsibilities of Leadership

Besides everything else, I face daily the pressure of my concern for all the churches.

2 CORINTHIANS 11:28

SERVICE

Jesus defined leadership as service, and His definition applies whether a leader works in secular or church organizations. Field Marshal Montgomery said that his war experience taught him that the staff must serve the troops and that a good staff officer must serve his commander while remaining anonymous himself.

In his book *Training of the Twelve*, A. B. Bruce wrote: "In other kingdoms they rule, whose privilege it is to be ministered unto. In the Divine commonwealth, they rule who account it a privilege to minister."[1] John A. MacKay of Princeton maintained that "servant" is the essential image of the Christian religion. The Son of God became the servant of God in order to do the mission of God. That image provides the pattern for mission societies, churches, and individual believers to fulfill their God-given mission.

The true leader is concerned primarily with the welfare of others, not with his own comfort or prestige. He shows sympathy for the problems of others, but his sympathy fortifies and stimulates; it does not soften and make weak. A spiritual leader will always direct the confidence of others to the Lord. He sees in each emergency a new opportunity for helpfulness. When God chose a leader to succeed Moses, it was Joshua, the man who had proved himself a faithful servant (Exodus 33:11).

D. E. Hoste spoke about the secrets of Hudson, whom Hoste has followed in leadership of the China Inland Mission:

> Another secret of his influence among us lay in his great sympathy and thoughtful consideration for the welfare and comfort of those about him. The high standard of self-sacrifice and toil which he ever kept before himself, never made him lacking in tenderness and sympathy toward those who were not able to go as far as he did in these respects. He manifested great tenderness and patience toward the failures of his brethren, and was thus able in many cases to help them reach a higher plane of devotion.[2]

APPLIED DISCIPLINE

Discipline is yet another responsibility of the leader, a duty often unwelcome. The self-discipline that is one of the central characteristics of a leader will eventually be applied consciously or unconsciously to those around him or her. Some will imitate the leader's disciplined life while others must be directed into that lifestyle by discipline. Further, the effectiveness and longevity of any Christian society requires godly and loving discipline to maintain divine standards in doctrine, morals, and conduct. Leaders preserve the standards through loving discipline.

Paul describes the spirit required in leaders who exercise discipline. "Brothers, if someone is caught in a sin, you who are spiritual should restore him gently. But watch yourself, or you also may be tempted" (Galatians 6:1). The fundamental ingredient in all discipline is love. "Warn him as a brother" (2 Thessalonians 3:15). "I urge you, therefore, to reaffirm your love for him" (2 Corinthians 2:8). The person who has faced up to his or her own problems and weaknesses is best able to help another in a way both loving and firm. The spirit of meekness will achieve far more than the spirit of criticism.

Approaching a disciplinary situation, the leader must remember five guidelines: (1) first, conduct a thorough and impartial inquiry; (2) then, consider the overall benefit of the disciplinary action to the work and to the individual; (3) do all in the spirit of love—be considerate always; (4) always keep the spiritual restoration of the offender in view; (5) pray it through.

GUIDANCE

Providing guidance is a third area of responsibility. The spiritual leader must know where he or she is going before presuming to lead others. The Chief Shepherd gave us the pattern. "When he has brought out all his own, he goes on ahead of them, and his sheep follow him because they know his voice" (John 10:4).

"The ideal leader," said A. W. Tozer, "is one who hears the voice of God, and beckons on as the voice calls him and them." Paul gave this challenge to the Corinthian Christians: "Follow my example, as I follow the example of Christ" (1 Corinthians 11:1). Paul knew whom he was following, where he was going, and could challenge others to follow him there.

It is not easy to guide people, even mature Christians, who have strong opinions of their own. The leader cannot assert his will recklessly. Said D. E. Hoste:

> In a mission like ours, those guiding its affairs must be prepared to put up with waywardness and opposition, and be able to desist from courses of action which, though they may be intrinsically sound and beneficial, are not approved by some of those affected. Hudson Taylor again and again was obliged either to greatly modify, or lay aside projects which were sound and helpful, but met with determined opposition, and so tended to create greater evils than those which might have been removed or mitigated by the changes in question. Later on, in answer to patient continuance in prayer, many of those projects were put into effect.[3]

INITIATIVE

A leader must initiate. Some leaders are more gifted at conserving gains than starting new ventures, for maintaining order than generating ardor. The true leader must be venturesome as well as visionary. He must be ready to jump-start as well as hold speed. Paul constantly took calculated risks, always carefully and with much prayer, but always reaching for what lay beyond.

The leader must either initiate plans for progress or recognize the worthy plans of others. He must remain in front, giving guidance and direction to those behind. He does not wait for things to happen but makes them happen. He is a self-starter, always on the lookout for improved methods, eager to test new ideas.

Robert Louis Stevenson called the attitude of safety and security "that dismal fungus."[4] Hudson Taylor took steps of faith that appeared to others as wildcat schemes. The greatest achievements in the history of missions have come from leaders close to God who took courageous, calculated risks.

More failure comes from an excess of caution than from bold experiments with new ideas. A friend who filled an important global post in Christian outreach recently remarked that when he surveyed his life, most of his failures came from insufficient daring. The wife of Archbishop Mowll said, "The frontiers of the kingdom of God were never advanced by men and women of caution."[5]

A leader cannot afford to ignore the counsel of cautious people, who can save a mission from mistakes and loss. But caution should not curb vision, especially when the leader knows God is in control.

To take responsibility willingly is the mark of a leader. Joshua was such a person. He did not hesitate to follow one of the greatest leaders of all history, Moses. Joshua had more reason than Moses to plead inadequacy, but Joshua did not repeat Moses's sin. Instead, he promptly accepted and set about the work.

When Elijah was taken up, Elisha did not flinch at stepping in. He accepted the authority conferred by the falling mantle and became a leader in his own right.

In each case these leaders were assured of their divine calling. Once that issue is settled, no one need hesitate to do what God has set before him or her.

Archbishop Benson lived in a different era, but his rules for life carry relevance today:

- Eagerly start the day's main work.
- Do not murmur at your busyness or the shortness of time, but buy up the time all around.
- Never murmur when correspondence is brought in.
- Never exaggerate duties by seeming to suffer under the load, but treat all responsibilities as liberty and gladness.
- Never call attention to crowded work or trivial experiences.
- Before confrontation or censure, obtain from God a real love for the one at fault. Know the facts; be generous in your judgment. Otherwise, how ineffective, how unintelligible or perhaps provocative your well-intentioned censure may be.
- Do not believe everything you hear; do not spread gossip.
- Do not seek praise, gratitude, respect, or regard for past service.
- Avoid complaining when your advice or opinion is not consulted, or having been consulted, set aside.

- Never allow yourself to be placed in favorable contrast with anyone.
- Do not press conversation to your own needs and concerns.
- Seek no favors, nor sympathies; do not ask for tenderness, but receive what comes.
- Bear the blame; do not share or transfer it.
- Give thanks when credit for your own work or ideas is given to another.[6]

CHAPTER 17

Tests of Leadership

God tested Abraham.
GENESIS 22:1

Then Jesus was led by the Spirit into the desert to be tempted by the devil.
MATTHEW 4:1

Everyone entrusted with spiritual authority can expect tests, temptations, and trials along the way. As difficult and inconvenient as these tests may be, they serve to purify and clarify leadership. The first chapter of James demonstrates that God allows, even plans, these experiences for our good and for our growth. Tests are meant to let us succeed, not fail. Tests display progress.

COMPROMISE

Can we waive a principle to reach agreement? Lowering standards is always a backward step, and compromise nearly always requires it.

The epic contest between Moses and Pharaoh is a classic example of the temptation to compromise. When Pharaoh realized that Moses meant to lead the Hebrews out of

Egypt, he used cunning and threats to frustrate him. "Worship God if you will," was his first overture, "but don't leave Egypt to do it." A modern equivalent would be: "Religion is okay, but don't be narrow about it. No need to let religion isolate you from the rest of the world."

When that approach failed, Pharaoh tried something else: "If you must go out of Egypt to worship, don't go far. Religion is fine, but no need to be fanatical about it. Stay as close to the world as you can."

Yet a third attempt played on natural affection: "Let the men go and worship, and the women and children stay here. If you must break with the world, don't force such a narrow lifestyle on everyone else in the family."

Pharaoh's last attempt was an appeal to greed: "Okay, go. But the flocks and herds stay. Don't let your odd religious commitments get in the way of business and prosperity."

With clear spiritual insight Moses cut through each evasion: "Not a hoof is to be left behind," he said (Exodus 10:26). So Moses passed with honors a great test of his leadership of God's people.

AMBITION

All great leaders—Moses too—face this test. During Moses's absence on Mount Sinai, the people of Israel turned to idolatry, and God became very angry, saying,"I will strike them down with a plague and destroy them, but I will make you into a nation greater and stronger than they" (Numbers 14:12).

Already Moses had heard more than enough of the people's constant complaining and frequent dalliance with paganism. Why not accept this divine proposal as a way to give the people their due, and start afresh with a smaller group that Moses could certainly control.

What a test, from the mouth of God Himself. Instead of personal ambition, Moses showed selfless nobility, genuine concern for God's glory, and compassion for the misguided people. Not for a moment did the thought of self-aggrandizement enter his lofty mind. Through prayer, Moses saved the apostate nation from judgment.

THE IMPOSSIBLE SITUATION

"How does this person face impossible situations?" John R. Mott would inquire as a way to separate leaders from followers. Mott encouraged leaders to deal with impossible tasks rather than easy ones in order to foster personal competence, teamwork, and faith. "I long since ceased to occupy myself with minor things that can be done by others," he said. A true leader steps forward in order to face baffling circumstances and complex problems.

Our own day presents leaders with difficult problems as never before. If leaders are to survive, they must view the difficult as commonplace, the complex as normal.

Moses faced an impossible situation when Israel reached the Red Sea. Behind them was the desert and Pharaoh's army; before them was water, and Israel had no boats. Moses was in a cul-de-sac, and the people were getting edgy. Complaints started flying as morale dropped: "Is it because there were no graves in Egypt that you have taken us away to die in the wilderness?" (NASB).

Moses, great man of faith, stayed himself on God. His orders must have sounded like sheer fantasy in the ears of the nation, but in point of fact that crisis was a defining moment of his leadership.

"Do not fear!" he cried, against every good reason to fear.

"Stand by!" he cried, as Pharaoh sped toward them.

"See the salvation of the Lord!"

So on that strange and wonderful day, the people of Israel saw their God in action, their hopes affirmed, their enemies crushed. The bracing lesson is that God delights to lead people, and then, in response to their trust, to show them power that matches every impossible situation.

Hudson Taylor faced many hard situations in his career to win China for Christ. He counted three phases in most great tasks undertaken for God—impossible, difficult, done.

Have you come to the Red Sea place in your life,
Where in spite of all you can do,
There is no way out, there is no way back,
There is no other way but through?
Then wait on the Lord with a trust serene
Till the night of your fear is gone;
He will send the wind, He will heap the floods,
When He says to your soul, "Go on."
In the morning watch, 'neath the lifted cloud,
You shall see but the Lord alone,
When He leads you on from the place of the sea
To a land that you have not known;
And your fears shall pass as your foes have passed,
You shall no more be afraid;
You shall sing His praise in a better place,

A place that His hand has made.
—Annie Johnson Flint[1]

FAILURE

Many people who appear to be at the height of their careers hide a great inner sense of failure. Alexander Maclaren, the great British preacher, delivered a wonderful address to a large crowd, but turned away overwhelmed with failure. "I must not speak on such an occasion again," he said.[2]

Were his expectations too high? Or did the devil bring him grief when he should have felt great joy?

How a leader handles failure (or simply feelings of failure) will set much of the agenda for the future. Peter appeared washed up as a leader after his denial of the Christ, but repentance and love reopened the door of opportunity, and Peter's leadership touched all the rest of Christendom. "Where sin abounded, grace did much more abound" (KJV).

Most Bible characters met with failure, and survived. Even when the failure was immense, those that found leadership again refused to lie in the dust and bemoan their tragedy. In fact, their failure led to a greater conception of God's grace. They came to know the God of the second chance, and sometimes the third and fourth.

The historian James Anthony Froude wrote: "The worth of a man must be measured by his life, not by his failure under a singular and peculiar trial. Peter the apostle, though forewarned, three times denied his Master on the first alarm of danger; yet that Master, who knew his nature in its strength and in its weakness, chose him."[3]

Successful leaders have learned that no failure is final, whether his own failure or someone else's. No one is perfect, and we cannot be right all the time. Failures and even feelings of inadequacy can provoke humility and serve to remind a leader who is really in charge.

JEALOUSY

Most leaders at some time face the problem of a jealous rival. Even Moses encountered that test. Jealousy is a common weapon of the devil.

Moses's first such challenge came from within his own family, his sister and brother. They had apparently forgotten that without Moses's noble decision to lead the people out of Egypt, they and all the rest of Israel would still be living under the slave master's lash.

Miriam by this time was elderly and should have known better. She promoted gossip against Moses because of his marriage to an Ethiopian. Race hatred is not the sin of this century alone. Miriam resented the intrusion of a foreigner and drew the weakling Aaron into her rebellion.

Not content with second place, Miriam and Aaron, led by the devil, tried to remove Moses by a coup. They cloaked their treachery in piety: "Has the Lord spoken only through Moses? . . . Hasn't he also spoken through us?"

Moses was deeply wounded, but he said nothing to vindicate himself. His main concern was God's glory, not his own position or privilege. "Now Moses was a very humble man, more humble than anyone else on the face of the earth" (Numbers 12:3). Yet though Moses maintained a dignified silence, God would not allow such a challenge to the authority of His servant to go without response.

Because the offense was public, judgment and punishment would also be public. "When the cloud lifted from above the Tent, there stood Miriam—leprous, like snow," the record states (Numbers 12:10). Such a drastic punishment points to the gravity of her sin, and once again Moses's greatness shines. His only response was to pray for his sister, and God graciously responded in mercy.

The lesson for the leader is plain. The person who fills a role appointed by God need not worry about vindicating his or her work when rivals become jealous or treacherous. Such a leader is safe in the hands of a heavenly Protector. Indeed, God shows how safe with His ominous words to Miriam: "Why then were you not afraid to speak against my servant Moses?" (Numbers 12:8).

Moses faced a second challenge from Korah and his henchmen, noted for their jealousy of Moses and Aaron. Korah wondered why these special two should enjoy the privilege of high office? Were not others (himself for one) equally deserving and qualified?

Once again Moses refused to vindicate himself against their charges. God intervened, judgment was rendered, and Moses stood higher than ever while the people grew in fear of God.

God will defend the leaders He has chosen. He will honor, protect, and vindicate them. Leaders need not worry about defending their rights or their office.

CHAPTER 18

The Art of Delegation

He chose capable men from all Israel and made them leaders of the people. . . . They served as judges for the people at all times. The difficult cases they brought to Moses.

EXODUS 18:25–26

One facet of leadership is the ability to recognize the special abilities and limitations of others, combined with the capacity to fit each one into the job where he or she will do best. To succeed in getting things done through others is the highest type of leadership. Dwight L. Moody, a shrewd judge of people, once said that he would rather put a thousand men to work than do the work of a thousand men.[1] D. E. Hoste said: "The capacity to appreciate the gifts of widely varying kinds of workers, and then to help them along the lines of their own personalities and workings, is the main quality for oversight in a mission such as ours."[2]

Thoughtful delegation will save the leader the frustrating experience of managing square pegs serving in round holes.

Delegation to others of responsibility, together with the authority to do the job, is not always relished by one who enjoys exercising the authority himself. He is glad to give the responsibility to others but reluctant to let the reins of power slip from his own hands. Also, some leaders feel threatened by brilliant subordinates and therefore are reluctant to delegate authority. Whatever the basic cause, failure to delegate authority is unfair to the subordinate and unlikely to prove satisfactory or effective. Such an approach tends to be interpreted as indicating a lack of confidence, and that does not promote the best cooperation, nor will it draw out the full abilities of those being trained for leadership. Failure to delegate is also a poor stewardship of human resources God has provided!

It is possible that the subordinate may not do the task as well as his superior, but experience proves that that is by no means necessarily the case. Given the chance, the younger person may do it better because he or she is better able to feel the pulse of contemporary life. But in any case, how is the younger leader to gain experience unless he or she has been delegated both the responsibility and authority for the task?

The degree to which a leader is able to delegate work is a measure of his success. A one-person office can never grow larger than the load one person can carry.

Failing to delegate, the leader is caught in a morass of secondary detail; it overburdens him and diverts his attention from primary tasks. People under him do not achieve their own potential. In some cases, insisting on doing a job oneself is a result of simple conceit.

Once a leader delegates, he should show utmost confidence in the people he has entrusted. A. B. Simpson trusted those in charge of the various schools he founded, leaving them free to exercise their own gifts.[3] If they failed, Simpson took it as a reflection of his own failed leadership, for he had selected them.

Subordinates perform better when they feel sure of the leader's support, whether a given project succeeds or fails, so long as they have acted within the bounds of their assignment. This confidence comes when responsibilities have been clearly defined in writing, to eliminate any misunderstandings. Failing to communicate clearly has led to many unhappy problems and unsatisfying outcomes.

Paul Super wrote of his association with John R. Mott:

> One of my greatest resources these ten years in Poland is the sense of his backing. My greatest pride is his belief in me. Surely one of my greatest motives is to be worthy of his support and to measure up to his expectations of me.[4]

One of the great biblical illustrations of the principle of delegation is the story of Jethro, father-in-law to Moses, recorded in Exodus 18.

Israel emerged from Egypt an unorganized horde of exslaves. By the time of Exodus 18, a new national spirit was developing. Jethro saw that Moses faced intolerably heavy burdens—he was dealing with problems from morning till night. Moses was the legislature; Moses was the judiciary; Moses was the executive branch of the new nation. His decisions were accepted by the people as God's will.

Jethro saw that Moses could not keep such a pace, and made two solid arguments for delegating some of the work. First, "you and these people who come to you will only wear yourselves out. The work is too heavy for you; you cannot handle it alone" (Exodus 18:18). Moses was at his limit, probably beyond his limit, of physical and emotional resources. Second, the current method of problem solving was too slow, and people were getting impatient. Sharing authority would speed up legal action, and the people would go away satisfied (Exodus 18:23).

Then Jethro proposed a two-part plan. Moses would continue to teach spiritual principles and exercise legislative leadership. He would also decide the hard cases at court. But much of his work would be delegated to competent, trustworthy subordinates.

Jethro spoke wisely, for if Moses had succumbed under the strain, he would have left chaos behind—no one trained to lead, no one in charge of anything. Failure to make provision for the succession of leadership has spelled ruin for many missions and churches.

Moses followed Jethro's advice and realized several benefits. He was able to concentrate on the biggest problems. The latent talents of many around him were discovered. Those gifted men, who could have become his critics had Moses continued alone, were now allies facing a common challenge. People-problems were solved with efficiency. And Moses laid the groundwork for effective leadership after his death.

Jethro encouraged Moses by articulating a spiritual principle of timeless relevance. "If you do this and God so commands, you will be able to stand the strain" (Exodus 18:23). Jethro placed his advice under the authority of God. God takes all responsibility for enabling His servants to do their work. Some tasks others can do better, and these should be delegated. But even if these secondary tasks are not done perfectly, still delegation is the better part of wisdom. Moses was probably better at judging than any of the seventy associate judges he appointed, but had he persisted alone, his career would have been cut short.

Jethro's spiritual discernment comes through in the qualifications he puts forward for the selection of this cadre: men of ability, for their work is formidable; men of piety, for fear of God is the beginning of wisdom; men of honor, who would shun bribes and greed.

It is a big mistake to assume more duties than we can discharge. There is no virtue in doing more than our fair share of the work. We do well to recognize our limitations. Our Jethros can often discern, better than we can, the impact of all our duties, and we should listen to them. If we break natural law—humans must sleep as well as work, for example—we cannot be exempt from repercussions. If we succumb to human persuasion and take on more than we should, God will accept no responsibility for the outcome.

Missionary leadership must be ready to delegate responsibility to nationals the moment they give evidence of spiritual maturity. Then the missionary must stand by them, ready to help but reluctant to intervene, guiding the national through trial and error so that he or she might learn spiritual leadership as the missionary did. Delegating in this way fulfills the essential task of discovering, training, and using the latent talents of national Christian colleagues. In the earlier stages, a wise watchfulness is necessary, but interfering should be reserved for acute needs only. The sense of being watched destroys confidence.

When W. E. Sangster was appointed general secretary of

the Home Mission Department of the Methodist Church in Britain, he divided labor between all his subordinates, assigned responsibilities, and offered supervision. He never regretted placing such trust. It was said of Sangster: "Perhaps his greatest grasp of leadership was knowing the importance of delegation and of choosing assistants with care. He was always a master of that art."[5]

Writing about the leader of a large missionary society, a member of his staff commented: "He had a great gift of leadership in that he never interfered with those who worked under him. Everyone was left to do his own work." Another member wrote, "He knew what people could do, and saw that they did it, leaving them to make the best of their opportunities, and investigating only if things went wrong."[6]

CHAPTER 19

Replacing Leaders

Moses my servant is dead. Now then, you and all these people, get ready to cross the Jordan River into the land I am about to give to them. . . . As I was with Moses, so I will be with you.

JOSHUA 1:2, 5

The ultimate test of a person's leadership is the health of the organization when the organizer is gone. This truth was behind Gamaliel's counsel to fellow Pharisees: "Leave these men alone! Let them go! For if their purpose or activity is of human origin, it will fail. But if it is from God, you will not be able to stop these men" (Acts 5:38–39). A work inspired by God and built on spiritual principles will survive the shock of leadership change and may even prosper as a result.

We sometimes demean God by assuming that the death of a great leader takes God by surprise, or sends God into emergency action. Though we may feel shock and anxiety, we need not tremble for the ark of God. Christian leadership is different from the worldly sort. God selects and prepares leaders for the kingdom (Mark 10:40). No work of God will be left destitute until its purposes are achieved.

Great movements are often thrown into crisis at the death of a founder. Such crises need not be fatal, however. Lyman Beecher said that he despaired when the first secretary of the American Board of Missions died. Then another leader arose and did so well that Beecher felt despair again when the second secretary died. At last, when the third secretary proved himself competent, Beecher began to feel confident that God's resources were equal to the task at hand. When Beecher himself was gone, some believed he could not be replaced. But all of Beecher's causes—temperance, orthodoxy, and foreign missions—found capable new leaders in God's time and way.[1] Indeed, no man, however gifted and devoted, is indispensable to the work of the kingdom.

God is always at work, though we cannot see it, preparing people He has chosen for leadership. When the crisis comes, God fits His appointee into the place ordained for him. Often such a replacement is not apparent to an organization, but time will reveal him.

God's greatest gifts to Israel, better than the land itself, were men like Moses and David and Isaiah. God's greatest gifts are always the servants through whom He works. His greatest endowment to the church was the gift of twelve men trained for leadership.

Imagine how distraught the Israelites were when the time approached for Moses to leave them. For four decades the entire nation had looked to him for problem solving and direction. Moses had interpreted the will of God for them. True, seventy elders served under him, but there was not another Moses. Adding to the sense of crisis was the timing of his death, just at the point of entry into Canaan.

The people could hardly believe that God had a new leader in reserve. But Joshua was in preparation, and the crisis brought him to the fore.

This situation is repeated throughout history; each generation learns the same lesson. The loss of an outstanding leader awakens doubts and fears. What will the Methodists do without Wesley? What will the Salvation Army do without Booth? What will our church do when the pastor moves?

The paths of glory lead always to the grave, but a new glory will be revealed. The greatest leader must inevitably be removed by death or some other cause, and the sense of loss will vary with the caliber of his leadership. But in retrospect it will usually be seen that the seeming tragedy has actually turned out to be in the best interests of the work.

Only after his removal are the character and achievements of a leader fully revealed. It was not until after Moses's death that Israel saw his greatness in the light of his completed work. "The emphasis of death makes perfect the lessons of the life."

At the same time, a leader's passing cuts his persona down to size in relation to the work of God. However great his achievements, no one is indispensable. The time comes when his special contribution is not the need of the hour. The most gifted leader has liabilities and limitations that become apparent when a successor comes along to advance the work. Often a successor with less fame and prestige than a founder is better able to develop the work because of the specific gifts he has. We must assume that Joshua was better equipped to conquer Canaan than Moses.

The departure of a strong and dominating leader makes

room for others to emerge and develop. Often when the weight of responsibility falls suddenly on his shoulders, a subordinate develops abilities and qualities he and others had not suspected he had. Joshua would never have developed into an outstanding leader had he remained one of Moses's lieutenants.

A shift in leadership also provides occasion for God to show His versatility in adjusting means to ends. His resources in any work He initiates are inexhaustible. If a man who possesses great gifts will not place them at the disposal of God, He is not defeated. God will take a man of lesser gifts that are fully available to Him and will supplement those gifts with His own mighty power. Paul implied this when he wrote to the Corinthians, 1 Corinthians 1:26–29:

> Brothers, think of what you were when you were called. Not many of you were wise by human standards; not many were influential; not many were of noble birth. But God chose the foolish things of the world to shame the wise; God chose the weak things of the world to shame the strong. He chose the lowly things of this world and the despised things—and the things that are not—to nullify the things that are, so that no one may boast before him.

God is surely eager to use the powers of naturally gifted people, but few of them are as willing as was Paul to place those gifts without reservation at God's disposal. When such people learn to rely not on their own power and wisdom but to depend on God, there is no limit to their usefulness in God's service.

Toward the end his life, A. B. Simpson was at a great convention when a respected New York minister observed that there was no one similarly qualified to continue leadership of the organization when Simpson's tenure was done. The minister suggested that a large endowment be established to ensure that the work continue. Simpson said nothing and did nothing. He believed that if his work was from God, nothing could dismantle it; if it were not from God, no good purpose was served by keeping it going.[2]

How Simpson rejoiced during the last months of his life, when he had retired from leadership in the Alliance, as reports came in of increased missionary offerings and progress on the foreign fields. The year after his death proved to be the most prosperous year in the history of the society to that date. No greater tribute could be paid to the quality of Simpson's leadership.

Only one Leader holds office forever; no successor is needed for Him. The disciples made no move to appoint a replacement for Jesus, tacit evidence that they were conscious of His abiding presence, their living Leader and Lord. At times the church has lost a vivid sense of Jesus' presence, but there has never been a panic cry from a leaderless army. The perils and distress of the church weigh deeply on Jesus' heart.

"We tell our Lord plainly," said Martin Luther, "that if He will have His Church then He must look to and maintain and defend it, for we can neither uphold nor protect it; and if we could, then we should become the proudest donkeys under heaven."

Since our Leader conducts His work in the power of an endless life—He is the same yesterday, today, and forever—changes in human leadership should not shake or dismay us.

CHAPTER 20

Reproducing Leaders

The things you have heard me say in the presence of many witnesses entrust to reliable men who will also be qualified to teach others.

2 TIMOTHY 2:2

With the words above Paul presses home a leader's responsibility to train others to lead. If he is to carry out his trust fully, the leader will devote time to training others to succeed and perhaps even supercede him. Barnabas's spiritual stature is seen in his entire freedom from jealousy when his protégé Paul surpassed his own leadership skills and became the dominant member of the team. It follows that a leader must provide subordinates with opportunity to exercise and develop their powers.

John R. Mott believed that leaders must multiply themselves by growing younger leaders, giving them full play and adequate outlet for their abilities. Younger people should feel the weight of heavy burdens, opportunity for initiative, and the power of final decisions. The younger leader should receive generous credit for achievements. Foremost they must be trusted. Blunders are the inevitable price of training leaders.

At a recent missionary conference, an Asian leader spoke frankly about the role of Western missionaries: "The missionary of today in the Orient should be less a performer, and more a trainer." This may not be true in every missionary setting, but it does highlight one of the great needs in current mission strategy.

Training new leaders is a delicate task. The wise trainer will not advertise the end he has in view. Bishop Stephen Neill spoke of the danger of this task:

> If we set out to produce a race of leaders, what we shall succeed in doing is probably to produce a race of restless, ambitious and discontented intellectuals. To tell a man he is called to be a leader is the best way of ensuring his spiritual ruin, since in the Christian world ambition is more deadly than any other sin, and, if yielded to, makes a man unprofitable in the ministry. The most important thing today is the spiritual, rather than the intellectual, quality of those indigenous Christians who are called to bear responsibility in the younger churches.

Lesslie Newbigin goes so far as to question whether the church ought to encourage the concept of leadership, so difficult it is to use without being confused with its non-Christian counterpart. The church needs saints and servants, not "leaders," and if we forget the priority of service, the entire idea of leadership becomes dangerous. Leadership training must still follow the pattern our Lord used with His twelve.[1]

Perhaps the most strategic and fruitful work of modern missionaries is to help leaders of tomorrow develop their spiritual potential. This task requires careful thought, wise planning, endless patience, and genuine Christian love. It cannot be haphazard, hurried, or ill-conceived. Our Lord devoted the greater part of His three years of ministry to molding the characters and spirits of His disciples.

Paul showed the same concern for training young Timothy and Titus. Paul's method for preparing Timothy for the church in Ephesus is deeply instructive.

Timothy was about twenty years old when Paul became his friend. Timothy tended toward melancholia, and he was too tolerant and partial to people of rank. He could be irritable with opponents. He was apt to rely on old spiritual experiences rather than kindle the flame of daily devotion.

But Paul had high hopes for him. Paul set about to correct Timothy's timid nature, to replace softness with steel. Paul led Timothy into experiences and hardships that toughened his character. Paul did not hesitate to assign him tasks beyond his present powers. How else can a young person develop competence and confidence if not by stretching to try the impossible?[2]

Traveling with Paul brought Timothy into contact with men of stature whose characters kindled in him a wholesome ambition. From his mentor he learned to meet triumphantly the crises that Paul considered routine. Paul shared with Timothy the work of preaching. Paul gave him the responsibility of establishing a group of Christians at Thessalonica. Paul's exacting standards, high expectations, and heavy demands brought out the best in Timothy, saving him from a life of mediocrity.

Paul Rees describes the experience of Douglas Hyde, onetime Communist but later a convert to Christ, as recorded in Hyde's book *Dedication and Leadership Techniques*:

> Easily one of the most fascinating stories in the book—a story connected with his Communist years—involves a young man who came to Hyde and announced that he wanted to be made into a leader. "I thought," said Hyde, "I had never seen anyone look less like a leader in my life. He was short, grotesquely fat, with a great, flabby, wide uninteresting face. . . . He had a cast in one eye, and spoke with a most distressing stutter."
>
> What happened? Well, instead of turning him away as a hopeless prospect, Hyde gave him a chance—a chance to study, to learn, to test his dedication, to smooth out his stutter. In the end he became a leader in one of the most Communist-infiltrated labour unions in Britain.[3]

The observant leader may discover latent talent in some quite unpromising people.

Frank Buchman, founder of Moral Rearmament, displayed many leadership gifts. He claimed that if he failed to train others to do his work better than he did it, he had failed. For many years he worked to make himself dispensable, a rare agenda for a founder.[4]

No work is more rewarding to a missionary than developing leaders, for the survival and health of the new churches the missionary plants will greatly depend on the spiritual caliber of the national Christians. Once the pioneer stage in any field has passed, the training of leadership should take high priority. One of a missionary's main goals should be the development of faith in promising young people who can, in time, lead the church.

Lest our training programs become too rigid and we discourage the exceptional person from service, we must always allow room for the unusual person, the one for whom there is no mold. God has His "irregulars," and many of them have made outstanding contributions to world evangelization. Who could have poured C. T. Studd into a mold? Such men and women cannot be measured by ordinary standards or made to conform to any fixed pattern.

One such missionary was Douglas Thornton, who made an indelible mark among Muslims in the Near East. He possessed rare gifts, and even as a young man did not hesitate to express opinions that seemed radical and impractical to his superiors. His biographer records:

> It is hardly surprising to learn that he felt constrained to write to his society a memorandum setting forth his views on the past, present and future of the work in Egypt. It is not a precedent that young missionaries after three and a half months on the field should be invited to follow, and on this occasion, too, heads were shaken. But Thornton was an exceptional man, and time has proven that his views and even his effusions were worthy of being studied. It was never safe to neglect them. Most juniors had best reserve their observations for a more mature season. But when the exceptional man arrives, two things have to be observed—the man has to learn to make his observations in the right way, so as to carry his seniors with him; the seniors have to learn how to learn from one who is possibly able, in spite of his want of local knowledge,

to benefit them enormously by his fresh and spontaneous ideas. Each is a difficult lesson.[5]

Leadership training cannot be done on a mass scale. It requires patient, careful instruction and prayerful, personal guidance over a considerable time. "Disciples are not manufactured wholesale. They are produced one by one, because someone has taken the pains to discipline, to instruct and enlighten, to nurture and train one that is younger."

When a person is really marked out for leadership, God will see that that person receives the necessary disciplines for effective service.

When God wants to drill a man
And thrill a man
And skill a man,
When God wants to mold a man
To play the noblest part;
When He yearns with all His heart
To create so great and bold a man
That all the world shall be amazed,
Watch His methods, watch His ways!
How He ruthlessly perfects
Whom He royally elects!
How He hammers him and hurts him,
And with mighty blows converts him
Into trial shapes of clay which
Only God understands;
While his tortured heart is crying
And he lifts beseeching hands!

How He bends but never breaks
When his good He undertakes;
How He uses whom He chooses
And with every purpose fuses him;
By every act induces him
To try His splendour out—
God knows what He's about!
—Author Unknown

CHAPTER 21

Perils of Leadership

. . . so that after I have preached to others,
I myself will not be disqualified for the prize.
1 CORINTHIANS 9:27

The perils of spiritual leadership are especially subtle, more so than for other callings. The leader is not immune from temptations of the flesh, but the greater dangers are in the realm of spirit, for the enemy Satan never fails to exploit the advantage in any area of weakness.

PRIDE

When a person rises in position, as happens to leaders in the church, the tendency to pride also increases. If not checked, the attitude will disqualify the person from further advancement in the kingdom of God, for "the LORD detests all the proud of heart" (Proverbs 16:5). These are strong and searching words! Nothing aggravates God more than conceit, the sin that aims at setting the self upon a throne, making of God a secondary figure. That very sin changed the anointed cherub into the foul fiend of hell.

Pride takes many forms, but spiritual pride is the most grievous. To become proud of spiritual gifts or leadership position is to forget that all we have is from God, and that any position we occupy is by God's appointment.

The victim of pride is often least aware of the sin. Three tests help us identify the problem:

The test of precedence. How do we react when another is selected for the position we wanted to fill? When another is promoted in our place? When another's gifts seem greater than our own?

The test of sincerity. In our moments of honest self-reflection, we often admit to problems and weaknesses. How do we feel when others identify the same problems in us?

The test of criticism. Does criticism lead to immediate resentment and self-justification? Do we rush to criticize the critic?

When we measure ourselves by the life of Jesus, who humbled Himself on the cross, we are overwhelmed with the shabbiness, even the vileness, of our hearts, and we cry:

Boasting excluded, pride I abase;
I'm only a sinner, saved by grace.
(James M. Gray)

EGOTISM

One of the repulsive manifestations of pride, egotism is the practice of thinking and speaking of oneself, of magnifying one's attainments, and relating everything to the self rather than to God and God's people. The leader who has long enjoyed the admiration of many followers stands in peril of this danger.

When Robert Louis Stevenson arrived in Samoa, he was invited to address students training for the pastorate at the Malua Institute. His talk was based on the Muslim story of the veiled prophet, a brilliant teacher who wore a veil because, he claimed, the glory of his presence was too great for men to bear the sight.

At last the veil grew ragged and fell off. Then the people discovered that the brilliant prophet was only an decrepit old man trying to hide his ugliness. Stevenson went on to make the point that, however grand the truths a preacher taught, however skillful the outward image of the leader, the time comes when the veil falls away and a man is seen by the people as he really is. Will the leader reflect the ugliness of egotism or the transfigured glory of Christ the Lord?

> It is a good test to the rise and fall of egotism to notice how you listen to the praises of other men of your own standing. Until you can listen to the praises of a rival without any desire to indulge in detraction or any attempt to belittle his work, you may be sure there is an unmortified prairie of egotistic impulse in your nature yet to be brought under the grace of God.[1]

JEALOUSY

This near relative of pride describes the person who is envious of rivals. Moses faced such a temptation through the loyalty of his own colleagues. When Eldad and Medad were "prophesying in the camp," an outraged Joshua reported, "Moses, my lord, stop them!" (Numbers 11:27–28).

But the great leader saw the situation for what it was,

an outbreak of God's Spirit among the assistants Moses had selected. "Are you jealous for my sake?" Moses replied to Joshua. "I wish that all the LORD's people were prophets" (Numbers 11:29). Envy and jealousy found no fertile ground in Moses's heart. God's work in others was to be encouraged, not snuffed out.

POPULARITY

What leader or preacher does not desire to be liked by his people? Being disliked is no virtue, but popularity can have too high a price. "Woe to you, when all men speak well of you," Jesus warned (Luke 6:26 RSV).

Personality cults have often developed around great spiritual leaders. Followers are awestruck at a leader's virtues, and show such fawning deference that the leader seems no longer merely human. Worse yet, sometimes the leader comes to enjoy his pedestal.

Paul faced this problem at Corinth. Christians there were splintering into camps promoting their favorite: some liked Apollos, others liked Paul. The apostle saw the danger and immediately put a stop to it. Neither of them warranted such favoritism, "but only God" (1 Corinthians 3:7). Any fervor, devotion, or loyalty the people in Corinth might have for spiritual leaders should be fastened tightly to the person of Jesus.

Spiritual leaders may be "esteem[ed] . . . highly in love for their work's sake" (KJV), but esteem that becomes adulation has degenerated. Leaders must work to attach the people's affection to Jesus. There is no fault in finding encouragement when one's service is appreciated, but the leader must altogether refuse to be idolized.

Stephen Neill said in a lecture to theological students: "Popularity is the most dangerous spiritual state imaginable, since it leads on so easily to the spiritual pride which drowns men in perdition. It is a symptom to be watched with anxiety since so often it has been purchased at the too heavy price of compromise with the world."[2]

Spurgeon also felt the danger of popularity pressing close to his heart:

> Success exposes a man to the pressure of people and thus tempts him to hold on to his gains by means of fleshly methods and practices, and to let himself be ruled wholly by the dictatorial demands of incessant expansion. Success can go to my head, and will unless I remember that it is God who accomplished the work, that He can continue to do so without any help, and that He will be able to make out with other means whenever He cuts me down to size.[3]

George Whitefield was immensely popular, and in his early years he enjoyed the acclaim. He recalled that he felt it was death to be despised and worse than death to be laughed at. But as his service and career progressed, he grew tired of the attention. "I have seen enough of popularity to be sick of it," he declared.

INFALLIBILITY

Spirituality does not guarantee infallible judgment. The Spirit-filled person is less likely to make mistakes of judgment than his secular counterpart, but perfection eludes us all, whatever our level of spiritual development. Even the apostles made mistakes that required divine correction.

Spiritual leaders who have given such a significant share of their lives to knowing God, to prayer, and to wrestling with the problems of renewal and revival may find it difficult to concede the possibility of misjudgment or mistake. Surely the leader must be a person of strength and decisiveness, to stand for what he believes. But willingness to concede error and to defer to the judgment of one's peers increases one's influence rather than diminishes it. Followers will lose confidence in a leader who appears to believe himself to be infallible. It is strange but true that a high level of genuine authority in one area of life often coexists with great humility in other areas.

INDISPENSABILITY

Many influential Christians have fallen before this temptation. It seems that Christians are especially prone to it. They cling to authority long after it should have passed to younger people. The author met a wonderful Christian in his nineties who was still superintendent of his church's Sunday school. Younger people were willing and available, but no one in the church had been able to approach this saint about retirement. One unfortunate consequence is that young people who have energy to fill a role are held back and stagnate.

Sometimes sincere and well-meaning followers encourage the notion of indispensability, which feeds a leader's ego and makes him even less objective about performance in office. And we do become less objective about our work as we get older.

The missionary who has raised a church to believe that he is indispensable has done the church an injustice. From the earliest days of the work, the missionary should be planning on working out of a job. National leadership needs to learn how to depend on the Lord, how to train its own spiritual leaders, and how to take responsibility for the work.

ELATION AND DEPRESSION

Every work of God includes days of frustration and days of joy. The leader is in peril of becoming overly depressed by the one and overly elated by the other. Discovering the balance here is not easy.

When the seventy disciples returned from their mission elated with results, Jesus checked their euphoria. "Do not rejoice that the spirits submit to you, but rejoice that your names are written in heaven" (Luke 10:20).

After the drama at Carmel (1 Kings 18), Elijah was so depressed that he wanted to die. The Lord corrected his self-pity in a most common manner, by insisting on two long sleeps and two decent meals. Only then did the spiritual lessons begin, and they made a lifelong difference to Elijah. His discouragement was unfounded: seven thousand faithful Israelites had not yet bowed to Baal. By running away, Elijah had deprived this remnant of leadership they desperately needed.

Not all our ideals and goals for the work of God will be realized. People we trust will disappoint us; cherished plans will fall victim to shortfalls or sickness; the sacrifices leaders make will be interpreted as selfish gestures. Bad things happen, but the spiritual leader should discern the reasons for depression and deal with it accordingly.

F. B. Meyer was an eternal optimist, ever hopeful, ever vigorous, ever confident of the triumph of good over evil. But he was also

> far too keen and thoughtful a man . . . not to be overcome now and again by the pessimistic views of life. He occasionally went down into the very depths of human despair. He had seen too often and too clearly the seamy side of life not to be sad and pessimistic now and then.[4]

Another kind of depression is described by Spurgeon in his lecture "The Minister's Fainting Fits":

> Before any great achievement, some measure of depression is very usual. . . . Such was my experience when I first became a pastor in London. My success appalled me, and the thought of the career which seemed to open up so far from elating me, cast me into the lowest depth, out of which I muttered my miserere and found no room for a gloria in excelsis. Who was I that I should continue to lead so great a multitude? I would betake me to my village obscurity, or emigrate to America and find a solitary nest in the backwoods where I might be sufficient for the things that were demanded of me. It was just then the curtain was rising on my lifework, and I dreaded what it might reveal. I hope I was not faithless, but I was timorous and filled with a sense of my own unfitness. . . . This depression comes over me whenever the Lord is preparing a larger blessing for my ministry.[5]

Seasons there are when all goes well. Goals are reached, plans find success, the Spirit moves, souls are saved, and saints blessed. When Robert Murray McCheyne went through times like this, he would kneel down and symbolically place the crown of success on the brow of the Lord, to whom it rightly belonged. That habit helped save him from assuming the glory for achievement that belonged to God alone.

Samuel Chadwick wisely said: "If successful, don't crow; if defeated, don't croak."[6]

PROPHET OR LEADER?

Sometimes we come to a fork in the path, and both ways look good and true. For example, a preacher with gifts of leadership faces a decision whether to be a popular leader or unpopular prophet. A. C. Dixon faced such a dilemma:

> Every preacher ought to be primarily a prophet of God who preaches as God bids him, without regard to results. When he becomes conscious of the fact that he is a leader in his own church or denomination, he has reached a crisis in his ministry. He must now choose one of two courses, that of prophet of God or a leader of men. If he seeks to be a prophet and a leader, he is apt to make a failure of both. If he decides to be a prophet only insofar as he can do without losing his leadership, he becomes a diplomat and ceases to be a prophet at all. If he decides to maintain leadership at all costs, he may easily fall to the level of a politician who pulls the wires in order to gain or hold a position.[7]

Dixon maximizes the differences between leader and prophet; in reality, however, the roles overlap. But situations develop in which a leader must choose between the hellfire of prophetic warning and the gentle prodding of pastoral work. Herein lies the peril.

Reuben A. Torrey, whom God used at the turn of the century to bring revival to half the world, faced such a choice. Dixon wrote of him:

> The thousands who have heard Dr. Torrey know the man and his message. He loves the Bible, and believing it to be the infallible Word of God, preaches it with the fervor of red-hot conviction. He never compromises. He has chosen to be a prophet of God rather than a mere leader of men, and that is the secret of his power with God and men.[8]

DISQUALIFICATION

Despite his success as a missionary and leader, Paul was never without a wholesome, watchful fear that he himself might be disqualified (1 Corinthians 9:27). To him this prospect was an ever-present warning against smugness and complacency. So should it be to all who are entrusted with spiritual responsibility.

The Greek work for "disqualified" (in other translations "castaway" or "disapproved") in verse 27 is used of metals that were not suitable for coinage. These metals could not survive the test; the refining process had left them below standard. Paul refers here to losing the coveted prize for failure to comply with the rules of the contest.

Paul's metaphor puts him in two roles here. He is a competitor in the context, and also the herald who announces the rules of the game and calls runners to the starting line. Paul feared that after acting as a herald (preaching), he himself should fail by the very standards he preaches. In that case, his position as herald would only serve to aggravate his own guilt, shame, and disgrace.

The failure before Paul's eyes here is failure of the body, and to guard against it requires rigorous self-discipline. Charles Hodge affirms that in Scripture the body is "the seat and organ of sin, and refers to our whole sinful nature. It was not merely his sensual nature Paul endeavored to bring into subjection, but all the evil propensities of his heart."[9]

Paul believed he could be disqualified not merely because of errors of doctrine or misjudgments of ethics but because of the body's passions. Paul worked toward mastering the body's appetites through disciplined moderation—neither asceticism on the one hand (such as causing oneself harm by denial of basic needs) nor self-indulgence on the other (losing strength through careless diet, for example). Paul was not willing to give in to bodily appetites, as if they were his master. He insisted on being in command of his own bodily needs and wants. A. S. Way rendered this passage: "I browbeat my own animal nature . . . and treat it, not as my master, but as my slave."

CHAPTER 22

The Leader Nehemiah

Remember me with favor, O my God.

NEHEMIAH 13:31

Nehemiah is one of the most inspiring leaders in the Bible. At times his methods seem somewhat vigorous, but they were used by God to achieve spectacular reforms in the life of his nation in an amazingly short time. An analysis of his personality and methods discloses that the methods he adopted were effective only because of the quality of his character.

HIS CHARACTER

The first impression a reader gains from this straightforward story is that Nehemiah was a man of prayer. For Nehemiah prayer was an ordinary part of living and working. Prayer was his first reaction on hearing the plight of emigrants in Jerusalem. Nehemiah was no stranger at the throne of grace (Nehemiah 1:4, 6; 2:4; 4:4, 9; 5:19; 6:14; 13:14, 22, 29).

He showed courage in the face of danger. "Should a man like me run away? Or should one like me go into the temple to save his life? I will not go!" (Nehemiah 6:11). Such firm fearlessness would inspire any discouraged people.

His genuine concern for the welfare of others was so obvious that even his enemies noticed (Nehemiah 2:10). He expressed his concern in fasting, prayer, and tears (Nehemiah 1:4–6). Nehemiah identified with his people in their sorrows and in their sins: "I confess the sins we Israelites, including myself and my father's house, have committed against you" (Nehemiah 1:6).

Nehemiah exhibited keen foresight. He knew that opposition was sure to arise, so he secured letters from the king for safe passage and for the resources to accomplish the task, "to make beams for the gates of the citadel . . . and for the city wall" (Nehemiah 2:8). He carefully planned his strategy.

Through all his adventures and boldness, there runs a strain of caution. He did not jump into the work immediately upon arrival but waited three days to appraise the situation (Nehemiah 2:11). And when he did set to business, he did not hold a tell-all press conference but kept his goals largely secret, even doing reconnaissance under cover of night.

Nehemiah could make clear decisions. He did not put off the tough call but cut to the heart and made a judgment. And his decisions were impartial; he did not play favorites. When censure was needed, he gave it to officials and executives as well as to workers (Nehemiah 5:7).

Nehemiah was uncommonly empathetic. He listened to grievances and took remedial action (Nehemiah 4:10–12; 5:1–5). He let people "weep on his shoulder." He sympathized with others.

Nehemiah was a realist; he understood the mechanics of the real world. "We prayed to our God and posted a guard day and night" (Nehemiah 4:9).

He accepted responsibility with the intention of following through on all assignments, the pleasant ones and the dirty ones, until the job was done.

Nehemiah was a vigorous administrator, a calm crisis manager, a fearless initiator, a courageous decision maker, and a persevering leader. He was resolute in the face of threats and vigilant against treachery—a leader who won and held the full confidence of his followers.

HIS METHODS

Nehemiah raised the morale of his colleagues, an important part of any leader's work. He built up their faith by redirecting focus away from "the impossible" toward the greatness of God. Throughout the record are such assurances as "the God of heaven will give us success" (Nehemiah 2:20) and "the joy of the LORD is your strength" (Nehemiah 8:10).

Faith builds faith. Pessimism dismantles faith. The spiritual leader's primary task is to build the faith of others.

Nehemiah encouraged others generously. When he arrived, the people were demoralized. First, he kindled hope by testifying to the vision and providence of God, and then secured their cooperation. "I also told them about the gracious hand of my God upon me and what the king had said to me. They replied, 'Let us start building.' So they began this good work" (Nehemiah 2:18).

Faults and failures must be corrected, but method makes all the difference. Nehemiah could point to people's shortcomings and find hope for a better day. Then his great personal discipline convinced the people that his optimism wasn't mere giddiness but the strength of deep conviction. And so he won their confidence and established his authority.

Nehemiah promptly faced potential weaknesses in the plan. Two cases illustrate.

The people were discouraged and tired. Opponents were making life miserable (Nehemiah 4:10–16). Garbage was piling up and hampering progress. Nehemiah first directed their vision to God, then put them under arms and deployed them at strategic points. He harnessed the strength of the family unit, ordering half a family to work while the other half stood guard and rested. The people recovered their courage as Nehemiah solved real problems through decisive action.

In the second instance the people were disillusioned by the greed of their own rich brothers (Nehemiah 5:1–15). Most people lived on mortgaged land; some had sold children as slaves to meet expenses. "Neither is it in our power to redeem them; for other men have our lands and vineyards" (Nehemiah 5:5 KJV). What an awkward mess: children of "have-nots," victims of an economy where wealth was held in the hands of a few, and those few were not about to release their grasp.

Nehemiah listened to their stories and sympathized with their suffering. He rebuked the nobles for their heartless usury (Nehemiah 5:7) and appealed for immediate relief (Nehemiah 5:11). So effective was his negotiation that the reply of the nobles was simply, "We will do as you say" (Nehemiah 5:12).

Nehemiah recovered the authority of the Word of God in the lives of the people (Nehemiah 8:1–8). Without the standard of God's Word, all the work would be for naught.

What does success matter if we have no standard, no vision of ultimate goals, no purpose larger than laying bricks on bricks? Nehemiah's greatest gift to the people was to show them why all this work was important. He restored the Feast of Tabernacles, which had not been observed since Joshua's day. He led the people to repentance through the reading of the law (Nehemiah 9:3–5). He purified the temple of pagan influence (Nehemiah 13:4–9). He encouraged tithing, established Sabbath rest, forbade intermarriage with pagan foreigners, and so recovered the special identity of Israel as God's chosen people.

Nehemiah could organize projects and people. Before setting plans he did a careful survey of resources and personnel. Some would have called it unglamorous paper pushing, time-consuming research studies, but Nehemiah called it careful preparation. He then established key objectives, assigned those to responsible leaders (men of faith and piety), and set them to work. All of this opened the leadership potential of others.

Nehemiah faced up to opposition without forcing a violent confrontation. He took insults, innuendo, intimidation, and treachery. He walked through it with his head high and his eyes wide open, with much prayer (Nehemiah 4:9). When he could, he simply ignored the adversary. Always he took precaution. Never did he allow opposition to deflect his energy from the central task. Always he kept faith in God (Nehemiah 4:20).

The test of spiritual leadership is the achievement of its objective. In Nehemiah's case, the record is clear:

"So the wall was completed" (Nehemiah 6:15).

A Final Word

Do you remember the questions and desires that motivated you to open this book? Were they questions about the wisdom of taking up leadership responsibilities or questions about setting them aside? Were you looking at a "breach in the wall" or considering an invitation to lead and wondering if you should step up? Were you wondering if you have what it takes to lead or wondering if you still have what it takes to lead?

Now you know that even though there's a lot involved in leadership, there's even more involved in spiritual leadership. If you feel overwhelmed as you finish this book, welcome to the life of a follower of Jesus. If spiritual leadership were easy, everyone would be doing it!

Spiritual leadership is not a calling we choose to pursue; it is a calling we choose to answer. We don't decide to become leaders; we decide to respond and keep responding to God's call in our lives. Along the way, whether we like it or not, that involves us in leadership.

The account of Nehemiah that closed this book presents the high bar of spiritual leadership—the kind of thoughtful, heartfelt, and wise practices we strive to emulate. But of all the biblical leaders whose style we've examined in these pages, the disciple Peter perhaps best represents many of the struggles we face on a day-to-day basis. One of the benefits we get from knowing Peter's life comes when we listen in on the last, crucial supervisory session between Peter and Jesus. Jesus helped Peter to clarify his commitment: "Simon son of John, do you truly love me more than these?" (John 21:15). Jesus restated Peter's job description: "Feed my lambs" (John 21:15). And Jesus gave Peter a central, overriding, "default" command: "Follow me!" (John 21:19).

Through all the highs and lows of leadership, in times of great certainty and crippling uncertainty, those who have led in rebuilding broken-down walls and bringing God's message of light and life into dark places have been those whose souls have never ceased to say "Yes" to Jesus' invitation, "Follow Me." And many of them turned out to be spiritual leaders. What answer to Jesus' invitation echoes in your heart and life today?

Notes

Chapter 1: An Honorable Ambition

1. Stephen Neill, "Address to Ordinands," *The Record*, 28 March 1947, 161. Neill (1900–1984) served in South India and later taught missiology.
2. C. W. Hall, *Samuel Logan Brengle* (New York: Salvation Army, 1933), 274. Brengle (1860–1939) was internationally sought as a holiness speaker during the early decades of this century.

Chapter 2: The Search for Leaders

1. Henry George Liddell (1811–1898) was dean of Christ Church, Oxford University, and chaplain to the Queen. Lewis Carroll wrote *Alice in Wonderland* for Liddell's daughter Alice.
2. Quoted in Paul E. Sangster, *Doctor Sangster* (London: Epworth, 1962), 109. William Sangster (1900–1960) was a leader in British Methodism.
3. Samuel Logan Brengle, *The Soul-Winner's Secret* (London: Salvation Army, 1918), 22.

Chapter 3: The Master's Master Principle

1. Paul S. Rees, "The Community Clue," *Life of Faith*, 26 September 1976, 3.

Chapter 4: Natural and Spiritual Leadership

1. Bernard L. Montgomery, *Memoirs of Field-Marshal Montgomery* (Cleveland: World, 1958), 70. Bernard Law Montgomery (1887–1976) made his mark in World War II as the first allied general to inflict a decisive defeat on the Axis at El Alamein in Northern Africa, October 1942. He was knighted that November. Chester Nimitz (1885–1966), quoted in Sanders's text without a citation, was commander of the Pacific Fleet and Pacific Ocean Areas during World War II. Charles George Gordon (1833–1885), also quoted without citation, was an eccentric but effective British military commander in China during the 1860s (for which he was tagged "Chinese Gordon") and in Africa, where he died at Khartoum trying to withstand an overwhelming army led by the Mahdi, a mystic leader in the Sudan.

2. Lettie B. Cowman, *Charles E. Cowman* (Los Angeles: Oriental Missionary Society, 1928), 251. John R. Mott (1865–1955) was a Methodist evangelist who served in the Student Volunteer Movement and the YMCA. His best-known book is *Evangelizing the World in Our Generation* (1900), which was also the motto he was widely known for. He was a founder of the World Council of Churches.
3. P. T. Chandapilla was general secretary for the Union of Evangelical Students of India from 1956–1971. His goal was to reach India's intellectuals with the gospel. Following Hudson Taylor, Chandapilla never asked for financial help. He worked closely with InterVarsity Fellowship and the International Fellowship of Evangelical Students.
4. Montgomery, *Memoirs*, 70.
5. Phyllis Thompson, *D. E. Hoste* (London: China Inland Mission, n.d.), 122.
6. A. W. Tozer, in *The Reaper*, February 1962, 459. Aiden Wilson Tozer (1897–1963) was a minister in the Christian and Missionary Alliance. Among his thirty books, the best known is *The Pursuit of God* (1948).
7. Paul E. Sangster, *Doctor Sangster* (London: Epworth, 1962), 109.
8. James Burns, *Revivals, Their Laws and Leaders* (London: Hodder Stoughton, 1909), 95.
9. Montgomery, *Memoirs*, 70.
10. B. Matthews, *John R. Mott* (London: S.C.M. Press, 1934), 346.
11. John Geddie (1815–1872), born in Scotland, was called the father of foreign missions in the Presbyterian Church in Canada. He went as a missionary to the New Hebrides (formerly called Aneityum) in 1848.
12. Matthews, *Mott*, 353.

Chapter 5: Can You Become a Leader?

1. R. E. Thompson, in *World Vision*, December 1966, 4.

Chapter 6: Insights on Leadership from Paul

1. William Barclay, *Letters to Timothy and Titus* (Edinburgh: St. Andrews, 1960), 92. Jeremy Taylor (1613–1667) was an Anglican bishop and chaplain to Charles I. He is known today for his devotional writings, especially *Holy Living* (1650) and *Holy Dying* (1651) written after Charles was beheaded and the victorious Oliver Cromwell was at his peak. Taylor was one of the most popular preachers of his day. Mencius (ca. 372–289 B.C.), the Chinese philosopher mentioned without citation in the third paragraph, was Confucius's greatest disciple. He promoted the cardinal virtues of love, righteousness, decorum, and wisdom. His Latinized name comes from Meng-Tzu, meaning Master Meng. He was known as the Second Sage.
2. C. W. Hall, *Samuel Logan Brengle* (New York: Salvation Army, 1933), 112.
3. John William Fletcher (1729–1785) was vicar of Madeley in Shropshire. Swiss by birth, he joined the Methodist movement within the

Church of England. He is remembered for his sanctity and his devotion to work among coal miners.

4. William Hendriksen, *1 and 2 Timothy and Titus* (London: Banner of Truth, 1959), 36. Dietrich Bonhoeffer, quoted but not cited, was a leader in Germany's underground church during the Third Reich. He was executed by the Nazis in 1945 just before Allied troops reached his prison camp.
5. Quoted in Barclay, *Letters*, 86.

Chapter 7: Insights on Leadership from Peter

1. William Barclay, *The Letters of Peter and Jude* (Edinburgh: St. Andrews, 1958), 156.
2. Paul S. Rees, *Triumphant in Trouble* (London: Marshall, Morgan & Scott, n.d.), 126.
3. J. H. Jowett, *The Epistles of Peter* (London: Hodder & Stoughton, n.d.), 188. Jowett (1863–1923), an English Congregationalist minister, was pastor of Fifth Avenue Presbyterian Church in New York, then succeeded G. Campbell Morgan at Westminster Chapel in London.
4. Stephen Neill, *On the Ministry* (n.p., n.d.), 107–8. Bishop of Azariah (1874–1945) was the first Indian bishop in the Anglican church. He founded the Missionary Society of Tinnevelly in 1903, then cofounded the National Missionary Society for the evangelization of India.

Chapter 8: Essential Qualities of Leadership

1. James Burns, *Revivals, Their Laws and Leaders* (London: Hodder & Stoughton, 1909), 182. Martin Luther (1483–1546) is generally credited with beginning the Protestant Reformation when he nailed "95 Theses" (statements outlining his understanding of the Scriptures contrasted to church teachings) on the church door at Wittenberg, Germany, in October 1517. Adoniram Judson (1788–1850), mentioned earlier, is widely known as a pioneer missionary to Burma.
2. Gustav Warneck (1834–1910) is generally recognized as the founder of the field of study called missiology. He held Germany's first university chair of mission, at Halle, in 1896.
3. Donald Grey Barnhouse (1895–1960) worked in Belgium and France before taking the pastorate of Tenth Presbyterian Church in Philadelphia. He edited *Revelation*, later *Eternity* magazine, and wrote extensively.
4. Amy Wilson Carmichael (1867–1951), missionary to India, founded the Dohnavur Fellowship to help neglected and abused children. Born in Ireland, she became the first woman to be supported on the mission field by the Keswick Missions Committee. She served fifty-six years without a furlough and wrote thirty-five books.
5. Phyllis Thompson, *Climbing on Track* (London: China Inland Mission, 1954), 116.

6. Florence Nightingale (1820–1910) was the heroine of the Crimean War and founder of modern nursing. Born to Italian nobility, she felt called to serve God at age seventeen and abandoned her family's wealth and privilege. Adulation flowed from her work in Scutari, Turkey, on behalf of British troops. She became a recluse, however, for the last four decades of her life.
7. N. G. Dunning, *Samuel Chadwick* (London: Hodder & Stoughton, 1934), 15. Chadwick lived from 1860 to 1932.
8. J. R. Andrews, *George Whitefield* (London: Morgan & Scott, 1915), 410–11. Barclay Buxton (1860–1946) mentioned immediately after this citation, was a missionary to Japan for forty-six years.
9. *World Vision*, January 1966, 5.
10. Brooke Foss Westcott (1825–1901) worked for twenty-eight years with Fenton Hort on *The New Testament in the Original Greek* (1881). His Bible commentaries are still read.
11. Powhatten James, *George W. Truett* (Nashville: Broadman, 1953), 266. Truett lived from 1867 to 1944.
12. Lettie B. Cowman, *Charles E. Cowman* (Los Angeles: Oriental Missionary Society, 1928), 259. Charles Cowman founded the Oriental Missionary Society, now known as OMS International, in 1901. Lettie Cowman wrote *Streams in the Desert*, one of the most-read devotional books of all time. William McKinley (1843–1901), mentioned immediately after this citation, was the twenty-fifth president of the United States. He died from an assassin's bullet wound suffered in Buffalo, New York.
13. W. H. T. Gairdner, *Douglas M. Thornton* (London: Hodder & Stoughton, n.d.), 80. Thornton (1873–1907) was educational secretary for the Student Volunteer Missionary Union. Henry Martyn (1781–1812), mentioned in the previous paragraph, was inspired to a life in missions after reading the diary of David Brainerd. He served as chaplain to the East India Company in Bengal, and translated the New Testament into Hindustani. Albert Benjamin Simpson (1844–1915) founded the Evangelical Missionary Alliance, later the Christian and Missionary Alliance, and wrote over seventy books.
14. Marcus Lane, *Archbishop Mowll* (London: Hodder & Stoughton, 1960), 202. Howard West Kilvington Mowll (1890–1958) served as an Anglican bishop in Canada, China, and Sydney (Australia).
15. Dunning, *Chadwick*, 20.
16. Theodore Roosevelt, in B. Matthews, *John R. Mott* (London: S.C.M. Press, 1934), 355. Roosevelt (1858–1919) was twenty-sixth president of the United States.
17. Phyllis Thompson, *D. E. Hoste* (London: China Inland Mission, n.d.), 155.
18. David Livingstone (1813–1873) began work in a cotton mill at age twelve, but taught himself Greek, theology, and medicine. In 1840 he went to Africa under the London Missionary Society. He was found by journalist Henry Stanley, working for the New York Herald, in 1871.

Stanley greeted the missionary with the simple yet oft-quoted words: "Doctor Livingstone, I presume."

19. Burns, *Revivals*, 181–82.
20. Ibid., 167–68. Luther's precise words at the Diet of Worms are the subject of historians' debates. Sanders' original text quotes from Burns. More recent historical data was used for the quotation in this edition. See James M. Kittelson, "The Accidental Revolutionary," in *Christian History*, Issue 34, 16. Quotations preceding Worms and near the time of Luther's death are reported as they appear in Burns.
21. William Law (1686–1761) was an evangelical devotional writer and mystic. He is best known for *A Serious Call to a Devout and Holy Life* (1728).
22. C. W. Hall, *Samuel Logan Brengle* (New York: Salvation Army, 1933), 275.
23. Robert Morrison (1782–1834) was an interpreter for the East India Company in Canton. He translated the Bible into Cantoese, and labored for twenty-seven years in China for about a dozen converts.

Chapter 9: More Essential Qualities of Leadership

1. Quoted in C. W. Hall, *Samuel Logan Brengle* (New York: Salvation Army, 1933), 278. Samuel Johnson (1709–1784), mentioned earlier, was an English poet, essayist, and lexicographer. His *Dictionary of the English Language* (1747) was the standard for a century.
2. Helmut Thielecke, *Encounter with Spurgeon* (Philadelphia: Fortress, 1963), 26. Charles Haddon Spurgeon (1834–1892), one of the best-known preachers of the nineteenth century, was pastor of the Metropolitan Tabernacle in London for thirty-two years.
3. A. E. Norrish, *Christian Leadership* (New Delhi: Masihi Sabiyata Sanstha, 1963), 28.
4. *Latin America Evangelist*, May–June 1965.
5. Robert E. Speer, *Christ and Life* (New York: Revell, 1901), 103. Frederick William Robertson (1816–1853) was ordained in the Church of England in 1840 and made his mark as a preacher among the working poor of Brighton. William Wilberforce (1759–1833), mentioned earlier, was a member of the British parliament whose work, strongly opposed by vested interest, eventually led to laws prohibiting slavery and the slave trade. In 1804 he helped form the British and Foreign Bible Society.
6. Ibid., 104. Joseph Butler (1692–1752), Anglican bishop, is remembered for his book *Analogy of Religion* (1736), probably the best defense of Christian faith to appear in the eighteenth century.
7. William Barclay, *Letters of Peter and Jude* (Edinburgh: St. Andrews, 1960), 258. John Chrysostom (ca. 347–407), mentioned earlier, is an "early church father." He was for ten years a monastic hermit, then deacon and priest in Antioch, then patriarch of Constantinople. He was exiled for preaching against vice and excess among the clergy and royalty.

8. J. C. Pollock, *Hudson Taylor and Maria* (London: Hodder & Stoughton, 1962), 35.
9. Ernest Gordon, *A. J. Gordon* (London: Hodder & Stoughton, 1897), 191.
10. Phyllis Thompson, *D. E. Hoste* (London: China Inland Mission, n.d.), 158.
11. A. E. Thompson, *The Life of A. B. Simpson* (Harrisburg, PA: Christian Publications, 1920), 204.
12. H. C. Lees, *St. Paul's Friends* (London: Religious Tract Society, 1917), 11.
13. A. W. Tozer, *Let My People Go* (Harrisburg, PA: Christian Publications, 1957), 36.
14. S. P. Carey, *William Carey* (London: Hodder & Stoughton, 1923), 256.
15. Lettie B. Cowman, *Charles E. Cowman* (Los Angeles: Oriental Missionary Society, 1928), 269.
16. Mrs. Hudson Taylor, *Pastor Hsi* (London: China Inland Mission, 1949), 164, 167.
17. Mark Clark (1896–1984) was a lieutenant general in the U.S. Army during World War II. He commanded the Fifth Army during the Italian campaign, and was commander of all United Nations troops in Korea during that conflict.
18. George Adam Smith, *The Book of Isaiah* (London: Hodder & Stoughton, n.d.), 229.
19. James Burns, *Revival, Their Laws and Leaders* (London: Hodder & Stoughton, 1909), 311.
20. *World Vision*, February 1966, 5.

Chapter 10: Above All Else

1. A. T. Pierson, *The Acts of the Holy Spirit* (London: Morgan & Scott, n.d.), 63. Arthur Tappan Pierson (1837–1911) was a preacher, writer, and missionary spokesman who also served as a consultant on the Scofield Reference Bible.
2. D. J. Fant, *A. W. Tozer* (Harrisburg, PA: Christian Publications, 1964), 73, 83.

Chapter 11: Prayer and Leadership

1. N .G. Dunning, *Samuel Chadwick* (London: Hodder & Stoughton, 1934), 19.
2. D. M. McIntyre, *The Prayer Life of Our Lord* (London: Morgan & Scott, n.d.), 30–31.
3. George Mueller (1805–1898) was a Plymouth Brethren leader who refused a salary, believing that God would supply his needs by prayer alone. He established an orphanage in Bristol for two thousand youngsters on the strength of prayer and promoted prayer during a seventeen-year world tour.

4. E. M. Bounds, *Prayer and Praying Men* (London: Hodder & Stoughton, 1921). Edward McKendree Bounds (1835–1913) was an American Methodist Episcopal minister who served churches throughout the South. He was a captain in the Confederate army.

Chapter 12: The Leader and Time

1. Michelangelo (1475–1564) was an Italian sculptor, painter, and poet. His famous works include the statue "David" and the ceiling of the Sistine Chapel in the Vatican. William James (1842–1910) was a Harvard psychologist and philosopher generally credited with popularizing a new approach to knowledge called pragmatism.
2. J. H. Jowett, *The School of Calvary or Sharing His Suffering* (reprinted, Alberta, Canada: Prairie Bible Institute, 1969).
3. Mary Slessor (1848–1915) went to Calabar, West Africa, in 1876, a region not controlled by any colonial power. Her sense of humor and courage won the confidence of warring chiefs, and she contributed immensely to the life of children and women.
4. J. Stuart Holden, *The Gospel of the Second Chance* (London: Marshall Brothers, 1912), 188.
5. W. Y. Fullerton, *F. B. Meyer* (London: Marshall, Morgan & Scott, n.d.), 70. Frederick Brotherton Meyer (1847–1929) was a Baptist preacher with a worldwide pulpit and a base in London. He was known for crusades against prostitution, alcoholic beverages, and prizefighting, and on behalf of unwanted children and unmarried mothers. John Wesley (1703–1791) is well known as the energetic cofounder of Methodism.
6. Paul E. Sangster, *Doctor Sangster* (London: Epworth, 1962), 314.
7. *Sunday School Times*, 22 November 1913, 713.

Chapter 13: The Leader and Reading

1. William Tyndale (ca.1494–1536) was the first to translate the New Testament into English, in 1525, from a base in Germany. He was arrested in 1535 and a year later burned at the stake. Before his death, he completed the translation of the first five Old Testament books and Jonah.
2. A. W. Tozer, "The Use and Abuse of Books," *The Alliance Weekly*, 22 February 1956, 2.
3. Harold J. Ockenga, *Christianity Today*, 4 March 1966, 36.
4. Francis Bacon, quoted in *The Alliance Weekly*, 14 March 1956, 2. Bacon (1561–1626) was a statesman and scholar who served Elizabeth I and James I. His many writings deal with scientific method, political theory, and the history of ideas. He was a loyal member of the Church of England.
5. Charles Finney (1792–1875) was trained in law but turned to ministry after his conversion in 1821. He led revivals through the Northeast, pastored churches, wrote books, opposed slavery and drink, and was

president of Oberlin College from 1851–1866. The book cited here was published in 1835.

6. C. W. Hall, *Samuel Logan Brengle* (New York: Salvation Army, 1933), 269.
7. Charles Thomas Studd (1862–1931) inherited a fortune, but gave it away and sailed to China as a missionary in 1885. He also served in India and Africa, and helped found the Student Volunteer Movement.
8. Muriel Ormrod, *The Reaper*, August 1965, 229.
9. Helmut Thielecke, *Encounter with Spurgeon* (Philadelphia: Fortress, 1963), 197.
10. *Sunday School Times*, 22 November 1913, 715.

Chapter 14: Improving Leadership

1. The reference is to John Bunyan's *The Pilgrim's Progress*, published in 1678 and now translated into hundreds of languages. Bunyan (1628–1688) wrote more than sixty books.

Chapter 15: The Cost of Leadership

1. Robert E. Speer, *Marks of a Man* (New York: Revell, 1907), 109.
2. Samuel Logan Brengle, *The Soul-Winner's Secret* (London: Salvation Army, 1918), 23.
3. The reference is to the famous 1925 book, *The Man Nobody Knows*, written by advertising advocate Bruce Barton. The book purported to show that Jesus was the keenest business mind, and hence the most successful salesman, of all time. Jesus' techniques could revolutionize the world, Barton argued.
4. Samuel M. Zwemer, *It Is Hard to Be a Christian* (London: Marshalls, 1937), 139. Samuel Marinus Zwemer (1867–1952) established missions to Muslims in the Middle East and was later professor of the history of religion at Princeton Seminary. He wrote over fifty books.
5. Lettie B. Cowman, *Charles E. Cowman* (Los Angeles: Oriental Missionary Society, 1928), 260.
6. Used by permission of the Christian Literature Crusade, Fort Washington, Pennsylvania.
7. Friedrich Nietzsche (1844–1900) was raised Lutheran, but as a scholar and university professor of philosophy, he became one of the most well-known atheists of the modern era. In every way he found reason to criticize Christian faith and life, except that he admired Jesus. Nietzsche went insane in 1889 but continued to publish attacks on the church, its mission, and its ethic.
8. W. H. T. Gairdner, *Douglas M. Thornton* (London: Hodder & Stoughton, n.d.), 225.
9. R. D. Abella, in *Evangelical Thought* (Manila: n.p., n.d.).

10. Phyllis Thompson, *Climbing on Track* (London: China Inland Mission, 1954), 116.
11. C. W. Hall, *Samuel Logan Brengle* (New York: Salvation Army, 1933), 272.
12. J. Gregory Mantle, *Beyond Humiliation* (Chicago: Moody, n.d.), 140–41.
13. Cowman, *Cowman*, 258.
14. Phyllis Thompson, *D. E. Hoste* (London: China Inland Mission, n.d.), 130–31.
15. Thompson, *Climbing on Track*, 115.

Chapter 16: Responsibilities of Leadership

1. Alexander Balmain Bruce (1831–1899) was professor of apologetics and New Testament at the Free Church College, Glasgow, from 1868 to 1899. He wrote *Training of the Twelve* in 1871.
2. Phyllis Thompson, *D. E. Hoste* (London: China Inland Mission, n.d.), 217.
3. Ibid., 158.
4. In *The Reaper*, May 1961, 89. Robert Louis Stevenson (1850–1894) was a British writer best known for *Treasure Island* and *Dr. Jekyll and Mr. Hyde.*
5. Marcus Loane, *Archbishop Mowll* (London: Hodder & Stoughton, 1960), 249.
6. Edward White Benson (1829–1896) became archbishop of Canterbury in 1882. His leadership of the Church of England was marked by concerns for education and the church in Wales.

Chapter 17: Tests of Leadership

1. Used by permission of Evangelical Publishers, Toronto, Canada.
2. Alexander Maclaren (1826–1910) was pastor for forty-five years at Union Chapel in Manchester, England. He was the first president of the Baptist World Alliance in 1905.
3. James Anthony Froude (1818–1894) was a British writer and historian attached to the Oxford Movement.

Chapter 18: The Art of Delegation

1. Dwight L. Moody (1837–1899) was one of America's foremost evangelists. He rose to national prominence after success in preaching meetings in Scotland and England during 1873–1875. He established educational institutions in Northfield, Massachusetts, and Chicago, Illinois (later called Moody Bible Institute).
2. Phyllis Thompson, *D. E. Hoste* (London: China Inland Mission, n.d.), 56.
3. A. E. Thompson, *The Life of A. B. Simpson* (Harrisburg, PA: Christian Publications, 1920), 208.
4. B. Matthews, *John R. Mott* (London: Hodder & Stoughton, 1909), 364.

5. Paul E. Sangster, *Doctor Sangster* (London: Epworth, 1962), 88, 221.
6. Phyllis Thompson, *Climbing on Track* (London: China Inland Mission, 1954), 99.

Chapter 19: Replacing Leaders

1. *Sunday School Times*, 8 November 1913, 682. Lyman Beecher (1775–1863) was one of America's leading revival preachers, a New England pastor, and president of Lane Seminary.
2. A. E. Thompson, *The Life of A. B. Simpson* (Harrisburg, PA: Christian Publications, 1920), 208.

Chapter 20: Reproducing Leaders

1. Lesslie Newbigin, in *International Review of Missions*, April 1950. Newbigin retired after forty years of missionary service in India.
2. H. C. Lees, *St. Paul's Friends* (London: Religious Tract Society, 1917), 135–41.
3. Paul S. Rees, "The Community Clue," *Life of Faith*, 26 September 1976, 3.
4. P. Howard, *Frank Buchman* (London: Heineman, 1961), 111. Frank Nathan Daniel Buchman (1878–1961) was a Lutheran minister who, discouraged with his work, moved to England in 1908. There he came in contact with the Keswick movement and experienced a conversion. In 1938 he launched the Moral Rearmament movement to promote love, honesty, purity, and unselfishness. The movement endured criticism from conservative Christians for alleged humanism. In Sanders's first edition, he makes a point of not endorsing "the merits" of Buchman's movement.
5. W. H. T. Gairdner, *Douglas M. Thornton* (London: Hodder & Stoughton, n.d.), 121.

Chapter 21: Perils of Leadership

1. Robert Louis Stevenson, in *The Reaper*, July 1942, 96.
2. Stephen Neill, in *The Record*, 28 March 1947, 161.
3. Helmut Thielecke, *Encounter with Spurgeon* (Philadelphia: Fortress, 1963).
4. W. Y. Fullerton, *F. B. Meyer* (London: Marshall, Morgan & Scott, n.d.), 172.
5. Quoted in Thielecke, *Encounter*, 219.
6. N. G. Dunning, *Samuel Chadwick* (London: Hodder & Stoughton, 1934), 206.
7. H. C. A. Dixon, *A. C. Dixon* (New York: Putnam's, 1931), 277. Amzi Clarence Dixon (1854–1925) served as pastor of Moody Memorial Church and the Metropolitan Tabernacle of London.
8. Ibid., 158. Reuben Archer Torrey (1856–1928), a Congregationalist minister, was first superintendent of the Moody Bible Institute (then

called Chicago Evangelistic Society) and pastor of Moody Memorial Church (then Chicago Avenue Church). He conducted crusades in Europe, Asia, and the Orient. He was later president of the Bible Institute of Los Angeles (now Biola College) and pastor of Church of the Open Door in downtown Los Angeles.

9. Charles Hodge (1797–1878), quoted here without citation, was professor of theology at Princeton Seminary. A conservative Presbyterian on matters of doctrine, he also believed that the Bible permitted slavery and condemned only its abuse, a position that caused him immense controversy during the peak of his career.

Spiritual Maturity

PRINCIPLES OF SPIRITUAL GROWTH
FOR EVERY BELIEVER

J. OSWALD SANDERS

Forethought

J. Oswald Sanders wrote no preface or introduction for *Spiritual Maturity*. As a reader, you will find yourself immediately engaged in Sanders' reflections on Scripture. This is not light reading—it is Light reading. The subjects will test your attentiveness. They will challenge your approach to God's Word.

If you take a moment to read through the table of contents, a pattern will be apparent. This book is a three-part reflection on the Trinity. Chapters 1–7 focus on God the Father; Chapters 8–14 on God the Son; Chapters 15–21 on God the Holy Spirit. Sanders gave deliberate equal consideration to the Triune God who is due our full attention.

This book invites the reader to experience the title. It is not just a "how-to" volume, but a "be" volume. Those who join the author in thinking about the most worthy subject of our hearts, minds, and souls immerse themselves in maturity. So, dive in. This is the deep end of the pool that represents grown-up reflection on God's ways with us.

These chapters are not cumulative. Sanders doesn't take us from point A to point B to point C. His subject is the revealed character of the Alpha and the Omega. We can start with any chapter and will be instantly challenged to understand God better even while we will be further convinced that we will never understand Him fully.

As we discover by keeping company with J. Oswald Sanders, spiritual maturity is not a position we reach or a goal we achieve. It is a life we find ourselves living. Those who have been prepared by their life in Christ will sense in this volume a selection of meaty dishes beyond the "milk of the Word" (see Hebrews 5:12–14). The taste will not be unfamiliar, but the required digestion will show us Sanders has served us a more substantial spiritual course than we are accustomed to at the table that is God's Word.

Prepare yourself for a deeply satisfying spiritual meal. Ask God to give you a hunger to take in as much of Him as possible. This is not fast food. Take your time. Savor the thoughts. Chew on the challenges. And let the truth you digest nourish your body, mind, and soul as you grow in spiritual maturity.

The Editors

PART ONE

The Overruling Providence of God

CHAPTER 1

The Overruling Providence of God

And we know that all things work together for good to them that love God, to them who are the called according to his purpose.

ROMANS 8:28

Reading: ROMANS 8:26–30

This sentence, interpreted in its context, can bring unlimited comfort and cheer to the Christian in time of testing. With Paul it was a matter of profound conviction: "And *we know* that all things work together for good." No room for question here. He had unwavering confidence in the overruling providence of his God. He believed that "God makes everything turn out for the best" (Scholefield). For him this conviction rendered complaining unthinkable since every event of life was either planned or permitted by God. It made possible of achievement his counsel of perfection, "In everything give thanks." It turned sighing into singing. It was a practical embracing of this truth which enabled him and his companion to sing at midnight even when plans seemed to miscarry and they were immured in a dungeon with bleeding backs. To him it mattered little whether physical conditions were propitious so long as he knew he loved God and was called according to His purpose. Everything, whether seemingly adverse or advantageous, would certainly turn out for the best. The important question is, Do we share Paul's joyous assurance?

Paul couches his statement in such categorical terms that it is impossible to remain neutral in the face of its astounding claim. If it were somewhat qualified or expressed in less dogmatic fashion, it would be easier to accept. When faced with devastating sorrows or reverses, it sounds rather glib and divorced from the grim reality of experience to say that it is all working together for good. But is it really so? Must this assertion be viewed with secret skepticism, or can it be embraced with joyous realism? Interpreted in its context, with full value given to each word, there is no verse in the whole of Scripture which will give such poise and serenity in the midst of tragedy, trial, or disappointment.

The key to the interpretation of the central statement, "All things work together for good," is that it must be neither isolated from its context nor divorced from its two conditional clauses—"to them that love God" and "to them that are called according to his purpose." These two clauses determine and limit its application. The simple fact is that all things do not without qualification work together for good for everybody. Nor does this verse claim that they do. Two things are presupposed. First, there must be correct *relationship* to God. The beneficiary under the promise is a member of God's family, enjoying and manifesting the family affection. Such a person is persuaded that He who did not spare His own Son would never permit or ordain anything which was not for his ultimate good. Love trusts even when it cannot discern. Then there is *partnership*. He is one of "the called" according to God's eternal purpose, and his plans have given way to God's plan. To him it is inconceivable that God's perfect design could be thwarted by anything really adverse to him. God is intermingling all things for his good. With his God, "accidents are not accidental and adversity is not adverse." The conclusion is that God's purpose unfolds to those whom He has called and who love Him in return. The promise has nothing for the man in rebellion against God and out of sympathy with His purposes. It is to the cold heart that this verse becomes a stumbling block. It glows with comfort when the heart is warm with love to God. But to be entitled to the comfort of the verse we must come within the category laid down by Paul.

The question inevitably arises, Can tragedy be good? Is ill health good? Is bereavement good? Is frustration good? Why does God permit these to strike us? In Paul's day there were four characteristic reactions to adversity. The attitude of the Epicurean was, "Let us eat and drink, for tomorrow we die." The Cynic defied fate to do its worst. The Stoic set his teeth and steeled himself to accept the divine will. Epictetus wrote:

> Have courage to look up to God and say, "Deal with me as Thou wilt from now on. I am as one with Thee; I am Thine; I flinch from nothing so long as Thou dost think that it is good. Lead me where Thou wilt; put on me what raiment Thou wilt. Wouldst Thou have me

hold office or eschew it, stay or flee, be rich or poor?
For this I will defend Thee before all men."

But in the text Paul epitomized the Christian attitude, not defiance or indifference or even resigned acceptance. The Christian joyously embraces adversity or sorrow, knowing that all things, whether propitious or adverse, are working together for his highest good.

Four truths full of comfort and encouragement emerge from this verse.

GOD'S PLAN IS BENEFICENT

"All things work together *for good.*"

The crux of the problem involved in the practical application of this verse lies in our interpretation of the two words "for good." The "good" promised by God in His long-sighted love may not always seem good and acceptable to us. Indeed His providences sometimes appear disastrous when viewed from a materialistic, temporal viewpoint. The good promised by God is *spiritual* rather than temporal, and some time may elapse before we discern its true beneficence.

It took years before the strange providences in the life of Job had their vindication. His afflictions had their rise in the malicious mind of Satan, but Job did not attribute them to blind chance or even to Satanic agency. He expressed his philosophy in the noble words, "The Lord gave, and the Lord hath taken away; blessed be the name of the Lord." When taunted by his wife he maintained his confidence in God. "What! Shall we receive good at the hand of God, and shall we not receive evil?" His stand of faith was abundantly vindicated by subsequent events. He emerged from his trials enriched and not impoverished. Through Job's cooperation, God took the evil acts of Satan and made them work out for good without in any way condoning the evil.

"We tend to interpret good in terms of animal comfort," writes Vernon Grounds.

> If we are exempt from disease, if our bodies are never stabbed by pain, if we always have money in our pockets or reserve in the bank, if we live in modern homes and enjoy the latest luxuries, if we can dress well and take long vacations at the seashore . . . that we consider good. Unfortunately we find ourselves victimized by a materialistic civilization, and despite our Christian faith we subtly equate comfort and goodness. In the same way we tend to equate success with goodness. . . . Or yet again we tend to equate pleasure with goodness. . . . And yet such equations are a million miles removed from Paul's basic teaching. And because all of these are false equations, we have trouble with Romans 8:28. Our failure to grasp Paul's conception of the good, changes what ought to be a soft pillow for our hearts into a hard problem for our heads.

Whate'er my God ordains is right;
He taketh thought for me.
The cup that my Physician gives
No poisoned draught can be,
But medicine due,
For God is true.

And on that changeless truth I build
And all my heart with hope is filled.

Few tragedies have highlighted this truth more than the fire at Serampore, India, on March 12, 1812. Within a few moments the sacrificial translation work of years of William Carey and his colleagues went up in smoke. The loss in paper for Bibles was immense. The newly cast Tamil type and Chinese metal type were a total loss. Portions of manuscripts, grammars, and dictionaries laboriously compiled perished. William Carey wrote, "Nothing was saved but the presses. This is a heavy blow, as it will stop our printing the Scriptures for a long time. Twelve months' hard labor will not reinstate us; not to mention the loss of property, mss, etc., which we shall scarcely ever surmount."

The loss of manuscripts referred to included portions of nearly all his Indian Scripture versions, all his Kanarese New Testament, two large Old Testament books in Sanskrit, many pages of his Bengali dictionary, all of his Telugu Grammar and much of his Punjabi, and every vestige of his well-advanced Dictionary of Sanskrit, the *magnum opus* of his linguistic life.

But there follows his affirmation of faith in words akin to those of our text. "God will no doubt bring good out of this evil and make it promote our interests." Before the ashes were cold, Carey's colleague, Marshman, wrote that the calamity was "another leaf in the ways of Providence, calling for the exercise of faith in Him whose Word, firm as the pillars of heaven, has decreed that all things shall work together for good to them that love God. Be strong therefore in the Lord. He will never forsake the work of His own hands."

In the midst of this desolating reverse, God's servants' grasp of this truth kept their hearts at peace. "It stilled me into tranquil submission, enabling me to look up and *welcome* God's will," said Marshman. Carey told how he had been hushed by the verse, "Be still, and know that I am God." Ward, the third of the famous trio, was found while the fires were still smoldering, not just submissive, but jubilant.

But how could this possibly be working together for good? It did not take long for the strategy of God to appear. "The catastrophe unstopped the ears of British Christendom. In the blaze of the fire they saw the grandeur of the enterprise; the facts were flashed out. And thus the destruction proved a beacon, and multiplied the Mission's zealous friends." So loud a fame it brought them as to reverse the nature of their risks. "The fire has given your undertaking a celebrity which nothing else could," wrote Fuller in a faithful warning. "The public is now giving us their praises. Eight hundred guineas have been offered for Dr. Carey's likeness! If we inhale this incense, will not God withhold His blessing, and then where are we?"

Then what is the nature of the good which Paul had in view? The answer is found in the context: "For whom he did foreknow, he also did predestinate to *be conformed to the image of his Son*" (Romans 8:29). Paul's conception was that anything which made him more like Christ was good, altogether irrespective of its reaction on his comfort or health or success or pleasure. Christlikeness does not always thrive in the midst of material comforts. Many of the most Christlike Christians have been plagued with ill health. Success in business has in many lives been the death knell of holiness. Seeking after pleasure often defeats its own ends.

GOD'S PLAN IS ACTIVE

"All things *work* together for good."

The heart that loves God discerns Him busily at work in even the most heartbreaking and unwelcome happenings of life. All things are turning out for the best because God is at work in them, transmuting bane into blessing and tragedy into triumph. His operation is not always clearly discernible. Indeed, it not infrequently seems that He is doing nothing. Carlyle, meditating on the enigmas of life, in the anguish of his heart said, "The worst of God is that He does nothing." But God is often most active when all seems most still. The working of God in nature is unseen but nonetheless effective. Under His invisible control the stars maintain their predestined courses and the restless ocean keeps within its appointed limits. We should never, in impatience at the seeming inactivity of God, take things into our own hands and try to be our own Providence. The daily happenings, whether tragic or joyous, are the raw material from which God is weaving the design of life. "This dance of plastic circumstance, machinery just meant to give the soul its bent." Introduce God into the events of life, and order emerges from chaos. "He is too kind to do anything cruel, too wise ever to make a mistake." No conceivable circumstances could better prosper God's plan or further our highest good.

GOD'S PLAN IS INCLUSIVE

"*All* things work together for good."

"All things" means exactly what it says. Everything in every sphere is under the beneficent control of God. It is the comprehensiveness of this statement which is so breathtaking. Bereavement, illness, disappointment, blighted hopes, nervous disorders, children who are giving concern, lack of fruit in service despite earnest endeavor to fulfill conditions of fruitbearing—surely these are not working together for good. Paul quietly asserts that such is the case. We may be willing to admit that life as a whole is subject to the overruling providence of God, but often we hesitate to believe that every detail of life is the object of His loving concern. Yet our Lord asserted this to be the case. Even the sparrow did not fall to the ground without His Father's knowledge. The circumstances of the Christian's life are ordained of God. There is no such thing as chance. Love refuses to believe that God is not interested in every detail of life. Everything is permitted and designed by Him for wise purposes. He will not cease His supervision for a moment.

Every adverse experience when rightly received can carry its quota of good. Bodily pain and weakness cause us to feel our frailty. Perplexity reveals our lack of wisdom. Financial reverses point up how limited are our resources. Mistakes and failure humble our pride. All these things can be included in the term "good."

GOD'S PLAN IS HARMONIOUS

"All things *work together for good.*"

They work into a preconceived pattern. The events of life are not related. The physician's prescription is compounded of a number of drugs. Taken in isolation, some of them would be poisonous and would do only harm. But blended together under the direction of a skilled and experienced pharmacist they achieve only good. Barclay renders the verse: "We know that God intermingles all things for good for them that love Him." The experiences of life when taken in isolation may seem anything but good, but blended together the result is only good.

In adverse circumstances unbelief queries, "How can this be working for good?" The answer is, "Wait until the Great Physician has finished writing the prescription." Who cannot look back on life to see that things considered disastrous proved in the ultimate to be blessings in disguise? The artist blends colors which to the unskilled eye seem far removed from his objective. But wait until he has finished his mixing.

Life has been likened to an elaborate tapestry being woven on the loom. For the beauty of the pattern it is imperative that the colors must not be all of the same hue. Some must be bright and beautiful, others dark and somber. It is as they are all worked together that they contribute to the beauty of the pattern.

Not until each loom is silent
And the shuttles cease to fly
Will God unroll the pattern
And explain the reason why;
The dark threads are as needful
In the Weaver's skillful hand,
As the threads of gold and silver
For the pattern He has planned.

In time of severe trial there is always the temptation, while assenting to the truth in general, to feel that our present circumstances are an exception. If that were so, the text is null and void, and the truth of the overruling providence of God in the affairs of men has no meaning. As tragedy upon tragedy overwhelmed Joseph—banishment from home, sale as a slave, unjust imprisonment—it was difficult for him to see these untoward events working together for his good. Yet in retrospect he said to his brothers, "But as for you, ye thought evil against me; *but God meant it unto good*" (Genesis 50:20).

In the events of life, "God has an end in view which is worthy of Him, and will command our fullest approbation when we cease to know in part." Even if called upon to face the wrath of man or devil we can confidently rest in the assurance that it will ultimately praise God, and that which cannot do so will be restrained.

Whate'er my God ordains is right;
My Light, my Life is He,
Who cannot will me ought but good,
I trust Him utterly:
For well I know
In joy or woe
We soon shall see, as sunlight clear,
How faithful was our Guardian here.

CHAPTER 2

The Prostrating Vision of God

I beseech thee, shew me thy glory.

EXODUS 33:18

Reading: EXODUS 33:11–23

This prayer of Moses has reechoed down the centuries. Successive generations of Christians have prayed for a vision of God, often without realizing the possible implications of such a petition. Not infrequently they have failed to recognize the answer when it was granted. John Newton, converted slavetrader, passionately longed for the transforming vision, but the answer to his urgent prayers came in a way which staggered and almost overwhelmed him. He has recorded this experience.

I asked the Lord that I might grow
In faith and love and every grace,
Might more of His salvation know
And seek more earnestly His face.
'Twas He who taught me thus to pray,
And He, I trust, has answered prayer;

But it has been in such a way
As almost drove me to despair.
I thought that in some favored hour
At once He'd answer my request
And by His love's constraining power,
Subdue my sins and give me rest.
Instead of that, He made me feel
The hidden evils of my heart,
And bade the angry powers of hell
Assault my soul in every part.
Nay more, with His own hand He seemed
Intent to aggravate my woe.
Crossed all the fair designs I schemed,
Blasted my gourds, and laid me low.
"Lord, why is this?" I trembling cried.
"Wilt Thou pursue this worm to death?"
"This is the way," the Lord replied,
"I answer prayer for grace and faith.
"These inward trials I employ
From self and sin to set thee free,
And cross thy schemes of earthly joy
That thou might'st find thy all in Me."

When we pray for a vision of God, what are we expecting? A glowing vision in the sky? A blinding flash of glory such as that which overwhelmed Saul of Tarsus? A thrilling, overpowering sense of spiritual exaltation? A study of the visions of God recorded in Scripture gives quite a different picture. In not one case did the vision immediately result in elation and ecstasy. With absolute consistency it produced in those to whom it came profound self-abasement. In every instance the experience was awe-full, not ecstatic. And the more intense the vision, the more complete the prostration before God.

If this is true, before we ask of God a vision of Himself, we should be prepared for the certain result. In the dazzling whiteness of the snow the cleanest linen appears soiled. Before the spotless purity and holiness of God, everything earthly is seen stained and unclean. In the light of the presence of God, Joshua the holy high priest appeared "clothed with filthy garments" and therefore disqualified for office (Zechariah 3:1–3). We have no grounds for expecting to be exceptions to this rule.

If we ask in what form the vision will come, we are not left in doubt. "God . . . hath shined in our hearts, to give the light of the knowledge of the glory of God in the face of Jesus Christ" (2 Corinthians 4:6). On the canvas of Holy Scripture, with master strokes and in vivid colors, the Holy Spirit has painted the face of Jesus Christ, image of the invisible God. And it is the same Spirit who will illumine the canvas to the one who longs to see His glory. He has no greater delight than to take of the things of Christ as recorded in His Word and in them to reveal the glory of God.

Although *Job,* possibly a contemporary of Abraham, lived in spiritual twilight he had an amazing concept of God and a lofty standard of life. His character was blameless in his own eyes. Conscious of inner integrity he claimed, "I am clean without transgression, I am innocent; neither is there iniquity in me" (33:9). This was not pious cant but the sincere expression of his inner probity. And not only was his character stainless in his own eyes, it was uniquely worthy in God's eyes. Addressing Satan, God asked, "Hast thou considered my servant Job, that there is none like him in the earth, a perfect and an upright man, one that feareth God, and escheweth evil?" (1:8). Few people have enjoyed to such a degree the approval of their own consciences and the commendation of their God.

Job was one of the very few whom God has called "perfect," thus affirming his blamelessness and integrity. How did this perfect man fare when in the crisis of his mounting trials there came to him the vision of God? He records it in a few pregnant words: "I have heard of thee by the hearing of the ear: but now mine eye seeth thee. Wherefore I abhor myself, and repent in dust and ashes" (42:5–6). *When confronted with the vision of God, the perfect man is reduced to abject self-abhorrence.*

The vision of God was granted to *Jacob* when, alone at the ford Jabbok, "there wrestled a man with him until the breaking of the day." In naming the spot Peniel, Jacob said with obvious awe: "I have seen God face to face, and my life is preserved" (Genesis 32:24, 30). How did the vision affect Jacob? He was compelled to spell out in terms of his own name, the shame of his character. "And he said unto him, What is thy name? And he said, Jacob"—supplanter, cheat, swindler. Before he could qualify for the blessing God would bestow on him, he had to confess his true nature. To his dying day he bore the marks of this encounter. *Confronted by the vision of God, the man who had succeeded in deceiving everyone else is compelled to acknowledge his own secret shame.*

Moses could boast of massive learning. He enjoyed the prestige of being called the son of Pharaoh's daughter. His ardent patriotism led him in fleshly impatience to attempt the deliverance of Israel. He would not wait for God to unfold His plan of campaign, and in consequence he had to hide from the wrath of the king. In the desert his impetuosity turned to passivity, until he was arrested by the divine vision. "And the angel of the Lord appeared unto him in a flame of fire out of the midst of a bush: and he looked, and, behold, the bush burned with fire, and the bush was not consumed. . . . God called unto him out of the midst of the bush, and said, . . . Draw not nigh hither: put off thy shoes from off thy feet; for the place whereon thou standest is holy ground. . . . And Moses hid his face; for he was afraid to look upon God" (Exodus 3:2–6). *In the man to whom was to be entrusted the deliverance of God's chosen people, the vision resulted in reverential awe and averted face.*

Elijah has been described as the grandest and most romantic character Israel ever produced. He is abruptly projected onto the stage of history in the Carmel drama. And what a man he was! So great was his power with God that he could lock the heavens at will. So little did he fear man that he dared to defy the king and indeed the whole nation. With Enoch he enjoyed the distinction of entering heaven without passing through the portals of death. How does this dauntless, rugged man of God survive the vision? "And, behold, the Lord passed by, and a great and strong wind rent the mountains . . . and after the wind an earthquake . . . and after the earthquake a fire; but the Lord was not in the fire: and after the fire a still small voice. And it was so, when Elijah heard it, that he wrapped his face in his mantle" (1 Kings 19:11–13). *He could remain defiant and petulant in the face of a majestic display of God's power, but he was broken and subdued by His voice of gentle stillness and hid his face.*

Isaiah the seer, to whom came the clearest foreshadowing of gospel truth, was haunted by no sense of inferiority. Lofty prophecy was mixed with scathing denunciation in his messages to the nation. He felt perfectly competent to call down woes on his contemporaries (3:9, 11; 5:8, 11, 20) until he saw the vision of God. "I saw also the LORD sitting upon a throne, high and lifted up, and his train filled the temple. Above it stood the seraphim: . . . And one cried unto another, and said, Holy, holy, holy, is the LORD of hosts: the whole earth is full of his glory. And the posts of the door moved at the voice of him that cried, and the house was filled with smoke" (Isaiah 6:1–5). On whom does he pronounce the next woe after this radiant vision? "Then said I, Woe is me! For I am undone, because I am a man of unclean lips . . . for mine eyes have seen the King, the LORD of hosts." *Lips which had mediated the Divine message were foul and unclean in the light of the holiness of God.*

The vision of God came to *Ezekiel* when he identified with his people in their distress and captivity in Babylon. "As I was among the captives by the river of Chebar . . . the heavens were opened, and I saw visions of God" (1:1)—visions of God's majesty and omnipresence, of His ceaseless activity and the glory of His rainbow-circled throne. "And above the firmament . . . was the likeness of a throne, as the appearance of a sapphire stone: and upon the likeness of the throne was the likeness as the appearance of a man above upon it. . . . And from the appearance of his loins downward, I saw as it were the appearance of fire, and it had brightness round about. As the appearance of the bow that is in the cloud in the day of rain, so was the appearance of the brightness round about. This was the appearance of the likeness of the glory of the Lord. And when I saw it, I fell upon my face" (1:26–28). *The fearless and faithful seer cannot bear the awful light of the throne on which sits the God of glory.*

Among the saintly men of Scripture, *Daniel* is in the front rank. He had held with distinction the post of Prime Minister through the reigns of five successive Oriental despots. That his head remained on his shoulders was remarkable tribute to his wisdom and integrity. His enemies could find no fault in him except that he prayed too much. Of Daniel alone is it recorded that an angelic messenger was sent to tell him how greatly he was beloved by God. Does he emerge unscathed from the beatific vision? Hear his confession: "I, Daniel, alone saw the vision: . . . I was left alone, and saw this great vision, and there remained no strength in me: for my comeliness was turned in me into corruption, and I retained no strength . . . and when I heard the voice of his words, then was I in a deep sleep on my face, and my face toward the ground" (10:7–9). *One of the most blameless of saints when confronted with the divine glory is prostrated at the corruption, not of his vices but of his virtues!*

In the midst of an experience of shattering self-revelation a young man wrote: "If I really thought that what I counted to be my prime virtue, my mental honesty, had been so complete a sham as this, I wouldn't be able to go on. And I want to go on. The lesson however is plain. I can't trust myself an inch. Whenever I am most pious, I am probably nursing the most vicious pride. I think it is better to stand at the mouth of the tunnel of personal evil and say, It is infinite. . . ."

After a fruitless night's fishing the vision came to *Peter*, and obedience to Christ's command resulted in a catch which broke the nets. Confronted with this miracle, Peter realized that Christ must either be omniscient in directing them to the shoal of fish, or omnipotent in directing the shoal of fish to them. When he glimpsed the glory of God in the face of Jesus Christ, he was overcome with his own defilement and unworthiness. "Depart from me," he cried, falling down at Jesus' feet, "for I am a sinful man, O Lord" (Luke 5:8). Actually this was the very last thing he wanted, but *when the man whom God would use to open the kingdom to Jew and Gentile saw the vision of God, he could think of no alternative to banishment from His presence.*

Saul of Tarsus, filled with mistaken zeal for God and lust for the blood of the hated Christians, was making his way toward Damascus. He was proud of the fact that he was a Hebrew of the Hebrews, the strictest of the Pharisees, and he was well satisfied with his ardor in the service of God. "Suddenly there shined round about him a light from heaven: and he fell to the earth, and heard a voice saying unto him, Saul, Saul, why persecutest thou me? And he said, Who art thou, Lord? And the Lord said, I am Jesus . . ." (Acts 9:3–5). *The glory of God shining in the face of the ascended Christ blinded and prostrated the man who probably came nearer than any other to justification by works.*

John the beloved was without doubt the sweetest and ripest saint of his day. He was the object of the special love of Christ, not on the grounds of favoritism but because he, more than any of the other disciples, appropriated it for himself. He alone was faithful in the judgment hall. Tradition bears abundant testimony to the charm of his personality and the purity of his devotion to Christ. In the ripe maturity of his old age he is granted the supreme vision of Christ: "one like unto the Son of man. . . . His head and his hairs were white like wool . . . his eyes were as a flame of fire . . . his voice as the sound of many waters . . . and his countenance was as the sun shineth in his strength" (Revelation 1:13–17). Surely if anyone is qualified to see the vision of God without being prostrated it will be this man who repeatedly pillowed his head on the bosom of incarnate deity. Not so. "And when I saw him," John wrote, "I fell at his feet as dead." *Earth's sweetest and most gracious saint falls as though lifeless in the presence of the transcendent majesty and holiness of God.*

A consistent pattern appears throughout these visions. First the vision, then self-abhorrence, self-abasement, the averted face, the sense of uncleanness, blindness, prostration, comeliness turned into corruption, self-banishment, falling as dead. Do we still desire to pray for a vision of God?

But there is still another side to the picture. God takes no pleasure in seeing His children lie in the dust. If He abases and humbles them, it is only that He may exalt them in due season. Humiliation is not an end in itself, it merely prepares the way for blessing. The open lesson of these visions surely is that God cannot entrust a man with any deep blessing, any important spiritual ministry, until there has come a complete collapse of self.

The collapse of Job's self-righteousness was quickly followed by the bestowal of double what he had lost, and the turning of his captivity through his intercessions for his friends. Jacob's vision resulted in a change of character which gave him new power with God and man. The rebuke of Moses' fleshly energy and apathy, with consequent loss of self-confidence, prepared him for the enormous task of delivering God's people. After Elijah's deflation he was encouraged by God and recommissioned for further service. Not only were Isaiah's unclean lips purged and his iniquity removed, but he received an enlarged commission. To Daniel, the sense of corruption gave place to joy in the privilege of being the vehicle of Divine revelation. Peter's deep conviction of unworthiness was a most important element in preparing him to become the mighty Pentecostal preacher. The vision marked Paul out as a chosen vessel to carry God's name before kings and Gentiles. The One who raised John from the ground entrusted him with writing the Apocalypse, the book which for two millennia has been the stay of a church in persecution. Each vision was the prelude to increased personal holiness and an enlarged sphere of service.

True, the vision of God inevitably leads to self-revelation, but always with a beneficent end in view. God does not aim merely to humiliate us. There is no need to fear being brought to an end of ourselves for "the end of self is the beginning of God." Indeed, we may welcome the vision of God if our deepest desire is to advance in holiness and to be of the greatest use to Him.

We may have the vision of God whenever we truly desire it, whenever we are willing for what it involves. And when it has been granted, there is no need to remain groveling in the dust abhorring ourselves. If we heartily repent of all that is amiss as it is revealed in the light of God's presence, we too will hear the words which came to Isaiah: "Thine iniquity is taken away and thy sin purged. . . . Go, and tell this people. . . ."

CHAPTER 3

The Undiscouraged Perseverance of God

The God of Jacob

PSALM 46:7

Thou worm Jacob

ISAIAH 41:14

Reading: GENESIS 32:1–32

No title of God is more startling than this—"The God of Jacob." No two characters seem more ill-matched. No single sentence more strikingly illustrates the undiscourageable perseverance of God.

The doctrine of the perseverance of the saints has always been prominent in Calvinistic theology, but its complementary truth has not always received equal emphasis. The perseverance of the saints is possible only because of the perseverance of God. Were it not for this, not one of us would be in the Christian race today. Paul had a magnificent confidence in the Divine perseverance. "Being confident of this very thing, that he which hath begun a good work in you will perform it until the day of Jesus Christ"

(Philippians 1:6). He directs our eyes from the pettiness and puniness of man to the might and majesty of God. He lifts us out of our own circumscribed circle into the grand sweep of a divine purpose which cannot fail.

Our God knows no unfinished task. He completes what He begins. Though Israel balked and thwarted Him at every turn, He persisted in His gracious disciplines until His purposes were realized, and in the Hebrew nation all the peoples of the earth were blessed. When one approach failed, He adopted another. If one generation refused to respond, He patiently began again with the next. Time and again succeeding generations of Israel turned to idolatry until at last the chastening of their final captivity in Babylon forever taught them its folly and futility. Never since has the Jewish nation worshiped idols.

Our Lord's perseverance was one of the unique characteristics of His life. It had been prophesied of Him, "He shall not fail nor be discouraged, till he have set judgment in the earth" (Isaiah 42:4). Nor did He. His loved disciples on whom He had pinned His hopes failed Him. To the very last their weakness and selfish ambitions overrode their love for Him. At the hour of His greatest need they all forsook Him and fled. It was not an enemy, but one of His own intimates, who sold Him into the hands of His bitter foes. Yet it was through these very men that He achieved His purpose. He cherished the unshaken confidence that His Father who had begun the good work would consummate it; no purpose of His would ever fail of fulfillment. We too can share this persuasion. We can trust our God to put the finishing touches to His own work.

The Bible record and Christian experience are replete with evidence of the tenacity and tireless patience of God's pursuing love. Francis Thompson fled from God through the years until he became a human derelict sleeping among the down-and-outs on the Thames Embankment in London. It was there that the love of God overtook and mastered him. In his magnificent poem, "The Hound of Heaven," he interprets this experience.

I fled Him, down the nights and down the days;
I fled Him down the arches of the years;
I fled Him, down the labyrinthine ways
Of my own mind; and in the mist of tears
I hid from Him, and under running laughter.
Up vistaed slopes I sped;
And shot, precipitated,
Adown Titanic glooms of chasmed fears
From those strong Feet that followed, followed after.

THE GOD OF JACOB

No more luminous illustration of this truth can be found in Scripture than God's pursuit of Jacob and its apogee in the incongruous title, "The God of Jacob." The God of Abraham, father of the faithful? Yes! The God of Moses, who talked with God face-to-face as a man to his friend? Yes! The God of Daniel, the beloved? Yes! The God of Jacob, the crooked, the grasping, the deceitful, the swindler? A thousand times, No! God would compromise His own character by linking His name with that of Jacob. And yet He has said, "Jacob have I loved. . . . The God of Jacob is thy refuge. . . . Fear not, thou worm Jacob." What is weaker, what is more worthless than a worm? And yet Jacob the worm, Jacob the worthless, subject of the relentless pursuing love of God, becomes a prince, having power with God and men.

THE SOVEREIGNTY OF HIS SELECTION

Had we been seeking a man to head up a nation through which to achieve a high and holy purpose and in whom all nations were to be blessed, Jacob would have been our last choice. Esau the magnanimous, Esau the largehearted would have been much higher on the list. Who else but God would have chosen a despicable character like Jacob? There is little that is attractive about this greedy, grasping, scheming man—so mean that he took advantage of his brother's extremity to filch not only his earthly inheritance but his spiritual authority. For Esau should have become the spiritual head of the clan on the death of his father.

To do Jacob justice, it should be noted that his parents showed little nobility of character. "Isaac loved Esau because he ate of his venison"—an undisciplined father, mastered by his appetite. Rebekah loved Jacob with an indulgent and ruinous love. She instigated and aided and abetted him in his deceit—an unscrupulous mother, mastered by an unholy ambition for her favorite son. Esau despised the spiritual and lightly relinquished his spiritual prerogatives. Jacob himself was cunning and mean, ready to exploit even his twin brother. Such was the family God selected for the display of His grace.

Heredity was dead against Jacob, but God is not limited by heredity. When His disciples asked Jesus concerning the blind man, "Who did sin, this man, or his parents?" Jesus replied, "Neither hath this man sinned, nor his parents: but *that the works of God might be made manifest in [through] him*" (John 9:2–3). Here is the key to God's selection of Jacob. He chose a worm that He might transform him into a prince.

The warped character of Jacob provides a striking background for the display of God's incomparable grace and for the revelation of His attitude toward the weakest of His children. If God chose only the strong, the noble, the brilliant for the achievement of His purpose, the vast majority of Christians would be disqualified. Paul in his familiar statement could have been justifying God in His selection of Jacob.

> *For ye see your calling, brethren, how that not many wise men after the flesh, not many mighty, not many noble, are called: but God hath chosen the foolish things of the world to confound the wise; and God hath chosen the weak things of the world to confound the things which are mighty; and base things of the world, and things which are despised, hath God chosen, yea, and things which are not, to bring to nought things that are: that no flesh should glory in His presence.* (1 Corinthians 1:26–29)

It is not generally recognized that Jacob was not a youth but a man of probably seventy years of age when he filched Esau's birthright; or that he was probably over eighty when he cheated him of his blessing. True, he lived to be 147, but he was a middle-aged man before these inglorious incidents took place. He was no callow youth but a mature man whose life pattern was set, a man who had obviously persisted in his crookedness for half a lifetime. Psychologists would say his character could never be radically changed at such a late hour, but God is not limited by the laws of psychology. He does not despair of us even when we despair of ourselves. His patience is never at an end. His resources are never exhausted.

THE DEPTHS OF HIS DISCERNMENT

There is an optimism in God which discerns the hidden possibilities in the most unpromising character. He has a keen eye for hidden elements of nobility and promise in an unprepossessing life. He is the God of the difficult temperament, the God of the warped personality, the God of the misfit. Only God saw the prince in Jacob. He has a solution for every problem of personality and temperament. When we surrender our lives into His hands for drastic and radical treatment, He will bring into play all His resources of love and grace.

"Jacob have I loved, but Esau have I hated" (Malachi 1:3; Romans 9:13) is one of the most perplexing statements of Scripture as it appears to attribute caprice to God. Two facts must be borne in mind. First, though the language sounds harsh to us, the word "hate" did not always carry the full meaning we give it today. Second, the statement as used both by Malachi and Paul referred primarily to nations—Israelites and Edomites, descendants of Jacob and Esau. God's selection of Jacob was not on the grounds of merit or character, for the choice was made while they were still unborn babes (Genesis 25:23). Paul is asserting that God, "in the exercise of His sovereign will has decreed that faith—not heredity or merit—is the eternal principle of sonship. In their national application 'love' and 'hate' are not the ground of election as we understand those subjective feelings. God is not arbitrary in His choice and cannot be charged with favoritism. The emotional terms indicate rather a national function and destiny. Judah, not Edom, was elected for progressive revelation in history."

But there is also a secondary and individual application of this statement. God's selection of Jacob and rejection of Esau was the outcome not of caprice but of discernment. Behind all Jacob's meanness and duplicity there lay a desire and a capacity for the spiritual. Time and again he did violence to it but still it persisted. Esau was generous and largehearted but behind this attractive exterior lurked a despising of the spiritual. He was a splendid specimen, preferring the gratification of sensual desires to the exercise of a spiritual ministry.

In spite of all his manifest weaknesses and failures, Jacob's desire for the spiritual provided God with a basis for His continued pursuit and subsequent dealings. For the Christian oppressed with the sense of his failure, there is enormous encouragement in this fact. It is human nature to notice the worst in the character of our fellowmen, but God is always looking for what is best. He clearly discerns the deepest spiritual yearnings of our hearts and works toward their realization. All His chastenings have that end in view. God appeared five times to Jacob. On each occasion he corrected some blunder of His intransigent child and on each occasion gave him a fresh opportunity.

THE PERSISTENCE OF HIS PURSUIT

The name "Jacob" means supplanter. Behind the word lies the idea of a determined and relentless pursuer who, on overtaking a foe, throws him down—the biography of Jacob in a single word! Jacob met his match and finally capitulated to the determined and relentless pursuit of the loving God who threw him at Jabbok. Had God not been undiscourageable in His pursuit, Jacob would never have become a prince with God. He would have remained an unlovely and unloved schemer. But in His gracious love God followed him relentlessly from his first encounter at Bethel until his final conquest thirty years later in the same spot. The divine pursuit was marked by four crises.

The first Bethel crisis occurred when Jacob filched the blessing from Esau. After the pangs of his hunger had been satisfied, Esau began to realize the implications of his twin brother's despicable action. On discovering that he had fled, the enraged Esau set off in pursuit. Meanwhile Jacob had his first encounter with God. With head pillowed on a stone, Jacob dreamed he saw "a ladder set up on the earth and the top of it reached to heaven: and behold the angels of God ascending and descending on it." Then God spoke, giving him absolute though totally undeserved promises of prosperity and protection, with the added assurance that all families of the earth would be blessed in his seed. Filled with awe he cried, "How dreadful is this place! This is none other but the house of God . . . and Jacob vowed a vow"—and forgot it! (Genesis 28:17, 20). But God did not forget.

Next came *the Peniel crisis.* Jacob was now over a hundred years old. He had spent twenty years serving his unscrupulous uncle Laban. It is instructive to note the disciplines to which God subjected Jacob in order to achieve His purpose. He put him with a man more mean, more grasping, more crooked than himself. All these years Jacob spent swindling and being swindled by his uncle. The supplanter was being supplanted, and the cheat, cheated. But it was this grueling discipline which ultimately led to his transformation. Might this be the reason in some lives for uncongenial home circumstances or working conditions? Could this be why some missionary has been placed with a difficult fellow worker? We would always choose pleasant conditions and congenial people with whom to work and live, but God is more concerned with our spiritual growth than with our temporal comfort.

It is reassuring to see that God was with Jacob through the whole of this experience and blessed him. He did not permit Laban to do him any injury (Genesis 31:7, 24, 29). Neither will our Laban ever do us any harm. To Jacob's credit be it said that he did not run away from his testing until God's time came. We are apt to chafe at our adverse circumstances and endeavor to evade them, but it will always be to our spiritual loss if we short-circuit the divine disciplines. God will remove them when they have achieved their appointed purpose. Our characters are perfected and enriched by the difficult people and difficult things of life.

While on his way home Jacob learned that Esau was on his way to meet him. Immediately fear begotten of a guilty conscience gripped him. Instead of calling on God and claiming His promised protection (Genesis 28:15), Jacob resorted to carnal scheming and sent carefully prepared and well-spaced gifts to pacify his brother. But the relentless pursuit of God continued. "And Jacob was left alone, and there wrestled a man with him until the breaking of the day."

It was God who began the wrestling match, not Jacob, but Jacob had remarkable powers of resistance. Apparently he thought he could get away with it as he had previously done. But the persistent pressure continued. It is a serious thing to resist a God who is intent to bless. When He found Jacob would not yield, God lamed him. Forever afterward he bore the marks of that terrible encounter. When he no longer had strength to resist, Jacob wrapped his arms around the Wrestler and refused to let Him go until he received the blessing. As though this was not the point to which God had been working for a lifetime!

Come O Thou Traveler unknown,
Whom still I hold but cannot see;
My company before is gone,
And I am left alone with Thee.
With Thee all night I mean to stay,
And wrestle til the break of day.
—C. Wesley

Before the blessing could be bestowed there had to be a collapse of the strong self-life of Jacob. He had to face up to the sin and shame of his own character. "What is thy name?" God asks him. "My name is Jacob"—supplanter, cheat, deceiver, confesses the now contrite penitent, and that confession was the distilled essence of a lifetime of failure. Sincerity is ever the precursor of blessing, and Jacob had now taken true ground before God. For him, Peniel, "the face of God," meant a confession of utter sinfulness and a consciousness of utter weakness. "I have seen God face to face and my life is preserved," he said with awe. It was at Peniel, too, that he received a further promise of blessing. "Thy name shall be called no more Jacob, but Israel," a prince of God, "for as a prince hast thou power with God and with men, and hast prevailed" (Genesis 32:28). He had prevailed by capitulating. God had succeeded in breaking his hardness. "Yea, he had power over the angel, and prevailed: he wept, and made supplication unto him" (Hosea 12:4).

Now that God had taken away his old name of shame, one would expect Jacob to live up to his new name. But no! He was as suspicious and scheming as ever. These ingrained qualities of his character died hard. Indeed they brought him to the *shameful and sordid Shechem crisis.* Actuated by fear of Esau, he did not complete his journey home but pitched his tent toward Shechem. Like his relative Lot, who was guilty of a similar act of folly at Sodom, he paid dearly for his act of unbelief. Tragedy engulfed his whole family because he would scheme his way out of trouble instead of trusting the God who had twice appeared to him. The subsequent story is one of rape and murder and fear. It is a costly thing to forget a vow or to withdraw a surrender.

Thirty years had elapsed since God first arrested him. Without doubt He would have been justified in abandoning so stubborn and rebellious a character. But God is not man. His love does not blow hot and cold. Instead of abandoning him, He graciously visited him again. "Arise, go up to Bethel, and dwell there: and make there an altar unto God, that appeared unto thee" (Genesis 35:1). This was the *second Bethel crisis.*

This time the disciplines of God over thirty years had done their work. Jacob did not linger. Immediately he gathered his family and hastened to Bethel. "And God appeared unto Jacob *again* . . . and blessed him." God is utterly undiscourageable in His purpose to bless His people. Once more Jacob heard the words, "Thy name shall not be called any more Jacob, but Israel shall be thy name: and he called his name Israel" (Genesis 35:9, 10). This time Jacob lived up to the privileges of his new name and did not backslide into his former scheming and deception. The disciplines of God had been effective and Jacob the worm finds his way into God's gallery of men of faith in Hebrews 11. "Where sin abounded, grace did much more abound."

There is no fundamental difference between one man and another. Only the incidence of temptation is different. In face of onslaughts of the common temptations such as jealousy, pride, ambition, money, or sex, the great majority of people commonly experience failure. They fall far below their own ideals. The same old sin revives, gathers strength, and masters them. The same tragic failure or flaw in character pursues them throughout life like a bloodhound. Paralysis of hope develops through a succession of defeats.

The devil preaches a message of despair. But in the typical life of Jacob, God is preaching the gospel of recovery. The laws of heredity are not the highest laws. The God of Jacob is preeminently the God of the second chance to Christians who have failed and failed persistently. The second chance does not avert the consequences of past failure, but even failure can be a stepping-stone to new victories. To the child of God, failure can have an important educative value. God does not waste even failure.

The outstanding lesson of Jacob's life is that *no failure*

need be final. There is hope with the God of Jacob for any disposition or any temperament. No past defeat puts future victory out of reach. When God has saved and apprehended a man, He pursues him with undiscourageable perseverance that He may bless him. He does not exclude from His royal service penitent men and women who have failed. Had God dismissed Peter for his failure, there would have been no great Pentecostal preacher. God will turn the tables on the devil by creating a wider ministry out of our very defeats.

CHAPTER 4

The Discriminating Disciplines of God

Doth the plowman plow all day to sow?

ISAIAH 28:24

Reading: ISAIAH 28:23–29

"Let Him Plow, He purposeth a crop." This reaction of Samuel Rutherford to the chastenings which came to him revealed a true insight into the divine disciplines and an attitude calculated to benefit most from them. The disciplines of life may be painful but they are never purposeless. "I grant that all chastening considered in the light of the immediate present, seems to be fraught, not with pleasure, but with pain; but in the long run it yields *a harvest of peace* to those who have been disciplined by it, *a harvest of righteousness*" (Hebrews 12:11 WAY). If we desire the harvest, we must welcome the discipline.

The paragraph under consideration occurs in one of Isaiah's greatest prophecies. "It is distinguished by that regal versatility of style which places its author at the head of the Hebrew prophets. Keen analysis of character, realistic contrasts between sin and judgment, clever retorts and epigrams, rapids of scorn and a spate of judgment—but the final issue, a placid stream of argument balked by sweet parable" (G. A. Smith). This "sweet parable" uses the methods of the farmer as typical of God's dealings with the nations and, in a secondary application, with the church and its individual members.

Isaiah highlights those qualities in God which give Him such a sure touch in His dealings with men. "For his God doth instruct him to discretion, and doth teach him" (v. 26). "The Lord of hosts . . . wonderful in counsel, and excellent in working" (v. 29). He is no mere experimenter in lives. He is moved neither by caprice nor prejudice. Every activity is dictated by the highest wisdom and executed in the deepest love. And through it all there is an exquisite discernment and discrimination. The means adopted are always those best suited to attain the end in view. Rightly received, an abundant harvest is assured.

The skill of the farmer, his careful judgment in the three main processes of husbandry—plowing, sowing, harvesting—is but a reflection of the skill and wisdom of the God who instructed him. If the farmer shows such deep discernment and exercises such careful oversight of his crops, Isaiah argues, will the God who counseled him be less discriminating in the much more delicate task of producing a harvest from our lives?

THE DISCRIMINATION OF HIS DISCIPLINES

Although the heavenly Husbandman permits the plowshare and harrows of sorrow or suffering to tear through the lives of His children, they are always guided and controlled by a supremely skillful hand. His ultimate purpose, a harvest, is ever kept in view. The three principal processes of farming are employed by Isaiah to illustrate the wisdom God exercises in His character training and tempering of the spirit.

Viewing the successive operations of plowing, sowing, and threshing as suggestive of the disciplines of life, three truths emerge from this parable.

God is discerning in their duration. "Doth the plowman plow all day to sow? doth he open and break the clods of his ground?" (v. 24). Of course he does not. "His God doth instruct him to discretion, and doth teach him" (v. 26). Plowing is only a means to an end. When the end is achieved, his plowing ceases. In the history of Israel God's discernment can be seen. For 430 years the plow of the Egyptian tyranny ripped through the stiff soil of the Hebrew nation, an unpromising wilderness in which God saw possibilities of a rich harvest. But there could be no harvest without plowing. As soon as the discipline of the Egyptian taskmaster's whip had achieved its purpose, it was removed. Not one day longer than was necessary to achieve the beneficent divine purpose did He permit His people to writhe under the oppression of their masters. As soon as they were ready to receive deliverance He led them into the rest and abundance and victory of Canaan. But only the severity of the discipline weaned them from Egypt.

The skillful farmer discriminates between one soil and another. Light and sandy soil requires only brief and light plowing. Stiff, sour clay requires totally different treatment if it is to produce a crop. It must be laid bare to the sun and drained. The plow must plunge deep into the subsoil, as deep as the share will go. Soil must be harrowed and harrowed again until the clods are broken down and a fine tilth secured in which the seed will germinate and grow. The farmer is discerning in the duration of his plowing. He does not continually tear up and harrow his land. He deals with each soil according to its need. Is not this the explanation of the differing incidence of suffering and sorrow and trial? The heavenly Husbandman can be trusted in the adaptation and timing and duration of the disciplines His love permits. We are safe in His hands.

The discipline is always preparatory to blessing and can bring nothing but blessing when rightly received. It is here that our responsibility lies. Food not digested is a bane, not a blessing. Disciplines not rightly received sour rather than sweeten the character. To querulously ask "Why?" when the chastening stroke falls is in effect to charge the all-wise and all-loving God with caprice. He does not rend the heart merely to demonstrate His power and sovereignty but to prepare for greater fruitfulness. He prunes every branch that does bear fruit to increase its yield. The discipline is purposeful. How do we react to God's plow? Does it soften, subdue, chasten us? Or does it harden and stiffen our resistance to His will? Does it sweeten or sour us?

Our reaction to family problems and financial reverses, to suffering and disappointment, to thwarted ambitions and disappointed expectations is all-important. If we submit, feeling that resistance is unavailing, that is better than continued rebellion. If we acquiesce in God's dealings, although without joy, that is higher ground. But it is when we embrace God's unexplained providences with a song that God is most glorified and we are most blessed. When Samuel

Rutherford lay in the Aberdeen prison, he used to write at the top of his letters, "God's Palace, Aberdeen."

Madame Guyon, a cultured Frenchwoman, was imprisoned for her faith from 1695 to 1705. Instead of repining at her lot, she joyously accepted God's will as her weal. "While I was a prisoner in Vincennes," she wrote, "I passed my time in great peace. I sang songs of joy which the maid who served me learned by heart as fast as I made them. And we together sang Thy praises, O my God. The stones of my prison walls shone like rubies in my eyes. My heart was full of that joy which Thou givest to them that love Thee in the midst of their greatest crosses." It was here she wrote one of her choicest hymns.

A little bird am I
Shut out from fields of air,
Yet in my cage I sit and sing
To Him who placed me there,
Well pleased a prisoner to be,
Because, my God, it pleaseth Thee.
Naught else have I to do,
I sing the whole day long.
And He whom most I love to please
Doth listen to my song.
He caught and bound my wandering wing,
But still He bends to hear me sing.
My cage confines me round,
Abroad I cannot fly,
But though my wing is closely bound,
My heart's at liberty.

My prison walls cannot control
The flight, the freedom of the soul.
O, it is good to soar
These bolts and bars above,
To Him whose purpose I adore,
Whose providence I love,
And in Thy mighty will to find
The joy, the freedom of the mind.

Job experienced the tearing of the plowshare through his life, but his reaction silenced the adversary who designed to make capital against God out of his failure. Satan had no answer to Job's noble statement, "The Lord gave, and the Lord hath taken away; blessed be the name of the Lord." God's confidence in Job was abundantly vindicated.

"These little troubles (which are really so transitory) are winning for us a permanent, glorious and solid reward out of all proportion to our pain. For we are looking all the time not at the visible things but at the invisible. The visible things are transitory; it is the invisible things that are really permanent" (2 Corinthians 4:17–18 PHILLIPS). It is when we turn our eyes away from the immediate and fix them on the ultimate that we are able to correctly interpret the disciplinary experiences of life.

He is careful in their choice. "Does he not rather, after leveling the surface scatter the dill and sow cummin, put the wheat in rows, barley in the appointed places, and rye around the border? His God correctly instructs and teaches him" (vv. 24–26 BERKELEY VERSION). The prudent farmer exercises the finest discrimination both in the evaluation of his seeds and in the selection of their situation. He is not haphazard in his methods. The more valuable seeds are given the most favorable position. The less valuable can fill in waste corners. Dill and cummin are small seeds used as a relish and therefore comparatively unimportant when compared with the essential wheat and barley. The farmer is always calculating what will pay him best and how he can get the maximum return from his land.

So it is with God. He never wastes His discipline. He knows which will produce the most luxurious harvest. Each is carefully selected by infinite wisdom. He regards our lives as the seed plots of eternity and pays attention not only to the seed but to the soil. The incidence and timing of His corrective dealings are meticulously correct. He who correctly instructs and teaches the farmer does not exercise less wisdom in His culture of a human heart. His selection is unerring, whether it be delay or denial, withholding or withdrawing, prosperity or adversity, joy or suffering. He always has a crop in view.

Are we less than the farmer in our assessing of relative values and in deciding priorities? It is in this that success, both temporal and spiritual, lies. We reap what we sow. If the soil of our lives is sown with the trivial and the carnal, they will produce after their own kind. If on the other hand we sow the primary and the spiritual, there will be an abundant harvest of holiness and joy.

He is considerate in their moderation. "For the fitches are not threshed with a threshing instrument, neither is a cart wheel turned about upon the cummin; but the fitches are beaten out with a staff, and the cummin with a rod.

Bread corn is bruised; because he will not ever be threshing it, nor break it with the wheel of his cart, nor bruise it with his horsemen. This also cometh forth from the Lord of hosts, which is wonderful in counsel, and excellent in working" (Isaiah 28:27–29).

The farmer has regard to the nature of the seed as well as its value and adapts his threshing technique accordingly. To treat each seed alike would irreparably damage some or leave others unseparated from the husk. He must apply exactly the correct length of time to achieve the end in view. Gentle tapping with a rod is sufficient for the dill but the wheat requires the *tribulum*, a heavy threshing-sledge. His intelligence and experience prevents the farmer from excess in his threshing method. As soon as the seed is separated from the restricting husk, the threshing process ceases.

God exercises a similar discretion and moderation in the methods He adopts to produce the harvest in the lives of His children. He does not use the heavy *tribulum* (from which our word "tribulation" is derived) where a light rod would achieve His purpose. His object is not the crushing, the destruction of the grain, but its purification and preservation. If He sends tribulation it is because no other means will produce the result. He employs no more force and for no longer than is necessary. Fruitfulness is the end of all discipline. True spirituality welcomes tribulation if it will produce a richer harvest for God. "I glory in tribulation," said Paul, and he certainly knew what he was speaking of. Never was nature more sensitive than his, but seldom has a man experienced more of the chastening rod.

THE PURPOSE OF GOD'S DISCIPLINES

There is infinite variety in the dealings of God both in their character and their incidence. No two people are treated alike by Him. He recognizes the uniqueness of personality, and this is reflected in His disciplinary method.

God's dealings have a threefold purpose.

Personal—to cultivate the soul. What we are is much more important than the amount we do. God is supremely concerned with the development of Christlike character. He purposes that every Christian should be "conformed to the image of his Son." Even His Son could be brought to maturity in the human experience necessary for His office as High Priest only through suffering. There is no substitute. Where discipline is not applied, or goes unheeded, there is no harvest of personal holiness and likeness to Christ.

It is recorded that when in His grace the Lord lavished kindness upon His people, the response was not gratitude but rebellion. "He made him ride on the high places of the earth . . . and he made him to suck honey out of the rock, and oil out of the flinty rock; butter of kine, and milk of sheep, with fat of lambs . . . with the fat of kidneys of wheat. . . . But Jeshurun waxed fat, and kicked" (Deuteronomy 32:13–15).

Character is often unevenly developed. "Ephraim is a cake not turned," said Hosea; a cake well-done on one side and undercooked on the other. God is not content with a partial sanctification, with Christians who are overdeveloped in some respects but deficient in others. It is to correct this inequality that He applies the fires of testing to the underdeveloped side of our characters.

Relative—to provide food for others. "Bread corn is bruised" is the Authorized Version rendering, and this is without doubt true, but it is not bruised in the threshing process or it would lose its value. The ASV is probably more accurate in its text. "Bread grain is ground; for he will not be always threshing it" (v. 28). The farmer does not needlessly crush the grain with the *tribulum*. Grain in the husk is useless for human consumption, and the objective of threshing is to separate the grain from the husk, so that the grain may be ready for consumption. Once it is threshed, it goes through the bruising and grinding process.

Bread corn is bruised! Shrink not, my soul,
From the plucking and the binding,
From the break and the grind:
The heart God breaks, He doth make whole.
The corn unshelled and thrown aside
Cannot for man's sore need provide.

Our Lord was "bruised for our iniquities" that He might become to us the Bread of Life to sustain us. "The disciple is not above his master, nor the servant above his lord. It is enough for the disciple that he be as his master, and the servant as his lord" (Matthew 10:24–25). We should not wonder, then, that bruising is the price of a spiritual ministry.

Ultimate—to prepare for Heaven. This life is but the kindergarten of Heaven; God would have us master the elementary spiritual lesson that where there is no cross, there can be no crown. Where the yoke is not taken, the rest is not enjoyed. But we are slow scholars and the lesson has often to be learned over and over again.

"We cease to wonder so much at the care God takes of human character," wrote Alexander Whyte, "and the cost He lays out upon it, when we think that it is the only work of His hands that shall last forever. It is fit, surely, that the ephemeral should minister to the eternal, and time to eternity, and all else in this world that shall endure or survive this world; all else we possess or pursue shall fade and perish, our moral character shall alone survive. Riches, honor, possessions, pleasures of all kinds; death with one stroke of his desolate hand shall one day strip us bare to a winding sheet and a coffin of all the things we are so mad to possess."

CHAPTER 5

The Perfected Strength of God

My strength is made perfect in weakness.

2 CORINTHIANS 12:9

Reading: 1 CORINTHIANS 1:25–2:5;
2 CORINTHIANS 12:7–10

There is an arresting difference between God's thoughts and man's concerning weakness and inadequacy. We are inclined to consider these justifiable excuse for shrinking from the difficult task. God advances these very qualities as reasons for tackling it. We maintain that we are too weak. God asserts that to be the very reason He chose us. Instead of the wise and mighty and noble filling the front ranks of God's army, we find the foolish, the weak, the despised, the nonentities. And why? That no human being might boast in the presence of God, and that His strength might be made perfect in our weakness. "Ye see your calling, brethren, how that not many wise men after the flesh, not many mighty, not many noble, are called: but God hath chosen the foolish things of the world to confound the wise; and God hath chosen the weak things of the world to confound the things which are mighty;

and base things of the world, and things which are despised, hath God chosen, yea, and things which are not, to bring to nought things that are" (1 Corinthians 1:26–28).

THE PRINCIPLE INVOLVED

An important spiritual principle is involved, which must be mastered by all who wish to be their best for God. God is not confined to the greatly gifted and exceptionally clever for the fulfillment of His purposes. Indeed, He can use them only as they abandon reliance on their purely natural abilities. All through history God has chosen and used nonentities because their unusual dependence on Him left room for the unique display of His power. When they are content to be nothing, He can be everything. He chooses and uses the richly endowed only when they renounce dependence on their own abilities and resources.

Paul does not say in the above paragraph that God did the best He could with the poor material at His disposal. He deliberately chose them, passing by the wise, the mighty, and the noble if they refused to renounce not their gifts and qualifications but dependence on these in attaining spiritual ends. This is surely a challenging and revolutionary thought—God will not use us in spite of our weakness and inadequacy but actually because of them. He refuses to use our most spectacular gifts and unique qualifications until we are weaned from reliance on them. Human weakness provides the best backdrop for the display of divine power.

An exaggerated emphasis on talents and qualifications has closed the door to the mission field for many a fine potential missionary. "They will offer their services to any society which will guarantee the full employment of their skills," writes L. T. Lyall. "This is necessary to satisfy their families and friends that all the long grind leading up to qualification is not going to be altogether wasted. Surely God must have allowed them to have this training in order to use it! Abraham laid down no such conditions. Nor did Paul. Nor did any of the outstanding missionaries between their day and ours. Most of them allowed their talents to fall into the ground and die, but they became fruitful missionaries. The Lord demands unconditional discipleship. A Christian is under orders. He must not ask to see the path before stepping out on it. It is for us to obey our omniscient Lord and leave it to Him to deploy us where He sees our qualifications can be most strategically employed. The current attitude of requiring assurance that one's qualifications will find adequate outlet may be an evidence of a lack of full surrender to the Lordship of Christ. If we believe God has given us a special stewardship in our training, can we not trust Him if it seems that He puts the gifts aside for a time—or even forever?"

"My strength is made perfect in weakness" was God's message to Paul. "When I am weak, then am I strong" was Paul's testimony (2 Corinthians 12:9–10). Of God's heroes it is recorded that it was "out of weakness [they] were made strong" (Hebrews 11:34).

William Wilberforce, the great Christian reformer who was responsible for the freeing of the slaves in the British Empire, was so small and frail a creature that it seemed even a strong wind might knock him down. But once Boswell heard him speak in public in advocacy of his great cause, and afterwards Boswell said, "I saw what seemed to me a shrimp mount the table, but as I listened he grew and grew until the shrimp became a whale."

"It is a thrilling discovery to make," writes J. S. Stewart, "that always it is upon human weakness and humiliation, not human strength and confidence, that God chooses to build His kingdom; and that He can use us not merely in spite of our ordinariness and helplessness and disqualifying infirmities, but precisely because of them. . . . *Nothing can defeat a church or soul that takes, not its strength but its weakness, and offers it to God to be His weapon.* It was the way of Francis Xavier and William Carey and Paul the apostle. 'Lord, here is my human weakness. I dedicate it to Thee for Thy glory.' This is the strategy to which there is no retort. This is the victory which overcomes the world."

THE PRINCIPLE ILLUSTRATED

Our trouble is not that we are too weak but that we are too strong for God. King Uzziah was "marvellously helped, till he was strong. But when he was strong, his heart was lifted up to his destruction" (2 Chronicles 26:15–16). Jacob became a prince having power with God and man only after the sinew of his strength withered under the touch of his Divine Antagonist. Paradoxical as it may seem, "the lame take the prey" (Isaiah 33:23). God calls our hindrances helps, and it is our direst extremity which affords Him His greatest opportunity.

Dwight L. Moody was innocent of formal education. His letters, many of which have been preserved, are full of grammatical errors. His physical appearance was not impressive. His voice was high-pitched and his tones nasal. But these handicaps did not prevent God using him to shake two continents. A reporter was sent by his newspaper to cover Moody's campaign in Britain, in which aristocracy and artisan alike turned to God, to discover the secret of his power. After considerable observation he reported: "I can see nothing whatever in Moody to account for his marvelous work." When Moody read the report, he chuckled, "Why, that is the very secret of the movement. There is nothing in it that can explain it but the power of God. The work is God's, not mine."

It is a secret joy to find
The task assigned beyond our powers,
For thus, if ought of good be wrought,
Clearly the praise is His, not ours.
—F. Houghton

But God does not confine Himself to the Moodys and Careys of the world. Think how He used Paul the apostle. He could be classed among the wise, the mighty, the noble. He had everything—intellectual power, emotional ardor, irresistible logic, quenchless zeal. But he placed reliance on none of these. "And I, brethren . . . came not with excellency of speech or of wisdom, declaring unto you the testimony of God. For I determined not to know any thing among you, save Jesus Christ, and him crucified. And *I was with you in weakness*, and in fear, and in much trembling. And my speech and my preaching was not with enticing words of man's wisdom, but in demonstration of the Spirit and of power" (1 Corinthians 2:1–4). He had everything, but he renounced dependence on his superb gifts and training and placed his sole reliance on his adequate God.

Moses, too, illustrates the principle. As the young scholar-prince, he was supremely self-sufficient and attempted single-handed the deliverance of his oppressed fellows. But he was not yet equipped for God's purpose. He was banished from Egypt to undertake a forty-year course in the university of the desert. So thoroughly did he master the difficult lesson of human weakness that he shrank from the call of God when it came to him. He adduced seven reasons why he should not do God's will, all of them based on his own weakness and incapacity.

His inventory of disqualifications covered lack of capability (Exodus 3:11), lack of message (3:13), lack of authority (4:1), lack of eloquence (4:10), lack of special adaptation (4:13), lack of previous success (5:23), and lack of previous acceptance (6:12). A more complete list of disabilities would be difficult to conjure up. But instead of pleasing God, his seeming humility and reluctance stirred His anger. "The anger of the LORD was kindledagainst Moses" (4:14). In point of fact the excuses Moses advanced to show his incapacity were the very reasons for God's selection of him for the task. Now, emptied of self-confidence and self-dependence, Moses would lean on his God.

For each of his disabilities God had a satisfying answer and an appropriate provision. The forgotten factor was that God's call always guarantees God's equipment for the task. His weakness became God's weapon when it cast Moses back on God's illimitable resources. Our "who is sufficient for these things?" can be merely the despair of unbelief. The joyous response of faith is, "Our sufficiency is of God."

The story of Gideon's victory by the three hundred

illustrates the principle from a different angle. In his response to the divine call Gideon affords a perfect example of conscious inadequacy. "O my Lord, wherewith shall I save Israel? Behold, my family is poor in Manasseh, and I am the least in my father's house" (Judges 6:15). But, encouraged by God's promise of victory and confirmatory signs, he responded to the call. The 32,000 followers who rallied to his side seemed pitifully inadequate to meet 135,000 Midianites, but they were "too many" for God (7:2). The courage test eliminated 22,000, but the remaining 10,000 were "yet too many" (7:4). These were again sifted by the drinking test, which was survived by only 300 eager and disciplined men. Gideon's band was now outnumbered by 450 to 1. Instead of arming them with the most potent weapons, God orders that their weapons shall be fragile pitchers, flaming torches, and rude trumpets. Had military strategy ever seemed more absurd? Yet God's picked and obedient men won the day. "All the host ran, and cried, and fled" before them (7:21). Totally inadequate numbers and equipment were more than compensated for by the omnipotence of God. The utter weakness of Gideon's band became His weapon for victory. And the reason for stripping the inadequate Gideon of human resources? "Lest Israel vaunt themselves against me, saying, Mine own hand hath saved me" (7:2), a reason akin to Paul's, "That no flesh should glory in his presence" (1 Corinthians 1:29).

"This is the strategy of God . . . that the world should know that Christianity—all the triumphs of faith in individual lives and the onward march and mission of the Church—is not to be explained by anything in man, any human virtue, prowess, ability (for in the light of the men involved any such explanation would be absurd). Therefore, the only possible explanation must be supernatural and Divine."

THE PRINCIPLE VINDICATED

Francis de L. Booth Tucker, a brilliant young officer in the Indian Civil Service, filled an important post. Rapid promotion lay ahead of him, but he had met and yielded to the claims of Christ. Becoming dissatisfied with his self-centered life, he longed to be able to do more for the morally and spiritually destitute people around him. He heard of the recently organized Salvation Army and its tremendous impact on the unprivileged classes in England. He resigned his post and threw in his lot with the new movement. He proceeded to England, and after a period of training returned to India as a Salvation Army missionary. However, despite his most sacrificial efforts, he seemed unable to bridge the gap between him and the needy Indian people. He was failing to achieve the very thing for which he had abandoned his worldly prospects. After much prayer he determined to adopt native dress, take a begging bowl as did their holy men, and live on what the poor people chose to give him.

With a companion he set out on his new venture, traveling barefoot on the burning midsummer roads. Native people who had never worn shoes were inured to the heat, but before long Booth Tucker and his companion found their feet a mass of blisters that made every step an agony. Coming to a village in the heat of the afternoon, they expected at least a drink of water and something to eat, but they were denied entry. Thoroughly dispirited, they lay down under a tree and fell asleep. While they slept some of the men gathered around them. One, amazed to see the blisters on their feet, said, "How much these men must care for us to suffer in this way to bring us their message. They must be good men and we have treated them badly." When the missionaries awoke, they were invited into the village, their feet were bound up, and food and drink were spread before them. Then followed the coveted opportunity of presenting the gospel message to these members of a criminal tribe. Thus began a movement which swept 25,000 into the kingdom. It was not his undoubted brilliance but his obvious weakness which opened the hearts of the people. When he was weak, then he was strong. His weakness became God's weapon. God's strength was perfected in his weakness.

CHAPTER 6

The Moral Antipathy of God

These six things doth the LORD hate . . . a proud look.

PROVERBS 6:16–17

Reading: ISAIAH 14:12–15; EZEKIEL 28:11–19

The Bible does not tell how sin entered the universe, but we are told how it entered our world and that it originated before it made its presence felt here. It is characteristic of Scripture revelation that while it does not tell us everything we would like to know, it tells us all we need to know to enable us to meet the exigencies of life and to live victoriously over sin and circumstances. To do this, it is not necessary that we know the primal origin of sin, but it is essential that we know the nature and character of the fundamental sin which has blighted the world ever since it was entertained by our first parents.

In Genesis, the original temptation to sin was presented by the devil, who himself had fallen from his lofty position. Two Old Testament passages throw light on the nature of his sin (Ezekiel 28:11–19 and Isaiah 14:12–15), passages which primarily refer to the king of Tyre and the king of Babylon.

But the meaning of these Scriptures obviously cannot be exhausted by mere men. The Ezekiel passage runs: "Thou sealest up the sum, full of wisdom, and perfect in beauty. Thou hast been in Eden the garden of God; every precious stone was thy covering. . . . Thou art the anointed cherub that covereth. . . . Thou wast perfect in thy ways from the day that thou wast created, till iniquity was found in thee. . . . and thou hast sinned; therefore I will cast thee as profane out of the mountain of God. *Thine heart was lifted up* [was proud] because of thy beauty. . . . I will cast thee to the ground." How reminiscent of the words of our Lord, "I beheld Satan as lightning fall from heaven" (Luke 10:18).

Or again the Isaiah passage: "How art thou fallen from heaven, O Lucifer . . . for thou hast said in thine heart, I will ascend into heaven, I will exalt my throne above the stars of God: I will sit also upon the mount of the congregation. . . . I will ascend above the heights. . . . *I will be like the Most High.* Yet thou shalt be brought down to hell."

The historical characters to whom these passages had primary reference could not exhaust the full significance of these extraordinary statements, which without doubt have a deeper meaning. This method of revelation of truth is employed elsewhere in Scripture, e.g., in the Messianic Psalms where the psalmist, though apparently referring to himself, made statements which in their fullness could refer only to the Messiah (Psalms 2, 22, and 110). This finds confirmation elsewhere in Scripture. So we have grounds for inferring that these passages have a secondary application to Satan, who occupied the lofty office of guardian and protector of the throne of God. He was the daystar, holding a position of unsurpassed glory near the Sun of Righteousness.

What caused his downfall? The fundamental sin of pride, the sin of seeking to establish a throne of his own. Instead of guarding the throne of God which he was set to protect, he struck at it and attempted to dethrone the Almighty. Pride led to self-exaltation which expressed itself in self-will. The essence of his sin was that he wanted to be independent of God. Pride is the self-sufficiency of a selfish spirit that desires only unrestrained independence. "I will set my throne on high. . . . I will make myself like the Most High." This is the fundamental sin which tries to enthrone *self* at the expense of God.

Though Satan was cast down, in his fall he wrested the scepter of sovereignty of the world from man, and now he rules as god of this world. In Eden he sowed the seeds of the same tragic sin. "In the day ye eat thereof . . . ye shall be as gods" (Genesis 3:5), he promised. Compare this with his "I will make myself like the Most High." Satan fell through pride. Adam and Eve fell through pride and implicated the whole human race in their ruin. You and I fall through pride, the fundamental sin which lies at the root of every other sin, the desire to be master of our own lives and to be independent of God. Since this is so, it is little wonder that pride leads the list in every catalog of sins compiled by the church.

GOD'S ANTIPATHY TO PRIDE

No sin is more hateful and abhorrent to God. Sins of the flesh are revolting and bring their own social consequences, but against none of those does God speak with such vehemence as He does of pride.

"Him that hath . . . a proud heart will not I suffer [endure]" (Psalm 101:5).

"The proud he knoweth afar off" (Psalm 138:6).

"These six things doth the LORD hate; yea, seven are an abomination unto him: a proud look" (Proverbs 6:16–17).

"Pride . . . do I hate" (Proverbs 8:13).

"Every one that is proud in heart is an abomination to the LORD" (Proverbs 16:5).

"A proud heart . . . is sin" (Proverbs 21:4).

"The loftiness of man shall be bowed down" (Isaiah 2:17 ASV).

"God resisteth the proud" (James 4:6).

No further words are necessary to express the hatred, the revulsion, the antipathy of God to pride and arrogance, to conceit and haughtiness. It is an abomination to Him. Can we condone what God hates? Can we entertain what is an abomination to Him? God opposes the proud and holds them at a distance. There is no point of meeting between a proud heart and God, but a broken and contrite spirit He will not despise.

THE ESSENCE OF PRIDE

The word "proud" in James 4:6 signifies literally "one who considers himself above other people." It is an offense to both God and man. The Greeks hated it. Theophylact called pride "the citadel and summit of all evils."

Pride is a *deification of self.* It thinks more highly of itself than it ought to think. It arrogates to itself the honor which belongs to God only. It caused Rabbi Simeon Ben Jochai to say, "If there are only two righteous men in the world, I and my son are the two. If only one, I am he." It was the sin of Nebuchadnezzar which brought him down to the level of the beasts. The valet of the last German Kaiser said, "I cannot deny that my master was vain. He had to be the central figure in everything. If he went to a christening, he wanted to be the baby. If he went to a wedding, he wanted to be the bride. If he went to a funeral, he wanted to be the corpse."

Pride is characterized by *independence of God.* It was at the heart of Adam's sin. Instead of being dependent on God, he desired to be as God and brought ruin on the whole race. Pride desires to be beholden to neither God nor man. It is perfectly self-sufficient, in striking contrast to the Son of God who said, "I can of mine own self do nothing" (John 5:30). He gloried in His dependence on His Father. Pride glories in being self-made.

It involves a certain contempt *for others.* "God, I thank thee, that I am not as other men are . . . or even as this publican" (Luke 18:11). It relegates every other mortal to a minor role in life. It uses other people as a backdrop to display its own brilliance. The proud man considers others beneath him, the *hoi polloi,* the common herd. Instead of pouring contempt on all his pride, he pours his contempt on others whom he esteems less worthy than himself.

Pride is *essentially competitive* in its nature. C. S. Lewis points out that no one is proud because he is rich, or clever, or good-looking. He is proud because he is richer, or more clever, or better looking than someone else. It involves a comparison which always goes in favor of the one who makes it.

THE MANIFESTATION OF PRIDE

Pride adapts itself to every temperament, accommodates itself to every situation. It is remarkably fluid. It can be humble or haughty at will. There is a form suited to every character. We do well to ask ourselves what are our particular forms of pride. Of face, race, place, grace? Of intellect, achievement, success, skill?

There is *intellectual pride*, for "knowledge puffeth up." This was the peculiar temptation of the brilliant Corinthians who prided themselves on their mental superiority. Seven of the eight passages in which "puffed up" is used occur in the Corinthian epistles. This form of pride tends to manifest itself in scornful superiority over those of limited intellectual gift, or who have been denied the opportunity of advanced education. It flourishes luxuriantly in the student to whom a new world of knowledge is opening and who has not yet learned that true learning begets humility, not conceit. It was different with Charles Dickens. People who met him for the first time would never have suspected that he was the most distinguished literary man of his time.

In the east we are reaping the harvest we have sown in our *racial pride* which despises those of a different color of skin or culture. Those who cherish this hateful attitude have not yet learned that differences of race and culture do not necessarily involve inferiority in any respect. Indeed, the longer contact we have with people of other races, the less foundation we discover for our vaunted superiority.

There is a *social pride* which preens itself on an accident of birth for which it can take no credit. It despises the common herd who do not move in such select circles of society. The lesson that nobility of character is not the exclusive possession of any one class or group has yet to be mastered. Charles Lamb once accosted one of these grandiose people with the remark, "Excuse me, sir, but are you—anybody in particular?"

But more abhorrent to God than any of these is *spiritual pride*, pride of grace. It is very possible to be proud of the spiritual gifts God has entrusted to us and to strut about ostentatiously, forgetting that we have nothing which we have not received, that grace is a gift, an undeserved favor. We can actually be filled with pride at the eloquence and brilliance of our sermon on humility. But the most perfect lens is that which allows us to forget the glass is there at all. Dr. John McNeill told of a lady who approached him at the close of a sermon on humility. "Yes, Dr. McNeill," she volunteered, "humility is my forte!"

Pride manifests itself in the inordinate assertion of self. The man in the grip of pride worships at the shrine of self. Like Narcissus gazing into the fountain, he is infatuated with himself. Seeing the image of his own beauty, Narcissus took it for a water nymph and fell in love with it. So infatuated was he that when he could not obtain the object of his passion, he committed suicide. He was the perfect example of the folly of being a lover of oneself.

The unbroken, proud man thirsts for and eagerly drinks in flattery and praise because it gratifies his self-love. He is elated when it is given, depressed when it is withheld. There is no one in the world about whom he delights to talk more than about himself. He will turn every conversation until it centers on himself. In the palace of Wurtzung there is a hall of glass known as the Hall of a Thousand Mirrors. You enter—a thousand hands are stretched out to greet you. You smile, and a thousand smiles greet your smile; you weep, and a thousand eyes weep with you. But they are all your own hands and smiles and tears. Such is the proud man, engrossed in himself, surrounded by self, imprisoned by self. The Master stands out in striking contrast to all such. In the delicate task of announcing His Messiahship to His own townspeople, He accomplished it without the use of the noun "I." Reading Isaiah 61:1 and 2 He said, "This day is this Scripture fulfilled in your ears." The only One whose prerogative it is to say "I," in His humility avoided its use.

Pride defiles everything it touches. There are germs which transform nourishing food into virulent poison. Pride transforms virtues into vices and blessings into curses. Beauty plus pride results in vanity. Zeal plus pride makes for tyranny and cruelty. Human wisdom compounded with pride brings infidelity. In speech, pride manifests itself in criticism, for criticism is always made from the vantage point of conscious superiority. Pride will find cause for criticism in everyone and everything. It lauds itself and belittles its neighbor.

Scripture is replete with illustrations of the folly and tragedy which follow in the train of pride. It was pride of his kingdom and power that moved King David to number Israel, a sin which resulted in divine judgment (1 Chronicles 21:1). Gripped by pride, Hezekiah showed his covetous enemies "all the house of his precious things, the silver, and the gold . . . and all that was found in his treasures" (2 Kings 20:13)—and lost them all. Nebuchadnezzar's pride fed on his own achievements. "Is not this great Babylon that I have built for the house of the kingdom by the might of my power and for the honor of my majesty?" But his haughty spirit went before a gigantic fall. "While the word was in the king's mouth, there fell a voice from heaven, saying . . . The kingdom is departed from thee. And they shall drive thee from men, and thy dwelling shall be with the beasts of the field: they shall make thee to eat grass as oxen." When his sanity was restored, the center of his worship was shifted from himself to God. "Now I Nebuchadnezzar praise and extol and honor the King of heaven" (Daniel 4:37). Pride is a species of moral and spiritual insanity.

Uzziah's heart was lifted up in pride by his supposed military might and success. "But when he was strong, his heart was lifted up to his destruction: for he transgressed against the LORD his God, and went into the temple of the LORD to burn incense upon the altar of incense. . . . leprosy even rose up in his forehead" (2 Chronicles 26:16, 19). Pride led him to intrude on the divine prerogatives and when he died, they said, "He is a leper." Herod lapped up the praise the people of Tyre accorded to his oration, "It is the voice of a god, and not of a man. And immediately the angel of the Lord smote him, because he gave not God the glory" (Acts 12:22–23). Peter's pride made him feel so superior in moral courage to his fellow disciples that he boasted, "Though all men forsake thee, yet will not I." It was not long before his boasting pride suffered a shattering blow when he "denied him with oaths and curses."

THE PROOF OF PRIDE

The subtlety of pride is seen in the fact that its victims are generally quite oblivious to their bondage, though all around can hear the clank of the chains. On one occasion a man said to his friend, "Well, I can thank God that whatever my other faults are, I am not proud." "I can well understand that," rejoined the other, "for of course you haven't very much to be proud about." "Haven't I, indeed?" was the indignant rejoinder. "I've got as much to be proud about as you have!" If we are honest with ourselves, it will not be difficult to discover the extent to which pride rules in our lives. There are infallible tests by which we can discover its hateful presence.

The Test of Precedence. How do we react when another is selected for the office we coveted? When another is promoted, while we are overlooked? When another is honored and we are ignored? When another outshines us? Does it stimulate jealousy and ill will, or can we really rejoice in another's advancement or greater ability? Do we, like Diotrephes, love to have the foremost place? It is true that the most difficult instrument in the orchestra to master is second fiddle. It was this test that came to John the Baptist when the crowds left him to follow Jesus, but he passed it with triumph. "He must increase, but I must decrease." "This my joy is fulfilled."

The Test of Sincerity. We will say all kinds of bad things about ourselves, but how do we feel when others say these same things of us? Many of our self-deprecatory statements are insincere and we realize them to be so when others affirm the same of us. Many a man declines office only that he might be pressed a little harder.

The Test of Criticism. What is our reaction to criticism? Do we immediately fly to justify ourselves? Does it arouse hostility and resentment in us? Do we immediately begin to criticize our critic? Such responses to criticism are the surest proof that we are in the grip of pride. We cannot bear to have people speak of us except with approbation. Humility will take criticism no matter from whom it comes, and will profit by it because it knows that where there is smoke there is fire, and there is usually some element of truth from which it can profit in the most scathing criticism.

The Test of Inferiority. People with an inferiority complex are not necessarily free from pride. Indeed, that very complex may be the clear index of a pride which is hurt because others do not accept them at their own valuation. It may be pride of a different kind but pride nonetheless. Our pride is hurt because we think people consider us inferior, whereas in our own heart of hearts, no matter how much we protest to the contrary, we do not feel as inferior as they appear to think.

THE CURE OF PRIDE

Pride must be radically dealt with. William Law wrote, "Pride must die in you or nothing of heaven can live in you. . . . Look not at pride only as an unbecoming temper, nor at humility only as a decent virtue. . . . One is all hell and the other all heaven." Steps on the road to cure are:

Perception. Humility, the antithesis of pride, has been defined by Bernard as the virtue by which man becomes conscious of his own unworthiness. We will never conquer a sin of which we are unconscious or over which we do not grieve. We must hate what God hates. Self-knowledge is not easy to come by, as we are all so prepossessed in our own favor. We see the splinter in our brother's eye with great clarity but, with strange inconsistency, fail to detect the plank in our own. We need to genuinely ask God to expose us to ourselves. When we see ourselves as we truly are, we will sink in self-abasement. Is it not true that we would not be very comfortable if others knew all our secret thoughts, saw all the pictures that hang on the walls of our imagination, perceived all our hidden motives, observed all our covered deeds, heard all our whispered words? Are we humbled that God knows us for the person we truly are? If we realize the facts about ourselves as they really are, all grounds for pride will be demolished. Do I know a lot? What I know is infinitesimal compared with what remains to be known. Am I clever? My cleverness is a gift for which I can take no credit. Am I rich? It was God who gave me the power to get wealth.

Chastening. As a preventive against loathsome pride in His children, God lovingly disciplines them. Paul had this experience. "And lest I should be exalted above measure through the abundance of the revelations, there was given to me a thorn in the flesh . . . lest I should be exalted above measure" (2 Corinthians 12:7). Do we recognize, in some crippling limitation, some painful malady, some thwarted ambition, the gracious ministry of God to deliver us from something worse, the ascendancy of pride?

Mortification. A prudent farmer cuts down weeds when they are young lest they spread their seeds and multiply. So let us observe the proud thought, confess it and put it away. Cherish the proud thought and you will find you have nursed a viper in your bosom. Pride is of the flesh and the Spirit will help us in killing it. "If ye through the Spirit do mortify the deeds of the body, ye shall live" (Romans 8:13).

Comparison. We compare ourselves among ourselves and come off fairly well in the comparison. But let us compare ourselves with the perfect Christ and if we are honest we will be overwhelmed with the tawdriness and shabbiness or even the vileness of our characters. While the disciples in their pride wrangled to secure first place, the Lord of glory donned the slave's smock and washed their dirty feet. It is striking that Satan tempted Christ with the very sin which had caused his own downfall, but where he succumbed, Christ triumphed.

Contemplation. The final secret is the contemplation of Christ. Our best efforts of self-discovery and self-discipline will be inadequate alone to root out this cancer. It requires a radical and supernatural change of heart, and this is what is promised. "Beholding . . . the glory of the Lord, [we are being] changed into the same image" (2 Corinthians 3:18). Pride shrivels and withers and shrinks away in the light of His humility. And again it is "by the Spirit of the Lord" that the transformation takes place. The Holy Spirit will always cooperate to the limit with anyone who comes to hate his pride and covets the humility of Christ.

CHAPTER 7

The Satisfying Compensations of God

Lo, I see four men . . . and the form of the fourth is like the Son of God.

DANIEL 3:25

Reading: DANIEL 3:1–30

In the days of our childhood this story seemed very remote and, while we may not have doubted its veracity, it appeared to be quite without relevance to the times in which we lived. But only recently a missionary of the China Inland Mission who had just returned from a visit to Burma told a comparable story of Titus, a former student of his in China. When he would not deny his faith, Communist officials in southwest China held him over a fire, then urged him to recant, but without success. The ghastly process was repeated until the chariot of fire carried him into the presence of his Lord, charred in body but dauntless in faith. So this story is right up-to-date, very relevant to those who even today may stand in Titus's place.

Picture the exact circumstances these three young men faced. Impressed by their caliber, Nebuchadnezzar had shown them favor, much to the displeasure of the Babylonian courtiers. Their jealousy was understandable. Do we relish seeing foreigners given privileged positions in our country? Are we without our own national jealousy? The courtiers determined that in some way they would remove these three interlopers. The edict that all must worship Nebuchadnezzar's golden image, erected to celebrate his victories and enhance his glory, provided a welcome opportunity.

The three young men had no doubt of the course they should adopt. Had Jehovah not commanded, "Thou shalt not make any graven image" and "Thou shalt have no other gods before me"? When they refused to bow to his image, "then was Nebuchadnezzar full of fury" (v. 19). If they would not bend to his will, they would burn in his furnace. "Heat the furnace seven times hotter than usual," he raged. Such is the background of the story.

THE RESOURCES OF FAITH

The magnificence of their faith is seen in their unwavering refusal to be disloyal to their God, with a seven-times heated furnace as the only alternative. Theirs was dauntless faith indeed. It was expressed in these sublime words, "O Nebuchadnezzar, we are not careful to answer thee in this matter. If it be so, our God whom we serve is able to deliver us from the burning fiery furnace, and he will deliver us out of thine hand, O king. But if not, be it known unto thee, O king, that we will not serve thy gods, nor worship the golden image which thou hast set up" (Daniel 3:16–18).

Note the resources of faith in their confession.

Faith in the ability of God to deliver them was their first resource. "Our God is able to deliver us." We all subscribe to the ability of God to do everything in general, but it takes the exercise of faith to believe that God is able to do the something in particular which is our concern—especially if we already feel the heat of the fiery furnace! Could anything have seemed more impossible than deliverance? Is my God able to deliver me in my particular furnace of trial? Am I willing to step out in faith and trust Him?

Confidence in the willingness of God to deliver them. "And He will deliver us out of thine hand." This is the second resource of faith. Many who concede the ability of God to do everything are not so confident of His willingness to intervene in their case. To know God is to be assured of His absolute willingness to intervene in the way He sees to be in our highest interests. The Lord did deliver the three men, but in a way they never envisaged. Indeed, at first it seemed that they were not to be delivered at all.

Thrice blest is he to whom is given
The wisdom that can tell
That God is on the field when He
Is most invisible.

When the leper appealed to Jesus for healing, he said, "Lord, if thou wilt, thou canst make me clean"—confident of His ability, but uncertain of His willingness. Jesus immediately corrected his mistaken concept with the words *"I will;* be thou clean."

But the faith of these young men was not at an end with

this second resource. Enshrined in the words "but if not," they had a third resource which rendered them invincible and fireproof.

Acceptance of the sovereignty of God. "But if not, be it known unto thee, O king . . . we will not worship the golden image." If we have this third resource of faith, if we can master this lesson, we are on the road to spiritual maturity. Even if God had not delivered them, their faith would not have been staggered. They knew it would be because He had some better thing for them. They recognized that it might not be God's purpose to exercise His ability in this way, and they were content to leave the issue in His hands. They understood the principle Jesus stated in parable, "Cannot I do what I will with mine own?"

Their attitude was, "Even if God does not do as we expect, our faith will not be stumbled, our confidence in Him and His love will remain unshaken. We know our God so well that we are prepared to accept His sovereign will even if we cannot understand it." In the event itself, there was apparent cause for their faith to stumble, for their courageous loyalty was rewarded by their being cast into the furnace after all. The onlooker might be justified in concluding that God was unconcerned, but their faith rose even to this test. To them, loyalty to their God was more important than life itself. They trusted Him where they could not trace His purposes. And God rewarded them on the scale of their magnificent trust; He had secret plans of grace and blessing of which they had never dreamed.

THE IMPLICATIONS OF FAITH

Thomas Carlyle once said, "The final question which each of us is compelled to answer is, 'Wilt thou be a hero or a coward?'" This question constantly confronts us in one form or another.

Faith is always confronted with a choice. We can choose either the high road or the low road. The choice for these young men was no easy one, nor will it be for us. Often it is an agonizing experience. Think of choosing between worshiping the king's image and being incinerated in the king's inferno! Nebuchadnezzar did not demand that they deny their faith, only that they bow to his image. In the days of the early church, the mere offering of a pinch of incense to the emperor would have spared many a martyr from being thrown to the lions. Faith always chooses the highest and best even though it be the most costly.

Faith always involves a risk. If there is no risk involved, no faith is necessary. If we can see the path ahead, we are walking by sight. What constituted Abraham the father of the faithful? The key to his whole life of faith is seen at its beginning. "Abraham went out, *not knowing whither* he went." He was willing to risk all on God. We exercise faith only when the way ahead is not clear, when we are so placed that we have no alternative if God lets us down. Not everyone enjoys taking such risks. Many who are bold as lions in taking physical risks are strangely timorous when it comes to taking a step of faith. We like to play safe, to have our plans cut-and-dried, to have an alternative ready. There is always a risk in the pathway of faith.

Faith always encounters opposition. The pathway of faith is not primrose-strewn, it is blood-marked. Abraham advanced from one test to another, each more difficult than the last. There was always opposition to be overcome, difficulty to be overleaped. Instead of repining at the difficulties we meet, we should rejoice at the fresh opportunity they afford for the exercise of faith. If we are advancing in the walk of faith, we can expect to encounter more opposition, inward and outward, than our fellows. How else could faith have its exercise? There would be no incentive to climb.

THE DELIVERANCE OF FAITH

There are two important lessons to master.

Deliverance from trial is not necessarily our highest good. God did not deliver the three men *from* the fiery furnace but He did deliver them *in* it. We must get away from the idea that deliverance from trial is the highest form of spiritual blessing. That is an attitude which is entirely alien to the spirit of the New Testament. Was it the attitude of the Lord whom we follow? Paul gloried in enduring tribulation, not in evading it. God could easily have prevented the three young men from being flung into the furnace. He had something much better for them. There has been too much emphasis in Second Advent teaching on escape from the tribulation which is to overtake this old world. Without engaging in any millennial controversy, we should be alive to an emphasis which is unwholesome. Our Lord categorically stated, “In the world ye shall have tribulation,” and it is the complacent church which knows little tribulation which makes little spiritual impact. God nowhere promises us immunity from trial. We learn more in a few days in the fiery furnace than we would learn in years out of it. We emerge from the trials with a greater God.

The incidence of trial is unequal. God does not treat all alike. This obvious fact causes some to be offended in God. These three young men were not concerned with God's treatment of others. They had their dealings directly with Him. We quickly run into spiritual trouble if we look around at God's dealings with others. Our Lord taught Peter a salutary lesson on this point. He was concerned lest John should receive preferential treatment. Jesus replied sternly, "What is that to thee? Follow thou me." James went from prison to the executioner's block. Peter went from prison to a prayer meeting. Peter won 3,000 souls. Stephen received 3,000 stones. We have to accept the fact that "the ways of the Lord are not equal." He does not deal with us on the mass-production principle. He delivers some *from* trial. He delivers some *in* trial.

Do we have a "But if not" in our spiritual vocabulary? Do we have this third resource of faith? Is our faith fire-proof? If wars should arise and son, daughter, husband, sweetheart be taken from our side, have we a "But if not" to carry us through that fiery furnace? If business should fail or financial reverses be experienced? If ill health grips us? When old age enfeebles us? When bereavement strikes? When desire for a life partner is not granted? When cherished plans are thwarted? If Christian work does not meet with the success we envisaged? When we are not designated to the mission station we expected or live with the fellow worker we would choose? Let us emulate the dauntless faith of the noble three who maintained their confidence in God in the face of seemingly unrewarded faith. "But if not, we will still go on trusting God," said the three men. They did not fall into self-pity or unbelief.

We may not always understand God's dealings with us at the time, and He nowhere undertakes to explain Himself. "What I do thou knowest not now, but thou shalt know hereafter" is His promise. In the meantime we learn many a lesson in the furnace of testing.

If all my days were summer, how could I know
What my Lord means by His "whiter than the snow"?
If all my days were sunny, could I say
In His fair land He wipes all tears away?
If I were never weary, could I keep
Close to my heart, "He gives His loved ones sleep"?
Were no graves mine, might I not come to deem
The life eternal but a baseless dream?
My winter and my tears and weariness,
Even my graves may be His way to bless.
I call them ills, yet that can surely be
Nothing but love that shows my Lord to me.

THE COMPENSATIONS OF FAITH

Their faith did not go unappreciated or unrewarded.

Companionship with the Son of God was their first joyous privilege. "Lo, I see four men loose, walking in the midst of the fire, and they have no hurt; and the form of the fourth is like the Son of God" (v. 25). In the furnace of affliction the Lord draws nearer than at any other time. It was not until they were "in the midst of the fire" that the Lord joined them. They acted in faith and He responded after they had risked all on Him.

Control of the flames was another compensation. God saw that the flames burned with a strange discrimination. "And the princes . . . saw these men, upon whose bodies the fire had no power, nor was an hair of their head singed, neither were their coats changed, nor the smell of fire had passed on them" (v. 27). The flames burnt only their bonds, enabling them to walk in fellowship with the Son of God in unfettered freedom. Can we not see in this one of the gracious compensations of the fires of testing?

Vindication of their own faith and of their God was one of the rewards of their unwavering confidence. Why the details about their bodies, and hair, and coats? And why no smell of fire? An anonymous writer says:

> High in rank and honor was the Babylonian god Izbar, the god of fire. Before the eyes of king and prince, governor, captains and counselors, this god must be defeated. The king had challenged the defeat by his own action. And now the defeat is overwhelming. On their own ground Jehovah has met these ardent believers in the god of fire, and they find that He is present, not merely as a tribal god in Palestine, but as the God of Heaven and earth in Babylon also, as able and willing to deliver only three of His children as to help thirty thousand if need were. Let us suppose for a moment that the three men had come out with the marks of fire partially upon them, or even with the smell of it, that here and there

the fire had singed either body or garment, and what would have been the attitude of the fire-worshipers? Something like this, "Ah, well, it is true Izbar has not been able to destroy them, but he has at least left his mark upon them. They will wear these clothes no more. Their friends will scarcely recognize them as the men they once were. The smell of the furnace will not soon leave them. They have not come out scatheless. Our Izbar is still a god to be reckoned with. They will not be so ready to disobey the king's mandate another time. They will not come out of the furnace, it may be, a second time as easily as they have done this time."

And so the whole moral effect of the protest of these three Hebrews would have been discounted. The dexterity of the world in evading direct issues of this kind is marvelous. But in this case evasion was impossible. Not one loophole of escape was left them. In awe they had to admit that Jehovah had conquered, that the miracle was perfect and unquestionable, and that "the smell of fire had not passed on" the three brave followers of the Most High.

There is many another similar illustration of an undaunted faith which had its "But if not" in the face of devastating alternatives. Each demonstrates a faith that is not only obedient to the Divine commands but triumphs over the Divine contradictions.

Job lost all—home, herd, family, health, even his wife's sympathy—yet in the midst of the holocaust his faith triumphed gloriously. "He shall bring me forth to the light, and I shall behold him." *But if not,* "though he slay me, yet will I trust him." Job had the third resource of faith.

Imagine the poignancy of Isaac's question to Abraham, "Where is the lamb for the burnt offering?" Abraham had his answer ready. "God will provide a lamb," *but if not,* I will still trust, accounting that God is "able to raise him up, even from the dead" (Hebrews 11:19). Such a thing as a resurrection had never been dreamed of, but Abraham's faith rose to the occasion and he received him back from the dead in a figure.

John the Baptist was languishing in prison. He was disappointed that he had received no message from Jesus, that He had taken no steps to liberate or even visit him. He sent his disciples with the question, "Master, am I mistaken? Art Thou He that should come, or look we for another? *But if not,* my faith is not stumbled. I will keep on looking for another."

The Lord Jesus was agonizing in prayer in Gethsemane, in such distress that bloody sweat forced its way through His pores. "Father, if it be possible, let this cup pass from me. *But if not,* thy will be done."

Can we wonder that Nebuchadnezzar was impotent against such a faith as this? The fire had no power over the bodies of the dauntless trio, and he had no power over their spirits. The world is powerless to lure or daunt men with a faith such as this. The devil is powerless to do more than burn their bonds and send them forth as God's free men.

In the world of today the testing flames may very well lick around us too. There is always an image somewhere demanding our worship. The form of the furnace may change with the years but the fact of it does not. The world may threaten to cast us into the furnace of social ostracism. If we do not bow to the god of popular custom, we will be fed to the flames of ridicule and unpopularity. It is not inconceivable that actual fires of persecution may rage around us yet. It is for us to be certain that we possess the fireproof faith of the three young men if we are to enjoy the abundant compensations of God.

PART TWO

The Supreme Vision of Christ

CHAPTER 8

The Supreme Vision of Christ

I saw . . . one like unto the Son of man.

REVELATION 1:12–13

Reading: REVELATION 1:9–20

The symbolic message of the book of the Revelation of Jesus Christ has ever been treasured most by a church passing through the fires of testing and persecution. For this reason it has special relevance for large segments of the world of today. Throughout history the self-revelation of God has always been appropriate to the contemporary needs of His people, and of no portion of Scripture is this more true than of the Apocalypse. To the exiled John is entrusted the privileged task of unveiling Christ in a character exactly suited to the needs of a harassed and persecuted church.

Such a message demands a sympathetic messenger and, that he might be thus prepared, God permitted John to be banished to Patmos where, according to Victorinus, along with a gang of criminals he had to work in the mines of that rocky island. It was on account of his loyalty to the Word of God and his testimony to Jesus Christ that he was in exile.

Indeed, early Christian tradition maintained that he was under sentence for failure to yield to the demands of emperor worship. From the vantage point of his identification with his Asian fellow believers in their tribulation, he was qualified to bring them the divine message. He sat where they sat.

Of this particular Lord's Day (by the second century this phrase had become the technical title for Sunday), John wrote that he "came to be in the Spirit," that state of ecstasy and elevated consciousness in which the prophet sees visions and hears words beyond his normal capacity to understand. It was as though he had been transported from the world of time and space into eternity. Paul had a similar experience. He was transported to "the third heaven" and heard "unspeakable words, which it is not lawful for a man to utter" (2 Corinthians 12:4). So entirely possessed and controlled by the Spirit was John that the outward world receded and the invisible world became tangible and real.

While in this ecstatic state John heard behind him "a great voice as of a trumpet" with its insistent, commanding clarity. It was the sound of a trumpet which summoned God's ancient people to their religious feasts. It was a trumpet voice which accompanied God's revelation of Himself at Sinai (Exodus 19:16; 20:18). It is not surprising that to one whose mind was steeped and saturated in the Old Testament Scriptures, the visions of the Apocalypse were communicated through Old Testament symbolism and imagery.

HIS UNIQUE PERSON

When John turned to see the speaker, he saw none other than the living Christ—"one like unto the Son of man"—whom he had last seen sixty years previously. No longer is He "despised and rejected of men, a man of sorrows and acquainted with grief," but He is now the transcendent triumphant Christ, clothed in inconceivable majesty and glory, standing in the midst of the seven golden lampstands which symbolized the seven churches of Asia. It was the very same Jesus on whose breast John had often laid his head, and yet how strikingly different from the days of His humiliation. The same, yet not the same; possessing the same human attributes, yet vested with awful power and majesty.

The vision was spiritual and the description symbolical, yet it presents to the mind a picture of Christ more vivid and impressive than any painting. It is not for us to endeavor from the imagery here used to conjure up a grotesque literal picture of the One whom John saw, but rather to interpret the symbols in which the inspired vision was given in the light of their use elsewhere in Scripture. Through the significance of the symbolism we can discover the meaning of the vision. Artists of all ages have endeavored to reproduce on canvas the face and form of Christ, but it is a remarkable fact that the Gospels contain not a line concerning His physical appearance, striking though that must have been. The only picture we have of Him is in the inspired words which present to us His moral and spiritual characteristics.

The first thing to impress John in the vision was *the clothing* of Christ. He was "clothed with a garment down to the foot, and girt about the paps with a golden girdle" (v. 13), a long flowing robe with a golden belt buckled at the breast. It was a garment fitted for dignified and majestic movement, the repose of sovereignty. It contrasted with the workaday robe which was girded at the loins, fitted for speedy service.

His function was suggested by His clothing. It was the robe characteristic of prophets, priests, and kings, and therefore it was eminently suited to the One in whom all three offices found their climax and fulfillment. It was the robe of the prophet, the bearer of the inspired message of God (Daniel 10:5). It was the garment worn by the high priest when engaged in his duty of trimming and supervising the shining of the lamps in the sanctuary. It was the robe of royalty (1 Samuel 18:4). Thus the One whom John saw is competent to impart the divine message to man, to introduce him into the holiest of all, and to reign over him in righteousness. There were no doubts in John's mind of the deity of this august Personage, for he ascribed to Him titles which in the Old Testament are used exclusively of God.

A full-length portrait of the exalted Lord follows, a sevenfold representation which in vivid colors and by graphic metaphor throws into bold relief His moral and spiritual attributes and His judicial powers.

"*His head and his hairs* were white like wool, as white as snow" (v. 14). The symbolism is drawn from Daniel. "I beheld till the thrones were cast down, and the Ancient of Days did sit, whose garment was white as snow, and the hair of his head like the pure wool" (Daniel 7:9). Here is the evident combination of antiquity and purity, of pre-existence and sinlessness. His is the great age and wisdom of eternity. "His is the age that is not aged, and the purity and holiness which are eternal." The raiment of the Ancient of Days glistened like snow in sunshine. When John saw the Son of Man on Mount

Tabor, "his raiment was white and glistering" (Luke 9:29), "shining, exceeding white as snow; so as no fuller on earth can white them" (Mark 9:3). Here is *holiness perfect and mature.*

"His *eyes* were as a flame of fire" (v. 14), symbol of that penetrating vision and infinite knowledge which is peculiar to omniscience. In Daniel's vision, His eyes were as "flaming torches" (10:6 RSV). This vivid symbol indicates His power to scrutinize and search every life, to penetrate the inner chambers of every imagination, to "bring to light the hidden things of darkness and make manifest the counsels of the heart." It appears again in Revelation 19:11–12. "And I saw heaven opened, and behold a white horse; and he that sat upon him was called Faithful and True, and in righteousness he doth judge and make war. His eyes were as a flame of fire, and on his head were many crowns." Here the emphasis is upon His consuming indignation as Executor of the righteous judgment of God against sin, "in flaming fire taking vengeance on them that know not God, and that obey not the gospel of our Lord Jesus Christ" (2 Thessalonians 1:8). But Christ's judgment, unlike ours, is based on perfect knowledge. "I know thy works" is His reiterated assurance to each of the seven churches, His assurance that every credit will be given. Nothing, whether favorable or adverse, can be concealed from the eyes of Him who possesses *perfect knowledge.*

"*His feet* like unto fine brass, as if they burned in a furnace" (v. 15). The symbolism here is not easy to interpret. The figure reappears in Revelation 2:18 and is followed by Christ's activity in judgment (vv. 23, 27). Christ walks among the churches and moves toward the consummation of God's eternal purpose. Brass in John's day was a compound of gold, copper, and silver, the strongest metal known. Here it is brass which has reached white heat in a furnace. One characteristic of brass was that it would not yield to heat. Christ, as man, could stand the furnace of God's holiness. Though walking in a world defiled by sin, He contracted no taint or corruption. But the figure could also suggest His inflexible and invincible procedure in judgment when, undeterred and unhindered by the opposition of man or devil, with glowing and flashing feet He treads down all the enemies of righteousness. "He treadeth the winepress of the fierceness and wrath of Almighty God" (Revelation 19:15). It is an awe-inspiring picture of God's irresistible and terrible judgment on rebellious man, and it is the Son of Man whose feet had walked unsullied through the corruption of the world, through whom it is effected. He will execute *perfect judgment.*

"*His voice* as the sound of many waters" (v. 15; Ezekiel 43:2). "The voice of his words like the voice of a multitude." What is more impressive than the roar of Niagara in full spate or a vast crowd in full throat? Such is the voice of Christ, inescapable, authoritative, commanding all men and nations. The same voice that once uttered the sweet invitation "Come unto Me" now resounds like the roar of a mighty cataract. As that loud, reverberating voice fell on John's ear, it was like the mighty waves that pounded Patmos's rocky shores—symbolic of the terribleness of the voice with which He will rebuke and sentence His foes within the church and without. There is a unique finality in the voice of Christ, for no word He spoke ever needed to be recalled. H. B. Swete remarks that the voice of God is not confined to one note. It can be terrible as the surge of the sea, or it can be the voice of gentle stillness, majestic in rebuke or tender in comfort. This is the voice of *perfect authority.*

"He had in *his right hand* seven stars" (v. 16). "The seven stars are the seven angels"—messengers or pastors—"of the seven churches" (v. 20). Christ is represented as holding in His powerful right hand the destiny of the churches. Any authority possessed by these messengers to the churches is derived from Him. He holds and upholds them and they are accountable to Him. He is the Possessor and Upholder of the churches, their Guardian and Sustainer, and the pastors whom He gives to them are secure in His powerful grasp. In the next verse, which records John falling at the feet of the majestic Christ, this same right hand is placed upon his head in reassurance. How safe the messengers to the church are under His *perfect control*!

"Out of *his mouth* went a sharp, two-edged sword" (v. 16). The interpretation of this symbol is found in Hebrews 4:12 (ASV): "The word of God is living, and active, and sharper than any two-edged sword . . . quick to discern the thoughts and intents of the heart"—truth piercing, dividing, discerning. The penetrating quality of the Word of Christ, the accuracy of His judgment and diagnosis of the deeds of men is in view, for the words which proceed from His mouth are to be the basis of all future judgment. "The word that I have spoken, the same shall judge him in the last day" (John 12:48). The power of the Word of Christ to reprove and punish is more prominent here than its power to convert, for the sword is the emblem of His judicial authority and power. It cuts into lives, lays bare sin, excises what should not be there, and destroys all that is not for the glory of God in the church. In His judgment Christ manifests *perfect discrimination.*

"*His countenance* was as the sun shineth in his strength" (v. 16). The countenance is the sum total of all the features. His entire appearance was like the sun at noon, shining in unclouded strength, too intense for the naked human eye. Was John recallingthe vision on the Mount of Transfiguration when "His face did shine as the sun"? The face which John saw now in vision was not "a visage marred more than any man's" but one that blazed with unbearable brightness, leaving an impression of dazzling splendor and awe-full majesty. The pastors are stars. The churches are lamps. Christ is the majestic Sun. Just as the sun is the supreme light-giver to the world, so Christ is the supreme Light-giver to the spiritual world. "And the city had no need of the sun, neither of the moon, to shine in it: for the glory of God did lighten it, and the Lamb is the light thereof" (Revelation 21:23). His countenance mirrors His perfect *moral glory.*

HIS UNIQUE PREROGATIVES

The effect of the vision on John was overwhelming. "When I saw him, I fell at his feet as dead" (v. 17). The vision of God always produces humiliation and prostration. John fell in awed worship and conscious unworthiness before the majesty of Him who is the effulgence of the Father's glory, the exact impress of His person (Hebrews 1:3).

Could this majestic, stupendous Personage be the same as the meek and lowly Man on whose breast he had laid his head? Yes, the heart that beats beneath the golden girdle is the same heart. The hands that control the seven stars are the same nail-pierced hands. The eyes that flash fire once wept tears of compassion over doomed Jerusalem. The voice has the same sweet cadences as moved the soldiers to say, "Never man spake like this man." The glowing feet are the very same feet as carried His bleeding body up the slopes of Mount Calvary. The mouth, out of which went the two-edged sword, once framed the invitation, "Come unto me . . . I will give you rest." The radiant countenance is the same as was once "marred more than any man."

But the real purpose of the vision was to encourage and strengthen John, not to terrify him. "He laid his right hand upon me, saying unto me, Fear not; I am the first and the last. . . . I am alive for evermore, Amen; and have the keys of hell and of death" (vv. 17–18). "I am Alpha and Omega, the beginning and the ending" (v. 8). This compassionate touch and further self-revelation of the Lord was sufficient to raise John to his feet and to reassure him. The nail-pierced hand, strong enough to uphold the universe, was gentle enough to comfort and impart strength to a prostrate, humbled worshiper.

HIS UNIQUE ASSERTIONS

In this vision our Lord made five unique assertions concerning Himself which afforded adequate grounds to dispel John's fears.

"I am Alpha and Omega" (vv. 8, 11), an assertion of the eternity of His Godhead. He is the God of all history, its beginning, its end, and the whole course in between, even as between the first and last letters of the Greek alphabet lies every possible form of speech. He is the perfect, complete, and eternal revelation of God. "In Christ, Genesis, the

Alpha of the Old Testament, and Revelation, the Omega of the New Testament, meet together: the last book presenting to us man and God reconciled in Paradise, as the first book presented man at the beginning, innocent and in God's favor in Paradise" (Jamieson).

"I am the beginning and the ending . . . the first and the last" (vv. 8, 11; cf. Isaiah 44:6). All things began with Him and all things will end with Him. He is the origin and goal of all creation. He is first, because before Him there was no God, and last, because after Him there will be no other. He is both Author and Finisher of faith. He is with us at birth; He will be with us at death.

"I am he that liveth and was dead" (v. 18), expressing the vivid contrast between the eternal life inherent in Christ and His voluntary surrender to the powers of death. Because He tasted death, He is able to say to death-ridden mankind, "There is no need to fear death. I have trodden that way, exhausted its power, and extracted its sting."

"I am alive for evermore" (v. 18), unto the ages of the ages. Death could not keep its prey. He now lives "in the power of an endless life." Others, like Lazarus, had returned to life only to die again. He rose from the dead and is alive forever. His having passed through death as a man and now living in fullness of life is basis for our confidence, since through Him death is but the gateway to fuller life. To a church facing the possibility of martyrdom, this truth was urgently needed to quell fear. "The church could not live if Christ were dead, but because Christ lives, the church cannot die."

"I have the keys of hell and of death" (v. 18), wrested in His resurrection from "him that hath the power of death,

the devil." Hades is conceived in Matthew 16:18 as a prison-house or walled city. It is the unseen world to which death is the portal. Keys are the symbol of authority. The keys of the unseen world are in Christ's hand and with them the destiny of all men. We need have no fear of going to any place the keys of which are in His nail-pierced hand. No longer need we fear the grim reaper, the king of terrors. Christ alone admits us to death and opens the way out on the other side. No one can wrest the keys from His control. Because He rose, we shall rise also.

Because this living, majestic, powerful Christ stands in the midst of His churches and holds their destiny in these hands, there is no cause for them or for us to fear.

CHAPTER 9

The Transcendent Worthiness of Christ

Thou art worthy to take the book, and to open the seals thereof: for thou wast slain.
REVELATION 5:9

Worthy is the Lamb that was slain to receive power, and riches,and wisdom, and strength, and honor, and glory, and blessing.
REVELATION 5:12

Reading: REVELATION 5:1–14

For more than forty years Samuel Chadwick, noted Methodist preacher, commenced each Lord's Day by reading this thrilling chapter. It might well be thought that continual reading would rob the passage of all inspirational power. But not so, and for two reasons. First, because of the inherent vitality of Scripture when illuminated by the Holy Spirit and applied by a sanctified imagination. Second, because in the vision of the ultimate and absolute triumph of Christ over all opposition, he found ever new inspiration for life and service. We, too, can kindle our heart's adoration at the same altar fire and in the strength of that vision fulfill the appointed task.

THE VISION OF THE LAMB

"I beheld, and lo, in the midst of the throne and of the four beasts [living creatures], and in the midst of the elders, stood a Lamb as it had been slain" (v. 6). John the Seer is introduced to a moving and majestic heavenly scene (4:1). A book or scroll, sealed with seven seals, rests in the right hand of Him who is seated on the throne. A mighty angel loudly challenges heaven and earth and hell to produce a champion qualified to break open the sealed scroll. In the breathless silence John anxiously scans the assembled myriads for the emergence of his champion. But there is not a stir. No volunteer appears. At last, overcome with dismay, he bursts into uncontrollable weeping because there is no one good enough to look on the scroll, much less to open it.

What is the seven-sealed scroll in which this cosmic crisis centers? Numerous interpretations of its significance have been advanced, for God has more than one book.

Is it *the sealed scroll of Holy Scriptures*? The Old Testament is undoubtedly a closely sealed book unless interpreted in the light of the advent and cross of Christ. To the Jews it is still sealed because they refuse to see Christ in it. How inscrutable are its mysteries without His cross and passion, but how open its message when He is seen on every page!

Is it *the sealed scroll of God's eternal purpose,* His final disposition of the affairs of the universe? The Lamb alone is qualified to interpret and disclose the mind and purpose of God and carry it forward to completion.

Is it *the sealed scroll of the covenant* between God and man which Christ fulfilled in His death, and by right of which He controls the destiny of the world and of the church?

Is it *the sealed scroll of history,* explaining the past and expounding the future? Apart from Christ, history is without final meaning, for real history is the history of redemption. History is His story. John was perplexed to find a satisfying interpretation of the history of his own times with its persecution, trial, and death. What were its meaning and issue? He discovers that the Lamb is the only interpreter of history, the only key to prophecy. He alone can authoritatively tell man where he is going.

De Brugh advances one of the most satisfying suggestions. The sealed scroll is *the title deed to man's inheritance*—an inheritance mortgaged through man's sin but redeemed through the sacrifice of the Lamb. In the scroll are outlined the successive steps by which He will recover it from the usurper and obtain actual possession of the kingdom already purchased for Himself and His elect.

It is significant that the most majestic vision of John's long life came to him when his eyes were wet with tears of conscious unworthiness. His distress was increased by the shattering realization that his disqualification was shared by all creation. "No man was found worthy"—morally fit, sufficiently strong—"to open and to read the book, neither to look thereon" (v. 4). He shared the dilemma of God in dealing with men who are utterly incapable of saving themselves. But God has His own solution for the dilemma.

"Stop weeping," the angel tells John. "Someone is approaching the Throne." But has he the necessary qualifications?

John is told that the champion is the Lion of the tribe of Judah. Turning to see the awesome Lion he sees a little Lamb encrimsoned with the blood of sacrifice. Christ is announced as the Lion but seen as the Lamb. Redemption is won by self-sacrifice, not by mere might. The Lamb becomes the focus of every eye as He advances to the Throne. Fearlessly He takes the scroll and breaks seal after seal. He alone can redeem man's forfeited inheritance, to which the scroll is the title deed. And His qualifications? Five wounds, mute evidence that He has paid the price of man's lost inheritance and discharged the mortgage.

This is an impressive picture of Christ—still bearing in Heaven the marks of His suffering and death, but evidencing also His divine prerogatives and attributes. The seven horns symbolize His omnipotence and the seven eyes His omniscience. The seven spirits sent out into all the earth are emblematic of His omnipresence.

As the Lamb takes the now-discharged mortgage deed, the assembled hosts burst into a spontaneous and unrestrained song of adoration, swelling to a crescendo in three ascending waves. Ten thousand times ten thousand and thousands of thousands of angels join the four living creatures and the twenty-four elders who raise the tune. The song swells louder and louder until "every creature that is in heaven, and on earth and under the earth, and such as are in the sea and all that are in them"—the universal chorus of creation—is drawn into this exulting paean of praise.

> Thou art worthy to take the book, and to open the seals thereof: for thou wast slain, and hast redeemed us to

> God by thy blood out of every kindred, and tongue, and people, and nation; and hast made us unto our God kings and priests: and we shall reign on the earth. . . .
>
> Worthy is the Lamb that was slain to receive power, and riches, and wisdom, and strength, and honor, and glory and blessing. . . . Blessing and honor, and glory, and power, be unto him that sitteth upon the throne, and unto the Lamb for ever and ever. (Revelation 5:9–10, 12–13)

"The final vision of the universe," writes William Barclay, "is a universe praising Christ; and it is our privilege to lend our voices and our lives to this vast chorus of praise, for that chorus is necessarily incomplete so long as there is one voice missing from it."

THE ASCRIPTION OF WORTHINESS

We are by nature essentially selfish beings. And even after we have been made partakers of the Divine nature, so strong is the power of the old life that we are usually more interested in receiving than in giving. Was not our Lord's ninth beatitude, "It is more blessed to give than to receive," a tacit correction of this tendency? In our relationship with God we are constantly at the receiving end. We commence our Christian life by receiving the atonement (Romans 5:11). We continue our Christian life by receiving the abundance of grace (Romans 5:17). We conclude our Christian life by being received into glory (1 Timothy 3:16). We are constantly tugging at God's skirts for some desired blessing, and He delights to have it so, but we forget that He too yearns to receive from us what we alone can give Him.

In one sense we cannot enrich Christ. But nothing is more gladdening to Him than the spontaneous voicing of our appreciation of His intrinsic worth, and nothing is more enriching to ourselves, for "it is in the process of being worshiped that God communicates His presence to men." Writing in this connection, C. S. Lewis says,

> To see what the doctrine really means, we must suppose ourselves to be in perfect love with God—drunk with, drowned in, dissolved by that delight which, far from remaining pent up within ourselves as incommunicable, hence hardly tolerable bliss, flows out from us incessantly again in effortless and perfect expression, our joy no more separable from the praise in which it liberates and utters itself than the brightness of a mirror is separable from the brightness it sheds. The Scottish catechism says that man's chief end is "to glorify God and to enjoy Him forever." But we shall then know that these are the same thing. Fully to enjoy is to glorify. In commanding us to glorify Him, God is inviting us to enjoy Him.

The perspective of eternity apparently corrects the outlook of the saints, for the universal throng sings with one voice, "Worthy is the Lamb *to receive* . . ." Then follows a sevenfold ascription of worthiness. These seven qualities are grouped under the single Greek article, as though to sum up in one glorious word all that can be given to the Lamb by men and angels.

THE HEPTAD OF PRAISE

The Lamb is worthy to receive:

Power. The French nation deemed Napoleon worthy to receive unlimited power. The German nation entrusted Hitler with unrestricted power. They discovered too late that their confidence was sadly misplaced. To their cost they proved the truth of Lord Acton's assertion: "Power tends to corrupt. Absolute power corrupts absolutely." These men were unworthy either to receive power or to exercise it. Only He who is all merciful is worthy to receive absolute power. The indelible marks of His passion and death are the guarantee that in His hands power will never be abused. It will never degenerate into tyranny or despotism. The scepter of universal sovereignty is held in a nail-pierced hand. The Lamb is worthy to receive power.

Riches. Although appointed heir of all things, Christ certainly did not receive riches during His earthly life. On the contrary, at times He had not anywhere to lay His head. He often depended on the women of his entourage for support. So poor was He that at His death His total personal estate consisted of the single garment left Him by the gambling soldiers. Small wonder Paul used His voluntary impoverishment to stimulate Corinthian liberality. "Ye know the grace of our Lord Jesus Christ," he exhorted, "that though he was rich, yet for your sakes he became poor, that ye through his poverty might be rich." True riches are moral and spiritual, not financial. "Love is the gold of glory." The unloved rich man is tragically poverty-stricken. Our Lord's becoming poor consisted in His leaving the harmony of Heaven for the discord of earth, the adoration of angels for the malignity of men. The Lamb has earned the right to receive and enjoy the true riches.

Wisdom. Not every learned man is a wise man. Wisdom is more than erudition. It is the ability to make the right use of knowledge. In his youth Solomon prayed for wisdom and his prayer was answered. When the queen of Sheba had seen all Solomon's wisdom, she said to the king, "Behold, the half was not told me: thy wisdom and prosperity exceedeth the fame which I heard" (1 Kings 10:7). Using the background of this very incident Christ said of Himself, "Behold, a greater than Solomon is here" (Matthew 12:42). Christ is the wisdom of God, the source and fount of all true wisdom (1 Corinthians 1:24).His infinite knowledge is always used for the highest and most beneficent ends. In His humiliation the wise men brought Him their gifts. In His exaltation the highest wisdom given is expressed in placing upon His head the crown of wisdom. The Lamb is worthy to receive wisdom.

Strength. There is a difference between physical and moral strength. Samson had physical strength but not moral strength. Physically powerful, he was morally and spiritually weak. Moral strength is the highest strength. The strength of the Lamb is full-orbed. He is the Strong Man who overcame the devil and spoiled his goods (Luke 11:22). There was no personal situation with which He did not cope. He manifested not only power to achieve, but also strength to endure. In the face of stupendous tests He revealed unparalleled spiritual strength. Who else ever "endured such contradiction of sinners"? Once crucified in weakness and shame, He is now robed in strength and majesty. We join the angels in ascribing to Him strength.

Honor. Honors in the realm of art or literature, music or science, sport or war are eagerly sought and highly prized. They are bestowed in just recognition of services rendered or excellence attained. But whose accomplishments can match the achievements of the Lamb? Who but He has redeemed from destruction men of every kindred and tongue and people and nation? True, on earth He experienced the deepest depths of dishonor in His death between two criminals. True, He refused to receive honor from men (John 5:44). But an adoring universe delights to ascribe to Him the honor He is worthy to receive.

Glory. This word is easier to illustrate than to define. It is something which belongs to God alone. It combines the ideas of splendor, radiance, renown. The noonday sun blinds us with the blaze of its glory. "We beheld his glory," wrote John of his vision of Christ on the Mount of Transfiguration when "his face did shine as the sun, and his raiment was white as the light" (Matthew 17:2). Of the same incident Peter wrote, "We . . . were eyewitnesses of his majesty" (2 Peter 1:16). The vision John had of Christ on Patmos was of One whose "countenance was as the sun shineth in his strength" (Revelation 1:16). John was yet to see the sun pale before the transcendent glory of the Lamb, for in Immanuel's land "the city had no need of the sun, neither of the moon, to shine in it: for the glory of God did lighten it, and the Lamb is the light thereof" (Revelation 21:23). The Lamb is worthy to receive glory.

Blessing. Blessing is ascribed praise, a wish or prayer for happiness and success. It is the will to return thankful praise for favors received. "It is the one gift that we who have nothing can give to Him who possesses all." The least we can do is to return praise for blessings conferred. Although we cannot enrich the Lamb, we can rejoice His heart by blessing His name. Limited though our concept of His glories may be, we can join the psalmist in his ascription of praise: "Bless the LORD, O my soul: and all that is within me, bless his holy name" (Psalm 103:1).

But so magnanimous is the Lamb that while He graciously accepts our ascription to Him of these seven qualities, He refuses to enjoy them alone. He must share them with all who are united to Him by faith and love. All that He is, He is for us. All that He has, He shares with us.

Do we ascribe *power* to Him who has been given "all power in heaven and on earth"? Then He assures us, "Behold, I give unto you power . . . over all the power of the enemy" (Luke 10:19). Or *riches*? "He became poor, that ye through his poverty might be rich" (2 Corinthians 8:9). Or *wisdom*? "Christ . . . is made unto us wisdom" (1 Corinthians 1:30). Or *strength*? "I can do all things through Christ which strengtheneth me," testified Paul (Philippians 4:13). Or *glory*? "The glory which thou gavest me I have given them" (John 17:22). Or *honor*? "Them that honor me I will honor" (1 Samuel 2:30). Or *blessing*? He "hath blessed us with all spiritual blessings" (Ephesians 1:3). "Bless the LORD, O my soul."

THE GROUNDS OF THE ASCRIPTION

The Lamb will accept no honors He has not won, and this chapter gives solid grounds for the sevenfold ascription showing it to be our logical act of worship. The late Dr. F. B. Meyer draws attention to five grounds for our ascription of worthiness.

His Sovereignty. "In the midst of the throne stood a Lamb," not sitting, but standing to rule His kingdom. Here Hebrews 2:9 has its fulfillment, "We see Jesus . . . crowned with glory and honor." No longer is He crowned with thorns, despised and rejected of men. In Him humanity has reached the throne of the universe and wields universal power.

The highest place that heaven affords
He holds by sovereign right;
As King of Kings and Lord of Lords
He reigns in glory bright.

His Character. "A Lamb . . . , having seven horns and seven eyes." No symbol occurs more frequently in Scripture than this, and none is more full of sacred significance. The word for "lamb" used here is found often in the Apocalypse, but in no other book is it applied to Christ. "It expresses endearment, the endearing relation in which Christ now stands to us, as the consequence of His previous relation as the sacrificial Lamb. So also our relation to Him" (Jamieson). Though clothed in majesty and glory, the Lamb is not an object of dread. If He has seven horns, symbol of His complete dominion over the world, He has also seven eyes, indicating the watchful care and wise providence of His Spirit over His people. In the Lamb there is a sublime combination of meekness and majesty, of mercy and might.

His Conquest. "The Lion of the tribe of Judah . . . hath prevailed to open the book, and to loose the seven seals thereof." Christ refused to be king by mere sovereign right or innate might as Son of God. He will gain and wear His crown as Son of man. When He stooped to become an infant, "He littered space with the glories He laid aside in His descent."

Hast thou not heard that my Lord Jesus died?
Then let me tell thee a strange story.
The God of power, as He did ride
In His majestic robes of glory
Resolved to light, and so one day
He did descend, undressing all the way.
The stars His tire of light and rings obtained,
The cloud His bow, the fire His spear.
The sky His azure mantle gained.
And when they asked what He would wear,
He smiled and said as He did go,
He had new clothes a-making here below.
—George Herbert

Entering the stream of our humanity and sharing all our sinless infirmities, step-by-step He fought His way back to the Throne. He was opposed at every step by the prince of darkness and his hosts. He went down to the grave, but He "death by dying slew." On the third day He returned, the keys of death and hell hanging at His girdle. He conquered once and for all every power of evil.

His Sacrifice. "Thou art worthy . . . *for thou wast slain*, and hast redeemed us to God by thy blood out of every kindred, and tongue, and people, and nation." "It is not the Lion of the tribe of Judah," wrote W. M. Clow, "not the Lamb in His innocence and undisfigured beauty who takes the fast-closed book and breaks the seals, but the Lamb slaughtered. It is

Christ in and by His cross who opens the book of God, gives the interpretation of the record and sets the hidden mysteries of providence and grace in clear light."

In the midst of the glories of Heaven, Christ crucified is central. We shall never be allowed to forget that we were not redeemed with shining silver or yellow gold, but with crimson drops of precious blood. The sentence pronounced on the first Adam was, "Thou shalt surely die." This sentence was exhausted on the last Adam: "Thou wast slain." His costly sacrifice was the climax of His glory, and because of it an adoring universe joins in an unending paean of praise.

His Achievement. "Thou hast made us unto our God kings and priests, and we shall reign on the earth." As the sacrificial Lamb He delivered us from the guilt and consequences of our sin. As the conquering Lion He met Satan in open conflict and defeated and disarmed him. He conquered sin and death and hell. He regained His throne but He is unwilling to occupy it alone. He must share it with those He has redeemed. So He constitutes His people kings and priests—each a king who reigns with Him, each a priest ordained to offer the sacrifices of praise and thanksgiving continually. Small wonder that when the slain Lamb took the book and broke the seals, they sang a new song, a song in which we can and must join:

Come, let us sing the song of songs,
The saints in heaven began the strain,
The homage which to Christ belongs,
Worthy the Lamb, for He was slain.
—James Montgomery

CHAPTER 10

The Unfinished Work of Christ

He ever liveth to make intercession.

HEBREWS 7:25

Reading: HEBREWS 5:1–6; 7:22–8:1

Without Christ's unfinished work—His intercession at the Father's right hand—the benefits of His finished work on the cross would never have reached us. The vast importance of that finished work can be gauged by the seemingly disproportionate space devoted in the Gospel records to the events surrounding His death. But Christ's costly work on Calvary would have been stillborn apart from the descent of the Holy Spirit at Pentecost and the presence of the Lord in Heaven. His unfinished ministry of intercession in Heaven is the capstone of His finished work on earth.

The heart of man, whether pagan or civilized, has ever craved a priest, a mediator who could represent him before his God. There seems to be a universal sense of a God who has been offended and must be appeased. There is the instinctive feeling that the one to set things right must be someone with compassion for human frailty and yet who has some special influence with God. In the dawn of history Job lamented, "Neither is there any daysman betwixt us, that might lay his hand upon us both" (9:33). This longing has resulted in the creation of orders of priests who men hoped could mediate with God on their behalf. Human priesthood reached its zenith in Judaism, but how imperfect a priesthood! Only in Christ, the Great High Priest, does this deep-seated yearning of humanity find complete satisfaction.

HIS QUALIFICATIONS AS HIGH PRIEST

The indispensable qualifications of the Jewish high priest were two. First, he must have *fellowship with man*, be linked to him by the ties of a common humanity. He must be "taken from among men" (Hebrews 5:1). Only thus would he be able to have compassion on those he was to represent. He must be "able to have a moderated feeling" toward them, neither too lenient nor too severe. Compassion is essential to the idea of priesthood.

But human qualifications, though necessary, are not sufficient for such a delicate and exalted office. He must have *authority from God* for his ministry. The appointment must enjoy the divine approval. "No man taketh this honor unto himself, but he that is called of God, as was Aaron" (Hebrews 5:4).

Does Christ meet these requirements? That He might help the race, He became part of it. He was indeed "*taken from among men*" and "in all things . . . made like unto his brethren" (Hebrews 2:17). In order that His identification with man might be complete, He came as a working man, not as a king, but sharing the pinch of poverty and the cark of care. He enjoyed the heights of popularity and suffered the extremes of isolation. But at the same time He received *authority from God.* He was not self-elected, but He was appointed by Him who said to Him, "Thou art my Son. . . . Thou art a priest for ever" (Hebrews 5:5–6).

Christ is morally and spiritually qualified to exercise His priestly ministry of intercession. "He ever liveth to make intercession for them." He "is holy, harmless, undefiled, separate from sinners, and made higher than the heavens" (Hebrews 7:25–26). He was born *holy* and lived a holy life. The word translated "holy" uniformly describes one who faithfully and meticulously does his duty to God. At the close of His life Jesus claimed, "I have glorified thee on the earth: I have finished the work which thou gavest me to do" (John 17:4). He was *harmless*, guileless, never deceived or hurt any man, and was therefore absolutely trustworthy. He was *undefiled*, stainless, free from any blemish which would unfit Him for approach to God. He was *separate from sinners*; not physically, for He constantly moved among them, but morally separate. He was entirely different from them in that while He experienced the full blast of temptations He conquered them all and emerged without sin. He was *made higher than the heavens*, exalted to the right hand of the Majesty on high.

HIS CAPABILITIES AS HIGH PRIEST

In this office Christ earns a triple honor.

He is able to succor. "Wherefore in all things it behoved him to be made like unto his brethren, that he might be a merciful and faithful high priest in things pertaining to God, to make reconciliation for the sins of the people. For in that he himself hath suffered being tempted, he is able to succor them that are tempted" (Hebrews 2:17–18). Being Himself truly human, He is able to meet man on the plane of his need. We are very willing to aid those requiring help, but so often we mourn our utter inability to do so. Our High Priest knows no such limitation. It should be noted that His ability to succor is grounded not in mere pity but in costly propitiation (2:17). Because He has suffered in thus making propitiation for our sins, He is able to succor us in our temptations and is adequate to deal with our sins and rebellion.

He is able to sympathize. We have not a High Priest who is unable to sympathize with our weaknesses (Hebrews 4:15). He never sympathizes with or condones our sin; and sinning man needs an Advocate to keep the way open through restoration. Because He has borne sin's penalty and exhausted its judgment, He is able to cleanse when there is heart confession. Our Lord is able to sympathize with our infirmities and weaknesses, which, though not sins, may easily degenerate into sin. Sympathy is the ability to enter into the experiences of another as if they were one's own. It reaches its highest power where one has suffered the same experiences. Since Christ was "tempted in all points like as we are," and has felt the tremendous pressure of sin upon His own spirit without yielding to its allurement, He is able to enter sympathetically into the experiences of those passing through the fires of testing.

He is able to save. "He is able also to save them to the uttermost that come unto God by him, seeing that he ever liveth to make intercession for them" (Hebrews 7:25). Because He thus lives forever as our Mediator and High Priest, He is able to bring to its final completion the salvation of all who draw near. The use of the present tense indicates "a sustained experience resulting from a continuous practice. 'He is able to be saving those who are continually coming,' i.e., those who make it a regular habit to draw near to God" (A. M. Stibbs).

Save is a spacious word and is used in Scripture in varying senses. In Matthew's Gospel the word is used in four different but closely related senses: deliverance from the power of sin (1:21), deliverance from danger (8:25), deliverance from disease (9:21), and deliverance from the condemnation of God (10:23; 24:13). One expositor suggests that while in Romans salvation is from death, hell, and judgment, in Hebrews it is deliverance from the pressure of things about and within us, from all that obscures the vision of Christ. Our Intercessor is able to save us completely, in the most comprehensive meaning of the term. There is no personal problem to which He is not able to provide the solution, no sin from which He is not able to deliver, no enemy from which He is not able to rescue His trusting child. And why? Because "He ever liveth to make intercession for them." Having offered a complete and perfect sacrifice for sin, He has passed within the veil and appears in the presence of the Father as our Advocate and Intercessor.

AN ILLUSTRATION OF HIS INTERCESSION

"Jesus Christ [is] the same yesterday, and today, and for ever" (Hebrews 13:8). If this is so, we can learn much from His ministry of intercession in the days of His flesh. Intercession is the act of pleading for another. Is it without significance that most of His prayers were intercessory in character? The only occasion on which He asserted His will in prayer was that we might be with Him and behold His glory (John 17:24). Every other prayer of His was intercessory.

Luke records Jesus' moving words to Peter: "Simon, Simon, behold, Satan hath desired to have you [plural, *all you disciples*] that he may sift you as wheat: but I have prayed for thee [singular, *Peter*], that thy faith fail not" (Luke 22:31–32). What a strengthening assurance this is in the light of what ensued. Through His intercession, Peter's faith would not fail. It was intercession anticipating a need of which the subject was entirely unconscious. Peter had no inkling that he was about to be exposed to a fierce attack of Satan. In the event, Peter failed, but his faith did not fail. By this incident our Lord intended to teach that similar intercession was typical of His ministry on behalf of His children.

It is of more than passing interest that two different words are used to describe Christ's ministry as Intercessor, the first of which is illustrated by the above incident. The author of Hebrews speaks of Christ as One "who maketh intercession for us." The term employed here is a picturesque word of rescue by one who "happens on" someone in trouble. It implies *presenting oneself unsought.* When need demands, He who neither slumbers nor sleeps comes to our aid unsought as He did to Peter. The otherword occurs in 1 John 2:1: "We have an advocate with the Father, Jesus Christ the righteous," a paraclete, *one who comes in response to a call* of need or danger. He comes at our call, pleads our cause, and restores us fully. So whether our need is conscious or unconscious, He ever lives to make intercession for us.

THE BASIS OF HIS INTERCESSION

Christ's intercession is grounded in His sacrifice on the cross. The "It is finished" of Calvary provided the basis for His unfinished work of intercession so clearly foreshadowed in the Levitical day of atonement (Leviticus 16). Once a year the high priest entered the Holy of Holies carrying blood and incense. The blood he sprinkled on the mercy seat. The incense he burned before the Lord on the coals in his censer. Even so our great High Priest after His ascension entered within the veil, presented the blood of His own sacrifice, accompanied by the fragrance of a life lived in absolute devotion to God, a sweet-smelling savor. This was *the climax of the incarnation.* Because the God-man, still bearing our humanity, represents us before the Father, we are accepted because of our union with Him, and can draw near to God with holy confidence. His very presence there is an unanswerable plea.

Five bleeding wounds He bears
Received on Calvary.
They pour effectual prayers,
They strongly plead for me.
Forgive him, O forgive, they cry,
Nor let that ransomed sinner die.
—*Charles Wesley*

THE MODE OF HIS INTERCESSION

"It is vain to ask *how*; in detail He thus acts for us," wrote Bishop Moule. "The essence of the matter is His union with

His people and His perpetual presence in that union, with the Father, as the once slain Lamb."

In our thinking, intercession is often associated with tearful supplication or agonizing entreaty. It is sometimes misconceived as a means of overcoming the apparent reluctance of God, but such ideas are entirely foreign to the intercession of Christ. He does not appear as suppliant before a God who must be coaxed into granting the desired boon. He appears as our Advocate, not to appeal for mercy on our behalf, but to claim justice for us—what we are entitled to in virtue of His sacrifice, what He has secured for us by His cross—from a God who is "faithful and just to forgive us our sins."

His intercession is not vocal. It is not an audible saying of prayers. In his great annual act of intercession, Aaron uttered not one word. The silence of the sanctuary was broken only by the tinkling of the golden bells on the hem of his robe. On the day of atonement it was the blood that spoke, not Aaron. It is the presence of our Intercessor, bearing in His body the evidence of His victory, that speaks for us.

Amintas was convicted of crimes against the Roman state and was being tried for treason. Hearing of his plight, his elder brother Aeschylus, who had lost an arm in the service of his country, hastened to the court. Bursting into the room he lifted his arm stump and, catching the eye of the judge, he said, "Amintas is guilty, but for Aeschylus' sake he shall go free." The judge acquitted him. Even so our Intercessor presents the tokens of His sufferings, and the Judge says of us, "They are guilty, but for My Son's sake they shall go free."

Jesus my great High Priest offered His blood and died;
My guilty conscience seeks no sacrifice beside:
His powerful blood did once atone,
And now it pleads before the throne.

His intercession is in perpetuity as He represents us before the throne of God. "Now to appear in the presence of God for us." On the cross He died to obtain salvation for us. Before the throne He lives to maintain us in salvation. Is not this the significance of the statement, "We shall be saved by his [risen] life" (Romans 5:10)? We could not hold out for a day in the Christian life were it not that He lives for us now to impart to us "all things that pertain unto life and godliness."

He receives and presents our prayers, mingling with our imperfect petitions the incense of His own merits. "There was given unto him much incense, that he should offer it with the prayers of all saints upon the golden altar which was before the throne" (Revelation 8:3). The prayers of all saints, passing as they do through the mind and heart of One who is always in harmony with the will and purposes of the Father, become His own as He presents them. Our prayers of faith do not ascend alone, they are steeped in His merits and because of that are mightily effectual.

To all our prayers and praises,
Christ adds His sweet perfume,
And love the altar raises
These odors to consume.

His intercession is personal. "He ever liveth to make intercession for us." This is His personal present occupation. He does not delegate this ministry to Gabriel. He discharges it Himself. He is never too busy to personally care for our concerns. As on earth, so in heaven, He is still One who serves.

Our need of His intercession is unremitting. H. de Vries writes in this connection,

> There is an impression among some believers that our Lord's intercession is required only when we are in extreme need or danger as Peter was when Satan desired to sift him as wheat, for then it was that Jesus prayed for him that his faith should not fail. And this would be correct if our Lord's intercession were like the city fire department which is called upon for help only when the house is on fire. The fact is that our house is always on fire and therefore always in need of His intercession. There is not a moment when we are not in need or danger, and therefore our Lord liveth evermore to make intercession for us. His intercession never ceases and is always prevailing. The very extent of our need and helplessness is the only limit to His intercession.

What confidence it should give us to know that at this very moment our great High Priest, One who knows our weakness and enters into our feelings, One who has passed through all phases of human life, is now appearing in the presence of God *for us*, able to keep in temptation, comfort in sorrow, succor in weakness. The realization of this glorious truth impelled the writer of Hebrews to sum up his treatise on the High Priesthood in these words:

"Now in connexion with what we have been saying *the chief point is that we have a High Priest* who has taken His seat at the right hand of the throne of God's Majesty in the heavens, and ministers in the Holy place" (Hebrews 8:1 WNT), a ministry which will continue as long as our need remains.

CHAPTER 11

Christ's Ideal of Character

Blessed are the poor in spirit.
MATTHEW 5:3

Reading: MATTHEW 5:1–11

In striking contrast to the thunderings and threatenings of the law, the manifesto of Christ's kingdom commences with a benediction. Blessedness is the keynote. And yet the pathway to this blessedness leads His followers through strange and unexpected territory. In a few concise and vivid word pictures Jesus outlines the ideal life, an ideal which was a reflection of the supremely attractive life He lived among men. He was the embodiment and example of His own lofty teaching in this pungent and penetrating sermon.

Jesus was an authority on blessedness. He was the blessed man depicted in Psalm 1 and was therefore qualified to reveal the qualities and attitudes of which this blessedness was the reward. How different they are from what one would expect—poverty, mourning, hunger, thirst, reviling, persecution. There must surely be some mistake, for how can these bring blessedness? It is a common idea that blessedness flows from the possession of wealth, the absence of sorrow, the gratification of appetite, being well spoken of and kindly treated. Christ's teaching cut right across this popular concept of happiness and indicated that the very experiences we are eager to avoid are the ones conducive to the deepest joy and most to be coveted.

"Blessed" is a word which has been ennobled by its use in the New Testament. It is derived from the Greek "to speak well of," and is akin to our word "happy" which in English etymology goes back to hap, chance, good luck. Originally it was used of Greek gods and men, but connoted largely outward prosperity. Jesus invested the word with a new dimension, giving it the sense of spiritual prosperity which is the outcome of pure character and a correct sense of values. It has been variously translated as "to be envied, to be congratulated, to be superlatively happy, to be spiritually prosperous, to be enviably fortunate, to be radiantly joyous."

Of the eight characteristics with their compensations which He listed, the first four relate to *our attitude to God* and the last four to *our attitude to our fellow men.* The first group are passive personal qualities, the second active social qualities. In his relations with his God, the superlatively happy person is conscious of:

A SENSE OF INADEQUACY

"Blessed are the poor in spirit: for theirs is the kingdom of heaven." Note, poor in spirit, not poor-spirited. Not merely diffident, but renounced in spirit. He is emptied of self-reliance. There is no hint of self-sufficiency. He considers himself insignificant. With Paul he confesses, "I know that in me . . . dwelleth no good thing."

It was the habit of Principal Cairns, the Scottish theologian, to say, "You first, I follow." Once on approaching the platform a great burst of applause greeted him. He stood aside and let the man behind him go first and began himself to applaud. He never dreamed the applause could be for him! Such is the blessed man.

It is significant that there are two words translated "poor." One refers to a laborer who is poor by reason of his circumstances, the other to a beggar who is poor by choice. The laborer has nothing superfluous; the beggar has nothing at all. It is the latter word, suggesting spiritual destitution, which is employed here. To be a beggar in spirit, to be bankrupt on the grace of God is an attitude to covet. The man of the world is proud of his independence and self-reliance. The blessed man, like his Master, confesses, "I can of mine own self do nothing." The typical attitude of the beggar is seen in Acts 3:5: "He gave heed unto them, *expecting to receive something of them.*" This man is broken of pride, and his sense of inadequacy for the demands of life, his consciousness of having empty hands, throws him back on the illimitable resources of God. His attitude is the complete antithesis of that of the Laodiceans who boasted, "I am rich, and increased with goods, and have need of nothing." Such poverty inevitably leads to spiritual affluence. Though himself poor, the blessed man makes many rich. He may not be a success by earthly standards but he enjoys the kingdom of Heaven.

A SENSE OF CONTRITION

"Blessed are they that mourn: for they shall be comforted." It is not the sorrow itself that is a blessed thing, but rather the comfort which God ministers to the sorrowing. There can be no comfort where there is no grief. "The man who knows nothing of sorrow is incomplete. One side of his nature has not been developed," wrote Archbishop Harrington Lees. "The happiness of the Gospel message is that it alone professedly deals with the common lot of sorrow, and gives the oil of joy for mourning. This is its initial undertaking: its final guarantee is 'no sorrow, nor crying.'"

The word "mourn" indicates a sorrow which begins in the heart, takes possession of the whole person, and is outwardly manifested. The special form of sorrow envisaged in this word is sorrow over spiritual failure or actual sin. The sense of spiritual poverty, of lukewarmness toward God, of distance from Him, of unlikeness to Christ inevitably leads to regret and contrition. The boasting and self-sufficient Pharisee did not mourn or beat his breast like the penitent publican, nor did he enjoy the experience of justification. The prodigal first recognized his abject poverty: "I perish with hunger"; then in true contrition he acknowledged his sin: "Father, I have sinned." It was only when Job had a vision of God that he said in deep self-abasement, "I abhor myself and repent in dust and ashes." He mourned over what might have been had he not been self-satisfied.

The paradoxical thing about this mourning is that it is not incompatible with rejoicing. Paul claimed to be sorrowful yet always rejoicing. The enjoyment of the comfort which God imparts to the contrite spirit is another of the ingredients of the superlatively happy life.

A SENSE OF MODESTY

"Blessed are the meek: for they shall inherit the earth." Meekness is not an invertebrate virtue, says one writer. It is not weakness or mere mildness of disposition, for our Lord claimed it as an element of His character, to be emulated by His disciples. Moses was meek (Numbers 12:3), but he certainly was not weak. It is the gentleness of strength in reserve, not of effeminacy. Meekness can fight with strength and vigor when the glory of God or the interests of the kingdom are at stake. It was the meek and lowly Jesus who with an upraised whip of cords expelled the mercenary traders from His Father's house. Nor is meekness mere good-naturedness which will take anything from anybody. Essentially it is that attitude of mind which does not insist on its own rights and is always ready to waive its privileges in the interests of others. It is always ready to renounce its own plans and to joyously embrace God's plans. Nietzsche preached that the world is ours if we can get it. Jesus preached that the world is ours if we *renounce* it; it is the meek, not the aggressive, who inherit the earth.

Of all qualities of character, meekness is probably the one least coveted. But Jesus extols it as a grace highly esteemed by God. "The ornament of a meek and quiet spirit, which is in the sight of God of great price" (1 Peter 3:4). The meek person is generally regarded as too good to make his way or count for much. Jesus refutes this concept by stating that it is he who inherits the earth. He is characterized too by a willingness to yield to others when principle is not at stake. He claims nothing, but the whole earth is his.

A SENSE OF DESIRE

"Blessed are they which do hunger and thirst after righteousness: for they shall be filled." One version renders it, "Blessed are they that are starving for righteousness, for they shall be crammed full." Jesus used these elemental human instincts to illustrate the passionate desire for holiness and likeness to Christ which commands the full response of God. These are the most intense and agonizing human appetites when denied satisfaction. When Sir Ernest Shackleton and his party were left without food for some time during one of their journeys in the Antarctic, he said it was extremely difficult to think of anything else but food. The person who has an unquenchable thirst and insatiable hunger for a holy life is one to be envied. Blessed starvation!

As pants the hart for cooling streams
When heated in the chase,
So pants my soul for Thee, my God,
And Thy redeeming grace.

It is noteworthy that the beatitude does not speak of hungering and thirsting after *happiness*. Happiness is the object of pursuit of the vast bulk of mankind, but generally it proves only an elusive mirage. Jesus teaches here that when a man makes the primary object of his pursuit not happiness but *righteousness*—a right relationship with God—he obtains superlative happiness to boot. "They shall be filled"—to repletion, both here and hereafter. "He satisfieth the longing soul, and filleth the hungry soul with goodness" (Psalm 107:9).

From indicating the ideal attitude of the subjects of His kingdom toward God, Jesus turns to their social relationships with their fellows. The person who is spiritually prosperous exhibits a fourfold disposition in testing circumstances—"strength with weakness at its mercy, purity in contact with defiling company, love which sees others at variance, rectitude suffering at the hands of tormentors. Each has its own beatitude, the fruit of a work of Divine grace."

A COMPASSIONATE SPIRIT

"Blessed are the merciful: for they shall obtain mercy." This beatitude has been correctly described as a self-acting law of the moral world. It is the man who shows mercy who receives mercy. We reap what we sow. It is possible for a man to hunger and thirst after righteousness, but for his righteousness to be hard and exacting. That quaint evangelist, Sam Jones, used to say that righteousness without mercy results in the indigestion countenance.

Like meekness, mercy is a distinctively Christian virtue which was little known among the non-Christian people. It has its source in a compassionate feeling and is expressed in the compassionate act. Mercy is shown to those who have no claim on it. If they have a claim to mercy, then it is only justice they receive. The man of a compassionate spirit is always ready to make allowances for those who have failed, or to put the best construction on ambiguous behavior. He does not judge harshly, remembering that he is not in possession of all the facts. We do well to bear in mind that our experience is only the rebound of our attitude. Mercy knows no retaliation.

A CLEAN HEART

"Blessed are the pure in heart: for they shall see God." The beatific vision is vouchsafed on earth only to those of pure heart. Purity here is an exclusive term employed in its widest meaning—purity of thought, imagination, motive, act. It signifies moral holiness or integrity, and refers especially to one who is without guile. Jesus bypassed mere external and ceremonial purity and enforced the absolute necessity of inner purity. Outward conformity to ceremonial requirements satisfies the heart of neither God nor man.

"Create in me a clean heart, O God," pleaded David in contrition, deeply conscious of his impurity and sin against his fellow men. The psalmist connected clean hands with a pure heart, recognizing his responsibility in human attitudes and relationships. There is no such thing as clearness of vision where there is not cleanness of heart. Too many are satisfied with outward presentability. They do not mind minor deviations from the path of moral rectitude so long as they can evade "losing face" with their own circle. The divine dictum is, "Without holiness no man shall see the Lord" (see Hebrews 12:14 KJV). There is a daily need of self-examination and appropriation of the cleansing of the blood of Christ.

To see God involves moral rather than physical vision, for God is Spirit. Sin beclouds the heart and obscures the face of God. To see God is to know God, to enjoy intimate fellowship with Him. Hypocrisy and insincerity are ruled out if one is to see God in this sense. With Christ in the heart as the indwelling fountain of purity, the maintenance of a clean heart becomes a glorious possibility. When this is experienced, it is possible to anticipate here on earth the day when we shall see Him face-to-face.

A CONCILIATORY MINISTRY

"Blessed are the peacemakers: for they shall be called the children of God." This beatitude is often read as though it referred to peacekeepers—keepers of a peace which was already in existence—or to peaceable men. Instead it refers to the one who makes peace in a situation where that peace has been broken. It is not a virtue, but an activity which is in view. Making peace is a much more costly ministry than maintaining peace. Our Lord "made peace by the blood of his cross." We can make peace only by allowing our own peace to be broken. There is always a cross in this ministry. In the presence of such a person, quarrels and discord die away. It is said of a noted British statesman that when he came into the House, no matter how bitter the debate or wrangling, it always withered away in his presence. And why? He lived in the presence of God. No matter how late the House sat, he always spent two hours in prayer and devotion before embarking on the work of the day. He carried the peace of God with him and radiated it wherever he went. This is a ministry which calls for uncommon courage and insight and tact. But what a ministry it is to bring together those who have been estranged. Paul used all his skill and tact in his endeavor to heal the breach between Euodias and Syntyche, as recorded in his Philippian letter (4:2).

The reward for the peacemaker is not to *become* a child of God but to *be called* a child of God. He is already a child of God. It is not his pedigree but his reputation that is in view.

As people see him going about his costly ministry of bringing peace, they see in him the image of his Master and recognize the family likeness.

A COURAGEOUS LOYALTY

"Blessed are they which are persecuted for righteousness' sake . . . when men shall revile you, and persecute you, and shall say all manner of evil against you falsely, for my sake. Rejoice, and be exceeding glad: for great is your reward in heaven." Even a peacemaker is not immune from the assaults and persecutions of his fellow men. The sinless Christ was not exempt from persecution and reviling. But note that the blessedness does not lie in the persecution or reviling. It is those who *have been persecuted*—for this is the correct tense—who *are* superlatively happy. It is the "afterward" of chastening. The blessedness consists in the joy of the special nearness of Christ in the time of trial. The man who is enviably fortunate, like the three young men in the fiery furnace, discovers that in the midst of the fierce fires of persecution, the Son of God walks with him and the fire does not kindle on him.

It must be observed, however, that all persecution does not bring this blessedness. There are three qualifying conditions. It must be:

Persecution "for righteousness' sake" (v. 10), not because of our own angularity or unwisdom. Many Christians bring unnecessary opprobrium upon themselves and the cause of Christ by their aggressive tactlessness. The persecution in view here comes upon us because we will do right at all costs, even if it results in social ostracism.

Reviling falsely based (v. 11), not which has been deserved. It is reviling which has no justification in either our words or actions which brings blessedness.

Persecution and reviling "for my sake" (v. 11). Ill treatment which arises from our loyalty to Christ and His righteousness will bring its own magnificent reward. The sharing of His sufferings is deeply appreciated by our Master. "Be glad and supremely joyful, for your reward in Heaven is strong, intense." This must have been a strikingly new concept to the Jews, who generally consider suffering and persecution as a curse from God.

Such is our Lord's lofty concept of ideal Christian character. Is it ours? Is it too high? God knows no standard but the character of His own Son. He purposes that we should all be conformed to the image of His Son, and it is the delight of the Holy Spirit to bring this about.

CHAPTER 12

Christ's Terms of Discipleship

Come to me. . . . Come after me. . . .

LUKE 14:26–27

Reading: LUKE 14:25–33

The New Testament is shot through with instruction on discipleship and its implications. It bulked largely in the teaching of our Lord but has been neglected or toned down in the teaching of His church. The reason is not far to seek. No teaching of Christ was more unpopular and unwelcome in His day, and succeeding years have seen little change in the human heart. The terms He laid down for thoroughgoing discipleship were so stringent that the crowds melted away from Him when they perceived its costliness.

Jesus was presented with a unique opportunity of capitalizing on the great popularity He had gained in recent months. "There went great multitudes with him" who hung on His every word. How will He improve this most favorable situation? Will He perform some sensational sign to further excite their curiosity? Will He flatter them to draw out their adulation? Will He offer some special inducement or indulgence to secure their allegiance? Instead, He seemed intent on alienating their sympathy by laying down conditions which appeared unnecessarily hard. A strange type of leadership this, to deliberately discourage those whose support He would surely be anxious to gain! We tend to scale down our demands in order to win the crowd. Jesus purposefully made following Him desperately hard and deliberately thinned the crowd of would-be disciples (see Luke 9:57–62).

In terms unmistakably clear, Christ indicated that being His disciple involved far more than an easy assent to a creed. It would be costly and exacting rather than thrilling and exciting. Instead of representing discipleship as easy and delightful, He emphasized its difficulties and dangers. He spoke more of the foes that would be encountered than of the friends who would be enjoyed. Not of silver slippers and primrose paths, but of rocky roads and shoes of iron. Never did He throw out a bait to secure a recruit, never did He conceal the cost of being His disciple. Everyone who followed Him would do so with eyes wide open. Browning correctly interpreted the teaching of our Lord.

How very hard it is to be a Christian!
Hard for you and me;
Not the mere task of making real
That duty up to its ideal,
Effecting thus, complete and whole,
A purpose of the human soul,
For that is always hard to do.

Dynamic leaders have always been alive to the fact that the finest response is made when the hardest challenge is presented. When Garibaldi was setting out to deliver his country from an invading horde, he encountered a group of idle young fellows and invited them to join him in his crusade. "What do you offer us?" they demanded. "Offer you? I offer you neither pay nor quarters nor provisions. I offer hunger, thirst, forced marches, battle, death. Let him who loves his country in his heart, not with his lips only, follow me." They followed him. The missionary enterprise has always been marked by discomfort and privation, hardship and danger in the noblest of all causes, and yet the imagination of youth has always been captured by the call to sacrifice.

The term "disciple" means "learner." But implicit in the word is the idea of one who learns with the purpose of translating the lessons into action. A Christian disciple is a volunteer learner in the school of Christ. Jesus first invites, "Come unto me," and then follows it with "Come after me." But not all who come to Him for salvation are willing to come after Him in sacrificial service. Though they ought to be, "disciple" and "believer" are not in practice synonymous terms.

J. Edgar Hoover, head of the Federal Bureau of Investigation in Washington, affirmed that Communism always stresses the relationship between theory and action. "To study the Communist 'masters' is to ready oneself for revolutionary action. Communists are not interested in preparing members to parade their Marxist IQs or pass academic examinations. Their knowledge must become a weapon to turn the world upside down for Communism. 'We study,' they say, 'for the sole purpose of putting into practice what we have learned.

It is for the Party and for the victory of the revolution that we study.'" Mr. Hoover pertinently asked, "Are we as Christians adapting to actual practice the teachings of Christ? Are our day to day actions in the secular world determined by our Christian beliefs?"

Why did our Lord make His terms of discipleship so exacting, when the inevitable result would be the loss of popular support? Because He was concerned more with *quality* than with *quantity*. He desired a band of picked men and women, a Gideon's band, on whose unwavering devotion He could count in days of crisis. He wanted trustworthy disciples on whom He could rely when building His church or battling with the powers of evil (Luke 14:29, 31). Once the disciple is convinced of the majesty and the glory of the Christ he follows and of the cause in which he is enlisted, he will be willing for any sacrifice.

Several centuries ago an invading Eastern king whose march had met with unbroken success neared the territory of the young chieftain Abu Taber. Hearing of his valor, the king was reluctant to kill him and instead sent an ambassador with terms of peace. When he heard the proposal, Abu Taber summoned one of his soldiers, handed him a dagger and commanded, "Plunge this into your breast." The soldier obeyed and fell dead at his feet. Calling another he ordered, "Leap over that precipice into the Euphrates." Without a moment's hesitation he leaped to his death. Turning to the ambassador Abu said, "Go, tell your master I have five hundred men like that, and that within twenty-four hours I will have him chained with my dogs." The king with his greatly superior numbers continued his advance, but numbers were of no avail against the fierce loyalty of Abu Taber's devotees. Before a day had passed the king was chained with Abu's dogs. It is quality that is important.

Christianity truly interpreted has never been popular. Indeed, a religion that is popular is far removed from the teaching of our Lord. "Woe unto you, when all men shall speak well of you! For so did their fathers to the false prophets," He warned (Luke 6:26). On the contrary, the Christian is truly blessed when men revile him and say all manner of evil against him falsely for Christ's sake (Matthew 5:11). We are invited to share not His popularity but His unpopularity. "Let us go forth therefore unto him without the camp, bearing his reproach" (Hebrews 13:13). We are to expect that "all who will live godly shall suffer persecution," not enjoy popular favor. We are invited to share "the fellowship of His sufferings" rather than to bask in His reflected glory. If we experience little of the "offense of the cross," it is because we, like Peter, are following Christ "afar off."

With utter sincerity Jesus affirmed, "Strait is the gate, and narrow is the way, which leadeth unto life, and few there be that find it," so we need not be surprised if the way of full discipleship is not crowded. Teaching such as this soon thins the crowd and eliminates the superficial. "As long as the church wore scars," said Vance Havner, "they made headway. When they began to wear medals, the cause languished. It was a greater day for the church when Christians were fed to the lions than when they bought season tickets and sat in the grandstand."

In His discourse, our Lord spoke of "counting the cost." There are two interpretations of this reference. One is that would-be disciples should carefully count the cost before they embark on the exacting road of discipleship. This is of course true, and is emphasized in the three irreducible claims of Christ which are the pith of the paragraph. But there is a strong body of opinion that the only way in which the passage reads logically and coherently is that it is Christ who is the tower builder, Christ who is the campaigning King. It is He who is doing the calculating and counting the cost. Can He afford to use as His builders and soldiers those whose commitment to Him is merely nominal and not sacrificial? The issues involved are so stupendous that He can afford to number me among His disciples only if I comply with His conditions, only if I am willing to follow Him to the death.

He enunciates three indispensable conditions of discipleship.

Touching the heart's affections—an unrivaled love. "If any man come to me, and hate not his father, and mother, and wife, and children, and brethren, and sisters, yea, and his own life also, he *cannot* be my disciple" (v. 26). We can be His disciples only if we love Him better than anyone else. Following Him involves a clash of loyalties. His incoming is divisive. Inevitably there come the contrasting claims of kin and Christ, and in the realm of the heart's affection Christ tolerates no rival.

"Hate" as used here sounds harsh and arbitrary, but the word is used in a relative, not in the absolute sense. It means simply "to love less." The unbalanced zealot will find no excuse here for a lack of natural affection. Jesus does not contradict Himself. There is no conflict between this demand and the command to honor father and mother. In the days when He spoke these words, becoming His disciple involved a man in discord with his family and ostracism by society. In Western lands there is little family or social cost involved, but this is far from the case on the mission fields. Declaring allegiance to Christ may involve a man in the loss of employment, of wife and children, even of life itself. And yet Christ does not scale down His demands.

Jesus was no ruthless iconoclast. He commanded filial and marital and parental love, but He knew that often "a man's foes are they of his own household." The crucial test is, will natural affection prevail over love to Him? In every crisis, love for Him must win the day if we are to be His disciples. The fact is that when He is thus given the preeminent place in our affections, every human relationship is enriched. Because we love Him more, it by no means follows that we will love our own kin less. The reverse is the case.

He further demands that love for Him shall triumph over our instinctive love of ourselves. "Yea, and his own life also." The condition passes over from the family circle to the central citadel of a man's own life. Christ is concerned that our deeply entrenched self-life shall be superseded once and for all. With Paul, the disciple will be able to say, "Neither count I my life dear unto myself."

If there is in our hearts no such unrivaled love for Christ, He affirms that we *cannot* be His disciples.

Touching life's conduct—an unceasing cross-bearing. "Whosoever doth not bear his cross, and come after me, *cannot* be my disciple" (v. 27).

Ramon Lull, the earliest missionary to the Muslims, tells how he became a missionary. He had been living a luxurious and pleasure-loving life. One day while he was alone Christ came to him carrying His cross and saying, "Carry this for Me." But he pushed Him off and refused. Again when he was in the silence of a great cathedral Christ came; again He asked him to carry His cross and again he refused. Christ came a third time, and this time, said Lull, "He took His cross and without a word left it lying in my hands. What could I do but take it up and carry it?" He did so, but it issued in his being stoned to death.

What did Christ mean by "His cross"? Certainly not physical infirmity, or temperamental weakness, or misfortune, trouble, or disease. These are unavoidable and are the common lot of all humanity, whether Christian or non-Christian. The fact that our Lord preceded His statements with His hypothetical "if" indicates that something voluntary is involved. In simplest terms, the cross stands for shame and suffering and death. It is a symbol of rejection by the world. Obviously, a real identification with Christ in the shame and suffering of His cross is implied. Bearing our own cross is a matter of choice. It is not thrust on us as was Jesus' cross on Simon of Cyrene. It signifies a willingness to share the scorn, the hatred, the ostracism of the world for His sake. A worldly disciple would be a contradiction in terms. Paul knew what was involved in this identification with a crucified Christ. "Being reviled, we bless; being persecuted, we suffer it: being defamed, we intreat: we are made as the filth of the world, and are the offscouring of all things unto this day" (1 Corinthians 4:12–13).

When we voluntarily embrace the adverse circumstances of life as instruments of death to the selfish and self-centered existence, we are bearing our own cross. Received aright, the sufferings, limitations, and trials of life will lead us to our true position as crucified with Christ. "Whoso looketh on the white side of Christ's cross and taketh it up handsomely, shall find it to him just such a burden as wings are to a bird" (Samuel Rutherford).

If we are unwilling for unceasing cross-bearing, we cannot be His disciples.

Touching personal possessions—an unqualified renunciation. "Whosoever he be of you that forsaketh not *all* that he hath, he *cannot* be my disciple" (v. 33). Our Lord's third requirement for discipleship is a full surrender of all, not a fine surrender of much. "All that he hath," are His words. In the Amplified New Testament, the word "forsake" is expanded thus: "renounce, surrender claim to, give up, say good-bye to." It is the absoluteness of our Lord's demand which is so staggering. It admits of no exceptions. He claims the right to dispose of everything in His disciple's possession as He in His wise love sees best.

With most people possessions, goods, property very easily become objects of love and devotion. "Things" can exercise a terrible tyranny over us. But we cannot serve God and mammon; we cannot give allegiance to two masters. Where the heart is divided between dual interests, discipleship is impossible. The lesson the Master was seeking to teach is that we are trustees of our possessions, not owners.

Discipleship will not necessarily involve a literal selling of all our possessions and giving away the proceeds, but it does not preclude such a possibility. The disciples claimed, "We have left *all* and followed thee." Paul said, "I suffer the loss of *all* things." Of the early church it was said, "Neither said any of them that *ought* of the things which he possessed was his own; but they had *all* things common" (Acts 4:32). Whatever else is involved in this condition, it means there must be such a real and deliberate renunciation and giving up our claim to all that we have, as will forever set us free from covetousness and selfishness. Our Master expects us to hold all that we have in a relaxed, inverted hand and not in a tightly clenched fist. Our attitude will be, "Lord, help Yourself to whatever You wish of mine."

Otherwise, we *cannot* be His disciples.

For obedience to these three unequivocal demands, some powerful motive is necessary. It is found in Christ's own example. He asks nothing of us He was not willing to do Himself. For love of us He "hated" His Father and His heavenly home, and came as the sinless God-man to live in a world of sin where often He had nowhere to lay His head. For our sake, Jesus "bearing his cross went forth into . . . Golgotha . . . where they crucified him" (John 19:17–18). For our eternal enrichment He renounced all that He had. "Though he was rich, yet for your sakes he became poor, that ye through his poverty might be rich" (2 Corinthians 8:9). Is the servant greater than his Lord? Shall we be reluctant to do for Him what He so willingly did for us? When we fulfill these three conditions, then and only then are we His disciples indeed.

CHAPTER 13

A Personal Letter from Christ

Unto the angel of the church of Ephesus, write . . .

REVELATION 2:1

Reading: REVELATION 2:1–7

A personal letter from the exalted Christ to a living church is indeed a memorable document, and it is a high privilege to be able to share its message. Though primarily directed to the church of Ephesus, it concludes with an individual and contemporary appeal, "He that hath an ear, let him hear . . ." In it there is appreciation tinged with pathos, commendation tempered by condemnation. Christ represents Himself as the One who walks among the seven golden lampstands, which in 1:20 are identified as the seven churches. He oversees and scrutinizes the shining of their lamp of witness. In His letter He passes moral judgment on the church from the vantage point of full and accurate knowledge. "I know thy works."

Ephesus was one of the notable cities of ancient times. Its citizens called it the metropolis of Asia. It was wealthy and cultured but utterly corrupt. Besides being an important commercial center, it was the focus of a vile form of heathen worship. It boasted the magnificent temple of Diana, one of the seven wonders of the world, which brought both wealth and notoriety. The church in Ephesus was uniquely privileged in the galaxy of spiritual gifts possessed by its founder and successive pastors. Paul, Apollos, Priscilla and Aquila, Timothy, and John had each contributed to its spiritual life. That they responded to and grasped the deep spiritual teaching they received is clear from the heights of spiritual truth to which Paul rises in his letter to them. The type of believer forming the nucleus of the church can best be gauged by the spiritual teaching they were able to assimilate.

By the time this letter was penned the Ephesian church had been established for forty years and its membership was of second- and third-generation Christians. The sublime new truths which had enraptured their forbears had now become commonplace. But much of the stability and strength of the previous generation was still in evidence, and for this Christ expresses His warm appreciation.

COMMENDATION

The tact and understanding of the Master stands out in clear relief in the opening sentence of His letter. It is noteworthy that when He has something to commend, He mentions that first, always a sound procedure in human relationships. He commended them without qualification for four virtues manifest in their midst.

They were ***loyal in labor***. "I know thy works, and thy labor, and thy patience" (v. 2). The whole life and conduct of the church is in view here, sacrificial toil and unflagging patience in the midst of weariness. The church was a hive of industry, full of good works. There was nothing passive about their patience. It was persistence in toil even to the point of exhaustion, and for this Christ warmly commended them. It is worthy of note that the three words used in this sentence occur also in Paul's letter to the Thessalonians where he commends their "*work* of faith, and *labor* of love, and *patience* of hope" (1 Thessalonians 1:3).

Then, too, they were ***intolerant of impostors***. "Thou canst not bear them which are evil" (v. 2). This was a church which would not condone impurity of any kind in its midst. There was sufficient spiritual virility to exercise a wholesome discipline, and for this they received divine commendation. The Ephesian church could bear anything except the presence of impostors in its midst.

As a church they were ***discerning in doctrine***. "Thou hast tried them which say they are apostles, and are not, and hast found them liars" (v. 2). From the tense of the verb it would appear that our Lord was referring to a recent crisis in which they had tested the doctrine of the Nicolaitans (v. 6) who posed as equal or even superior to the original apostles, and had condemned them. Forewarned by Paul in his farewell address (Acts 20:29), they had been on the watch for the "grievous wolves" to which he alluded. Here were believers who were careful of what they listened to and thus they were not deceived. But not only did they test their words, they tested their deeds also, and rejected them. For this Christ, who is the Truth, commended them. "Thou hatest the deeds of the Nicolaitans, which I also hate" (v. 6). Ignatius bore this testimony to the Ephesian church: "Ye live according to the truth and no heresy hath a home among you: nay ye do not so much as listen to anyone if he speak of aught else save concerning Jesus Christ."

Finally, they were ***patient in persecution***. "[Thou] hast borne, and hast patience, and for my name's sake hast labored, and hast not fainted" (v. 3). In the midst of raging fires of persecution they had displayed a remarkable staying power.

With such an amazing and deserved commendation from the Christ, whose "eyes were as a flame of fire," this church surely has grounds for self-congratulation. What more could be expected of her? How gratified we would be if all our churches merited such praise. But Christ's penetrating eye saw a fatal defect beneath the fair exterior. His listening ear detected a missing note in the harmony of its worship.

COMPLAINT

"Nevertheless I have somewhat against thee, because thou hast left thy first love"—you have abandoned the love you had at the first. The prophetic word of the Lord Jesus had already come true (Matthew 24:12). At first blush this may not seem a matter of tremendous importance against the background of their many admirable qualities, but such a view is terribly superficial. Is it a small thing to a wife if her husband abandons the love he had for her at the first? A beautiful home, a large bank account, good social position would be as ashes to her if he withdrew his love. No suffering is so poignant as that of unrequited love.

It would appear that some crisis had come in the history of this loyal, busy, orthodox church which had caused their early love for Christ to wane. Had they become so ardent in the consuming task of maintaining good works that their love for Christ had cooled off? Were they so busy hating the deeds of the Nicolaitans that they had ceased to love Christ? Loss of love for Christ is no trifle. The work and labor and patience of the newly converted Thessalonian Christians each had an inspiring motive—faith, love, hope. But for the second-generation Ephesian believers, faith and love and hope had fallen by the way, and all that was left was work, labor, patience. Without the inspiring motives their work became a burden and their orthodoxy a dead thing. It takes ardent love for Christ to make these activities of lasting spiritual value. Toil and zeal and even self-sacrifice are no substitute for love.

Men do not think loss of love for Christ a very serious thing, but He views it as a sin of such terrible dimensions that unless it is repented of, it would result in the destruction of the witness of the church. It would have failed in the very purpose for which it was brought into being.

COUNSEL

First the exalted Christ calls on the church to *remember*. "Remember therefore from whence thou art fallen" (v. 5). There is a time to look backward and a time to look forward. Memory can exercise a salutary ministry when it is brought into play. We have a fatal facility for forgetting unpleasant or unwelcome facts or truths. If we love Christ less today than we did in the early days of our new life, He says we have fallen. We may not have fallen into gross sin, but we have fallen out of love with Christ. Let us think back to see if there was a time when our love for Christ was more passionate, more sacrificial than it is today. "Remember" is in the imperative mood; our Master is commanding us to put our memories to work. It is true that love is likely to be more demonstrative in its early stages than later, but as love matures it will run ever deeper and more strongly. Has this been our experience?

Jeremiah's prophecy has a poignant paragraph. "The word of the LORD came to me, saying, Go and cry in the ears of Jerusalem, saying, Thus saith the LORD; I remember thee, the kindness of thy youth, the love of thine espousals, when thou wentest after me in the wilderness, in a land that was not sown" (Jeremiah 2:1–2). God remembered with sad joy the glow and warmth of His people's early love for Him, a love which was then selfless and sacrificial. But now that glow had faded. He recalled with wistful grief its four beautiful characteristics.

He remembered ***the kindness of their love***. "I remember the kindness of thy youth," the early days when they loved Him more than anyone or anything else; when they showed a sensitive and solicitous concern for His feelings; when they considered and consulted Him in everything large and small. The touchstone of all activity was, "Will this please Him?" Has the center of our life shifted so that the question has become, "Will this please me?" Correctness of relationship does not take the place of the kindness of love.

The devotion of their love in early courtship was fresh in His memory. "I remember the love of thine espousal." Newly awakened love is a very beautiful thing. When Hudson Taylor was traveling by train in France, a young and obviously newly married couple entered his compartment. They were entirely oblivious of their fellow traveler. The bride could hardly take her eyes from her lover's face. She anticipated every wish. They were entirely absorbed in each other. Mr. Taylor said, "My heart cried out, O that I had such a love for my Lord!"

God recalled with deep appreciation ***the exclusiveness of their love.*** "Thou wentest after Me." He was the center of their world and around Him everything revolved. Personal devotion to Him motivated their whole life. But now "Me" had degenerated into "It." It is perilously easy for devotion to the Lord's Person to deteriorate into devotion to the Lord's work.

Ramon Lull, the Spanish nobleman and brilliant university professor of the thirteenth century, turned from his alluring prospects to evangelize the Muslims. Twice he was banished from the country. He spent a year and a half immured in a dungeon. As an old man, when taken to a wall and stoned to death, his last words were, "Jesus only." Shortly before he died he said, "He that loves not lives not, and he that lives by Christ shall never die." The terms of his consecration vow were, "To Thee, O Lord God, I offer myself, my wife, my children, and all I possess," and to his dying day he never revoked the exclusiveness of his love for Christ.

When persecution was raging in Holland, Geleyn de Muler was told to recant and give up reading the Bible or suffer death by fire. He had a wife and four children. "Do you love your wife and children?" asked Titelman. "God knows that were the heaven a pearl and the earth a globe of gold, and were I owner of all, most cheerfully would I give them up for my family, even though our fare be only bread and water. But not *for Christ.*" He was strangled and burned.

God was not forgetful of ***the sacrifice of their love***. "Thou wentest after me in the wilderness, in a land that was not sown." Theirs was an uncalculating love, a love which was prepared for risks. In the glow of their first devotion they were willing to sacrifice everything if only they could be with Him, for the one thing love cannot endure is distance. Loneliness, privation, hunger, poverty held no terrors if they had the compensation of His presence. There is not much to allure in a wilderness, the place of temptation and testing. It was a "land not sown," with no security, no prospects; but this could not quench the ardor of their love. There was no certainty of harvest and no assurance for the future, yet in spite of this they followed Him there. He remembered with deep joy the kindness of a love that renounced all other loves and prospects simply to be with Him.

Next Christ called on the church at Ephesus to *repent* (v. 5). He issues an imperative demand for an immediate change of mind, attitude, and conduct before it is too late. It is a word which combines the intellectual and the volitional. It was not sufficient for the Ephesians to feel badly about their sin of having fallen out of love with Christ; they had to fall in love with Him afresh, and this was in their power to do. The expression "thou didst leave thy first love" almost implies some crisis, some definite point of time when the chilling wind began to blow. Pilgrim found the lost roll exactly where he left it. It may be that for some of us it will be necessary to take a mental pilgrimage to the occasion when we lost the love we had at the first.

Finally, He calls on them to *reform*. "Do at once the works you did at the first." Again it is an imperative. They are to resume the works they used to do, and the implication is that the change of mind toward Christ coupled with a renewal of the former activities, which then sprang from a glowing love for Christ, would once again kindle the fire of love in the heart. Love is a matter of the will as well as of the emotions. When adjustment is corrected, love will return again.

Christ enforced His commands with a solemn warning. "Repent, and do the first works; or else I will come unto thee quickly, and will remove thy candlestick out of its place, except thou repent" (v. 5). Apparently this appeal was effective for a period, and love for Christ was again apparent in the Ephesian church, but not for long. The lamp of witness guttered out and history tells the sequel. Ephesus is now only a squalid village set in the ruins of her former glory, and Christian testimony is nonexistent. Trench records a visitor to the village finding only three Christians there, and these so ignorant that they had hardly heard the names of Paul or John.

This letter has a contemporary message and warning to the church of our day. Where other things are magnified and fostered in the life of the church at the expense of fervent love for Christ, the congregation may remain intact but the lampstand has in reality been removed—having a name to live, but dead.

COMPENSATION

The letter does not close on a negative note. It began with commendation; it ends with compensation. "To him that overcometh will I give to eat of the tree of life, which is in the midst of the paradise of God" (v. 7). Here is a glorious promise to the one who is obedient to the exhortation and warning of his Lord. He who overcomes receives something better than the food offered to idols with which the Ephesian believers were tempted. He will have free access to the tree of life which was forbidden to Adam in Eden. He will be given to eat of the tree of life—to feed on Christ Himself. What man lost in the primal sin in Eden is gloriously restored to the overcomer in any age.

CHAPTER 14

A Reigning Life Through Christ

It is a far greater thing that through another Man, Jesus Christ, men by their acceptance of His more than sufficient grace and righteousness should live all their lives like kings.

ROMANS 5:17 PHILLIPS

Reading: ROMANS 5:12–21

"Living all their lives like kings." What an alluring picture of the Christian life Paul presents in these few words! And when he wrote of kings he was not referring to a limited constitutional monarchy such as we know today. Now the king or queen is largely a symbol, while executive power is vested in Parliament and the prime minister. Then, the king possessed absolute and despotic powers which were beneficent if he was a good man, tyrannical if he was a bad man. With this concept of kingship in mind, the full significance of Paul's statements becomes clear. But this idea of the Christian life seems far removed from the actual lives most Christians live.

RIVAL SOVEREIGNTIES

Four regions are alluded to in Romans chapter 5.

"*Death* reigned from Adam to Moses" (v. 14).

"*Sin* hath reigned unto death" (v. 21).

"Even so might *grace* reign through righteousness" (v. 21).

"*They* . . . shall reign in life" (v. 17).

To use Paul's imagery, there are two eternally antagonistic dynasties endeavoring to capture and reign over the citadel of Mansoul—the dynasty of sin and death, and the dynasty of grace and righteousness. Between the two stands the Christian whose decision determines which dynasty shall have the ascendancy. Zoroastrianism sees the whole universe as a battleground between these two dynasties, between the god Ormuzd and the god Ahriman. That which settles a man's destiny is the side he chooses in the cosmic conflict.

We are left in no doubt of the divine purpose and provision. "They shall reign in life." "Even so, might grace reign." God intends His children to live triumphant, not defeated lives. Paul himself testified, "But thanks be to God, for He always leads me in His triumphal train, through union with Christ" (2 Corinthians 2:14 WILLIAMS). The picture is of a king who has returned from a triumphant campaign and is being honored by his emperor and nation.

ROYAL PRIVILEGES

The idea of royalty is normally associated with certain desirable characteristics whose spiritual counterparts should appear in the life of the Christian. In the reigning Queen of England, even though she does not exercise the absolute powers of the royalty of Paul's day, we both expect and find a ***nobility of character***. Consciousness of her royal descent and strict self-discipline have produced in her a dignity and bearing which becomes one in her exalted position. We look in her for ***charm of personality***, nor are we disappointed. To rich and poor alike she shows the same gracious interest and concern. On her royal tours, no matter how exacting the demands or how exhausted she has become, there is no loss of charm and winsomeness. Then, too, there is a ***consciousness of authority*** begotten by constant exercise of the prerogatives which her royal position confers on her. Those who come in contact with her are conscious of her authority and take no liberties. She suffers from no ***limitation of wealth***. For her, to desire is to have. No matter what riches are displayed in clothing or jewels, there is always the impression of unlimited resources as yet untouched. She enjoys, theoretically at any rate, an ***unfettered freedom***. The whole land is hers, and others enjoy its use only by grant from her. She can go where she will, do what she likes throughout her whole realm.

What a fascinating picture of Christian living this vivid picture portrays: nobility, charm, authority, wealth, freedom. Our God invites us to believe that these spiritual qualities and prerogatives may and should be enjoyed by every child of the King of kings. If we do not manifest and enjoy them, it is not because they are beyond our reach, but only because we are living below our privileges. God is always liberal with His gifts. If it is love He bestows, it is "love that passeth knowledge." Or joy, it is "joy unspeakable and full of glory." Or peace, it is "peace that passeth all understanding." Our God is the God of the superlative.

Mrs. Hetty Green was a recluse who lived in a closely sealed apartment in an American city. She was fabulously wealthy, having inherited $20,000,000 of railway stock. On her death it was discovered that in place of an underskirt, she wore newspapers sewn together! In this way she was able to save some money, but it could not be said that she was living up to either her privileges or her resources!

Must we not admit that we too live on a scale far below our spiritual resources? We are not always "more than conquerors." Instead of reigning over ourselves, our circumstances, our sins, we are frequently under their dominion. We wistfully read the categorical assurance, "Sin shall not have dominion over you," but have to confess with confusion of face, "O LORD our God, other lords beside thee have had dominion over us" (Isaiah 26:13). The alluring promise of Romans 5:17 remains a tantalizing mirage. Instead of being robed in royal apparel, we are wearing our old newspapers. "I know full well that this is an experience into which all do not enter," wrote Dr. W. M. Clow. "It is a range of well-being and felicity to which some men dare not aspire and other men do not crave to attain. *All our lives are lived on a needlessly low level.*"

THE ROYAL SUBJECTS

Reigning implies subjects. What are they? The reign of sin and death is the reign of a power over a personality. The reign of grace and righteousness is a reign of a personality over a power. "They shall reign." The rights of royalty over powers which would impoverish and tyrannize have been bestowed on us.

Sin. "Sin shall not have dominion over you." If we are living under the dominion of sin it is either because we are ignorant of the way of deliverance or because deep in our being we do not want to be delivered. It is not because full provision for liberation has not been made in the death and resurrection of Christ and the indwelling of the Holy Spirit. Because "death hath no more dominion over Him," says Paul, "sin shall not have dominion over you" (Romans 6:9, 14). Besetting sin holds many of us in its vise-like grasp and throttles our spiritual life. But we can reign over every form of sin. No longer need our special besetment mar our spiritual experience.

Circumstances. We either reign over our circumstances or they reign over us. There is no middle path. We are their playthings or they are our subjects. In the closing verses of Romans 8, Paul lists the worst possible circumstances in which the believer could find himself—tribulation, distress, persecution, famine, nakedness, peril, sword—and then adds, "Nay in *all* these things we are more than conquerors *through him* that loved us" (Romans 8:35, 37). No concessions need be made to the weakness of the flesh when the triumph of Christ is our triumph.

Frustration. This word has become very popular in the psychological jargon of our day, because it characterizes so many who, not having submitted to the lordship of Christ, have found life purposeless and frustrating. There need be no frustration to the person who has embraced the will of God as his rule of life. It was prophesied of Jesus before His birth and abundantly evidenced in His life, "I delight to do thy will, O my God" (Psalm 40:8). This does not sound like frustration. When life has as its supreme purpose the doing of God's will, that is a source of endless joy and delight.

Inadequacy. What is usually advanced as an excuse for low-level living and scanty spiritual service may in reality prove a great blessing. "Blessed are the poor in spirit"—the inadequate—said our Lord. But inadequacy brings blessedness only when it throws us back on the limitless resources of Christ. Pleading our inadequacy does not please God, as Moses learned. When He calls to any task, the call carries with it the implication that all necessary enabling will be given. Paul's testimony was, "I can do all things through Christ which strengtheneth me."

Emotional States. No tyranny can be more despotic than that of our feelings and nothing more devastating to those with whom we live and work. In many homes there is a state of constant tension, if not violent discord because some member or members know nothing of reigning over their emotional states. They diffuse an "atmosphere" wherever they go. Other members of the family look covertly at them when they come down in the morning to discover in which way the wind is blowing, what kind of feeling is in the ascendancy. We should bear in mind that feelings are not irresponsible things. They are but the reflection of our inner state. If we ourselves are undisciplined, our feelings will be undisciplined too. If we are right at the center of our being in our relationship with the Lord, we will be right at the circumference as well. We should *live in the realm of the will,* not of the emotions. We become what we choose. Reigning is not an emotional state. It is the purposeful exercise of conscious prerogatives. God means that we should ascend the throne and reign over our feelings.

Fears. The writer to the Hebrews speaks of those who "through fear . . . were all their lifetime subject to bondage."

Bound, who should be conquerors,
Slaves, who should be free.

Fear frequently has a basis in reality, but more often it is something intangible, a nameless dread that grips and benumbs the spirit. Some people are afraid of everything. They fear people, the past, the future; they fear everything unknown; they fear undertaking responsibility and making decisions, and "fear hath torment" (1 John 4:18). But it is gloriously possible for us to reign over all our fears, for "He hath said, I will never leave thee, nor forsake thee. So that we may boldly say, The Lord is my helper, and I will not fear." Note that two things are involved in reigning over fear—confidence in the assured companionship of God, and the fixed determination of the will, because He is our helper, that we will not fear. The ever-present God is there to reinforce the weak human will.

THE ROYAL RESOURCES

If the verse we are studying means anything, it means that there is no spiritual blessing which we can ever need or desire which God has not made available to us. Note the inventory of the resources at our disposal: "His more than sufficient grace," "the free gift of righteousness." We may give intellectual assent to the theological truth that God's grace is more than sufficient for our needs, and yet experimentally it may be absolutely untrue. The resources are available but they may be unappropriated.

It is to be noted that our "living like kings" and "reigning in life" are never apart from Christ. Paul makes this abundantly clear. "They shall reign in life *by one, Jesus Christ.*" Our reigning in life is the direct outcome of His reign in us. If He reigns in us, we reign in life. He has already made available to us the spoils of His victory but they await our appropriation.

"God . . . *hath blessed us* with all spiritual blessings . . . in Christ" (Ephesians 1:3).

"He that spared not his own Son, but delivered him up for us all, how shall he not *with him* also freely give us all things?" (Romans 8:32).

"All things are yours . . . and ye are Christ's; and Christ is God's" (1 Corinthians 3:21, 23).

These verses make it crystal clear that God has no favorites. There is no difference in bestowal between one Christian and another. There are no handicapped believers where royal resources are concerned. All may share alike. The only difference is in reception.

It may be asked, since these resources are available to all in Christ, why is there so little evidence of their possession in lives of Christians as a whole? Can the head be rich and the body poor? Yes, when the blood flow is restricted. Faith is the blood of the spiritual life and when faith is not functioning, spiritual penury is the inevitable result.

THE ROYAL SECRET

"They that *receive* . . . shall *reign*," Paul asserts. Receiving and reigning are conjoined twins. One cannot live separated from the other. What God has joined, man cannot put asunder. If some become spiritual giants while others remain spiritual pygmies, it is because some have been great receivers while others have allowed God's more than sufficient grace to remain unappropriated.

Appropriation lays hold of God's facts and turns them into factors of Christian experience. It claims God's promises, being "fully persuaded that what he had promised, he was able also to perform." It staggers "not at the promise of God through unbelief." We each have the same spiritual resources to our credit as the greatest saint who ever lived. The degree in which we "live like kings" and "reign in life" will be the degree in which we draw on them and turn them into the currency of experience. In His matchless parable of the prodigal son, our Lord made it clear that the wonderful father "divided unto *them* his living"—to the elder brother equally with the younger son. And yet the former complained, "Thou never gavest me a kid that I might make merry with my friends." The difference was not in the bestowal but in the appropriation. The prodigal son at least did his father the honor of receiving what he had been given.

Our enjoyment of spiritual blessings is strictly limited to our appropriation of them. We enjoy not what we long for, or hope for, or even ask for, but only what we receive. We can sigh for a reigning experience all our lives, but it becomes ours only when we appropriate the assurance of His promise, "They that receive . . . *shall* reign," and only then. Canaan was given to Israel by God but they did not enjoy its blessings and benefits for many years—not until they personally appropriated it by walking over it. They could have entered forty years sooner had they received and made their own what God had already given them.

If we have a credit at the bank, there is no necessity to implore the teller to give it to us. We only need to claim what is ours by passing across a check. There are said to be thirty thousand promises made to the child of God, but they are of no more value to us than statements in the newspaper if we do not personally appropriate them.

Towering above the City Hall in Philadelphia is a statue of William Penn, the Quaker founder of the commonwealth of Pennsylvania. He was on very good terms with the Indians, and in recognition of his kindness they one day told him that they would give him as much land as he could walk around in a day. He took them at their word. Next morning he rose very early and walked all day long. It was late at night when he returned. He was met by a group of Indians with quizzical smiles on their faces. "Paleface has had a very long walk today," they said. But they kept their promise, and Penn received all the land which is now the city of Philadelphia. Will God be less faithful to His promises?

It may be objected that the illustrations used are of tangible things, whereas spiritual blessings are intangible and the appropriation of them seems more difficult. But do we not appropriate intangible things constantly? Love may be lavished without stint, but it is not enjoyed until it is believed and received. Forgiveness may be freely bestowed but it brings no release until it is believed and received. Our Lord enunciated an unalterable law of the spiritual life when He said, "According to your faith be it unto you." You will get only what you take.

The late Dr. F. B. Meyer recounted how he learned the royal secret of appropriation. He was addressing a large gathering of children who became increasingly unruly. He found his patience rapidly ebbing out and knew that he was about to lose his temper, over which he had never fully reigned. He was ashamed of his failure but was unable to do anything about it. In his extremity he cried in his heart, "Thy patience, Lord!" Immediately it seemed as though a lump of the cooling patience of Christ dropped into his heart. All anger and annoyance completely died and he was able to bring the meeting to a blessed conclusion.

The experience was so striking, so decisive, and the deliverance so complete that he knew he had discovered a valuable secret. He testified that ever afterwards he used the same formula. He retained the words, "Thy . . . Lord!" and put between them whatever was his present need. Did he feel lonely? "Thy companionship, Lord!" Did fear grip? "Thy serenity, Lord!" Did impurity tempt? "Thy purity, Lord!" Was he feeling critical of others? "Thy love, Lord!" God had given him "all things that pertain unto life and godliness," and he appropriated them just as the need arose. He found Christ to be the complement of his every need. He proved, as will we, that there is a world of difference between the faith that asks and the faith that appropriates. Only those who receive, reign in life.

PART THREE

The Spirit—The Breath of God

CHAPTER 15

The Spirit—The Breath of God

There came a sound from heaven as of a rushing mighty wind [breath].

ACTS 2:2

Reading: JOHN 20:19–23; ACTS 2:1–4

Stuck between Easter and Pentecost." This arresting diagnosis of the spiritual condition of many Christians is worthy of careful thought and personal application. It is possible to rejoice in the fact that Christ is risen without passing on to experience the enduement with power promised by the risen Christ, of which Pentecost was the prototype. Why the vast discrepancy between the spiritual power wielded by the early church and that exercised by the church of our day? The simple explanation is that we cannot have the fruits without the roots. The early church achievement was the outcome of the early church enduement. Scripture makes it satisfyingly clear that this unction and its replenishment are as available to the Christian of today as on the Day of Pentecost.

Pentecost was the necessary complement of Calvary. Like an ellipse, the Christian faith and Christian experience revolve around these twin centers. Without Pentecost, Calvary would have failed of its purpose and been ineffectual to redeem a lost world. It would have been like perfecting a costly machine and neglecting to provide the motive power. The great facts on which redemption is based—our Lord's virgin birth, virtuous life, vicarious death, and victorious resurrection—had been completed for more than forty days, and yet nothing had happened—until the Day of Pentecost. Only then did the machinery of redemption swing into motion.

The Day of Pentecost witnessed the coalescing of the sovereign purpose of God and the spiritual preparation of the men to whom He was entrusting its fulfillment. The exact timing of the descent of the Spirit had been indicated centuries earlier. The feast of Pentecost was to be celebrated fifty days after the feast of Passover (Leviticus 23). The Day of Pentecost must follow fifty days after "Christ our Passover" was sacrificed for us. And it did, with all its blessed accompaniments.

Two of the great revivalists of a past generation were Jonathan Edwards and Charles G. Finney. Edwards viewed revival as a sovereign act of God which could in no way be influenced by man's preparations or endeavors. Finney, on the contrary, maintained that God was always ready to bestow revival, and that man could have it whenever he was ready to pay the price in heart preparation. The Day of Pentecost demonstrated that both were right and both were wrong. The Holy Spirit descended only "when the day of Pentecost was *fully* come" (Acts 2:1). No amount of self-emptying or heart preparation on the disciples' part would have induced His descent on any other day. But this sovereign act of God coincided with deep humbling and self-abasement on their part. The Spirit would not have come upon men and women in whose hearts there had been no prior preparation. The ten days of waiting and prayer had produced an intolerable craving for the fulfillment of "the promise of the Father" (Luke 24:49). At Pentecost God's sovereign purpose and man's essential preparation came to maturity, and immediately there followed a spontaneous divine intervention. "There came . . . from heaven" three supernatural phenomena.

"And suddenly there came a sound from heaven as of a rushing mighty wind, and it filled all the house where they were sitting" (Acts 2:2). This was a corporate experience, signifying the mysterious renewing and purifying of the Spirit in the church.

"And there appeared unto them cloven tongues like as of fire, and it sat upon each of them" (Acts 2:3). This was an individual experience, symbolizing the Spirit's melting, warming, purging ministry.

"They were all filled with the Holy Ghost, and began to speak with other tongues, as the Spirit gave them utterance. . . . Now when this was noised abroad, the multitude . . . were confounded, because that every man heard them speak in his own language" (Acts 2:4, 6).

This was the outcome of the Spirit-empowered witness of men and women with tongues aflame as they spoke of the wonderful works of God—a reversal of Babel. Then, they were confounded because one language became many. Now, they are confounded because many languages became one.

While there was a dispensational and historical side to

Pentecost, it had also personal and practical implications for the early disciples and for us who have believed on Christ through their word (John 17:20). They themselves knew that something momentous had happened in them. Instead of hiding behind closed doors "for fear of the Jews" (John 20:19), "they spake the word of God with boldness" (Acts 4:31) and ate their food "with gladness . . . praising God, and having favour with all the people" (2:46–47).

The multitudes assembled in Jerusalem knew that something inexplicable had happened to the disciples. In their endeavors to explain this miraculous change, the mockers said, "These men are full of new wine." They were nearer the truth than they suspected, and yet infinitely removed from it. Ready as ever with his answer, Peter replied in effect, "Yes, they are intoxicated, but not from an earthly source. Their inebriation springs from another Spirit" (Acts 2:14–18). They were intoxicated, not with the devil's stimulant, but with the Divine Stimulus. Men usually resort to stimulants because they are conscious of inadequacy and inability to cope with the exigencies of life. They must have some external stimulus. God, who knows the full extent of human inadequacy, has made adequate provision for this universal need. Paul refers to it in his antithetical exhortation, "Be not drunk with wine, wherein is excess; but be filled with the Spirit" (Ephesians 5:18). He Himself is the Divine Stimulus.

The extent of the transformation the coming of the Holy Spirit effected in the waiting disciples was staggering. The risen Christ became vividly real to them. They preached as though He was at their very elbow. They received entirely new insight into the significance of familiar Old Testament

Scriptures. Linking passage with passage, Peter was able to say with assurance, "This is that which was spoken by the prophet" (Acts 2:16). Their speech became authoritative and incisive, and their Spirit-given words produced deep conviction (Acts 2:37). They left saving impressions on the minds of their hearers, and they became utterly fearless in their witness (Acts 4:31).

One of the most significant changes in their attitude was their willingness to submerge themselves in the interests of the progress of the gospel. Hitherto there had been constant strife for precedence among them. Now they are a self-forgetful team with one objective—to preach Christ. Dr. A. B. Simpson made a challenging statement in this connection: "Not many rivers flow into the sea. Most rivers run into other rivers. The best workers are not those who demand a separate sphere of influence and prestige for themselves, but are content to empty their streams of blessing into other rivers."

Such was the transformation wrought in the early Christians by the advent of the Holy Spirit. How can a comparable experience of His transforming power take place in our lives? The first message of the risen Lord to His disciples throws light on this very question of personal participation in the blessing and benefits of the Holy Spirit's ministry:

> Then the same day at evening, being the first day of the week, when the doors were shut where the disciples were assembled for fear of the Jews, came Jesus and stood in the midst, and saith unto them, Peace be unto you. And when he had so said, he showed unto

> them his hands and his side. Then were the disciples glad, when they saw the Lord. Then said Jesus to them again, Peace be unto you: as my Father hath sent me, even so send I you.
>
> And when he had said this, He breathed on them, and saith unto them, Receive ye the Holy Ghost. (John 20:19–22)

In order that we may understand the significance of our Lord's symbolical act of breathing on—or, better, into—the disciples, we should note that the word "Spirit" is derived from the Latin *spiritus*—breath. We "inspire" when we breathe in and "expire" when we breathe out. The Greek word for the Spirit, *pneuma*, also means wind or breath. The Hebrew word for Spirit, *ruach*, has the same significance. Job, adopting the Hebrew poetic device of the repetition of ideas said, "The Spirit of God hath made me, and the breath of the Almighty hath given me life" (33:4), thus identifying "the breath of the Almighty" with "the Spirit of God." In doing so he used a figure of speech which is consistently used of Him throughout Scripture. He is so called because He is the direct emanation of God, the manifestation of His very presence.

It was the breath of God which produced order out of chaos in the beginning (Genesis 1:2). Man became a living soul by God breathing into his nostrils the breath of life (Genesis 2:7). Ezekiel witnessed lifeless corpses become a living army when in obedience to the Divine command he prayed, "Come from the four winds, O breath, and breathe upon these slain, that they may live" (37:9).

With this in mind, let us consider the symbolic act of

Christ, in which He graphically revealed to His disciples the source of their power. First, there was the twice-repeated bestowal of peace (John 20:19, 21). Next the Great Commission: "As my Father hath sent me, even so send I you" (20:21). Then the imparting of the Spirit. "He breathed on [into] them, and saith unto them, Receive ye the Holy Ghost" (v. 22), without whose aid they would be powerless to execute His commission. This was a miniature anticipation of the full-scale bestowal of the Spirit at Pentecost, and it teaches a valuable lesson. It is as though He were saying, "All you have to do is to breathe in, to take the Holy Spirit I impart to you now. He is the power to enable you to fulfill My commission."

This graphic outbreathing and inbreathing illustrates the method of reception of the Spirit. The disciples breathed in what Christ breathed out. Could any illustration be more simple? On the Day of Pentecost God breathed out—"there came a sound from heaven as of a rushing mighty wind [breath]." They breathed in, and "they were all filled with the Holy Ghost." Breathing in is simply the equivalent of receiving. When we breathe in, the same life-giving qualities as are in the atmosphere are in us. When we breathe in or receive the Holy Spirit, that which is peculiar to Him becomes peculiar to us, just as when we place iron in the fire, the fire enters the iron and the iron partakes of the properties peculiar to the fire.

It is a familiar law that nature abhors a vacuum. In breathing we create a vacuum by breathing out and fill the vacuum by breathing in. If we are to know either an initial or a renewed experience of the filling of the Spirit, there must first be the abandoning of every other dependence, a breathing out, and then the appropriating of His sufficiency and power as our own, a breathing in.

Dr. J. Wilbur Chapman, noted American evangelist who with Charles Alexander exercised a mighty evangelistic ministry around the world, was at one time deeply concerned at the lack of fruitfulness in his ministry. "What is the matter with me?" he inquired of Dr. F. B. Meyer. "So many times I fail, so many times I am powerless. What is the reason?" "Have you ever tried breathing out three times without breathing in once?" was the quiet rejoinder. Dr. Chapman needed no further explanation.

It might be objected that in this age, which is the dispensation of the Holy Spirit, there is no need for the believer to receive the Holy Spirit since, as Paul says, "If any man have not the Spirit of Christ, he is none of his" (Romans 8:9). This is, of course, true, but not every believer *knows* that he has the Spirit or knows the Spirit whom he has (John 14:17). When Paul met the twelve disciples at Ephesus, he asked, "Did ye receive the Holy Spirit when ye believed? And they said unto him, Nay, we did not so much as hear whether the Holy Spirit was given" (Acts 19:2 ASV). If they were true believers they were indwelt by the Holy Spirit, but their ignorance of the fact deprived them of the benefits of much of His ministry in their lives. It was only with the advent of Paul that they knew anything of His power. Was it not this very possibility of ignorance which caused Paul to write to the Corinthian Christians, "Know ye not that ye are the temple of God, and that the Spirit of God dwelleth in you?" (1 Corinthians 3:16). In its full sense "receiving" involves conscious volition. Possession and conscious reception do not always go together.

There is not much benefit to me in having a check for $1,000 in my pocket if I do not know it is there; or if while knowing it is there I have no conception of its value. I have received it in the sense that I possess the piece of paper. But in actuality I have not received it until I present it at the bank and receive its value in cash.

If this be true, it is our part to breathe out—to exhale from our lives all that is impure and unworthy, and then to breathe in—to consciously appropriate the Holy Spirit for ourselves in His absolute sufficiency. He has been sent to be the Savior's representative to guide, control, empower. When we receive Him in this capacity, He who dwelt in us unconsciously is now able to exercise His gracious ministry with our full knowledge and consent.

Breathe on me, Breath of God
Fill me with life anew,
That I may love what Thou dost love,
And do what Thou wouldst do.

CHAPTER 16

The Transforming Power of the Spirit

But we all, with open face beholding as in a glass the glory of the Lord, are changed into the same image from glory to glory, even as by the Spirit of the Lord.
2 CORINTHIANS 3:18

Reading: 2 CORINTHIANS 3:1–18

How may we acquire likeness to Christ?" This verse provides a satisfying answer to this wistful question of many hearts. There is not only one answer to that question, for there are many varieties of Christian experience, and the fullness of blessing is not experienced by all in the same manner or through the same aspect of truth. But this paragraph sets out in unmistakable terms one of the great secrets of conformity to the image of Christ.

The context of this alluring possibility draws a striking contrast between the old covenant of law and the new covenant of grace—the passing glory of the one, the surpassing splendor of the other—between Moses with face veiled and the believer with veil removed. The requirement of the old covenant was that man, by his own unaided effort, should live up to the exacting standard of God's holiness in the decalogue, a requirement which led only to deep despair. The supreme revelation of the new covenant was that transformation of character into the likeness of Christ comes not by painful striving, but by beholding and believing and the operation of the Holy Spirit in the heart of the believer. The old covenant which came by Moses was a ministration of death and condemnation, but the new covenant which was ushered in by the death of Christ was a ministration of righteousness and life (vv. 7–8). The aspiration of Moses under the old covenant was expressed in his request, "I beseech thee, shew me thy glory." The realization of this aspiration in the new covenant is seen in the text, "We all, with open face beholding . . . the glory of the Lord, are changed into the same image."

AN OBJECTIVE VISION

"We all with open [unveiled] face beholding as in a glass the glory of the Lord." Transformation of character begins not with subjective introspection, but with an objective vision of the glory of the Lord and the Lord of glory. It is "Christ Jesus, who of God is made unto us . . . sanctification [holiness]" (1 Corinthians 1:30). And where may this captivating vision be seen? Not in illuminated heavens but in the written Word—the mirror which reveals His perfect manhood, His flawless character, His unique Person, and His mediatorial work. Concerning the Word of God, Jesus said, "Search the scriptures . . . they are they which testify of me" (John 5:39). Paul asserts that "the light of the knowledge of the glory of God" may be seen "in the face of Jesus Christ" (2 Corinthians 4:6). But where can that face be authentically seen? Not on a painter's canvas, for the most beautiful painting is only the projection of the artist's conception of Christ. It can be seen only in the records of His inspired biographers who under the guidance of the Holy Spirit have given us with meticulous accuracy a full-length portrait of Him.

The Jews saw the face, but they missed the glory because a veil lay over their minds, a veil of prejudice and hatred and unbelief far more impenetrable than the veil which concealed Moses' radiant face (v. 7). But, says Paul, through Christ this veil is taken away (v. 14). And now "we all"—not a select group of especially holy people—"with unveiled face" may gaze at His glory. The glory here referred to is, of course, the moral glory of Christ, His excellences of character and conduct, which shine out everywhere in the Scriptures.

A SUBJECTIVE TRANSFORMATION

"Are being changed into the same image." This objective vision has a subjective purpose, that we might be changed into His likeness. God is not satisfied with us as we are. Nor are we satisfied with ourselves as we are if we really know ourselves. The Son of Man was to the Father such an object of delight, He so perfectly fulfilled all His purposes and conformed to His standard, that He plans for all His children to be "changed" or, as the word is, "transfigured" into His likeness. When our Lord was transfigured before His disciples, for a moment He drew aside the veil of flesh which concealed His innate and essential glory and allowed the three on the mount to briefly glimpse it. "We beheld His glory, the glory as of the only begotten of the Father," said John several decades later. "We were eyewitnesses of

His majesty," said Peter, another of the favored three on the Mount of Transfiguration. We have no such inherent and essential glory. The Divine purpose for us is not mere external imitation but internal transformation. And the transformation will not be transient and evanescent. We shall not lose the glory as did Moses. "The children of Israel could not steadfastly behold the face of Moses for the glory of his countenance; which glory was to be done away" (v. 7). Ours is to be glory retained and transmitted. "For if that which is done away was glorious, much more *that which remaineth* is glorious" (v. 11).

And the method of transformation? "Beholding." Not a despairing struggle against that which captivates, but a steady, concentrated gazing on Christ and a confident relying on the Holy Spirit to effect the change.

The word used here for "beholding" may with equal propriety be rendered either "beholding" or "reflecting." As we behold His glory, we are changed into His likeness. As we are changed, we reflect as in a mirror the image into which we are transformed. Reflecting is the inevitable result of beholding.

It is the law of life that we become like those we constantly gaze at. The eye exercises a great influence on life and character. The education of a child is conducted largely through the eye. He is molded by the manners and habits of those he constantly sees. This is the explanation of the powerful influence of movies on young people. They become like that on which they gaze. Look on the streets of a large city and you will see counterparts of famous actresses. Their fans copy them in dress, in speech, in behavior. We become like those we admire. Alexander the Great studied

Homer's *Iliad* and as a result he went out to conquer the world. William Cowper, the celebrated poet, when a young and sensitive boy, read a treatise in favor of suicide. Who can doubt that when, later in life, he attempted to destroy himself, it was the influence of the book which had gripped him in earlier days. In the spiritual realm, how many famous preachers have numerous smaller editions of themselves among their admirers!

On one occasion the writer was holidaying at an isolated spot. When the Lord's Day came, the only church service of any kind was conducted by a Salvation Army soldier, an illiterate farmer. His text was the one at the head of this chapter. He was not eloquent. He did not evidence deep learning. Some of his exegesis was questionable. But his reiteration of his text etched four words indelibly on the mind—*"beholding, we are changed."* His radiant face and obvious joy in the Lord were exemplification of the truth of his claim. "A glance of faith may save, but it is the gaze of faith which sanctifies," said Robert Murray McCheyne. A hurried glance at Christ snatched after lying abed too late will never effect a radical transformation of character.

Dr. A. B. Simpson sees us here as the photography of God, the Holy Spirit developing and perfecting Him in the midst of our lives. If the image is to be perfect, the sitter must be in focus. The veil must be removed. The sitter must remain quite still with steadfast gaze since it is a time exposure. After the image has been transferred to the sensitive film in the moment of exposure, there follows the process by which the acids etch away all that conceals the likeness of the subject. This is the ministry of the Holy Spirit who, as we yield to His influence, removes all that is unlike Christ and imparts to us His own perfections.

But we are also to *reflect* the glory of the Lord as Moses did after his forty days' sojourn in the mount in the presence of the glory of God. When we behold the glory of Christ in the mirror of Scripture, His glory shines upon us and into us, and then it is reflected by us. With Moses it was a transient and fading reflection of the glory, but it need not be so with us. It should be our constant aim to ensure that we are an accurate reflection of Christ to the world of men around us. It is very possible for His image in us to be distorted and blurred in the course of transmission, as our own image has been in a funfair mirror. Since unbelieving men can know Christ only by what they see of Him in us, how important that we do not misrepresent Him, that we do not display our own carnal attitudes instead of His moral beauty and glory. What they see of Christ reflected in us should turn their antagonism and indifference into wistfulness and faith.

A PROGRESSIVE EXPERIENCE

"*We are being changed* into His likeness from one degree of glory to another." Translators render this sentence differently, but in them all there is the idea of progression. "Through successive stages of glory," "in ever increasing splendor," "from a mere reflected to an inherent glory," "from one degree of radiant holiness unto another." One thing is clear. It is not the purpose of God that our Christian experience should be static. There lie ahead of us endless possibilities of growth into the likeness of Christ. These words clearly show that Christlikeness in all its fullness is not the result merely of some moment of high and holy exaltation, but that it is a progressive experience. The inward change produced in us by the Holy Spirit is to be daily transforming us more nearly to the image of our Lord. We are transfigured by the renewing of our minds.

THE TRANSFORMING AGENT

"Even as by the Lord the Spirit." "The Lord the Spirit," as it is in the original, is an unusual phrase and poses a theological problem. William Barclay comments, "Paul seems to identify the Risen Lord and the Holy Spirit. We must remember that Paul was not writing theology; he was setting down experience. And it is the experience of the Christian life that the work of the Spirit and the work of the Risen Lord are one and the same. The strength, the light, the guidance we receive come alike from the Spirit and from the Risen Lord. It does not matter how we express it so long as we experience it."

We need to see in this transformation our responsibility and the Holy Spirit's ministry. The change into the likeness of Christ is not automatic. It involves moral endeavor and activity. We are not only to "let go and let God," we are also to "put off" and "put on" certain things, and this involves definite activity of the renewed will. It is not the inevitable result of passive daydreaming about Christ. Our part is to "behold the glory of the Lord" in active, expectant faith. The Spirit then exercises His prerogative of revealing the glory of Christ and reproducing that likeness in ever-increasing splendor. We behold Him, but we trust and expect the Holy Spirit to change us into Christ's likeness. The transforming work is entirely His as He ministers and imparts to us all the values and virtues of the Person and work of Christ. We behold in silent adoring contemplation; He works into the fabric of our lives what we see in Jesus.

In achieving this, the Spirit exercises both a negative and a positive ministry. First, He *reveals to us the things in our life and character which are unlike Christ* and which therefore must go. Everything alien to the perfection of Christ must be "put off." This revealing ministry is not pleasant; indeed, it can be devastating, for despite our protestations of unworthiness we are all greatly biased in our own favor. We do not enjoy others evaluating us as we profess to evaluate ourselves. But if we sincerely desire to be transformed, we will be willing to part with everything that mars Christ's image in us. God cannot "put off" these manifestations of unlikeness to Christ. It is something which we alone can do and must do. Paul indicates elsewhere things which must be put off if we are to be assimilated into Christ. "Anger, wrath, malice, blasphemy, filthy communication out of your mouth. Lie not one to another" (Colossians 3:8–9).

But the Spirit not only reveals what must be discarded. He enables us to do it. "If ye *through the Spirit* do mortify the deeds of the body, ye shall live," were Paul's bracing words (Romans 8:13). We are not left to our own unaided efforts as were those who lived under the old covenant. We have a mighty Paraclete whose supreme delight it is to aid us to the limit when our hearts are set on becoming like Christ in character and conduct.

Then *the Holy Spirit reveals the graces and blessings which should and could be ours* and enables us to appropriate them. One of the tragedies of many Christian lives is the poverty of their experience when contrasted with the vastness of their unclaimed privileges. "Blessed be the God and Father of our Lord Jesus Christ," wrote Paul, "who *hath* blessed us with *all* spiritual blessings . . . in Christ." "All *things* are yours. According as his divine power *hath given* unto us *all things* that pertain unto life and godliness." There is no grace which we behold in the character of our Lord which may not be ours in increasing measure as we look to the Spirit to produce it in us.

"Beholding . . . we are changed."

CHAPTER 17

The Purging Fire of the Spirit

Then the fire of the L*ORD* *fell.*

1 KINGS 18:38

Reading: I KINGS 18:1–40

This story is one of the most dramatic in the Old Testament. Everything about it is vivid and colorful. The characters are spectacular, the issues tremendous, the outcome glorious. Elijah, the lone prophet of Jehovah, was one of the most remarkable characters of Israel's history. He appears suddenly as the prophet of the crisis, the champion of Divine rights. He disappears as suddenly to the accompaniment of a chariot of fire and a whirlwind. The New Testament has more to say of him than of any other prophet. Stepping out of the unknown, his first public act was to lock the heavens by his prayers so that no rain fell for three and a half years—in this instance a judgment on an idolatrous nation.

Though we have no record of his early life, there had undoubtedly been a private preparation for so powerful a public ministry. Such a career as his could only be the outcome of a personal encounter with God. In secret he had received his prophetic call. By secret tests he had so come to know God as to be absolutely sure of Him. Through secret fellowship with God he had been completely delivered from the fear of man. Physically, he was a suntanned sheik of rugged and austere appearance. Morally, he was a man of courage, faith, and zeal!

Character is revealed in crises, and the secret of Elijah's life is epitomized in these words: "LORD God of Abraham, Isaac, and of Israel, let it be known this day that thou art God in Israel, and that I am thy servant, and that I have done all these things at thy word" (v. 36). The true man is seen in the place of prayer. Three facts emerge:

He ***had a consuming passion for the glory of God***. "Let it be known that thou art God." This came first in his thoughts. His soul was filled with a holy jealousy for God's glory.

He ***was content to be the slave of Jehovah***. "Let it be known that I am thy servant." He acknowledged God's absolute ownership.

He ***was implicitly obedient to the divine commands***. "I have done all these things at thy word."

The gathering of Israel (v. 19) was not the work of a moment. Judging by the outcome, it is not difficult to believe that Elijah spent much time in waiting on God and receiving from Him the plan of campaign. Such sublime confidence in God as he displayed could only be the outcome of prolonged communion with God. Elijah knew his God.

Elijah's dramatic challenge grew out of his deep concern over the apostasy of the nation. On the throne was the weakest and wickedest king Israel had known. Even before his marriage it is recorded that "Ahab . . . did evil in the sight of the Lord above all that were before him." To this he added another base distinction."As if it had been a light thing for him to walk in the sins of Jeroboam . . . he took to wife Jezebel . . . and went and served Baal, and worshipped him. . . . and Ahab did more to provoke the Lord God of Israel to anger than all the kings of Israel that were before him" (16:30–33). Instead of Jehovah, Baal enjoyed pride of place in Israel's worship. It was at this juncture when true religion and morality had almost disappeared that Elijah dramatically walked onto the stage of Israel's history.

THE CHALLENGE OF THE FIRE

"The God that answereth by fire." There could be no compromise between the worship of Jehovah and the worship of Baal. The two contrasting systems of religion could not live together in peaceful co-existence. It is the man of God who precipitates the crisis. God always has His man to match the hour. He prepares him in secret and then manifests him in the hour of crisis. God is never without His witness. There is always a Luther or a Calvin, a Wesley or a Whitefield, a Moody or a Torrey or a Graham.

The grandeur of Elijah's character is nowhere more strikingly apparent than in the drama on Carmel. True, he was "a man of like passions" with us, but he was also a man of unlike courage and faith. Like Martin Luther, the lonely prophet fearlessly faced the assembled religious might of the nation. In the language of his day he proclaimed, "Here I stand, I can do no other." He threw down the gauntlet and challenged the false gods to a test of strength with his God.

The test was eminently fair. Since Baal was the god of fire, let the test be his own element. "The god that answereth by fire, let him be God," was Elijah's reasonable suggestion. No objection could be raised. The issues were crystal clear. "If Jehovah be God, follow Him, but if Baal, then follow him." The crisis hour had come, and they must take one turning or the other.

THE SIGNIFICANCE OF THE FIRE

"The Lord descended . . . in fire." The significance of the test by fire was not lost on the people of Israel. They could all recall occasions in their national history when God had answered by fire, and they knew that the fire was the manifestation of the presence of God.

God manifested His presence to Moses in the burning bush. "Behold, the bush *burned with fire*, and the bush was not consumed. And God called unto him out of the midst of the bush" (Exodus 3:2, 4). The presence of God on Mount Sinai was evidenced by fire: "And Mount Sinai was altogether on a smoke, *because the Lord descended on it in fire*" (Exodus 19:18). The presence of God in the midst of His people was symbolized by the fire which hovered over the Tabernacle by night. "And the glory of the Lord filled the tabernacle. . . . and *fire was on it* by night, in the sight of all the house of Israel" (Exodus 40:35, 38). There was a similar manifestation of the divine presence at the dedication of the temple. "Now when Solomon had made an end of praying, *the fire came down from heaven* . . . and the glory of the Lord filled the house" (2 Chronicles 7:1). The presence of the fire was proof of the presence of God.

Such was the significance of the symbol of fire in Old Testament times. But what is its meaning for us today? In the New Testament it is symbolic of the presence and energy of the Holy Spirit. Announcing the ministry of the Messiah, John the Baptist said, "He shall baptize you with the Holy Ghost, and *with fire*" (Matthew 3:11). His prophecy was fulfilled. On the Day of Pentecost when the Holy Spirit came with power upon the assembled disciples, the chosen symbol was prominent. "There appeared unto them cloven tongues *like as of fire*, and it sat upon each of them" (Acts 2:3). There is therefore justification for the view that the symbolism of fire in its present-day application is the presence and power of the Holy Spirit.

In Elijah's day the holy fire had disappeared from the altars of Jehovah; and false fire was burning on the altars of Baal. The glory had departed, and no man could rekindle the sacred flame. When Nadab and Abihu "offered strange fire before the Lord," they died, for there can be no substitute for the true fire of God.

In our day, the greatest lack in the life of the individual Christian and of the church is the fire of God, the manifested presence and mighty working of the Holy Spirit. There is little about us that cannot be explained on the level of the natural. Our lives are not fire-touched. There is no holy conflagration in our churches to which people are irresistibly drawn as a moth to a flame. It is the absence of the fire of God which accounts for the insignificant impact the church is making on a lost world. It never had better organization, a more scholarly ministry, greater resources of men and means, more skillful techniques. And yet never did it make a smaller contribution to solving the problems of a distraught world. Our prayer should be, "Lord, send the fire." What else can meet the need of the hour?

THE FALLING OF THE FIRE

"Then the fire of the LORD fell." The falling of the fire was the crux and climax of the Carmel drama. All else had been preparatory to this moment. Important spiritual lessons can be learned from what preceded it. If we can discover the fundamental factors, we will discover the source of spiritual revival. "Then the fire . . . fell." When?

The fire fell ***at a time of national apostasy***. Jehovah worship was at its lowest ebb and Baal worship had captured the field. Spiritual darkness enveloped the whole land. God does not limit the bestowal of His blessings to times when conditions are most propitious. It is when the darkness is deepest that the light is most needed, and no one will be disposed to minimize the darkness of the hour in which we live. No vivid imagination is required to see a real parallel with conditions in our day. Satanic forces are abroad. The church exerts little influence on the nation, although there are still the seven thousand who have not bowed the knee to Baal.

The fire fell ***when Elijah obeyed God without hesitation***. Earlier God had said to him, "Hide thyself." "So he went and did according unto the word of the LORD" (1 Kings 17:3, 5). Now comes the unequivocal command, "Go, show thyself unto Ahab; and I will send rain upon the earth" (18:1). It is not difficult to appreciate how little Elijah wished to meet Ahab, his implacable enemy. For three years the vindictive Ahab had been seeking his life. He could not forget that it was Elijah's prayer that had closed the heavens and smitten the land with drought. But before the drought could be relieved, Elijah must obey the word of the Lord.

His obedience was just as prompt as when he was told to hide himself. "And Elijah went to show himself unto Ahab" (18:2). The falling of the fire and the coming of the rain were a direct result of Elijah's obedience to facing Ahab, the personification of moral and spiritual evil. We will seek in vain the falling of the fire of God if there is some reserved area in our lives concerning which we refuse to obey God. If He is pressing on us the necessity of some act of obedience, restitution, apology, or witness, we refuse to obey at our own cost. He cannot move in blessing until there has been obedience.

The fire fell ***after the ruined altar had been repaired***. "He repaired the altar of the Lord that was broken down" (v. 30). The ruined altar spoke volumes. An altar is a symbol of worship. Carmel, it would appear, had been a secret meeting place for the people of God, but the altar had fallen into disuse and disrepair. The worship of Jehovah had ceased. Before the fire can fall, the altar must be rebuilt. Elijah took the twelve stones—he did not recognize the division between the northern and southern kingdoms—and rebuilt the altar. His objective was a reunited nation with the manifested presence of God among them. The fire of God falls when there is spiritual unity among God's people. If there is some altar in our lives which has fallen into disrepair, the fire will not fall until it is reerected. What does the altar preeminently typify? Did Christ not offer Himself on the altar of the cross? Only when the cross in its full significance is restored to its central place will the fire of the Lord fall.

The fire fell ***when the whole offering was placed on the altar***. "He . . . cut the bullock in pieces, and laid him on the wood" (v. 33). The fire of God never falls on an empty altar. The dismembering of the sacrifice is not without its spiritual significance. It is easy in a moment of exaltation and high resolve to place the whole life on the altar, but it is in the members of the body that the consecration has to be lived out, as F. R. Havergal so beautifully says in her consecration hymn. It begins with "Take my life," but it proceeds, "Take my hands . . . my feet . . . my voice . . . my love." It is not one great initial dedication only, but continuing acts of surrender. God will not be satisfied with a partial surrender. Ananias and Sapphira presented part to God, pretending it to be all, but at what tragic cost to themselves. Abraham was called upon by God to surrender to God the worst thing in his life and the best thing in his life. He had to surrender Ishmael, son of his carnal unbelief, and send him away from his paternal tent into the wilderness. He had to place on the altar Isaac, son of his sublime faith, and lift the sacrificial knife. Then the fire of the Lord fell on Abraham and there came the divine response, "In thy seed shall all the nations of the earth be blessed; because thou hast obeyed my voice." The last piece of the sacrifice had been placed on the altar. We cannot deceive God. He knows when the altar is full and His response will not tarry. When Elijah placed the last piece of the sacrifice on the altar, there was the flash of flame.

The fire fell ***after the counterfeit had been excluded***. "Fill four barrels with water, and pour it on the burnt sacrifice, and on the wood . . . and the water ran round about the altar" (vv. 33, 35). Elijah allowed no room for false fire.

Three times in his challenge to the prophets of Baal he stipulated, "Put no fire under." There was to be no trickery, no insertion of a secret spark. But he was equally strict with himself. Every precaution was taken against deception. He wished it to be clear that the fire which fell on his altar was kindled in Heaven. "Come near unto me," he invited the people. He had nothing to fear from their scrutiny. So sure was he of his God that he heaped difficulties in the way. The water would soon have quenched any hidden spark. His was the faith that laughs at impossibilities. Not many have a buoyant faith like this. Our inclination would be to help God out by pouring gasoline on the sacrifice for easier ignition! Elijah wished it to be evident that he had no alternative but God. It is for us, too, to guard against counterfeit, the substitution of the psychic for the spiritual, or mass hypnotism for the power of the Holy Spirit.

The fire fell ***after Elijah had prayed the prayer of faith***. Elijah said, "LORD . . . let it be known this day that thou art God in Israel, and that I am thy servant, and that I have done all these things at thy word. Hear me, O LORD, hear me, that this people may know that thou art the LORD God" (vv. 36–37).

What a contrast this, to the frenzied yelling of the priests of Baal as they leaped on their altar, calling on their unresponsive god and cutting themselves with lances till the blood gushed out! But no fire from Heaven fell in answer to their frantic cries. Before offering the prayer of faith Elijah had laughed the laugh of faith. The silence of Heaven proved the futility of their claims for Baal. So sure was he of the response of Jehovah that with withering sarcasm he taunted them and their god. "Cry aloud: for he is a god; either he is talking, or he is pursuing, or he is in a journey, or peradventure he sleepeth, and must be awaked" (v. 27). In this utterance Elijah had so committed both himself and his God that God could not let His servant down. Such a display of confidence was well-pleasing to God. "The immortal test of Elijah, made in the presence of an apostate king, and in the face of a backslidden nation and an idolatrous priesthood on Mount Carmel, is a sublime exhibition of faith and prayer," wrote E. M. Bounds.

No sooner had this simple prayer for the vindication of God and His servant been offered than there was a flash from Heaven. "Then the fire of the LORD fell." The fire did not fall in stages. The prayer of faith was immediately followed by the fire from Heaven. Sacrifice, wood, stones, water, alike offered no resistance to the heavenly flame. Elijah's heart's desire was realized. The supremacy of Jehovah was established. The presence and power of the true God was once again manifest among His people. The honor of both God and His servant was vindicated. The pretensions of the Baal worshipers were demolished. When our prayers are motivated by the desire "that the Father may be glorified in the Son," we too shall see the fire fall.

THE ACHIEVEMENT OF THE FIRE

The falling of the fire ***brought all Israel onto their faces***. "And when all the people saw it, they fell on their faces: and they said, The LORD, he is the God; the LORD, he is the God" (v. 39). The testimony of the man of God was vindicated by fire from the God who Himself is a consuming fire.

They could not deny the evidence of their eyes. A godless world will begin to pay attention to our witness when they see the fire of God in our midst, the manifestation of the presence and power of the Holy Spirit at work among us.

The falling of the fire ***resulted in the death of the false prophets***. Elijah's first act was to command Israel to bring with their own hands the priests of Baal to be killed. All rivals to the true God must be overthrown. The falling of the true fire automatically involved the removal of the false fire from the altars of Baal. Only the fire from Heaven gave Elijah the moral authority for such a purging as this.

The falling of the fire ***accomplished patent impossibilities***. Whoever heard of stones being consumed? And yet it was done. At Pentecost the fire of God accomplished the impossible in the lives of the apostles. Cowardice was burnt up and gave place to courage, doubt to faith, self-seeking to selflessness and a passion for the glory of Christ. Qualities of character which previously were conspicuous by their absence now flourished.

After the Great Plague in London there came the Great Fire when a large portion of the city was devastated. Some time afterward it was observed that strange and exotic flowers which had never before been seen sprang up in the vacant lots. Seeds which had long lain dormant in the cold soil suddenly sprang into life with the heat of the fire. The fire of God falling on a believer will achieve in ten minutes what he could not achieve in himself in ten years.

'Twas most impossible of all
That here in me sin's reign should cease,

Yet shall it be? I know it shall,
'Tis certain though impossible.
The thing impossible shall be;
All things are possible to me.
—C. Wesley

The falling of the fire ***left nothing but ashes.*** All that was combustible was consumed; only that which was indestructible remained. Fire can do no more to ashes. The fire of God will consume the carnal and superficial and leave only that which is of eternal value. Ashes have two characteristics. The slightest breath of wind will move them, and they invariably move in the direction of the wind. The life on which the fire of God has fallen will be especially sensitive to the promptings of the Holy Spirit and will always move in the direction of God's will.

O Thou who earnest from above
The pure celestial fire to impart,
Kindle a flame of sacred love
On the mean altar of my heart.
There let it for Thy glory burn
With inextinguishable blaze;
And trembling to its source return
In humble prayer and fervent praise.
—C. Wesley

CHAPTER 18

The Mighty Dynamic of the Spirit

And made them to cease by force and power.
EZRA 4:23

Not by might, nor by power,
but by my Spirit, saith the Lord.
ZECHARIAH 4:6 RSV

Reading: EZRA 4:1–24; ZECHARIAH 4:1–10

The patriotic remnant of Israel had returned to Jerusalem from their exile in Babylon. They carried with them a decree of King Cyrus authorizing the rebuilding of the temple, and work on the project had begun with great enthusiasm. They had not progressed far, however, before they encountered organized opposition. By guile and falsehood, adversaries had secured a counterdecree from Artaxerxes King of Persia, ordering that the work cease forthwith. Armed with this document, the exultant enemies went in haste to the Jews at Jerusalem and by force and power made the work cease (Ezra 4:20–24).

Discouraged and disheartened by this unexpected turn of events, instead of calling on the God who had so magnificently prospered their expedition, the patriots spiritlessly gave up. "Then ceased the work of the house of God . . . unto the second year of the reign of Darius." The first round had been won by the adversaries of God and Israel.

It would be easy to condemn their lack of spirit and lack of confidence in God, were we unfamiliar with the intricacy and treachery of our own hearts. Under less testing circumstances we have doubtless made no better showing.

THREE CRIPPLING HANDICAPS

The Jews were working under great handicaps. They were confronted with *the antagonism of neighboring races* who had the ear of the king. The advantage was with them. They varied their tactics to suit the changing situation. First, *infiltration*. "Let us build with you." When this failed, they tried *discouragement*. "They discouraged them." Then *intimidation*. "They made them afraid to build." Not content with this, they aimed to produce *frustration*. They "hired counselors against them, to frustrate their purpose." And lastly, they wrote an *accusation* against them (Ezra 4:1–6).

How familiar these tactics of the adversary seem in the semi-totalitarian world of our own day. Incidentals have changed but the pattern remains constant. Christian minorities the world around encounter similar opposition in their struggle to maintain their faith and testimony.

They suffered from *lack of resources.* In his proclamation Cyrus had generously ordered that the expenses incidental to the rebuilding of the temple be paid from the royal treasury (Ezra 6:4), but now Artaxerxes' decree had canceled this provision. Deprived of this source of revenue, they were left bankrupt of the financial and military resources necessary for their great task. Worse still, the noble and lofty ideals which had inspired their venture had faded, and they were becoming reconciled to their failure.

But the most serious handicap of all was the *disqualification of their leaders*. Their governor, Zerubbabel, though a man of royal descent, had proved a broken reed. In the face of the organized campaign of their adversaries, he had wilted. He was no Winston Churchill who, on learning of the defection of France in World War II, said to his cabinet, "Gentlemen, I find this rather exhilarating." Zerubbabel began well but did not display staying power and gave no inspiration to his discouraged people.

Joshua the high priest, the spiritual leader of the nation, was doubtless the holiest man of his day. Yet in Zechariah 3:3 he is seen standing before God "clothed with filthy garments" and consequently disqualified to minister on their behalf before God. Finding themselves without effective leadership, either temporal or spiritual, it is little wonder that the difficulties loomed before the people as an impassable mountain (Zechariah 4:7).

THE VISION OF HOPE

Just at this critical juncture a message of hope comes to Zechariah in the form of a vision. Was it mere coincidence or by divine ordering that the phrase used by the angel in the vision was the very one used by Ezra to recount the manner in which the work had been halted? Had work on the house of God been stopped by the "force and power" of their enemies? That was no reason for them to lose heart. "The hands of Zerubbabel have laid the foundation of this house; his hands shall also finish it" (Zechariah 4:9). It would be achieved, however, "not by might, nor by power, but by my Spirit, saith the LORD" (RSV). Despite the virulence of the opposition, despite their lack of resources, despite the incompetence of their leaders, victory was assured so long as they followed the Divine strategy. Success depended on neither Zerubbabel nor Joshua; on neither human force nor human power, but on the power of the Holy Spirit.

In vision Zechariah saw a lampstand, "all of gold, with a bowl upon the top of it, and his seven lamps thereon, and seven pipes to the seven lamps . . . and two olive trees by it, one upon the right side of the bowl, and the other upon the left side thereof" (Zechariah 4:2–3). The bowl which served as a reservoir for the oil was continually fed with oil from the two olive trees.

The primary application of the vision would not be missed by Jews familiar with the golden lampstand in their temple. They knew God had chosen their nation to be a light-bearer in the world. But in this they had failed dismally, and the light of testimony was all but extinguished. In His letters to the seven churches of Asia our Lord clearly indicated that the function Israel had failed to fulfill had passed over to the church, and borrowing the imagery of the vision, we are warranted in applying its symbolical teaching to the church of our day.

THE FUNCTION OF THE CHURCH

The primary task of the church as symbolized in the figure of the lampstand is to bring the light to a world shrouded in darkness. What other function has a lamp? Responsibility for reaction to the light is not ours. In the Revelation, Christ is seen standing in the midst of seven lampstands, each of which represented a living church, scrutinizing and appraising the shining of their lamp of testimony (Revelation 1:13, 20). Just as the golden candlestick was the sole means of illumination in the tabernacle, so the church is the only medium of light to a lost world. It exists to give light, and if it fails here it fails everywhere. God has made no alternative provision. "Ye are the light of the world," He said. And the light is *derived* light, reflected from Him who said, "I am the light of the world." How gross is the darkness of the contemporary world! What idolatry and superstition, what cruelty and suffering, what vice and crime, what materialism and cynicism! It is in this very context the church and the individuals who comprise it are to shine as lights.

But how is the church to fulfill its function? The vision supplies the secret. The church possesses no inherent light-giving power. Though illuminating, the lampstand was not itself luminous. It could not generate light, it could only bear it. It derived its light from a source outside itself. Surmounting the lampstand was the reservoir, always full, unfailingly pouring its supply of oil through the golden pipes to the flaming lamps. The bowl in turn was kept full from the olive trees which continually poured into it a stream of golden oil.

The significance of the oil is clearly indicated—"My Spirit." The church can give light only through the continual supply and enabling of the Holy Spirit. The *bowl* would surely symbolize Christ who is the reservoir of all the divine power and resources. "In him dwelleth all the fullness of the Godhead bodily. And ye are complete in him," wrote Paul. The fullness of the Spirit is always at high-water mark in His glorious nature. Every needful quality for effective light-bearing is stored in Him; on His fullness we may hourly draw. He it was who poured out the Holy Spirit on His waiting people on the Day of Pentecost. "Having received of the Father the promise of the Holy Ghost, he hath shed forth this, which ye now see and hear" (Acts 2:33). It is still He who imparts the same enduement today.

PROSCRIBED METHODS OF WORK

"Not by might, nor by power." The task of the church will never be achieved by purely human means. "Not by might, nor by power . . . saith the Lord." The phrase "not by might" may be rendered "not by an army," i.e., collective power, force of men or of means. Sometimes it means "wealth," sometimes "virtue" in an ethical sense, or "valor." But in all its usages the underlying thought is of human resources.

"Power" here also signifies force, but rather the prowess and dynamic of an individual. It is never used in a collective sense. Taking both words together the phrase would mean that success in the church's task depends on neither the combined strength of men organized to assist one another, or on the prowess and drive of any single individual.

It depends only and entirely on the agency of the Holy Spirit. And why? Because the task of the church is superhuman, and any resources of men and means, of skill and dynamic, are at best only human. If the task were only that of creating a visible organization, they might be adequate, but the church is infinitely more than a visible organization. It is a supernatural organism which can be nurtured and sustained only by spiritual means. The great danger faced by the church today is lest, in the midst of careful planning and seeking improved methods, she forget the superhuman factor without which her task will never be encompassed.

Hudson Taylor placed great emphasis on this vital truth. "The supreme want of all missions," he wrote, "is the manifested presence of the Holy Ghost. Hundreds of thousands of tracts and portions of Scripture have been put in circulation; thousands of gospel addresses have been given; tens of thousands of miles have been traversed in missionary journeys, but how small has been the issue in the way of definite conversions! There has been a measure of blessing, but where are the ones that chase a thousand, and the twos that put ten thousand to flight? . . . It is *Divine power* we need and not machinery. If the tens or hundreds we now reach daily are not being won to Christ, where would be the gain in machinery that would enable us to reach double that number?"

The Jewish patriots had to learn that success depended not on absence of opposition, but on clever leadership, not on human resources, but on the indispensable working of the mighty Holy Spirit.

DIVINELY APPOINTED MEANS

"By my Spirit, saith the LORD" (RSV). If we wish to enjoy the benefits of electric light, we must obey the laws of electricity. We have the benefit of a power only when we conform to its laws. Just so, we will experience the power of the Holy Spirit as we abandon every other dependence and obey "the law of the Spirit." If we are to illumine the world's darkness, it will be only as we submerge ourselves in the Golden Oil and allow the fire of the Holy Spirit to touch into flame the wicks of our lives. The great need of the world is of lives incandescent with the flame of God.

In the vision, one factor indispensable to light-bearing is never mentioned—the wick. Yet without it there could be no light, no contact between oil and flame. The wick exists only to be consumed. So long as it saves itself there will be no illumination. In the process of giving light, the believer's life is gradually consumed. Each time Jesus healed someone, He was conscious of virtue going out of Him. It was said of Him, "The zeal of thy house hath eaten me up." We will never be, like John the Baptist, burning and shining lights if we are not prepared to be consumed in the process. There must inevitably be exhaustion in self-outpouring, but we have the compensating assurance that "though our outward man perish, our inward man is renewed day by day."

Power for light-bearing is not inherent in the wick; it has no illuminating power. By itself it will emit only acrid smoke and black smudge. It is only the medium between oil and flame. It cannot conserve its own supply, but it is constantly dependent. It is always on the verge of bankruptcy. Withdraw it from the oil and the light becomes darkness.

In Old Testament times one of the functions of the priests was to remove with golden snuffers the encrustation from the wick, otherwise there would have been no clear shining. Sometimes our High Priest must use the golden snuffers to remove from our lives things which encrust and hinder the clear shining of the light. He performs this office through His Word applied in power to the heart by the Holy Spirit. Let us cherish this ministry, painful though it be.

It is by the dynamic of the Spirit alone that the church can fulfill its function, not by resources of intellect or finance or zeal. Propaganda, organization, and brilliance are no substitute for the Holy Spirit. New techniques and better methods have their place, but they do not dispense with the need for the dynamic of the Spirit. We will see success in our missionary work only when He has prepared the way for our coming. Where missions have flourished, there is evidence of the Spirit having been at work before the advent of the missionary, producing heart-hunger, creating expectation, causing disillusionment with their religions and persuading them of the insufficiency of the light they had.

What is implied in the phrase, "but by my Spirit"? That in all Christian work the superhuman factor is of supreme importance. True, it operates through the human, but it is the human interpenetrated by the Divine as the wick is saturated with the oil which is the Holy Spirit. Then we will not rely on our argument or persuasion to win converts and build up believers in their faith. We will trust Him to manipulate circumstances and overcome obstacles in our path. We will expect Him to enable us to "finish the work."

What a privilege is ours—to have the flame of God

consume us as we bring light to a world enveloped in midnight darkness! On reaching the shores of India, Henry Martyn said, "And now, let me burn out for God." He did—in six short years, but with an incredible legacy of achievement in Bible translation left behind Him.

And when I am dying, how glad I shall be,
That the lamp of my life has been blazed out for Thee;
I shall not care whatever I gave
Of labour or money one sinner to save;
I shall not care that the way has been rough;
That Thy dear feet led the way is enough
And when I am dying, how glad I shall be,
That the lamp of my life has been blazed out for Thee.

CHAPTER 19

The Missionary Passion of the Spirit

Ye shall receive power, after that the Holy Ghost is come upon you: and ye shall be witnesses unto me . . . unto the uttermost part of the earth.

ACTS 1:8

Reading: ACTS 13:1–13; 16:6–10

The Holy Spirit is the Executor of the Great Commission and Administrator of the missionary enterprise. In the great missionary manual of the New Testament, the Acts of the Apostles, we meet His name on almost every page. The history related is one sustained narrative of His activity through the church.

In preparation for His approaching departure, Christ promised a Vicegerent and Representative who would be the disciples' Companion and Counselor. "If I go not away, the Comforter [Paraclete] will not come unto you; but if I depart, I will send him unto you" (John 16:7). On the Day of Pentecost they exchanged Christ's physical presence for His omnipresence in the person of His Spirit. From the moment of the Spirit's advent the consuming passion and main preoccupation of the Lord began to be fulfilled. The promise had been that when the Spirit came upon them they would be witnesses to Christ (Acts 1:8). The fulfillment was specific. "They all began to speak as the Spirit gave them utterance." And their speech was mightily effective.

In the record of their missionary activity it is everywhere apparent that the acts of the apostles—and of the churches too—are traced beyond the human channel to the Divine source. The main actor is the Holy Spirit, and men are but His instruments in the achieving of the divine purpose. From first to last the Holy Spirit is the prime mover and chief worker.

The Day of Pentecost marked two significant events in the onward march of Christianity. First, *the inauguration of the Holy Spirit* into His twofold office as Comforter and Enduer. As Comforter, He was imparted to His fearful and sorrowing disciples by the risen Christ in fulfillment of His promise (John 16:7), when He breathed on them and said, "Receive ye the Holy Ghost" (John 20:22). The promise of the Son was of the Holy Spirit as Comforter.

The promise of the Father was the Holy Spirit as Enduer, and it too found its fulfillment on the Day of Pentecost. "Behold, I send the promise of my Father upon you: but tarry ye in the city of Jerusalem, until ye be endued with power from on high" (Luke 24:49). "And they were all filled with the Holy Ghost" (Acts 2:4). It was only as the vastness of the task committed to them began to break in upon their consciousness that the disciples felt their great lack of power. On this memorable day when Babel was reversed, God graciously gave them an initial experience of the Spirit's empowering. There, men were confounded because one language became many. Here, they were amazed because many languages became one. It was this epoch-making event which marked the real beginning of the missionary enterprise. The gospel in one day penetrated a score of countries and was spoken in a score of tongues.

The inauguration of the Paraclete into His twofold office was accompanied by another epoch-making event, *the institution of the church*, the mystical body of Christ, a living and irresistible organism. In the days of His flesh, our Lord in Person provided a perfect vehicle through which the Holy Spirit could bring to pass the world purpose of God. But now with the removal to Heaven of His glorified physical body, His mystical body, the church, was to become the instrument of the Holy Spirit. Everything Christ did when on earth was done through the empowering of the Spirit; ideally this was to be true of His church as well. The baptism of the Spirit had a corporate significance, for by it all believers of all ages were incorporated into the mystical body of Christ. "For by one Spirit are we all baptized into one body" (1 Corinthians 12:13). This body through its members was charged with the responsibility of bringing the good news of salvation to the whole world. The gospel was to be preached "in all the world for a witness unto all nations" (Matthew 24:14). The power for this witnessing they would find in the enduement of the Spirit.

ENDUER OF THE MISSIONARIES

In His final utterance, the ascending Lord linked the advent of His Spirit with the bestowal of power for the effective worldwide witness which was His supreme objective. "But ye shall receive power, after that the Holy Spirit is come upon you: and ye shall be witnesses unto me both in Jerusalem, and in all Judea, and in Samaria, and unto the uttermost part of the earth" (Acts 1:8). Christ's words were fulfilled not many days after, when "devout men out of every nation under heaven" heard their Spirit-given testimony. The Day of Pentecost was a sample of which subsequent missions were to be a facsimile.

The specific manner of the fulfillment was clearly stated. "And they were all filled with the Holy Ghost" (Acts 2:4). This was not an experience confined to those of the pentecostal company, nor did it occur only on an isolated occasion. Peter, for example, experienced subsequent fillings as recorded in Acts 4:8 and 31. The repeated emphasis on this subject throughout the Acts is significant, showing that these early missionaries took seriously their Master's command not to engage in their ministry until they were endued with power from on high. And this enduement is the essential missionary equipment today, for apart from the Holy Spirit there can be no effective witness.

The idea behind the expression, "filled with the Spirit," was not of a passive receptacle to be filled but of a vibrant human personality to be controlled by a Divine Personality. Passivity was out. Every faculty of the disciple was in fullest and highest exercise, but no resistance to the control of the beneficent Holy Spirit was offered.

It is noteworthy that the term "filled" as used in Acts 2:4 and Ephesians 5:18 frequently carries the sense of "controlled." For example, "And [they] were filled with fear"

(Luke 5:26). "Because I have said these things unto you, sorrow hath filled your heart" (John 16:6). These people were gripped and controlled by their fear and sorrow. Thayer in his lexicon says in this connection, "That which takes possession of the mind is said to fill it." We are filled with the Spirit when we voluntarily allow Him to possess and control our whole personality and bring it under the Lordship of Christ. When He fills us, He exercises His control from the center of our personality. He constantly enlightens our intellects to appreciate and appropriate the truth as it is in Christ Jesus. He purifies and stabilizes our emotions, fixing them on Christ. He reinforces our wills to obey the commandments of Christ. Rather than obliterating our personalities He releases and enhances them. In this way the Holy Spirit infused new life and power into the lives of the disciples to equip them for their tremendous responsibilities.

This enduement of the Spirit was the normal and essential equipment of the missionary and for it there is still no substitute.

ADMINISTRATOR OF THE MISSIONARY ENTERPRISE

As Executor of the great commission and Administrator of the missionary enterprise, the Holy Spirit is given great prominence in the records of the achievements of the early church. His authority at the commencement of the new dispensation was vindicated by His strange work of judgment in the case of Ananias and Sapphira. The sin of lying to the Holy Ghost brought on both of them the dire penalty of sudden death. "Why hath Satan filled thine heart to lie to the Holy Ghost? . . . Thou hast not lied unto men, but unto God" (Acts 5:3–4). God would have men know that it was no light thing to trifle with the Holy Spirit whom He had appointed as Executor of His purposes on earth. It is not without significance that the first word in the history of missions among the Gentiles is, "The Holy Ghost said, Separate me . . ." (Acts 13:2).

His first administrative activity is in *the calling of the missionary.* In the missionary call the initiative is with the Holy Spirit, not with the volunteer or with the church. The paragraph recounting the call of Barnabas and Saul (Acts 13:1–4) throws clear light on this subject. "Separate me Barnabas and Saul for the work whereunto I *have called them,*" was the message of the Holy Spirit. The Divine call precedes any activity of church or missionary. The church's responsibility was to let them go, to recognize the Spirit's appointment and act upon it. It is worthy of note that the Holy Spirit selected the ablest men for His purpose, and the church made no demur. The responsibility of the missionary was to respond to the call. In the final analysis, judgment of fitness lay neither with the individual nor with the church leaders but with the Holy Spirit. Their part was to be sensitive to His leading and obedient to His command. The church did not vote on the issue. The candidates did not submit sheaves of testimonials. The missionaries were discovered to a group of spiritual leaders while in an attitude of prayer and self-denial they "ministered to the Lord." But it has not ever been so. Especially in the early days of modern missions, missionaries went out in the teeth of the overwhelming opposition or indifference of a church insensitive to the voice of the Spirit—mighty men such as Ramon Lull and William Carey. But though neglected by men they were not forgotten by the Holy Spirit who called them.

Then the Holy Spirit *sent out the missionaries* with the church as consenting party. "When they had fasted and prayed, and laid their hands on them, they sent them away. So they, *being sent forth by the Holy Ghost*, departed unto Seleucia" (Acts 13:3–4). The fellowship of the church was symbolized in the laying on of hands, but the authorizing thrust came from the Holy Spirit who was the real Consecrator. The church dedicated and commissioned those whom the Spirit had already consecrated. Without the prior ordination of the Spirit, the laying on of hands by men is in vain.

The selection of the sphere of work was also the prerogative of the Spirit, not of the missionaries. The Holy Spirit alone knows the strategy of the Lord of the harvest whose interests He serves. This is strikingly illustrated in the journeys of Paul. On their first journey the Spirit guided the missionaries to Cyprus, on the sea route to Asia and the Roman world. Concerning their second missionary journey we read, "Now when they had gone throughout Phrygia and the region of Galatia, and were *forbidden of the Holy Ghost* to preach the word in Asia, after they were come to Mysia, they assayed to go into Bithynia: but *the Spirit suffered them not*" (Acts 16:6–7). The Holy Ghost alone knows which are the strategic centers and who is best fitted to serve there. Carey planned to go to the South Seas. The Spirit designated him to India. Barnardo felt called to China. The Spirit retained him in England. Judson's objective was India. The Spirit directed his steps to Burma.

And in the light of subsequent events, how important it was to the missionary enterprise that they heeded His leading!

Asia and Bithynia were to receive the gospel in due time, but for the present the Divine strategy was that the message should travel westward to Europe, whence would stem the great missionary enterprise. Europe was ripening for the harvest. The Anglo-Saxon race were to be the missionary pioneers, and five-sixths of all missionary work has been done through their instrumentality. Paul was sufficiently sensitive in spirit to respond to the Spirit's restraint. He did not press forward in self-will but drew apart to discover in prayer and consultation the geographical will of God for him and his companions. It should be noted that the expansion of the church and its extension to unexpected quarters was due to the constraint of the Holy Spirit rather than to the deliberate planning of the missionaries.

The Spirit too *determines the timing of the missionary program.* How very slow God at times appears to be. Why wait seventeen years from the completion of the events on which Christianity is based before fully launching His universal missionary program, and then why send out only two? Why so paltry a task force in the face of such appalling need? We have to learn that God's thoughts are higher than our thoughts, that His ways are past finding out. It is our part to heed the restraints of the Spirit and wait on Him for the revelation of His timing. We must learn that there is such a thing as the tide of the Spirit. He is working to a meticulously accurate timetable, and in our own spheres of responsibility we disregard His timing to our own loss and disappointment.

The appointment of fellow workers is also in the sphere of the Spirit's authority. Saul did not choose his own fellow worker—he was assigned by the Holy Spirit. Even the brilliant and deeply taught apostle was not sent forth by the Spirit without a more experienced and spiritually strong senior. The placing of Saul with Barnabas was no chance happening. Barnabas was mature, experienced, a "son of consolation." To his gracious gifts the Holy Spirit added the intensity, the fiery zeal, the restless urgency, the brilliant intellectual powers of Saul, who had long been preparing in the school of God. Together they made a wonderful blending of gifts. But even in a team so spiritually alert and gifted there later came a rift over Barnabas's nephew, John Mark (Acts 15:39). Even this regrettable incident was overruled by the Spirit, in that two preaching bands were created instead of one.

Another activity of the Spirit is *the leading of the missionary to strategic converts*. One outstanding example is the call of the Spirit to Philip to leave the thriving revival which was in progress in Samaria and in which he was playing such an important role, for "Gaza, which is desert." On the face of it this seemed the opposite of sound judgment. But when Philip in obedience to the Spirit's voice reached Gaza his arrival exactly synchronized with that of a vastly influential man in search of Christ and His salvation (Acts 8:29). It was the reward of his unquestioning obedience to be invited to explain the gospel to a prepared seeker who embraced Christ on the spot. And through this convert, none other than Ethiopia's chancellor of the exchequer, the gospel penetrated into that kingdom. Apart from the Spirit's intervention Philip would never have gone to Gaza, and Ethiopia would have remained without the gospel. Every mission field provides similar if less spectacular examples.

One of the acute problems of missionary work is the pressure of the powers of darkness. At times these pressures seem too great to be borne, but here too the Holy Spirit is active in *empowering against Satanic opposition.* Elymas the sorcerer withstood Barnabas and Saul, seeking to turn the deputy Sergius Paulus away from the faith. "Then Saul . . . *filled with the Holy Ghost* . . . said, O full of all subtlety and mischief . . . wilt thou not cease to pervert the right ways of the Lord? . . . Thou shalt be blind" (Acts 13:9–11). He experienced the cooperation of the Holy Spirit in dealing with Satan-inspired opposition. The Spirit first imparted to him spiritual insight to discern the source of the disturbance, and then spiritual authority to deal with it. He boldly unmasked the nature, origin, spirit, and aim of Elymas's opposition, and he solemnly invoked the judgment of God.

Then, too, the Holy Spirit *sustained the missionaries amid opposition and discouragement,* when the Jews in their hostility to Christ expelled them from their coasts. The strange sequel was, "And the disciples were filled with joy, and with the Holy Ghost" (Acts 13:52). They were lifted above their circumstances and were able to rejoice amid their trials. They found indeed that the Holy Spirit was the Divine Stimulus and Comforter.

It was the Holy Spirit who *directed the church in the appointment of its leaders.* It was not done by majority vote. "Take heed . . . to all the flock [of God], over the which *the Holy Ghost hath made you overseers*" (Acts 20:28). It was He who assigned the pastors to the flock. The appointments were His prerogative from lowest to highest, not of the officers themselves. For even the humblest service within the church, the men must be controlled by the Spirit (Acts 6:3).

At the first church council in Jerusalem, the presence and *presidency of the Holy Spirit* was clearly recognized by the delegates present. His was the deciding voice in any matter of doubt. The chairman's wording of the decision of the council was clear indication of the place accorded to Him in their deliberations. "*It seemed good to the Holy Ghost,* and to us" (Acts 15:28). He was accorded the place of first importance in their findings.

The importance the early missionaries attached to the work of the Holy Spirit can be gauged by the care with which they introduced converts and believers to His ministry (Acts 8:17; 9:17). Paul traced the ineffectiveness of the twelve men at Ephesus to their ignorance of the Spirit's filling and empowering (Acts 19:2–6). Is this not a strong case for a very early indoctrination of converts on this crucial subject?

When the church and its missionaries concede to the Holy Spirit the supreme place in their planning and activities, we can expect to see spectacular advance on the mission fields of the world. But the plain fact is that even where His prerogatives are not entirely ignored, He is afforded little opportunity to display His power.

It was otherwise with Jonathan Goforth under whose ministry powerful revivals took place in China and Korea. He was deeply concerned to see revival in his work, and with that end in view set himself to make an intensive study of the Person and work of the Holy Spirit. He then began to preach what he was learning to the Christian groups he visited. Deep conviction and confession of sin followed, and an increasing number of conversions.

While speaking in one Chinese city to a heathen audience, which filled the street chapel, Goforth witnessed a stirring in people's hearts such as he had never seen before. When speaking on the text, "He bore our sins in his own body on the tree," conviction seemed written on every face. When he asked for decisions, practically everyone stood up. Then, turning about, seeking one of ten evangelists who accompanied him to take his place, he found the whole band with a look of awe on their faces. One whispered, "Brother, He for whom we have prayed so long was here in very deed tonight." Everywhere they went in succeeding days, many souls sought salvation. They had conceded to the Holy Spirit His rightful place in the missionary enterprise and reaped their reward in His mighty working in their midst.

One of the most thrilling stories of the moving of the Spirit on the mission field is that of the Lone Star Mission in Ongole, India. After fifteen years of sacrificial work, only ten converts had been won. In view of a heavy deficit, the Baptist Missionary Union in 1853 was deciding to close down the station. Dr. Colver made an eloquent plea for the little church, won at such cost. Dr. Edwin Bright, the Secretary, followed with a speech which concluded, "Who is the man who would write the letter or carry the message to that little church of ten members, telling them that American Baptists had resolved to abandon them?" He strode up and down the platform saying, "And who shall write the letter?"

That night, Dr. Samuel Smith, author of "My Country, 'Tis of Thee," could not sleep. During the debate a map had been hung, the mission stations being marked with stars. Burma was thickly studded, but Nellore stood alone in India. Someone had referred to the lone star. Taking pencil and paper, Dr. Smith wrote:

Shine on, Lone Star, thy radiance bright
Shall spread o'er all the eastern sky;
Morn breaks apace from gloom and night!
Shine on and bless the pilgrim's eye.
Shine on, Lone Star, I would not dim
The light that gleams with dubious ray.
The lonely star of Bethlehem
Led on a bright and glorious day.
Shine on, Lone Star, in grief and tears,
And sad reverses oft baptized;
Shine on amid thy sister spheres:
Lone stars in heaven are not despised.
Shine on, Lone Star; who lifts a hand
To dash to earth so bright a gem,
A new 'lost pleiad' from the band
That sparkles in night's diadem?
Shine on, Lone Star, the days draw near
When none shall shine more fair than thou;
Thou, born and mused in doubt and fear,
Wilt gather on Immanuel's brow.
Shine on, Lone Star, till earth redeemed,
In dust shall bid its idols fall;
And thousands where thy radiance beamed
Shall crown the Saviour Lord of all.

At breakfast, Judge Harris, the chairman, asked Dr. Smith his opinion. He produced the poem. He read it at the meeting with much feeling. It shook the audience, and men wept. A vision of hope dawned.

And the result? A great movement of the Spirit crowned their faith. In a single day 2,222 baptisms took place. Thirty years later the Ongole church had 15,000 members, the largest Baptist church in the world.

CHAPTER 20

The Spirit and Speaking with Tongues (1)

They . . . all . . . began to speak with other tongues as the Spirit gave them utterance.

ACTS 2:4

Reading: 1 CORINTHIANS 12:6–11; 28–31

The phenomena accompanying the descent of the Holy Spirit on the Day of Pentecost bore clear witness to the release of a new spiritual power, the dawning of a new era. The polyglot crowds were confounded by the spectacular gift of speaking with tongues bestowed on the apostles. They were amazed but deeply impressed by the fact that "every man heard them speak in his own language."

Speaking with tongues occurred also on two subsequent occasions when the Holy Spirit descended on Gentile groups in Caesarea and Ephesus. On this foundation of fact has been erected the great superstructure of what is generally termed the Pentecostal movement. The majority of adherents of this group of churches holds that speaking with tongues is the necessary accompaniment and evidence of the baptism or enduement with the Holy Spirit. The movement has experienced spectacular growth during the past half-century. In the United States of America it is the fastest growing of all church groups. This alone should stimulate inquiry into its claims and Scriptural basis. If we are missing some blessing which God has for us, we should know it. If the movement, though sincere, is mistaken in some of its emphases, we should know it.

Pentecostalism is not a heresy, for it denies no doctrine of evangelical Christianity. Indeed, it contends earnestly for the faith. We must therefore bear in mind that even though we may not agree with the views of Pentecostals, they are fellow members of the body of Christ. That adherents of this movement are mistaken on certain points we believe, but many of them are utterly sincere and intensely earnest. Pentecostalism may perhaps, without any desire to be offensive, best be described as a spiritual infatuation. And an infatuation is seldom overcome by cold and logical argument. To approach those in the emotional, almost ecstatic grip of this teaching merely with a series of syllogisms, even if supported by appropriate Scriptures, will generally leave them entirely unmoved. They are in the enjoyment of something which they are not willing to surrender for what they consider to be the cold and unsatisfying doctrine of many evangelical churches.

May it not be that hungry Christians and new converts have been driven into the arms of this group because it holds out the promise of something more vital, more satisfying, more dynamic than the type of Christianity they encounter in our churches? As they compare the zeal and fervor of the early church with the lukewarmness of most churches of our day, have they not grounds for following something which promises a repetition of early church power? Has our teaching in this connection been inadequate or defective? We do well to be challenged by the virility of the Pentecostal movement around the world, both in its home ministry and its missionary outreach.

THE PENTECOSTAL GIFT

What was "the promise of the Father" for which our Lord commanded His disciples to wait in Jerusalem? It was not the gift of tongues, but enduement with power from on high, and these two things are quite distinct and separable (Luke 24:49). The evidence of having received the enduement was to be effectiveness in witness. When our Lord amplified the promise as recorded in Acts 1:8, He made it clear that the result of the coming of the Spirit upon them would be the power of effective and extensive witness to the risen Christ: "Ye shall receive power, after that the Holy Ghost is come upon you: and ye shall be witnesses unto me . . . unto the uttermost part of the earth." It is true that this enduement was accompanied by "speaking with other tongues, as the Spirit gave them utterance" (Acts 2:4), but this was neither the gift itself nor even its most significant evidence, as Pentecostals claim.

OTHER TONGUES AND UNKNOWN TONGUES

In order to meet this assertion, several preliminary questions must be answered:

Are the "other tongues" of Pentecost and the "unknown tongues" of 1 Corinthians 14 one and the same? It should be noted that "unknown" used in connection with "tongues" in 1 Corinthians 14 (KJV) is not in the Greek. The ASV correctly translates simply "tongues." "Other" tongues occurs only once—in Acts 2:4. In Acts 10:46 and 19:6 the rendering is simply "with tongues," and in the latter passage the addition of "and prophesied" would seem to make a distinction between ecstatic utterances and plainly spoken teaching.

In his commentary, E. H. Plumptre asserts that apart from the Day of Pentecost, the tongues were not "the power of speaking in a language which had not been learned by the common way of learning, but the ecstatic utterance of rapturous devotion." His contention has much scriptural support.

At Pentecost ***all*** spoke in tongues (Acts 2:4). This was not true of the believers at Corinth (1 Corinthians 12:30).

At Pentecost the tongues were understood by all (Acts 2:6). At Corinth they were understood by none (1 Corinthians 14:2, 9).

At Pentecost they spoke to men (Acts 2:11, 17). At Corinth they spoke to God (1 Corinthians 14:2).

At Pentecost no interpreter was necessary (Acts 2:6). At Corinth speaking with tongues was forbidden if an interpreter was not present (1 Corinthians 14:23, 28).

At Pentecost speaking with tongues was a sign or credential to believers (Acts 11:15). At Corinth it was a sign to unbelievers (1 Corinthians 14:22).

At Pentecost speaking with tongues brought salvation to others (Acts 2:41). At Corinth it edified those who spoke (1 Corinthians 14:4).

At Pentecost strangers were filled with awe and marveled (Acts 2:7–8). At Corinth Paul warned that if all spoke with tongues in a church assembly, strangers would say they were mad (1 Corinthians 14:23).

At Pentecost there was perfect harmony (Acts 2:1). At Corinth there was confusion (1 Corinthians 14:33).

Since there is such a marked difference between these two manifestations of the gift of tongues, it would be questionable exegesis to build a system of doctrine on the identity of the two occurrences. If the "tongues" of 1 Corinthians 14 are not identical with those of Acts 2, what were they? The "other tongues" spoken on the Day of Pentecost were other than their native tongues. "Each one began to speak in a language he had not acquired, and yet it was a real language understood by those from various lands familiar with them. It was not jargon, but intelligible language." The "tongues" of 1 Corinthians 14 were ecstatic, vocal utterances, fervent and rapturous religious expressions, not necessarily intelligible to speaker or hearer except through the gift of interpretation. This description would fit in with the whole teaching of the chapter.

William Barclay comments: "This phenomenon was very common in the early church. In it a man became worked up to an ecstasy and in that state he poured out a quite uncontrollable torrent of sounds in no known language. Unless these sounds were interpreted, no one had any idea what they meant. Strange as it may seem, in the early church this was a highly coveted gift. It was a dangerous gift. For one thing it was abnormal and greatly admired and therefore the person who possessed it was very liable to develop a certain spiritual pride in his gift; and for another thing, the very desire to possess it produced, at least in some, a kind of self-hypnotism and a kind of deliberately induced hysteria which issued in a completely false and deluded and synthetic speaking with tongues."

But it must be remembered that this kind of ecstatic utterance is not by any means the sole prerogative of Pentecostalism. It is familiar to both Islam and Hinduism, to Mormonism and Spiritism. This fact alone should cause one to view with reserve any claim that speaking with tongues is the necessary and only evidence of the Spirit's baptism or enduement. One writer claims, "In nearly all religions at the point where fervor merges into fanaticism, there are similar manifestations." Speaking with tongues, then, may be the working of the Spirit of Error as well as the Spirit of Truth.

CAN THERE BE GENUINE "TONGUES" TODAY?

Two views are held on this question. The first is well expressed in the words of Sir Robert Anderson, stated with his characteristic conviction. "It is not a matter of opinion but of fact that whereas the Pentecostal gifts and evidential miracles hold a prominent place in the narrative of The Acts and in the teaching of the Epistles written during the period historically covered by The Acts, the later Epistles are silent with regard to them. The natural inference is that the miracles and gifts had ceased, and the Epistles of Paul's last imprisonment give proof that this inference is right."

Supporting the same view, Dr. G. Campbell Morgan wrote: "We must remember that these signs were initial, they were incomplete. They produced no final result. They were necessary to arrest the attention of Jerusalem. . . . They were Divine, direct and positive, but they were transient, never repeated because never needed."

A reasonable case can be presented in support of this view, although it is by no means conclusive. In 1 Corinthians 13, which separates the cataloging of spiritual gifts in chapter 12 from the instruction in the worthy exercise of those gifts in chapter 14, these words occur: "Whether there be prophecies, they shall fail; whether there be tongues, they shall cease; whether there be knowledge, it shall vanish away. For we know in part, and we prophesy in part. But when that which is perfect is come, then that which is in part shall be done away" (1 Corinthians 13:8–10).

Proponents of the view that the Pentecostal gifts and evidential miracles have passed away maintain that 1 Corinthians 13:10 refers not to the final consummation, but to the full revelation of God's truth which was reached in the writings of Paul. In Ephesians 4:8–16 which gives chronologically the last list of spiritual gifts, the miracle gifts are omitted. And even of the gifts mentioned, two—apostles and prophets—are now withdrawn. With the coming of maturity and completeness, the three special gifts—knowledge, prophecy, and tongues—have passed away and ceased, because they have fulfilled their purpose. They were needed only while revelation was incomplete (See Hebrews 2:3–4). These gifts were the accompaniment of spiritual immaturity, and Paul said in this connection, "When I became a man, I put away childish things."

So the argument runs. It rests, not on any clear statement of Scripture, but rather on a series of reasonable deductions. The writer has used this line of argument with some enamored of the viewpoint of Pentecostalism, but entirely without success. There are no categorical Scriptural statements to which one can appeal as the end of all argument. On the contrary, several unequivocal scriptural statements can be advanced against it.

> "Forbid not to speak with tongues."
> (1 Corinthians 14:39)
> "I would that ye all spake with tongues."
> (1 Corinthians 14:5)
> "I speak with tongues more than ye all," said Paul.
> (1 Corinthians 14:18)

In the face of such clear statements, to class *all* speaking with tongues in the present as spurious, "nothing but jargon and hysteria," would be rather sweeping and would hardly carry conviction with believers who hear in the inspired writings of Paul the voice of the Holy Spirit.

That most modern speaking with tongues may justly be classed as jargon and hysteria is not denied. Its fruits have not proved in the main to be the fruit of the Spirit. Even when interpretations are given, the subject matter is often puerile and adds nothing that is not much better stated in Scripture. Writing on this point, Dr. R. A. Torrey, who studied deeply the early development of this movement, while believing that much of it was spurious, said, "We do not deny the possibility of God's giving a man in our day the gift of tongues." When the movement was just gathering momentum, Rev. George W. Soltau, a reliable Bible expositor, wrote, "Then is there no such thing as speaking with tongues? Verily there is.

. . . To whom has it been given? It would appear from such information as is at hand, that the real blessing has been given *in private*, often unexpectedly and without any seeking for it, and that it has been bestowed for the purposes of worship and adoration, not for soul-winning and display. There are some few cases of such gift being bestowed in public meetings, and such have been accompanied by a spirit of gentleness, humility, sobriety, and love."

The writer has personally known such a case as that referred to, when the manifestation came in private and unsought, and resulted in worship and adoration. After a few occurrences it ceased and never recurred.

CHAPTER 21

The Spirit and Speaking with Tongues (2)

Do all speak with tongues?

1 CORINTHIANS 12:30

Reading: 1 CORINTHIANS 14:1–33

EVIDENCE OF BAPTISM OF THE HOLY SPIRIT

The majority of Pentecostals hold the view that speaking with tongues is the essential evidence of the baptism or enduement of the Spirit. They contend that without this manifestation the baptism of the Spirit has not been experienced or His fullness bestowed, but only a measure of the Spirit's presence and power. This belief is based on the fact that at Jerusalem on the Day of Pentecost, at Caesarea in the house of Cornelius, and at the church gathering at Ephesus the baptism of the Spirit was evidenced by speaking with tongues (Acts 2:4; 10:46; 19:6). It is of interest to note the cases in the book of Acts in which there is no question of this experience having such accompanying manifestations.

A study of the three occurrences mentioned reveals that in each case there was a significant reason for the bestowal of the gift of speaking with tongues.

At Pentecost the urgency and emergency of the occasion was the reason. The feast of Pentecost had drawn a great company of Jews from the surrounding nations. Many were about to return home. With the crucifixion, resurrection, and ascension of Christ now in the past, the foundation facts of the gospel were complete. The descent of the Spirit with the accompanying manifestations had aroused the interest of the whole city. If the immense crowd was to be evangelized, if the explanation of these significant events was ever to reach them, it must be now. Without the gift of tongues the witness could not have reached the men of these fifteen nations because of the language barrier. So in the exercise of His sovereign will, the Holy Spirit bestowed the gift, and the divine purpose of the initial evangelization of these nations was achieved. There is no record of an identical repetition on any subsequent occasion.

At *Caesarea* the reason was different. The speaking with tongues was rendered necessary by the reluctance of Peter to obey the Lord's command to take the gospel to Cornelius the Gentile. His attitude was exactly representative of that of the church at Jerusalem. In order to convince both Peter and the church that God had bestowed the identical gift on the Gentiles as on the Jews, God graciously gave a repetition of the manifestation at Jerusalem, but without its polyglot languages or evangelistic implications.

At *Ephesus* the Jewish brethren had heard nothing of the subsequent history of the movement which began with

John the Baptist, and in which they had participated. They did not know all the facts of redemption or of the gift of the Holy Spirit. But through Paul's teaching their experience was linked with that of the church at Jerusalem and with the firstfruits from among the Gentiles at Caesarea by the same evidential gift of tongues, but again without the evangelistic accompaniments of Pentecost.

It would appear then that the purpose of the gift of tongues in these cases was not as evidence of the gift or fullness of the Holy Spirit but of the identity of the blessing bestowed on each of these occasions. It is noteworthy, too, that at Jerusalem, Caesarea, and Ephesus, *the gift was bestowed without being sought or expected, and in each case at one and the same meeting.* There is no precedent here for the "tarrying meetings" which have characterized the Pentecostal churches. The gift was bestowed in each case on the assembled company, not on selected or specially prepared individuals.

For the above reasons it cannot be maintained on the strength of these passages that speaking with tongues is the sole evidence of the Spirit's baptism and enduement. If this were the case, its practical effect would be to make it the most important of all spiritual gifts and, therefore, to be sought above all others. Paul's emphasis, however, is in exactly the opposite direction. Prophecy is everywhere given precedence over tongues, which gift he classes as of least importance. He exhorts the Corinthian believers to "covet earnestly the best [greater, ASV] gifts," thus indicating that some spiritual gifts are greater and more to be desired than others. While positively urging the Corinthians to earnestly desire to prophesy, he says concerning tongues that they are not to be forbidden.

Of no gift does he point out more clearly the possibility of abuse, and no other gift is so hedged around with restrictions and regulations. "In the church," he said, "I had rather speak five words with my understanding, that by my voice I might teach others also, than ten thousand words in an unknown tongue" (1 Corinthians 14:19).

THE PURPOSE OF "TONGUES"

It may be questioned, since this gift required such strict regulation and was so open to abuse and counterfeit, whether it is of any real value. The fact that it was bestowed by the Holy Spirit is sufficient evidence that in its pristine purity and when exercised within the divinely sanctioned restrictions, it was neither unnecessary nor useless. If that were so, we would have no explanation of or justification for the gift of interpretation.

The gift of tongues attested the beginning of a new era and also served the important function of authenticating and confirming the inspired spoken word when as yet there was no written New Testament. God bore witness with His preachers by means of "signs and wonders, and with divers miracles, and *gifts of the Holy Ghost*, according to his own will" (Hebrews 2:4). It could also be the genuine expression of devotion and as such serve a beneficent purpose. We must be careful not to so exaggerate its inferiority to the other gifts as to impugn the wisdom of the Holy Spirit in bestowing it.

RULES GOVERNING THE GIFT

While indicating that such ecstatic utterance need not be encouraged but should not be forgotten, Paul does surround its exercise with restrictive regulations. He did not question the reality of the gift but he was well aware of its dangers, for ecstasy and hysteria and self-hypnotism are very difficult to distinguish. If it be conceded that there may be genuine speaking with tongues today, it must be accepted as a corollary that its genuineness will be attested by its conformity to the requirements of Scripture. It was permitted on the understanding that everything was to be done "decently and in order" (1 Corinthians 14:40). From Paul's instructions the following facts emerge:

The bestowal of all spiritual gifts is the sovereign prerogative of the Holy Spirit (1 Corinthians 12:11). Therefore, no such gift can be demanded as of right. We cannot dictate to Him which spiritual gift we shall have.

We are urged to desire earnestly the greater gifts, that is, those most to the edification of the church (1 Corinthians 14:12). The Corinthian church disregarded this counsel and majored in the spectacular, to its own confusion and loss.

The primary object of the bestowal of any gift is the edification of the church (1 Corinthians 14:12). If any professed manifestation of the gift does not do this, it is either counterfeit or being abused.

If anyone desires to speak with a "tongue" in public, he must first ascertain whether it can be interpreted (1 Corinthians 14:28).

In the church, speaking in a "tongue" was to be confined to two or three, and each in turn. They must speak in succession and not all at once. Failing this, the tongue was to be suppressed (1 Corinthians 14:28).

If the exercise of the gift produces confusion rather than order, that is *prima facie* evidence that it is spurious, for God is not the author of confusion (1 Corinthians 14:33).

REASONS FOR CAUTION

We recognize those who hold these views as fellow believers and many of them as devout Christians. But we must appraise the movement in the light of its fruits and possible dangers. One of its great dangers lies in its tendency to subordinate the primary and essential to the incidental and secondary. Exaltation of the spectacular tends to make the great central truths of Christianity subordinate to subjective spiritual manifestations and the experience which such manifestations produce. Any teaching which does this is at once suspect.

Several dangers confront this teaching.

Spiritual Pharisaism. Of course this is possible in any Christian circle, but it is a special peril in a movement which claims to possess special or distinctive truth. The claim that the gift of tongues is the prime evidence of the Spirit's baptism or filling and that this gift is more in exercise in Pentecostal assemblies than in other churches tends to beget a superior attitude. One of their number once said to the writer, "Of course we live on a higher plane than you do." This may very well be true, but it would have come better from other lips. But in fairness it must be said that this attitude would be deplored by the more spiritual of their members as it would by us.

Openness to Counterfeit. It is an indisputable fact that of all the spiritual gifts, this is the one most open to abuse and counterfeit. The fact that heterodox and anti-Christian movements also experience this phenomenon is clear indication that the manifestation can emanate from hell as well as from Heaven. Satan delights to debase and imitate all that is good and holy and pervert it to his own base uses. The physical and spiritual realms are very closely interrelated, and it is easy to mistake one for the other. Fleshly enthusiasm and excitement can easily be mistaken for spiritual ardor.

Divisive Tendencies. To one who knows anything of the history of the Pentecostal movement, this point needs little elaboration. Both on the mission field and in the homelands there has been a constant history of division, both within the movement itself and in numberless evangelical congregations. It is sad that this movement which considers itself the Holy Spirit movement par excellence, instead of being characterized by the unity of the Spirit, is noted rather for its divisive tendencies. In view of this, Paul's counsel to the believers in Rome is apposite: "Mark them which cause divisions and offenses contrary to the doctrine which ye have learned; and avoid them" (Romans 16:17). Not all Pentecostal groups cause division, and this verse should not be interpreted as a blanket rule to boycott these believers.

Emotional Excesses. If in our conventional religion the emotional element tends to be unduly suppressed, exactly the opposite is the peril of this movement. F. W. Robertson comments: "The Holy Ghost may mingle with man in three ways—with his body, and then you have what is called a miracle; with his spirit, and then you have that exalted feeling which finds vent in what is called 'tongues'; or with his intellect, and then you have prophecy. In the case of 'tongues' men felt and could not logically express that feeling. . . . The clear understanding vanished into ecstasy; the utterer, unless he controlled them, was carried away by his feelings."

This state of ecstasy was so pleasurable, and so excited the admiration and emulation of others, that in the Corinthian church, with its penchant for the spectacular, it became the prime object of pursuit, as in the Pentecostal assemblies today. Instead of steady continuance in well-doing, they tended to spend their time exhibiting intense feeling, and this uncontrolled religious emotion overpowered reason and sense. Mere natural and animal feeling was passed off as spiritual fervor. The same trends have been present in Pentecostalism, not infrequently accompanied by grievous and gross excesses.

The late Dr. Arthur T. Pierson, who conducted an exhaustive worldwide investigation into the progress and characteristics of the movement, summarized the considerations which should govern approach to the subject.

> The infallible Scriptures and not human experience alone can be the ultimate court of appeal.
>
> The gifts most to be sought are those most to edification.
>
> All spiritual gifts that are genuine are promotive of peace and harmony.
>
> All true endowments of the Spirit lead to humility and docility of temper.
>
> Any gift sought for its own sake or for self-glory is a delusion and a snare.

All undue human influence is inconsistent with the supremacy of the Spirit of God.

Whatever has a divisive and centrifugal tendency is open to the gravest suspicion.

We need to be always on the alert to detect Satanic devices and counterfeits.

POSITIVE TEACHING ON THE SPIRIT

One question remains to be answered. *How can we best help those obsessed by this teaching and prevent others from embracing it?*

We should early give to all Christians to whom we have the responsibility of ministering, full and positive teaching concerning the work of the Holy Spirit, the significance of Pentecost, and how they may personally appropriate the Spirit's fullness. When souls turn to Christ we should take the earliest opportunity of leading them into such an experience. This important aspect of teaching should not be postponed until they attain greater maturity. It is this experience which will bring them to maturity. It is amazing how much spiritual truth a young convert can absorb. It is our conviction that if this were a regular procedure in our churches, there would be much less backsliding and more rapid advance in holiness.

Where believers have been drawn into the Pentecostal movement, or are attracted by it, special care should be taken to meet the situation in a spiritual manner and not with carnal weapons. A frontal attack would be much more likely to drive them into it than to rescue them from it. On one occasion the writer was invited to give a series of addresses in a church which was on the point of being split on this very issue. In the whole series he neither mentioned Pentecostalism nor made any indirect attack on the movement. Instead, clear and positive teaching was given on the Holy Spirit and how He could meet their every need for a holy life and effective service. The Spirit bore witness to the Word, and not one member left to join the Pentecostal church.

The method to adopt when others are being attracted by the promise of an experience of ecstasy and power is to show from Scripture and demonstrate by personal experience that when the Spirit controls the life there is holiness and joy and power in witness. If we ourselves have never enjoyed the Spirit's fullness, our first duty would be to appropriate that fullness for ourselves. Then we will be able to demonstrate in practice as well as by precept what Paul calls the "more excellent way."

Paul's great hymn of love is not placed where it is in the Corinthian epistle by mere chance. Its lofty theme was introduced of set purpose, and its objective is clearly stated. "But covet earnestly the best gifts: and yet show I unto you a more excellent way"—than even spectacular spiritual gifts, the way of Christian love. The highest gift, unless motivated by and exercised in the spirit of pure love, is utterly valueless spiritually. "Make love your aim," pleads Paul, "and earnestly desire the spiritual gifts"—but not the one without the other. This is the "more excellent way."

Epilogue

The New Testament knows three types of Christians—the spiritually mature, the spiritually immature, and the spiritually decadent. It is tragically possible for the believer either to fall short of maturity or to fall back from it. The Scripture searchingly diagnoses the cause of such failure and prescribes its cure. The foregoing chapters are calculated to meet in part the need of each class and to show that satisfaction for every aspiration after a closer walk with God may be found in correct adjustment to the three members of the Holy Trinity.

It is for the spiritually immature to move on from an elementary interest in Divine truth to a full and deep experience of God in Christ. The panacea for spiritual degeneracy is found in retracing the steps which led to the failure and in a fresh appropriation of His more than sufficient grace. True spiritual maturity produces not so much a sense of having attained as a passionate purpose to "go on to maturity."

From the pages of His Word we have been awed by the holiness of God and His antipathy to sin. We have realized anew the beneficence of His providence and the discernment of His disciplines. We have been humbled by His infinite patience in perfecting Christian character and the promise of His strengthening presence in the midst of trial. Such a view of God is calculated to beget a holy reverence, a restful confidence, and a comforting assurance that He is ordering our lives with infinite care and skill.

We have turned our eyes upon Jesus, have glimpsed His glory and majesty, the sublimity of His life and the triumphs of His death. We have seen Him impaled on a cross and seated high on a throne. We have heard His stringent conditions of discipleship and have envisioned the possibility of a life of kingly reigning through Him. We bow at His feet in worship and self-surrender.

Some of the supremely important ministries of the Holy Spirit have passed before us in review. His inspiring and transforming power, His purging and cleansing activity, His irresistible dynamic and missionary passion have assured us that He is one with Father and Son in their purpose to lead us "on to maturity." That life alone is spiritually mature which yields without reserve to the sanctifying influences of the Blessed Three.

Spiritual Discipleship

PRINCIPLES OF FOLLOWING CHRIST FOR EVERY BELIEVER

J. OSWALD SANDERS

Introduction

The initial call of Christ to the men with whom He planned to associate in His purpose of world evangelization was a call to discipleship.

> As Jesus walked beside the Sea of Galilee, he saw Simon and his brother Andrew casting a net into the lake, for they were fishermen.
>
> *"Come, follow me,"* Jesus said, "and I will make you fishers of men." (Mark 1:16–17)

His charisma was such that "at once they left their nets and followed him" (v. 18). In the ensuing days He gave the same call to others.

After He rose from the dead, but before He ascended to heaven, Jesus gave to these same men (and to us) the command "Go and *make disciples* of all nations," adding the assurance "Surely I am with you always, to the very end of the age" (Matthew 28:19–20). This is the true calling and function of the church. It is the privilege and responsibility of the whole church to respond in obedience and give the whole gospel to the whole world.

Today discipleship is a standard subject for study in churches and groups. Seminars on discipleship abound, and there is no question of the importance of the subject. But when the lives of many Christians are put alongside the lifestyle Jesus prescribed for disciples and demonstrated Himself, there is a vast discrepancy. It is one thing to master the biblical principles of discipleship, but quite another to transfer those principles into everyday life.

It is not without significance that the word *disciple* occurs in the New Testament 269 times, *Christian* only 3 times, and *believers* 2 times. This surely indicates that the task of the church is not so much to make "Christians" or "believers" but "disciples." A disciple must, of course, be a believer; but according to Christ's conditions of discipleship (Luke 14:25–33), not all believers are disciples of the New Testament stamp.

The word *disciple* means "a learner," but Jesus infused into that simple word a wealth of profound meaning. As used by Him and by Paul, it means "a learner or pupil who accepts the teaching of Christ, not only in belief but also in lifestyle." This involves acceptance of the views and practice of the Teacher. In other words, it means learning with the purpose to obey what is learned. It involves a deliberate choice, a definite denial, and a determined obedience.

Today one may be regarded as a Christian even if there are few, if any, signs of progress in discipleship. It was not so in the early church. Then discipleship involved the kind of commitment Peter spoke about when he protested to the Lord, "We have left everything to follow you!" (Mark 10:28).

The temper of our times is for instant gratification and short-term commitment—quick answers to prayer and quick results with a minimum of effort and discomfort. But there is no such thing as easy and instant discipleship. One can commence a walk of discipleship in a moment, but the first step must lengthen into a lifelong walk. There is no such thing as short-term discipleship.

To some who have been nurtured on the "easy believism" doctrine, the radical demands of Christ may seem excessive and unreasonable. The result is that after they have traveled a short distance, and the path grows more steep and rugged, they are like the disciples mentioned in John 6:66: "From this time many of his disciples turned back and no longer followed him." He is looking for men and women of quality for whom there is no turning back.

In this book I have not dealt with the mechanics of discipleship but rather with its standards—the underlying principles that are to be incorporated into the lifestyle of the disciple. There is also encouragement for those who have failed in this area to step out again.

CHAPTER 1

The Ideal Disciple

Blessed are you . . .
MATTHEW 5:11

It is more than a coincidence that whereas the last word of the Old Testament, which enshrines the Old Covenant, is "curse," the first word of our Lord's first recorded sermon under the New Covenant is "blessed." This latter word is the keynote of His kingdom.

The Old Covenant of law could pronounce only a curse on those who failed to fulfill its demands. The New Covenant, which was sealed with Christ's blood, does not reduce the law's demands but imparts the desire and the dynamic to fulfill them. The "thou shalt, thou shalt not" of the Old is replaced by the "I will, I will" of the New.

In the Beatitudes (Matthew 5:3–12), Jesus set forth the characteristics of the ideal subjects of His kingdom—qualities that were present in perfection in the life and character of the One who announced them. It is a fascinating exercise to match each of those virtues to the life and ministry of the Lord.

In His Sermon on the Mount Jesus addressed His words primarily to His disciples but did so in the hearing of the crowd (v. 1). "His disciples came to him, and he began to teach them." So this is a message for disciples.

He directed their attention away from the idea of being satisfied with mere outward presentability to an immeasurably higher and more demanding lifestyle. The standard He set is so high that no one can live the life depicted in the Sermon who is not the one depicted in the Beatitudes. The whole Sermon is revolutionary, but nowhere more so than in these verses. They cut right across the popular idea of the definition of blessedness and happiness.

Many think that if they had abundant wealth, absence of sorrow and suffering, good health, a good job, unrestricted gratification of appetites, and kind treatment from everyone, that would be blessedness indeed. But Jesus completely reversed that concept and substituted many of the very experiences we would like to sidestep—poverty, mourning, hunger, thirst, renunciation, persecution. True blessedness is to be found along this path, He told them.

The word *blessed* can be rendered "O the bliss!" or "to be envied, to be congratulated," and it is applied to eight conditions of life that divide into two groups.

FOUR PASSIVE PERSONAL QUALITIES

Christ begins by calling four passive personal qualities blessed.

Spiritual Inadequacy. "Blessed are the poor in spirit, for theirs is the kingdom of heaven" (v. 3), or "O the bliss of those who feel inadequate!"

On the surface those words have a hollow ring to those whose lives are plagued by that debilitating condition. Of course it is to the poor in spirit that our Lord is referring here, not to the poor in pocket. There is no virtue in poverty per se; it is certainly not an automatic blessing.

There are two words for "poor" in Greek. One means someone who has nothing superfluous; the other, one who has nothing at all, is bankrupt, and has no resources. It is this second meaning that Jesus referred to. The lesson is clear. The person who is to be envied is the one who, in consciousness of his spiritual bankruptcy, is cast back on God and draws on His limitless resources. As Luther said, "We are all beggars, living on the bounty of God." But such poverty leads to spiritual affluence. "Theirs is the kingdom of heaven."

Spiritual Contrition. "Blessed are those who mourn, for they will be comforted" (v. 4), or "O the bliss of the penitent!"

This is another paradox. It is as though one said, "How happy are the unhappy!" This quality is the product of the poverty of spirit of the first beatitude. It is not bereavement that is primarily in view, although that need not be excluded. The word *mourn* conveys the idea of grief of the deepest kind. It is mourning over sin and failure, over the slowness of our growth in likeness to Christ—mourning over our spiritual bankruptcy.

There are two mistakes that the disciple may make. One is to believe that Christians must never be happy and laughing; the other, that Christians must always be happy and laughing. As a wise man said, "There is a time for everything . . . a time to weep and a time to laugh, a time to mourn and a time to dance" (Ecclesiastes 3:1, 4).

No one attains full maturity without the experience of sorrow. There is room for the disciple to mourn over the slowness of his growth and the paucity of his spiritual attainment altogether apart from any actual sin in his life.

Mourning and bliss are not incompatible, for Jesus said, "Blessed are you who weep now, for you will laugh" (Luke 6:21). The blessedness is in the comfort God gives, not in the mourning itself. "They will be comforted."

Spiritual Humility. "Blessed are the meek, for they will inherit the earth" (v. 5), or "O the bliss of the humble!"

Humility is an exotic flower in our sooty and smoggy world. It is no native of earth and is little esteemed by man in general.

The word *meek* is more than amicability or mere mildness of disposition. Its meaning has been weakened by the line in the children's hymn "Gentle Jesus, meek and mild." He was meek but was far from mild. The impression the hymn leaves is that Jesus was rather weak and ineffective. In fact, He was the very reverse of weak.

Was it mildness He displayed when, alone and with uplifted whip, He drove the materialistic traffickers with their sheep and cattle out of the Temple? He was anything but servile and spineless. When He asked the disciples who men said that He was, they replied, "Some say John the Baptist; others say Elijah"—two of the most rugged characters in the Bible! The word *meek* was used of a horse that had been broken and domesticated, giving the idea of energy and power, controlled and directed.

In heaven, the seven angels sing the Song of Moses and the Lamb (Revelation 15:3)—Moses, the meekest man on earth, and Jesus who said, "I am meek and lowly in heart" (KJV). But both could blaze with sinless anger when the interests of God were at stake. Meekness is no spineless quality.

This virtue challenges the world's standards. "Stand up for your rights!" is the strident cry of our day. "The world is yours if you can get it." Jesus said, on the contrary, that the world is yours if you renounce it. The meek, not the aggressive, inherit the earth. The meek have an inheritance. The worldly have no future. "They will inherit the earth."

Spiritual Aspiration. "Blessed are those who hunger and thirst for righteousness, for they will be filled" (v. 6), or "O the bliss of the unsatisfied!"

The blessing promised here is not for mere wistfulness or languid desire. It is for those who have a passionate craving not after happiness alone but after righteousness—a right relationship with God. The truly blessed person is the one who hungers and thirsts after God Himself, not only the blessings He gives. David knew that aspiration when he wrote, "As the deer pants for streams of water, so my soul pants for you, O God" (Psalm 42:1).

The discovery that happiness is a by-product of holiness has been a joyous revelation to many. We should therefore "follow after holiness." God is eager to satisfy all the holy aspirations of His children. "They will be filled."

FOUR ACTIVE SOCIAL QUALITIES

The ideal disciple will have four active social characteristics.

Compassionate in Spirit. "Blessed are the merciful, for they will be shown mercy" (v. 7), or "O the bliss of the merciful!"

It is always to the undeserving that mercy is extended. If it were deserved, it would no longer be mercy but mere justice.

It is possible to have a passion for righteousness and yet lack compassion and mercy for those who have failed to attain it. Mercy is the ability to enter into another's situation and be sympathetic toward his plight or problem. Like meekness, this is a distinctively Christian grace. We are naturally geared more to criticism than to mercy.

Pity can be sterile. To become mercy, it must graduate from mere emotion to compassionate action. Although mercy does not condone sin, it endeavors to repair its ravages. Mercy encourages the one who has fallen to begin again.

Our personal experience will be the rebound of our attitudes and reactions. Just as in physics, where action and reaction are equal and opposite—those who are merciful will be shown mercy, and if we are shown mercy, we will be merciful. "They will be shown mercy."

Pure in Heart. "Blessed are the pure in heart, for they will see God" (v. 8), or "O the bliss of the sincere!"

Cleanness of heart brings clearness of vision. The emphasis here is on inward purity and reality in contrast to external respectability.

The revelation of God envisaged here is not granted to the mighty intellect unless that is accompanied by purity of heart. It is more than an intellectual concept that is in view; it is not a matter of optics but of moral and spiritual affinity. Sin befogs the vision. The word *pure* here means "unadulterated," free from alloy, sincere, and without hypocrisy. "They will see God."

Conciliatory in Spirit. "Blessed are the peacemakers,

for they will be called sons of God" (v. 9), or "O the bliss of those who create harmony!"

It is not peace lovers or peacekeepers who qualify for this beatitude, but peacemakers. Nor is it those who maintain an existing peace, but those who enter a situation where peace has been broken and restore it. The beatitude speaks not of a pacifist but of a reconciler.

Very often peace can be made only at a cost to the peacemaker himself. It was so with our Lord. He made peace by the blood of His cross (Colossians 1:20). He achieved it by allowing His own peace to be broken. The disciple is to follow in His train. To be a lover of peace is good. To be a promoter of peace is better. "They will be called sons of God."

Unswerving in Loyalty. "Blessed are those who are persecuted because of righteousness, for theirs is the kingdom of heaven. Blessed are you when people insult you, persecute you and falsely say all kinds of evil against you because of me. Rejoice and be glad, because great is your reward in heaven" (vv. 10–12), or "O the bliss of the sufferer for Christ!"

What was done to the Savior will be done to the disciple. But even insult, reviling, injury, and persecution can work blessing—not in the persecution itself but in the divine compensations it brings.

The tense of the verb conveys the sense, "Blessed are those who *have been* persecuted." The blessing is in the results that flow from it. Suffering is the authentic hallmark of Christianity. "Even if you should suffer for what is right, you are blessed," said Peter (1 Peter 3:14).

But not all persecution is blessed. Sometimes Christians bring it on themselves through unwise and unchristian actions. For persecution to bring blessing, there are three conditions:

1. It must be for righteousness' sake, not as a result of our angularity or fanaticism or tactlessness.
2. The evil-speaking must have no basis in fact; it must not be something that is the outcome of our sin or failure.
3. It must be for Christ's sake—suffering that arises from our consistent loyalty to Him.

"Great is your reward in heaven."

CHAPTER 2

Conditions of Discipleship

Anyone who does not carry his cross and follow me cannot be my disciple.
LUKE 14:27

As usual, Jesus was surrounded by the thronging crowds, who were listening to His every word. "Large crowds were traveling with Jesus" (Luke 14:25), fascinated by the novelty, winsomeness, and challenge of this new teaching, for it was still in the days of His popularity.

The situation presented Him with a unique opportunity to capitalize on their feverish interest. The whole nation was looking for a charismatic leader who would help them throw off the galling Roman yoke—and here was someone superbly qualified for the task. All He needed to do was to perform a few spectacular miracles and then lead them in a great insurrection.

Did He flatter them, offer some inducement, perform some miracle to win their allegiance? It seemed as though He were intent on alienating their interest and actually discouraging them from following Him. He began to thin their ranks by stating in the starkest of terms the exacting conditions of discipleship.

The line Jesus took with the impressionable crowd was the exact opposite of much evangelism today. Instead of majoring in the benefits and blessings, the thrills and excitement, the adventure and advantages of being His disciples, He spoke more of the difficulties and dangers they would meet and the sacrifices that would be involved. He placed the cost of being His disciple very high. He never concealed the cross.

Robert Browning captures this aspect of the Lord's message in one of his poems:

How very hard it is to be a Christian!
Hard for you and me,
Not for the mere task of making real
That duty up to its ideal,
Effecting thus complete and whole
A purpose of the human soul,
For that is always hard to do.

It is a well-proved fact that dynamic leaders in all ages and in all spheres have always met with the best response when they confronted people with the difficult challenge rather than the soft option. The appeal to self-interest inevitably draws the wrong kind of follower.

In the early stages of World War II, when the highly mechanized German armies were sweeping forward almost unchecked, the French resistance collapsed. Great Britain was left alone with its "contemptible army" on foreign soil to face alone the German colossus.

I well remember a speech by Prime Minister Winston Churchill at that critical juncture. It outlined in starkest terms the ominous situation in which the nation was placed, with inadequate weapons, weak defenses, and the possibility of an invasion imminent. He uttered no soft words of comfort but challenged the whole nation to rise to the occasion.

> We will fight them on the streets;
> We will fight them on the beaches . . .
> All I offer you is blood and sweat and tears.

Instead of depressing them, his words galvanized the nation into a superhuman war effort that turned the tide and won the day.

Why did Jesus impose such stringent terms? Had He been prepared to soften His conditions of discipleship the crowds would have swept along behind Him, but that was not His way. He was looking for men and women of quality; mere quantity did not interest Him.

In His message to the crowds concerning the conditions on which they could be His disciples, Jesus employed two illustrations:

> Suppose one of you wants to build a tower. Will he not first sit down and estimate the cost to see if he has enough money to complete it? . . . Or suppose a king is about to go to war against another king. Will he not first sit down and consider whether he is able with ten thousand men to oppose the one coming against him with twenty thousand? (Luke 14:28, 31)

Jesus employed these illustrations to demonstrate His disapproval of impulsive and ill-considered discipleship. Like the builder, He too is engaged in a building program—"On this rock I will build my church" (Matthew 16:18). Like the king, He too is engaged in a desperate battle against the devil and the powers of darkness.

In this building and battling, Jesus desires to have associated with Him disciples who are men and women of quality—those who will not turn back when the fighting grows fierce. Are we disciples of this caliber?

The message Jesus proclaimed was a call to discipleship—not to faith alone but to faith and obedience. Jesus gave a solemn warning: "Not everyone who says to me, 'Lord, Lord,' will enter the kingdom of heaven" (Matthew 7:21). Obedience is evidence of the reality of our repentance and faith. Our obedience does not achieve salvation, but it is evidence of it.

Present-day preaching finds little place for repentance, yet without repentance there can be no regeneration. Many have been encouraged to believe that because they have come forward to an appeal or signed a decision card, or prayed to receive Christ, they are saved—whether or not there is any subsequent change in their lives.

It needs to be reiterated, as John MacArthur wrote, that "saving faith is more than just understanding the facts [of the gospel] and mentally acquiescing. It is inseparable from repentance, submission, and a supernatural eagerness to obey. The biblical concept of saving faith includes all those elements."

It is sad but true that whenever the way of the cross and its implications are preached, superficial believers, whose conversion experiences have been shallow, fall away.

There are three indispensable conditions for true discipleship:

AN UNRIVALED LOVE

The first condition of discipleship is an unrivaled love for Christ. In the realm of the disciple's affections He will allow no rival.

The reader will have noticed that in Luke 14:25–33 one statement is repeated three times: "he cannot be my disciple." Each occurrence of the clause is preceded by a condition to which there is no exception.

> If anyone comes to me and does not hate his father and mother, his wife and children, his brothers and sisters—yes, even his own life—*he cannot be my disciple.* (v. 26)
>
> Anyone who loves his father or mother more than me is not worthy of me. (Matthew 10:37)

The use of the word *hate* here has been the cause of considerable misunderstanding. The word Christ used is far removed from the normal connotation of the word in today's usage. He does not tell us in one breath to love and honor our parents and then in the next to hate them. Jesus was using the language of exaggerated contrast. *Hate* here means simply "to love less." So the disciple is a follower of Christ whose love for Him transcends all earthly loves.

But note that because we love Christ supremely does not mean we will love our relatives less than we love them now. Indeed, the very reverse can be the case; for when Christ holds first place in our affections, our capacity to love will be greatly expanded. Romans 5:5 will then have a fuller meaning for us: "God has poured out his love into our hearts by the Holy Spirit, whom he has given us."

Sometimes a clash of loyalties arises at this point, and the disciple must choose which love will prevail.

When the China Inland Mission (now Overseas Missionary Fellowship) had to withdraw from China, one of the countries to which they transferred operations was Thailand. The mission was assigned several provinces with a population of about four million in which there were no churches and no missionary work.

In one town, the first to be converted was a high school girl named Si Muang. Her heart opened to the gospel as a flower opens to the sun. She soon realized that she had to confess her faith in Christ to her parents, who were ardent Buddhists. She was under no illusions as to the possible outcome.

Overcoming her fears, she confessed her faith to her mother. Her mother was furious and told Si Muang that she must either renounce this new religion or leave home—a painful dilemma for a young girl to face, especially as she was the only Christian in the town. The conflict was fierce. Would she give Christ an unrivaled love and "hate" her father and mother, brothers and sisters? That is what she did, and she was turned out of her home. The Lord did not desert her, and some months later she was received back.

There was yet another area that came under this condition of discipleship: "Yes, even his own life." The disciple's love for Christ is to be supreme over self-love. We are not to hold even our own lives dear. Love of self is soul-destroying, but love of Christ is soul-enriching. If the disciple is not prepared to comply with this condition, the words are categorical: "He cannot be my disciple" (Luke 14:26).

AN UNCEASING CROSS-BEARING

"Anyone who does not carry his cross and follow me *cannot be my disciple.*" (Luke 14:27

"Anyone who does not take his cross and follow me *is not worthy of me.*" (Matthew 10:38)

To understand what Jesus meant by His command to carry the cross, we must think what that expression would have meant to the people of that day.

What is the cross of which Jesus spoke? Those words were said before He went to the cross. In common parlance people speak of some physical infirmity, some temperamental weakness, some family problem, as their cross. One woman referred to her bad temper as her cross.

"Oh, no!" was the reply. "That is the cross of the unfortunate people who have to live with you."

Those are not the circumstances the Jews would have associated with a cross—they are just the common lot of man. Crucifixion was an all too familiar sight to them. They would have thought of the cross as an instrument of agonizing suffering and eventual death.

What did the cross mean to Jesus? It was something He took up voluntarily, not something that was imposed on Him; it involved sacrifice and suffering; it involved Him in costly renunciations; it was symbolic of rejection by the world.

And it is to cross-bearing of this nature that the disciple is always called. It involves a willingness to accept ostracism and unpopularity with the world for His sake. We can evade carrying the cross simply by conforming our lives to the world's standards.

Contrary to expectation, taking our cross and following Christ is not a joyless experience, as the saintly Samuel Rutherford knew: "He who looks at the white side of Christ's cross, and takes it up handsomely, will find it just such a burden as wings are to a bird."

If the disciple is unwilling to fulfill this condition, Jesus said, "He cannot be my disciple."

AN UNRESERVED SURRENDER

"Any of you who does not give up everything he has cannot be my disciple." (Luke 14:33)

The first condition had to do with the heart's affections; the second with life's conduct; the third with personal possessions. Of the three, the third condition is probably the most unwelcome of all in our covetous and materialistic age. Did Jesus mean what He said to be taken literally? Everything?

What was the Lord really asking for? I do not think He meant that we are to sell all that we have and give it to the church, but He was claiming the right of disposal of our possessions. He has given them to us only as trustees, not as owners.

This was the test Jesus put to the young man who came inquiring about eternal life: "Jesus answered, 'If you want to be perfect, go, sell your possessions and give to the poor, and you will have treasure in heaven. *Then come*, follow me'" (Matthew 19:21). He had to choose between Christ and his many possessions. He flunked the test, and because he was unwilling to forsake all, he disqualified himself from being a disciple of Christ. Christ must be given preeminence over all earthly possessions.

There are two ways in which we can hold our possessions. We can hold them in our clenched fist and say, "These are mine to do with as I like." Or we can hold them with our hand inverted, the fingers lightly touching, and say, "Thank You, Lord, for loaning me these possessions. I realize I am only a trustee, not an owner. If You want any of them back again, tell me, and I will let them go." The latter is the attitude of the disciple.

Our attitude toward our possessions is a clue to the reality of our discipleship. When we are thinking of our stewardship of money, what is our attitude? Is it, "How much of my money will I give to God?" Or is it, "How much of God's money will I keep for myself?"

In view of the stringency of those conditions, it may be asked, "Has the Lord the right to demand them as conditions of discipleship?" The answer is that He is asking nothing that He has not first done Himself.

Did He not love His Father supremely, more than He loved mother, brothers, sisters, and His own life also?

Did He not carry and die on a literal, agonizing cross to secure our salvation?

Did He not renounce all that He had as heir of all things? When He died, His personal estate consisted of the loincloth that the soldiers left Him after gambling away His outer garments.

Jesus, I my cross have taken,
All to leave and follow Thee;
Destitute, despised, forsaken,
Thou, from hence, my all shalt be:
I will follow Thee, my Saviour
Thou didst shed Thy blood for me,
And though all the world forsake Thee,
By Thy grace I'll follow Thee.
—H. F. Lyte

CHAPTER 3

Evidences of Discipleship

By this all men will know that you are my disciples, if you love one another.
JOHN 13:35

It is significant that Jesus did not command His followers to go and make believers, or converts, of all nations. His clear, unequivocal command was: "All authority in heaven and on earth has been given to me. Therefore go and make disciples of all nations" (Matthew 28:18–19).

A disciple is simply "a learner." The word comes from a root that means "thought accompanied by endeavor." So a disciple of Christ can be defined as "a learner of Jesus who accepts the teaching of his Master, not only in belief but in lifestyle." It involves acceptance of the views and practices of the Teacher and obedience to His commands.

When J. Edgar Hoover was head of the Federal Bureau of Investigation in Washington, he interviewed a young Communist who volunteered this statement: "We Communists do not learn in order to show what a high IQ we have.

We learn in order to put into practice what we have learned." That attitude is the essence of true discipleship.

The Communist Party requires of its members absolute commitment. One of their leaders asserted, "In Communism we have no spectators." Lenin went further and said that they would not accept into membership anyone with any reservation whatsoever. Only active, disciplined members of one of their organizations were eligible for membership.

When we respond to Christ's call to discipleship, we enter His school and place ourselves under His instruction. Originally "Christian" and "disciple" were interchangeable terms, but they cannot be so used today. Many who would wish to be classed as Christians are unwilling to comply with Christ's stringent conditions of discipleship.

Jesus never led His disciples to believe that the path of discipleship would be primrose-strewn. He coveted men and women who would follow Him through thick and thin. He was aiming more for quality than for quantity, so He did not tone down His requirements in order to gain more recruits.

In the course of His teaching ministry, Jesus enunciated three fundamental principles to guide His disciples in their service.

THE CONTINUANCE PRINCIPLE

Jesus then said to the Jews who had believed in him, "*If you continue in my word you are truly my disciples*, and you will know the truth and the truth will make you free." (John 8:31–32 RSV)

This gives us the *inward* view of discipleship, permanent continuance in the words of the Master, the attitude of scholar to teacher. Where that is absent, discipleship is nominal and lacks reality.

What is the significance of "my word" in the passage? In a sense it is indistinguishable from Himself, for He is the living Word. The sense here, however, is that of the whole tenor and substance of His teaching. It stands for His message as a whole, not favorite passages or pet doctrines but the whole range of His teaching.

His conversation with the two disciples on the Emmaus road is revealing in this connection: "Beginning with Moses and all the Prophets, he explained to them what was said in all the Scriptures concerning himself" (Luke 24:27).

To continue in His Word (or to "hold to [his] teaching," as the New International Version has it) was to make it their rule of life in daily practice. Our discipleship begins with the reception of the Word. Continuance in the Word is the evidence of reality.

Columba was an evangelist who left his native Ireland in AD 563 to bring the gospel to Scotland. He realized that he would face great difficulties and would be tempted to return home. A mound on the beach where he buried his boat when he landed was mute testimony to the reality of his purpose to obey the Lord's command to "make disciples of all nations." He committed himself to discipleship without any reservations.

At a conference in Ben Lippen, South Carolina, a young woman was giving testimony to her call to service. In the course of her message she held up a blank sheet of paper, saying that it contained God's plan for her life. The only writing on it was her signature at the bottom. Then she said,

"I have accepted God's will without knowing what it is, and I am leaving it to Him to fill in the details." She was a true disciple, and she was on safe ground. With such a yielded will, the Holy Spirit would be able to guide her mental processes as she moved along the path of life.

Some decide to follow Christ on impulse, making their decision on the crest of a wave of enthusiasm that too often proves short-lived. It was with such a person in mind that our Lord stressed the importance of first counting the cost before making a decision with such far-reaching implications. An impulsive decision often lacks the element of intelligent commitment, with the result that when its implications become more clear, the cost proves too great and they fail to continue in the word of Christ.

Others are willing to follow Christ—on a short-term basis. However, there is no such thing in the New Testament as short-term discipleship. The location in which our discipleship is exercised may be for only a short term, but total commitment is involved. The short-term disciple does not burn his bridges behind him, or bury his boat as Columba did. He never ventures as far as the point of no return.

A young man said to me: "I think I will take a trip to Asia and look around and try it out. If I feel comfortable about it, I might possibly return as a missionary." But in giving His Great Commission the Lord did not make the comfort of the messenger a deciding factor. One whose commitment was so desultory would be no asset to the missionary force.

That great Methodist preacher Samuel Chadwick stated the implications of discipleship in stark terms that recognize the lordship of Christ: "We are moved by the act of God. Omniscience holds no conference. Infinite authority leaves no room for compromise. Eternal love offers no explanations. The Lord expects to be trusted. He disturbs us at will. Human arrangements are disregarded, family ties ignored, business claims put aside. We are never asked if it is convenient."

Having said that, it should be noted that God is not only a sovereign Lord who can do as He wills, but also a loving Father whose paternity will never clash with His sovereignty. That reassuring truth is clearly stated in Isaiah's words: "Yet, O LORD, you are our Father. We are the clay, you are the potter" (Isaiah 64:8). The fatherhood of God is our guarantee that His sovereignty will never require of us anything that will not in the long run be in our highest interests (Hebrews 12:10).

Continuance in Christ's Word is not automatic; it is the result of strong purpose and self-discipline. It demands taking time, not only to read the Scriptures but to meditate on them, turning them over in the mind in the same way the cow chews the cud. It will include memorization—hiding His Word in our hearts. Further, it will need to be "mixed with faith." Without that, our reading will bring little spiritual profit. Of the Hebrew Christians it was said, "The message they heard was of no value to them, because those who heard did not combine it with faith" (Hebrews 4:2).

There is a striking parallel and a vital connection between Colossians 3:16–25 and Ephesians 5:18–6:8. It will be noted that the same results that follow being filled with the Spirit (Ephesians 5:18) are attributed in Colossians to letting the Word of Christ dwell in us richly (Colossians 3:16). Is not the obvious conclusion that these two are Siamese twins?

We will remain filled with the Spirit just so long as we let the Word of Christ dwell in us richly.

THE LOVE PRINCIPLE

"A new command I give you: Love one another. As I have loved you, so you must love one another. By this *all men will know that you are my disciples, if you love one another.*" (John 13:34–35)

Those verses give the *outward* view of discipleship and have to do with our relations with our fellow men.

On Saturday evenings it was the custom in the home of the godly Samuel Rutherford to prepare for the Lord's Day by going through the catechism with his family. Question and answer went around the table.

One evening the exercise was interrupted by a knock at the door. The hospitable Rutherford invited the stranger to join the family circle. When it was the stranger's turn to answer, the question was, "How many commandments are there?"

"Eleven," he replied.

Rutherford was astonished that a so obviously well-educated man should be so ignorant, so he corrected him. The stranger, however, justified his answer by quoting the words of Jesus: "A new commandment I give to you, that you love one another" (John 13:34 NASB).

Rutherford extended hospitality to him for the night. As he was walking to the church on the morning of the Lord's Day, he heard a voice raised in prayer behind the hedge and recognized the voice of the stranger. It was a wonderful prayer, and the surprised minister waited until the stranger emerged.

"Who are you?" he inquired.

"I am Archbishop Ussher, the Primate of Ireland," was the reply. "I had heard so much about your piety," he continued, "that I took this method of finding out for myself."

As they talked, their hearts flowed together in their common devotion to the Lord. Not surprisingly the archbishop was invited to preach, and you can guess his text: "A new commandment I give to you."

As we have seen, a disciple of Christ is one who not only studies His teaching but obeys His commands as well. In that instance the command is accompanied by example—"As I have loved you, so you must love one another" (John 13:34).

Aversion and affinity are alike irrelevant. We are to love our fellows, not because we like them or because they are attractive. Our love must not be selective—because of family or social ties, or because they are neighbors geographically—but simply because we are obligated to share the love of Christ with others.

How did Jesus express His love? We are to express it in the same way.

His was Selfless Love. Even in the noblest human love there is usually some element of self-interest. We love, in part, because of what we receive from it—the happiness it brings. Our Lord's love was entirely disinterested and unselfish.

It was Forgiving Love. The only one who can forgive is the one against whom the offense has been committed. Although He was doubted, denied, betrayed, and forsaken, the Lord's love was not quenched—"as I have loved you."

When He told Peter that his forgiveness was to extend not to seven offenses but to seventy times seven, He was only illustrating the extent of His love for His failing disciples.

It was Sacrificial Love. In His earthly life Jesus gave Himself without stint. When He forgave the needy woman who crept up and touched the fringe of His garment, "at once Jesus realized that power had gone out from him" (Mark 5:30). His service was always at cost to Himself. There was no limit to the sacrifices He was prepared to make. It is the highest love that gives without any prospect of return.

The supreme evidence of discipleship, the authentic badge, is genuine love for one another. When people see it exemplified in Christians' lives, they will say, "These are true disciples of Christ. We can see it by the warmth of their love for one another." We can preach, pray, give, and even sacrifice, but without this love we gain nothing, and are spiritual nonentities (1 Corinthians 13:2).

One writer remarks that the lesson Jesus taught was not only for advanced scholars. It is equally applicable to those in the kindergarten class. This love will be developed at first in private between scholar and Teacher, but it must soon become public evidence of discipleship.

THE FRUIT PRINCIPLE

"If you remain [continue] in me and my words remain in you, ask whatever you wish, and it will be given you. This is to my Father's glory, *that you bear much fruit, showing yourselves to be my disciples.*" (John 15:7–8)

This passage reveals the *upward* view of discipleship. A fruitless disciple of Christ is a contradiction in terms. If there is no real fruit in our lives, we cannot claim to be true disciples.

What constitutes the "fruit" of which the Lord spoke? Primarily the fruit is for God and His glory, and only secondarily for man. It is manifested in two areas.

Fruit in Character—in the inward life. "The fruit of the Spirit is love, joy, peace, patience, kindness, goodness, faithfulness, gentleness and self-control" (Galatians 5:22–23).

The fruit of the Spirit's working in our lives is expressed in nine winsome graces. A tree is known by its fruit. The disciple is recognized by his likeness to Christ in inward character. It was to this end that Paul toiled. "I seek the fruit which increases to your credit" (Philippians 4:17 RSV).

Fruit in Service—in outward ministry. "Open your eyes and look at the fields! They are ripe for harvest. Even now the reaper draws his wages, even now he harvests the crop for eternal life, so that the sower and the reaper may be glad together" (John 4:35–36). Fruit is seen when souls are won for Christ, discipled by concerned disciples, and led on to spiritual maturity.

The fruit bearing that is an authentic mark of discipleship is not automatic but conditional. Jesus made this clear when He said, "I tell you the truth, unless a kernel of wheat falls to the ground and dies, it remains only a single seed. But if it dies, it produces many seeds" (John 12:24). He thus links fruit bearing with the cross. And did He not exemplify this principle in His own death? A single kernel of wheat fell into the ground at Calvary and died, but on the Day of Pentecost it produced three thousand kernels, and fruitage has resulted ever since.

The operative words in the statement in John 12 are "unless" and "if." The glorious possibility of "much fruit" lies in our own hands. "It is enough for the student to be like his teacher, and the servant like his master" (Matthew 10:25). It is as we apply the cross to our lives and die to the self-dominated life that the Spirit can make our lives fruitful.

CHAPTER 4

Tests of Discipleship

I will follow you, Lord; but . . .
LUKE 9:61

As our Lord was walking along the road on His way to Jerusalem, He took the opportunity of giving His disciples a challenging insight into what was involved in following Him (Luke 9:57–62). He cited the cases of three men, each of whom acknowledged His lordship and His right of command. Each was a candidate for service, but at the very outset of his candidacy, each found himself faced with a stringent test of the reality of his discipleship.

In His reply to the first candidate, Jesus presented the path of discipleship under the figure of plowing a field, and a straight furrow from which there was to be no deviation. Everyone who becomes a disciple of Christ, by that action puts his hand to the plow; but there are many influences to deflect him from turning a straight furrow. Three of these emerge from this passage.

THE IMPULSIVE VOLUNTEER

"I will follow you wherever you go" (Luke 9:57).

In a burst of enthusiasm he made a voluntary and unconditional offer of service to the Lord. His sincerity was not questioned. He was a volunteer prepared to go anywhere after Jesus. Surely Jesus would warmly welcome this enthusiastic soul into His entourage.

But Jesus knew what was in men. John made this startling statement about His insight: "He knew men so well, all of them . . . he himself could tell what was in a man" (John 2:24–25 NEB). He discerned that while this candidate was genuine, he was not yet ready for service.

He would have been a good "catch" for the Lord, for Matthew tells us he was a scribe (8:19 NASB); but Jesus saw in him a too-fast follower. He saw that his enthusiasm would be likely to evaporate in times of testing.

The man would doubtless have expected to be welcomed with open arms by the new Teacher and would have been surprised at the Lord's cryptic and cautious response. Jesus had discerned a similarity between this man's response and Peter's protestation: "Even if all fall away on account of you, I never will" (Matthew 26:33).

A generous impulse ought not to be stifled, but Jesus saw in that volunteer one who had spoken without counting the cost involved. He did not reject his offer of service but made a cryptic statement that would open his eyes to the realities of the situation: "Foxes have holes and birds of the air have nests, but the Son of Man has no place to lay his head" (Luke 9:58).

In effect Jesus asked him, "Do you realize where your enthusiasm may lead you?" He was always transparently honest with would-be followers because He wanted their allegiance to be intelligent. So He sifted the man's motives as He sifts ours: "Take your time. Are you willing to face the sacrifices? Foxes and birds have their homes, but are you prepared to be homeless? Are you prepared to accept a lower standard of living for My sake?"

Bishop Ryle rightly maintained that nothing causes so much backsliding as enlisting disciples without letting them know what they are taking in hand. Such a charge could never be laid at Christ's door.

That was the test of poverty. The enthusiast must become the realist.

Although casualties are no less inevitable in spiritual warfare than in temporal military campaigns, it is not fair to send soldiers into battle without first briefing them on what is to be expected, and that is what Jesus was doing.

In these days of the welfare state, there is a growing demand for security against "the slings and arrows of outrageous fortune," and not every candidate for service is prepared to forgo this privilege. Before ever he embarks on missionary service, many a candidate displays an unhealthy interest in retirement benefits and holidays and working hours. Discipleship is a whole-time job and a whole life job.

I recently received a letter that contained this challenging statement:

> Our modern emphases are so experience-orientated, and so centered on happiness and warm feelings instead of holiness and hard thinking, that some Christians' faith is nearer to the Buddhist's search for peace in the environment than to the message of the cross in history.

In the economic flux of our times we are learning painfully that there is no security in material things. They can be swept away overnight. The Lord offers us no security except in Himself. But is not that sufficient? Let us emulate adventurous Abraham who left the security of sophisticated Ur of the Chaldees and went out, "even though he did not know where he was going" (Hebrews 11:8). But though he had to tread an unknown path, he persevered because "he was looking forward to the city with foundations, whose architect and builder is God" (Hebrews 11:10). He had broken with the tyranny of the material.

There is indeed a cost in loyal discipleship, but there is also assurance of abundant compensation. It is impossible to outgive God. We may lose in material things but never in terms of joy and fulfillment here and eternal bliss hereafter.

THE RELUCTANT CONSCRIPT

"Lord, first let me go and bury my father" (Luke 9:59).

The second candidate for service did not volunteer. He responded to the Lord's call, "Follow me." But his response held a reservation. What he really meant was, "Let me attend to my home affairs first." If the first man was too fast, this candidate was too slow. To him, discipleship was a matter of only secondary importance.

Matthew informs us that the second man was already a follower of Jesus when he was called (8:21), so it is apparent that he was dragging his feet and putting other things before his commitment to Christ. True, he said in effect, "I will follow you," but he added an unacceptable rider—"when it suits my convenience." His devotion to Christ was casual, not vital. He was not ready to take the decisive step to burn all his bridges behind him. The Lord's cryptic reply was a challenge to do just that.

At first our Lord's reply seems rather harsh and unfeeling. Was it not natural and right for the man to attend his father's funeral? In Palestine it was required of elder sons to carry out the funeral ceremonies of their parents. He would have been adjudged unfilial if he did not do so. But there is another side to the story.

During a visit to the Holy Land, Sir George Adam Smith, a noted expositor, heard a man with whom he was traveling use exactly the same expression. On making inquiry he discovered that there was no literal funeral involved. His father was alive, but it was a colloquial saying in common use and really meant, "Let me attend to my family interests." Another traveler in the East heard a man use the same expression with his father sitting alongside him!

In His reply, "Let the dead bury their own dead, but you go and proclaim the kingdom of God" (Luke 9:60), Jesus implied that if he would put God's interests first, his family interests would not suffer. In any case, even if a literal funeral was involved, there would doubtless be other relatives who did not share his discipleship and were not concerned about the interests of the kingdom who would attend to the funeral arrangements. All other interests must come second if one is to be a true disciple. He must learn—and so must we—that where there is a clash of interests, Christ can be divisive.

God is not indifferent to family relationships and responsibilities. He does not speak with two voices, urging great care and compassion in those relations on the one hand and then making harsh, contrary demands on the other. But even home ties must come second to His requirements.

In setting out the conditions of discipleship in Luke 14, Jesus further clarified the issue: "If anyone comes to me and does not hate his father and mother, his wife and children, his brothers and sisters—yes, even his own life—*he cannot be my disciple*" (v. 26). When Christ is given unrivaled love and obedience, Jesus promised wonderful compensation; and no one would be the loser.

This can be much more than an academic problem in Christian service, especially in the realm of missions. The call of God comes to some disciples to leave home and preach the kingdom overseas. What of aged parents and other relatives left behind?

Where there is an absolute need and there are no other acceptable alternatives, the right course would be for the candidate to stay at home until the situation changes. Otherwise, despite the pull of natural affection, the course for the committed disciple is clear. "Go and proclaim the kingdom of God" (9:60). Unsympathetic or unspiritual relatives and friends may be critical, but our primary loyalty is to our Lord and Master.

In these days when there are so many unstable and broken marriages, there is in many churches a commendable emphasis on the importance of maintaining strong family ties. But even this good thing can get out of balance.

I recently talked with a family man who had attended seminars that rightly stressed the importance of parents spending quality time with their children. But he carried that exhortation to an unscriptural extreme. "I must give my whole time to my family," he said. "I am not going to any church meetings during the week, and I am not taking on any church responsibilities so that I can give time to my family." To such a man the Lord would be likely to give an answer similar to that given to the reluctant conscript.

If the first test of discipleship was that of poverty, the second is the test of urgency.

THE HALFHEARTED VOLUNTEER

"I will follow you, Lord; but first let me go back and say good-by to my family." (Luke 9:61)

If the first candidate was too fast, and the second too slow, the third was too pliable. His limited commitment had a "but" in it, and like the response of his predecessor, it had an ominous "me first" sound as well. It was to him that the Lord gave the most solemn and heart-searching challenge of all: "No one who puts his hand to the plow and looks back is fit for service in the kingdom of God" (v. 62).

Christ's reply uncovered the nature of that man's problem: his heart was back at his home, not with his Master. Jesus saw that soon he would be looking back and then turning back. There is so much to deflect us from the path of full discipleship. Many like this man are willing for a limited commitment, yet there is always a "but" in their following.

Two fine and gifted young people had completed their first term of missionary service and had showed great promise. We had great hopes for them. As they left for furlough, my colleague said to me, "I don't think we will see them back again." I strongly disagreed with him, for I had detected no such indication. I asked him why he had formed that opinion. He replied in three words—"She never unpacked." With greater discernment than mine, he had detected signs that her heart had never been weaned from home. They never returned.

Those who insist on putting earthly relationships first are the ones most likely to be deflected. The third disciple was yielding to the backward tug of earthly relationships. Our subtle adversary is very skilled in playing upon our natural affections. The tense of the verb our Lord used indicates not a single backward look but a developing habit—"keeps on looking back." And which of us has not felt that backward pull?

Elisha's response to the call to follow Elijah affords a striking contrast to the attitude of the reluctant volunteer.

> So Elijah went from there and found Elisha. . . . He was plowing with twelve yoke of oxen, and he himself was driving the twelfth pair. Elijah went up to him and threw his cloak around him. Elisha then left his oxen and ran after Elijah. "Let me kiss my father and mother good-by," he said, "and then I will come with you."
>
> "Go back," Elijah replied. "What have I done to you?"
>
> So Elisha left him and went back. He took his yoke of oxen and slaughtered them. He burned the plowing equipment to cook the meat and gave it to the people, and they ate. Then he set out to follow Elijah and became his attendant. (1 Kings 19:19–21)

In a literal sense he burned his bridges behind him. It is to such total commitment that our Lord is calling us. But like the early disciples, we are inclined to say, "This is a hard saying."

What this volunteer was proposing was a postponement of service. There are very many who say, "Oh, I am willing to go"—but they don't go. The backward pull is too strong. A growing affection for one who does not share the vision; ambition and the allurement of material prosperity; the easier path of comfort and indulgence rather than the rugged path of self-denial—these and many other considerations encourage the backward look.

The conflict can be agonizing. I had a conversation with a student at Cambridge University in England. The student had heard the call of God to missionary service, but he faced a difficult choice. His father, who owned a business with two thousand employees, wanted him to come into the business and in due course manage it. But there were features about it that would have prevented him from responding to the divine call. It was a moving experience to be with that young man as he wrestled with the problem and made a costly decision.

Jesus said in the plainest words: "No one who puts his hand to the plow and looks [keeps on looking] back is fit for service in the kingdom of God." Let us pray this prayer:

Keep me from turning back!
My hand is on the plow,
My faltering hand.
The wilderness and solitary place,
The lonely desert with its interspace,
Keep me from turning back.

The handles of my plow
With tears are wet,
The shares with rust are spoiled,
And yet, and yet,
My God, my God,
Keep me from turning back.
—Anonymous

CHAPTER 5

The Disciple's Master

Ye call me Master and Lord: and ye say well; for so I am.
JOHN 13:13 KJV

Jesus Christ . . . is Lord of all.
ACTS 10:36

The question of authority is one of the burning issues of our times. It is challenged in every sphere—in family, church, school, and community. This revolt against constituted authority has been responsible for the disastrous breakdown in law enforcement, with a consequent upsurge in crime and violence.

Without some central authority, society will disintegrate into chaos and anarchy. Every ship must have a captain, every kingdom a king, and every home a head if they are to function aright.

If this is true of society in general, it is no less true in the kingdom of Mansoul, as Bunyan termed it—in the lives of individual men and women. The crucial question to answer is, "In whose hands does the final authority rest?" For the Christian there are only two alternatives. The authority rests in the Master's hands or in mine. Scripture leaves us in no doubt as to who should hold it—"[He] is Lord of all."

LORDSHIP SALVATION

In recent times in evangelical circles there has developed strident debate around what has been termed "lordship salvation," a name that has been applied to the view that, for salvation, a person must believe in Christ as Savior and submit to His authority. Some, at the other end of the spectrum, go so far as to say that to invite an unsaved person to receive Jesus Christ as Savior and Lord is a perversion of the gospel, and is adding to the scriptural teaching about salvation. "All that is required for salvation is believing the gospel message," says Thomas L. Constable.

On either side are godly men whose love for the Lord is beyond question, and each view aims to preserve the purity of the gospel presentation in our day. There must, therefore, be mutual respect, but both positions cannot be right.

In my view, it is defective teaching to divorce the Saviorhood of Christ from His lordship. Salvation is not merely believing certain doctrinal facts; it is trusting in and embracing the divine Person who is Lord of the universe and who atoned for our sins.

To suggest that a person can exercise saving faith in Christ while knowingly rejecting His right to lordship over his life, seems a monstrous suggestion. In salvation we are not accepting Christ in His separate offices. To deliberately say, "I will receive Him as Savior, but I will leave the matter of lordship until later, and then decide whether or not I will bow to His will," seems an impossible position, and cannot be sustained by Scripture.

Having said that, I would concede that many have genuinely believed in Christ who, through inadequate teaching, were never confronted with Christ's claim to lordship, and therefore they have not knowingly rejected it. The proof of the reality of their regeneration would be that as soon as they learn of Christ's claim, they submit to His mastery.

Christ's call was not merely to believe in Him but to be His disciple, and that involves more than "making a decision" or believing certain doctrinal facts. A disciple is one who learns of Christ with the purpose of obeying what he or she learns. Jesus did not commission His disciples to go and make *believers* of all nations, but *disciples*; the terms are not synonymous, although there can be no salvation without believing (Matthew 28:19–20).

When Peter preached the first sermon to the Gentiles in the house of Cornelius, he said, "He is Lord of all." But Peter had not always recognized and bowed to His lordship. When, prior to that visit he saw a vision of a sheet being let down from heaven, containing all kinds of animals, reptiles, and birds, he heard a voice say, "Get up, Peter. Kill and eat."

"Surely not, Lord!" Peter replied. "I have never eaten anything impure or unclean" (Acts 10:13–14). He set his opinion against the Lord and received a well-deserved rebuke. If Christ were lord of his life, he could not have said, "Surely not," to Him. If he said, "Surely not," that was a negation of His lordship.

Have we not sometimes done what Peter did? When the Holy Spirit has prompted us to pray, to witness, to give, to break with some sin, to respond to a call to missionary or other service, have we said, in effect if not in words, "Surely not, Lord"?

When speaking to a large crowd, Jesus concluded His

message with these challenging words: "Why do you call me, 'Lord, Lord,' and do not do what I say?" (Luke 6:46). Acknowledging Christ's lordship is more than repeating the chorus "He is Lord, He is Lord."

Mahatma Mohandas Gandhi was a patriot and mystic. He sincerely admired Jesus as a man, but on one occasion he said, "I cannot accord to Christ a solitary throne, for I believe God has been incarnated again and again." He was willing to concede to Him equality with Buddha, Muhammad, Confucius, Zoroaster, and the rest, but not a unique and solitary throne. Yet that is exactly what He demands and deserves.

"O Lord, our God, other lords besides you have ruled over us," said Isaiah (26:13). Note that he did not say "instead of you," but "besides you." Israel did not want to entirely reject Jehovah, but they invited other gods to share their allegiance. But God will tolerate no rivals, no divided loyalty. No normal wife would be willing to share her husband's love with another woman, but that was what Israel had done.

The "other lords" take various forms. With some it may be business, with others sports, or money, or some avocation that takes the place that is due Christ. The danger is that these "other lords," though legitimate in themselves, may take an inordinate place in our time and affection and may eventually oust the real Lord.

Ideally the coronation of Christ as lord of the life should take place at conversion. When we present the gospel to a seeking soul, we should follow the example of the Lord and not conceal the cost of discipleship. Christ was scrupulously open and honest on this point. Unfortunately, that is not always done.

It is noteworthy that immediately on his conversion Paul realized what his only possible attitude should be toward Jesus. As soon as he got the answer to his question, "Who are you, Lord?" and realized that Jesus was indeed the Son of God, he asked a second question, "What shall I do, Lord?" (Acts 22:8–10). That was a clear, unequivocal submission to His lordship. His subsequent life proved that he never withdrew that allegiance. It should be remembered that in New Testament times a confession of Christ as Lord meant an irreversible change in public life. It needs to be clearly stated and strongly emphasized in our day that the Lord Jesus Christ has absolute and final authority over the whole church and every member of it in all details of daily life.

Seeing that our adversary the devil is always trying to seduce the disciple from following Christ, it is not surprising that some disciples do withdraw their allegiance. When Christ's teaching runs counter to their worldly and carnal desires, they take the reins of life back into their own hands.

But Christ will not reign over a divided kingdom. If there was a time when Christ was really crowned as king in your life, it is salutary to ask the question, "Is Christ still king of my life in daily practice?" Thank God that even if allegiance has been withdrawn, on confession of that sin we can renew that coronation, and He will graciously reassume the throne.

WHAT IS INVOLVED IN CHRIST'S LORDSHIP?

Let us examine what submitting to Christ's lordship really means.

Full Submission to His Authority. "In your hearts set apart Christ as Lord" (1 Peter 3:15).

The verb is in the imperative, so it calls for a definite act of the will, by which we take our place at the feet of Christ in absolute surrender. Paul states that this was the objective of His death and resurrection: "For this very reason, Christ died and returned to life *so that He might be the Lord* of both the dead and the living" (Romans 14:9).

In one of the Napoleonic wars, Lord Nelson defeated the French navy. The defeated admiral brought his flagship alongside Nelson's vessel and went aboard to make his surrender. He approached Nelson smilingly, with his sword swinging at his side. He held out his hand to the victor.

Nelson made no response to this gesture but said quietly, "Your sword first, sir." Laying down the sword was a visible token of surrender.

So, like Paul, we must lay down the sword of our rebellion and self-will. Henceforth His will becomes the law of our lives. Our consistent attitude will be: "Thy will be done [in me] as it is done in heaven." Submission means the complete surrender of our rights. That sounds like a frightening prospect, but the experience of millions has proved that it is the path of unimagined blessing.

Make me a captive, Lord,
And then I shall be free,
Force me to render up my sword
And I shall conqueror be.
—George Mathieson

Recognition of His Ownership. He is "Lord of all" (Acts 10:36).

The word *Lord* here carries the idea of an owner who has control of all His possessions. Unless we recognize that fact in practice, Christ's reign over us is purely nominal. We are His by creation, and we are His by purchase. Now we are His by self-surrender. All that we have we hold as trustees, not as owners. But His gifts are to be enjoyed. God "richly provides us with everything for our enjoyment" (1 Timothy 6:17).

The story of Sir John Ramsden of Huddersfield, England, provides an interesting sidelight on this aspect of truth. I have checked the accuracy of the story with an old man from Huddersfield, who, when a boy, used to run messages for a Quaker and was rewarded with an orange and a penny.

When quite a young man Sir John saw that Huddersfield was destined from its location in Yorkshire to become a great industrial center. Property was certain to acquire a greatly increased value in the near future. He therefore began quietly to purchase houses and lands, and in a few years he was possessor of the whole of the town, with the exception of a cottage and garden that belonged to a Quaker gentleman.

All the overtures of the real estate men having proved futile, Sir John Ramsden himself called upon the Quaker to see what he could accomplish by personal influence. The usual courtesies having passed between the knight and the Quaker, Sir John Ramsden said, "I presume you know the object of my visit."

"Yes," said the Quaker, "I have heard that thou hast bought the whole of Huddersfield with the exception of this cottage and garden, and I have been earnestly solicited by thy agents to sell this. But I do not want to sell. The cottage was built for my own convenience and suits me well.

The garden, too, is laid out to suit my tastes. Why should I sell them?"

Sir John Ramsden said, "I am prepared to make you a very generous proposal. I will put a golden sovereign on every inch of ground covered by this cottage and garden, if you will sell." Sir John felt sure a proposal of such nature would not be in vain. So he inquired, "Will you sell?"

"No," said the Quaker with a mischievous twinkle in his eye. "Not unless thou'lt put them on edge." That was altogether out of the question, and somewhat chagrined, the knight rose to leave. As he was going, the Quaker said, "Remember, Sir John, that Huddersfield belongs to thee and to me."

Although the Quaker owned a very small part of the town, he could walk over all the rest of Sir John's town to reach the part that belonged to him.

In every life in which Christ's claims are recognized only in part, a similar situation arises. Satan can say to Him, "That disciple belongs to You and to me! He is a Christian worker, but I control part of his life." Where Christ is not lord in practice, life becomes a battleground of conflicting interests.

Unquestioning Obedience. "Why do you call me, 'Lord, Lord,' and do not do what I say?" (Luke 6:46).

Obedience from the heart is the true and unmistakable evidence of the reality of Christ's lordship in our lives. Disobedience vitiates all our professions of loyalty. Our performance speaks more loudly than our professions. The test is not what I say but what I do.

Were it not for Calvary's revelation of the heart of God, we might well fear God's sovereignty and think His demands tyrannical. Calvary has set that fear to rest once for all.

There was a man in Germany, a village organist, who one day was practicing on the church organ, playing a piece by that master of music, Mendelssohn.

He was not playing it very well, and a stranger stole into the church and sat in the dimness of a back pew. He noted the imperfections of the organist's performance, and when the latter had ceased playing and was preparing to depart, the stranger made bold to go to him and say, "Sir, would you allow me to play for a little?"

The man said gruffly, "Certainly not! I never allow anybody to touch the organ but myself."

"I should be so glad if you would allow me the privilege!"

Again the man made a gruff refusal. The third time the appeal was allowed, but most ungraciously.

The stranger sat down, pulled out the stops, and on that same instrument began to play. And, oh, what a difference! He played the same piece, but with wonderful change. It was as if the whole church was filled with heavenly music.

The organist asked, "Who *are* you?"

In modesty the stranger replied, "My name is Mendelssohn."

"What!" said the man, now covered with mortification. "Did I refuse you permission to play on my organ?"

Let us not withhold any part of our lives from the mastery of Christ.

It may be that you are thinking, *I recognize Christ's claim to lordship of my life, and I want to live under His lordship, but my will is so weak. It lets me down at the crucial moment.*

How can I maintain recognition of His lordship? How can I keep Him on the throne of my life?

Paul anticipated this dilemma when he wrote, "No one can say ["keep on saying" gives the tense of the verb], 'Jesus is Lord,' *except by the Holy Spirit*" (1 Corinthians 12:3).

The Holy Spirit is sent to enable the disciple to keep Christ on the throne of the believer's life, and He delights to do it. He will detach our hearts from the world and attach our affections to Christ. He will empower our weak wills and make them strong to do the will of God.

Other lords have long held sway,
Now Thy name alone to hear,
Thy dear voice alone obey,
Is my daily, hourly prayer
Let my heart be all Thine own,
Let me live to Thee alone.
—*F. R. Havergal*

CHAPTER 6

The Disciple's Senior Partner

May the grace of the Lord Jesus Christ,
and the love of God, and the fellowship [partnership]
of the Holy Spirit be with you all.

2 CORINTHIANS 13:14

When a merchant is operating an expanding business venture, he is sometimes hampered in its development by a lack of capital. So he inserts an advertisement in the newspaper: "WANTED, a partner with capital, to join in developing a promising business."

The business of living the Christian life as it should be lived is too lofty in its ideals and too exacting in its demands for us to engage in it alone. We desperately need a partner with adequate capital to make it a success.

Certain statements of Scripture bring us face-to-face with the paucity of our spiritual capital. They make demands that are patently impossible for the unaided human nature. Verses such as those that follow, far from encouraging us, tend to fill us with dismay when we review our past performance.

"Be perfect, therefore, as your heavenly Father is perfect." (Matthew 5:48)
It is written, Be ye holy; for I am holy. (1 Peter 1:16 KJV)
Always giving thanks to God the Father for everything. (Ephesians 5:20)
Do not be anxious about anything. (Philippians 4:6)
Pray without ceasing. (1 Thessalonians 5:17 KJV)

What an impossible standard! How could ordinary men and women hope to reach such heights of spiritual attainment? "I can understand Paul getting high grades, but I'm no Paul!"

But is God so unreasonable as to make impossible demands and then hold us responsible for our failure? Our conscious spiritual inadequacy underlines our need of a partner who has adequate spiritual resources on which we can draw.

Here, as everywhere else, our bounteous God has anticipated our need and meets it through the operations of His Holy Spirit. That provision is implicit in the familiar benediction: "The fellowship of the Holy Spirit be with you all" (2 Corinthians 13:14).

The Greek word for "fellowship" is the familiar word that has recently come into common use in religious circles, *koinonia*. It is defined as meaning "partnership, participation in what is derived from the Holy Spirit."

Without straining the text, that is the staggering suggestion that the third Person of the Trinity is willing to become the active, though secret, Partner of the disciple in his walk and witness.

Five times in the New Testament *koinonia* is translated as "partner." It is used of a partnership in a fishing business: "They signaled their partners in the other boat to come and help them" (Luke 5:7). Thus "the partnership of the Holy Spirit" is a concept that is textually and etymologically supported.

THE PERSONALITY OF THE PARTNER

Most who read these pages will believe in the doctrine of the personality of the Holy Spirit—that He is not a mere power or influence that we can use for our purposes, but a divine Person. We believe the doctrine, but do we always recognize and honor Him as such in daily life? It is so easy to forget Him or to ignore Him unconsciously, and yet He is active in every aspect of life.

When Jesus was breaking the news of His approaching departure and the consequent coming of the Comforter to His disciples, He uttered four pregnant words that call for a searching of our hearts. He had already said: "If you really knew me, you would know my Father as well" (John 14:7). Then He added:

> If you love me, you will obey what I command. And I will ask the Father, and he will give you another Counselor to be with you forever—the Spirit of truth. The world cannot accept him, because it neither sees him nor knows him. *But you know him,* for he lives with you and will be in you. (John 14:15–17)

In those passages Jesus speaks of our knowing Him, knowing the Father, and knowing the Holy Spirit. The

Father concept in reference to the Godhead is familiar to us because we have fathers (although some fathers may be far from ideal). But we can conceive of God as a perfect Father. We *know* God as our Father.

Similarly, it is not too difficult for us to form a concept of Jesus as the Son of God, for He came to earth and revealed Himself as the Son of Man and fully identified Himself with our humanity, even to the extent of assuming our sinless weaknesses. We *know* Jesus as our Savior and Lord.

But can we say with equal definiteness that we *know* Him, the Holy Spirit, as a divine Person who is worthy of equal love and reverence with the Father and the Son? Do we enjoy His personal help and empowering in daily life; or is He just a mystical, shadowy figure of whom we have no clear concept?

It is helpful in this connection to consider the significance of the words "another Counselor" or Comforter. In Greek two words mean "another." One means "another of a different kind"; the other, "another of exactly the same kind." It is the second that Jesus used. He was assuring His disciples that His personal Representative whom He was sending was exactly like Himself. This Representative would be just as loving, tender, and caring—so much so that there would be an advantage to them in His own departure (John 16:7). Does that not dispel some of the shadow that tends to shroud His real personality? *He is exactly like Jesus.*

Since He is willing to be Partner with us in daily life, should we not get to know Him better?

THE PURPOSE OF THE PARTNERSHIP

If an earthly partnership is to be successful, it is of prime importance that there be a warm and trustful relationship between the partners. Also, if friction is to be obviated, they must be one in both aims and ideals.

I was once appointed executor of an estate that involved a business partnership. The surviving partners, although upright in character, held entirely opposing views of the direction the business should take. Ultimately, the dissension became so acute that the only course possible was to dissolve the partnership and sell the business. For success, there must be mutual trust and confidence and unity of aim.

The Holy Spirit has been sent to transact big business for the kingdom of God, nothing less than to participate in the redemption of a lost world. In this vast enterprise He seeks our partnership as He oversees the interests of Christ on earth.

Jesus spelled out the Spirit's primary ministry in six words: "He will bring glory to me" (John 16:14). Just as Christ's aim was to glorify His Father (John 17:4), so the aim of the Holy Spirit is to glorify Christ. If we are truly partners with the Spirit, then that will be our consuming objective too. So long as our genuine ambition is to glorify Christ, we can count on the aid of our Senior Partner, whether in home, school, office, or pulpit.

THE POSITION OF THE PARTNERS

Some businesses operate quite successfully with one member being a working partner and the other being a silent partner. The latter, though not involved in the day-to-day conduct of the business, makes an essential contribution by providing the capital for the operation. He, of course, shares proportionately in the profits.

The Holy Spirit, however, will not consent to be a sleeping partner, although He may be a secret Partner in the sense that He is not visible in the partnership business. He must be accorded the role of Senior Partner and have control of the whole enterprise if there is to be a harmonious and successful operation.

Could not many of our failures be attributed to the fact that we arrogate to ourselves the role of senior partner instead of ceding it to Him? Have we been guilty of trying to make use of Him instead of allowing Him to make use of us?

The story of Gideon illustrates this point. He became a powerful instrument in God's hands because he recognized correctly the relative positions of the Holy Spirit and himself: "Then the Spirit of the Lord came upon [clothed himself with] Gideon" (Judges 6:34).

Gideon's personality voluntarily became a garment, so to speak, in which God could move among men. He was thus enabled, through Gideon, to achieve a notable victory on behalf of His people.

When Dwight L. Moody and his wife were vacationing beside the Syrian Sea, an old man greatly amazed Moody by saying, "Young man, honor the Holy Spirit or thou shalt break down."

"I was angry," Moody said, "but he was right. I was troubled, and prayed until there came a night when Third Heaven found me. Since then my soul has known the mystery of Moses' burning bush which burned with fire, but was not consumed."

If in our service we honor the Holy Spirit, and consistently respect His position as Senior Partner, we will not be prone to suffer from the contemporary malady of "burnout." We will not be undertaking work for God in our own strength or embarking on enterprises He has not initiated. The last word in any decision must lie with the Senior Partner.

PARTICULARS OF THE PARTNERSHIP

If a partnership is to run harmoniously, the terms of partnership must be clearly understood and set out in writing, down to the last particular. It is unwise to enter into a partnership arrangement, even though it be with friends, without a signed and sealed deed of partnership setting out the mutual privileges and responsibilities of the partners.

What does Scripture have to say about the terms on which the Holy Spirit will be able to work with us? I will suggest five that usually have their counterpart in a human partnership agreement:

The Business Shall Be Conducted According to the Partnership Agreement. The Spirit-breathed Word of God is, of course, our deed of partnership. No contingency can arise in our work for the kingdom for which provision has not been made there. Our first duty is to acquaint ourselves with those provisions and conform our lives to their demands.

The Partners Shall Devote Their Whole Time, Abilities, and Energies to Furthering the Partnership Business. There is no question of the Holy Spirit's failing to honor His obligations. The risen Lord assured us of His cooperation and empowering: "You will receive power when the Holy Spirit comes on you; and you will be my witnesses" (Acts 1:8).

Like his Lord, the disciple should be willing to subordinate personal interests and comforts to the concerns of the kingdom. He should not enter into secret alliances with competitors or others whose interests are adverse—the world, the flesh, or the devil.

The Capital to Be Contributed by Each Partner. It is at this point we come face-to-face with our spiritual bankruptcy. What have we got to contribute? James M. Gray states our position in verse:

Naught have I gotten but what I received,
Grace has bestowed it since I have believed.
Once more to tell it would I embrace,
I'm only a sinner, saved by grace.

My only contribution to the partnership assets is my redeemed personality with its powers and possibilities. Because I was made "in the image of God," I am acceptable to my Partner despite my penury. So I present my contribution:

All for Jesus, all for Jesus,
All my being's ransomed powers,
All my thoughts, and words and actions,
All my days, and all my hours.

But what will the Holy Spirit contribute? He has been authorized to make "the unsearchable riches of Christ" available to us (Ephesians 3:8). "All the treasures of wisdom and knowledge" are part of the capital (Colossians 2:3). Why do we not appropriate more of what has been given to equip us for effective service?

A young man was suddenly launched into a business that expanded rapidly. He was quite unknown in business circles, and he himself had very little capital. Yet he did not appear to be financially embarrassed. What they did not know was that an anonymous wealthy man, discerning the capabilities of the young man, had said to him, "You begin a business, and I will stand by you financially." The mystery was solved. It is in this sense that the Holy Spirit is our divine Standby.

In the Event of Any Disagreement or Dispute Arising, the Matter Shall Be Referred to an Arbitrator. Who is the arbitrator if I fail to fulfill the terms of the partnership agreement? If the dove of peace has flown from my heart, that will be evidence that I am out of harmony with my Senior Partner; I will have grieved the Holy Spirit. An honest confession of sin and failure and a renewal of obedience will secure the return of the dove of peace. One rendering of Philippians 4:7 has it: "May the peace of God be enthroned in your heart as the arbitrator in all disputes."

The Distribution of Profits. In our association with the Holy Spirit, we are given the best of the bargain all the way through. Unlike other partners, He seeks nothing for Himself. In spite of our negligible contribution to the capital, He turns all the profits over to us, and we are constituted "heirs of God and co-heirs with Christ" (Romans 8:17).

THE PRIVILEGES OF THE PARTNERSHIP

What abundant benefits accrue to us through our association with our Lord's Representative on earth!

In Bible Study. The Spirit of truth is both inspirer and interpreter of the Scriptures. He illumines the sacred page as we traverse it under His guidance. He delights to unfold before our eyes the glories, virtues, and achievements of the Savior. He imparts "the light of the knowledge of the glory of God in the face of Christ" (2 Corinthians 4:6).

In the Prayer Life. He is called the "spirit of grace and supplication" (Zechariah 12:10), and in this role He "helps us in our weakness [for] we do not know what we ought to pray for" (Romans 8:26). Much of the barrenness of our prayer lives can be attributed to our failure to appropriate the promised help of our Partner.

In Our Service. We can draw upon His mighty power to enable us to do everything that is within the scope of the will of God. The risen Christ promised this equipment: "You will receive power when the Holy Spirit comes on you" (Acts 1:8).

In Our Character. The passion of the Holy Spirit is to transform us into the likeness of Christ, as Paul intimates:

> And we, who with unveiled faces all reflect [behold] the Lord's glory, are being transformed into his likeness with ever-increasing glory, which comes from the Lord, who is the Spirit. (2 Corinthians 3:18)

With that light on the all-too-familiar benediction, it should have much more meaning for us.

CHAPTER 7

The Disciple's Servanthood

I am among you as one who serves.

LUKE 22:27

No servant is greater than his master.

JOHN 15:20

In Isaiah's prophecy, the phrase "servant of the Lord" is used in three distinct senses. It is used of the nation of Israel: "But you, O Israel, my servant, Jacob, whom I have chosen . . . I said, 'You are my servant'" (41:8–9).

It is used of the children of God: "This is the heritage of the servants of the LORD, and this is their vindication from me, declares the LORD" (54:17).

It is used anticipatively of the Messiah, Christ: "Here is my servant, whom I uphold, my chosen one in whom I delight" (42:1).

God selected Israel from among the nations to represent Him on earth and to be a light among the godless nations of the world, but they failed Him at every turn. Christ, the promised Messiah, rendered the perfect devotion and service that Israel had failed to give and met the highest ideals of both His Father and of man. In chapter 42:1–4, a messianic passage, Isaiah depicts the ideal Servant of Jehovah and the qualities He will display.

In the incident when Jesus washed His disciples' feet as servant, He said to them, "I have set you an example that you should do as I have done for you. . . . No servant is greater than his master" (John 13:15–16). His attitude is the pattern for the disciple. Only twice in Scripture is Christ specifically stated to be our example: once in connection with service, and significantly, the other in connection with suffering (1 Peter 2:21).

The supreme revelation of lowly service recorded in John 13 was no new office for our Lord, for He is "the same yesterday and today and forever" (Hebrews 13:8). He was only manifesting in time what He had always been in eternity. On that occasion He acted out the master principle of service—that the highest honor lies in the lowliest service. He revealed to us that the life of God is spent in the service of humanity. There is no one so perpetually available as He. He rules all because He serves all.

Jesus was no revolutionary in the political sense, but in no area was His teaching more revolutionary than in that of spiritual leadership. In the contemporary world the term *servant* has a lowly connotation, but Jesus equated it with greatness: "Whoever wants to become great among you must be your servant, and whoever wants to be first must be slave of all" (Mark 10:43–44).

Most of us would have no objection to being a master or a mistress, but servanthood and slavery have little attraction. And yet that is the way the Master went. He knew that such an otherworldly concept would not be welcomed by an indulgent and ease-loving world of men. But He did not reduce His standards to attract disciples.

It should be noted that in stating the primacy of servanthood in His kingdom, He did not have in mind mere acts of service, for those can be performed from very dubious motives. He meant the spirit of servanthood.

Principles of the Lord's life that are to be reproduced in the lives of those of us who are His disciples include:

DEPENDENCE

"Here is my servant, whom I uphold." (Isaiah 42:1)

That is one of the amazing aspects of the self-emptying of Christ in His incarnation. In becoming man, Jesus did not divest Himself of any of His divine attributes or prerogatives, but He did empty Himself of self-will and self-sufficiency. Although He was "upholding all things by the word of his power" (Hebrews 1:3 KJV), so closely did He identify Himself with us in all the sinless infirmities of human nature that He too needed the divine upholding. His own words testify to this: "I tell you the truth, the Son can do nothing by himself" (John 5:19); "My teaching is not my own. It comes from him who sent me" (John 7:16); "These words you hear are not my own; they belong to the Father who sent me" (John 14:24).

Taken together, those verses indicate that Jesus chose to be dependent on His Father for both His words and His works. Are we as dependent as He was? This divine paradox is one of the amazing aspects of His incarnation, when He took "the very nature of a servant" (Philippians 2:7). The Holy Spirit will be able to use us to the measure that we adopt the same attitude. The danger is in our being too independent.

ACCEPTANCE

"My chosen one in whom I delight." (Isaiah 42:1)

Although the Father met with little more than disappointment with His servant Israel, He found delight in the attitudes and achievements of His Son. On two occasions He broke the silence of eternity to declare His pleasure in Him. Christ was a servant who never failed to shed abroad the fragrance of a self-forgetful ministry. It rose to heaven as an aromatic cloud. We, too, are God's chosen ones, "accepted in Him."

SELF-EFFACEMENT

"He will not shout or cry out,
or raise his voice in the streets."
(Isaiah 42:2)

One rendering is, "He will not be loud and screamy." The ministry of God's servant would not be strident and flamboyant but modest and self-effacing. That is a most desirable quality in a day of blatant self-advertisement, of TV brashness and mounting decibels.

The devil tempted Jesus on this point when he challenged Him to create a stir by jumping from the parapet of the Temple. But He did not fall into the tempter's snare. On the contrary, He silenced those who would blazon His miracles abroad. Often He stole away from the adulation of the crowd. He performed no miracle to enhance His own prestige.

It is recorded of the cherubim, those angelic servants of the Lord, that they used four of their six wings to conceal their faces and feet—a graphic representation of contentment with hidden service.

EMPATHY

"A bruised reed he will not break,
and a smoldering wick he will not snuff out."
(Isaiah 42:3)

The weak and erring, the failures, are often crushed under the callous tread of their fellow men. But the ideal Servant specializes in ministry to those who are generally despised or ignored. No life is so bruised and broken that He will not restore it.

Ambitious and self-seeking Christian workers, like the priest and the Levite, pass by on the other side of the street in order to devote themselves to a higher stratum of society. They are not willing to keep teaching the elements of the gospel to simple believers, or to endeavor to encourage backsliders onto the narrow way. They want a ministry more worthy of their powers.

Jesus, however, found delight and satisfaction in stooping to serve those whom most choose to ignore. His skillful, loving care caused the broken reed once again to produce heavenly music and fanned the dimly burning wick into a glowing flame. He never entirely crushed or condemned the penitent. It is noble work to care for those whom the world ignores.

How dimly Peter's wick burned in Pilate's judgment hall! But what a brilliant flame blazed on the Day of Pentecost. The Master Himself fanned the spark so effectually in that private interview that it kindled the Pentecost conflagration.

E. Stanley Jones said, "Jesus was patient with and hopeful for the weak and faltering and sinful. And yet He did not compromise and accommodate Himself to their imperfections and sins. He held them to victory and not to defeat."

OPTIMISM

"He will not falter or be discouraged till
he establishes justice on earth." (Isaiah 42:4)

The New American Standard Bible has it, "He will not be disheartened or crushed." A pessimist will never be an inspiring leader. We will look in vain for pessimism in the life or ministry of the pattern Servant. He was a realist but not a pessimist. He evinced an unshakable confidence in the fulfillment of His Father's purposes and in the coming of the kingdom.

It is not by accident that the words "falter" and "discouraged" in verse 4 are the same in the original as "break" and "snuff out" in verse 3. The implication is that though God's Servant engages in a gracious ministry to bruised reeds and smoking wicks, He is neither one nor the other. The essential elements of hope and optimism will be justified by the achievement of His objective.

ANOINTING

"Here is my servant . . . I will put my Spirit on him."
(Isaiah 42:1)

By themselves the five preceding qualities will be insufficient equipment for divine service. In truth the disciple needs a touch of the supernatural. That was supplied for God's ideal Servant in the anointing of the Spirit. "God anointed Jesus of Nazareth with the Holy Spirit and power, and . . . he went around doing good and healing all who were under the power of the devil" (Acts 10:38).

All that He did was through the empowering of the Holy Spirit. Until the Spirit descended on Him at His baptism, He created no stir in Nazareth; then world-shaking events began to happen.

The same Spirit and the same anointing is available to us. We should not attempt what our divine Exemplar would not do—embark upon ministry without being anointed by the Spirit.

God does not give the Spirit by measure (John 3:34). It is only our capacity to receive that regulates the supply of the Spirit. What happened to our Lord at Jordan, and to the 120 when they were all filled with the Spirit on the Day of Pentecost, must happen to us if we are to fulfill God's ideal for us as His servants.

MINISTRIES OF THE SERVANT

The disciple is called to be both a minister and a priest:

"*You will be called priests of the* Lord, *you will be named ministers of our God.*" (Isaiah 61:6)

The priests ministered to the Lord. The Levites ministered to their brethren. It is the privilege of the disciple to minister to both, and we must therefore keep in balance the worship of God and service to man.

We are to offer spiritual sacrifices in the sanctuary and to engage in the other duties of the house of God as well.

The Servant is responsible to mediate the light of the gospel, as a light to the nations, and to rescue the captives from the prison house of sin (Isaiah 42:6–7). But His supreme responsibility is to glorify God. "You are my servant, Israel, in whom I will display my splendor" (Isaiah 49:3).

In reviewing His earthly life, the ideal Servant summarized the whole in one sentence, which is for our emulation: "I have brought you glory on earth by completing the work you gave me to do" (John 17:4).

CHAPTER 8

The Disciple's Ambition

So whether I am at home or away from home,
it is my constant ambition to please Him.
2 CORINTHIANS 5:9 WILLIAMS

It is the responsibility of the disciple to be the best he or she can be for God. To please Him is a most worthy aim. He wants us to realize the full purpose of our creation; He does not want us to be content with bland mediocrity. Many fail to achieve anything significant for God or man because they lack a dominating ambition. No great task was ever achieved without the complete abandonment to it that a worthy ambition inspires.

Fred Mitchell was a pharmacist before he became the British Director of the China Inland Mission. He told me that when he was a student, he and a friend took a course in optometry. One day the latter made a startling statement that bordered on the realm of fantasy. "One day I am going to be King George's optometrist," he said. With predictable skepticism Fred replied, "Oh, yes?" Fred then asked me, "Do you know who is the King's optometrist today? That same young man." He was in the grip of a master ambition that channeled his life in a single direction, and he reached his goal.

We would do well to ask ourselves if *we* have any such clearly defined ambition. Are we making the most of our lives? Are we exercising our maximum influence for our Lord?

THE PLACE OF AMBITION

Our English word *ambition* is not a New Testament word. It is derived from the Latin and has the doubtful distinction of meaning "facing both ways to gain an objective." A modern illustration of this word would be the electioneering tactics of an unprincipled and ambivalent politician canvassing for votes.

Worldly ambition can have a variety of ingredients, but it usually follows three main lines: *popularity*, fame, the desire to build a reputation; *power*, the desire to wield authority over one's fellows; *wealth*, the desire to amass a fortune, with the power that brings. The fatal flaw with such ambitions is that they all focus on *self*.

Even secular writers have seen the seamy side of such ambition, which has justifiably been termed "the last infirmity of noble minds." With his uncanny insight into the heart of man, Shakespeare put these words into the mouth of Cardinal Wolsey: "Cromwell, I charge thee, fling away ambitions. By that sin fell the angels, how can man then, the image of his Maker, hope to profit by it?"

But not all ambitions warrant these strictures. Paul employed a word that had a nobler ancestry and could be rendered "a love of honor." So 2 Corinthians 5:9 could be rendered, "So we make it a point of honor to please him."

Further, Paul asserts that "to aspire to leadership is an honorable ambition" (1 Timothy 3:1 NEB). Of course in this connection the motivation would be the determining factor. Too many disciples are content with the status quo and cherish no ambition to improve their spiritual condition and fulfill a more useful ministry.

At the Lord's command Jeremiah communicated to Baruch the divine exhortation: "Should you then seek great things *for yourself*? Seek them not" (Jeremiah 45:5). This injunction was not a blanket prohibition of ambition. The operative words are "for yourself." Baruch was counseled to forswear self-centered ambition. Jesus made clear that an ambition to be great is not in itself necessarily sinful (Mark 10:43). It was ambition to be great from unworthy motives that He denigrated. God needs great people whose dominant ambition is to further the glory of God.

THE TEST OF AMBITION

James and John were both ambitious men, but their ambition was almost entirely self-centered and therefore unworthy. Their ambition peeps out of their request of the Lord. "Let one of us sit at your right and the other at your left in your glory" (Mark 10:37). They actually asked Him to reserve the best seats for them in His coming kingdom! It was pure, unadulterated selfishness and warranted the rebuke it received: "Not so with you" (v. 43). The kingdom of God is founded on self-sacrifice, not on selfishness. James and John asked for a crown of glory; Jesus chose a crown of thorns. They wanted to rule over their fellows; He told them that the road to greatness was by serving, not by ruling. This is a tremendously important lesson for the disciple to master.

The ambition of Count Nikolaus Zinzendorf, founder of the great missionary Moravian Church, was enshrined in these words: "I have one passion: it is He, He alone!" This Christ-centered passion and ambition was imprinted on the church he led. It pioneered a world missions program in a day when missionaries were few. For a hundred years there arose night and day an unbroken stream of prayer from the church at Herrnhut. His was a worthy ambition that found its center in Christ and reached the world.

We can test the quality of our own ambition with this measuring stick: "Will the fulfillment of my ambition bring glory to God and make me more useful to Him in reaching out to a lost world?"

A MASTER AMBITION

David Brainerd, early missionary to the Indians of the United States, was so consumed with a passion for the glory of Christ in the salvation of souls that he claimed: "I cared not how or where I lived, or what hardships I endured, so that I could but gain souls for Christ."

Paul was a passionately ambitious man, even before his conversion. He could do nothing by halves. I was "exceedingly zealous," he declared (Gal. 1:14 KJV). Always impatient of the confining status quo, he constantly strained toward new goals and horizons. There was in him a compulsion that would brook no denial.

His conversion did not quench the flame of his zeal but rather caused it to leap higher. Whereas his old ambition had been to efface the name of Jesus and exterminate His church, now he had a passion to exalt the name of Jesus and establish and edify His church. His new ambition found its center in the glory of Christ and the advancement of His kingdom.

In later life Paul wrote:

> It has always been my ambition to preach the gospel where Christ was not known, so that I would not be building on someone else's foundation. Rather, as it is written: "Those who were not told about him will see, and those who have not heard will understand." (Romans 15:20–21)

One writer suggested that Paul suffered from spiritual claustrophobia. His early commission had been to "Go . . . far away to the Gentiles" (Acts 22:21), and he was ambitious to discharge that trust. He was haunted by the "regions beyond," and every true disciple should share that ambition.

Henry Martyn, brilliant scholar and gallant missionary, expressed his master ambition in these words: "I desire not to burn out for avarice, to burn out for ambition, to burn out for self, but looking up at that great Burnt-offering, to burn out for God and His world."

Paul's ambition was fired by two powerful motives. First was the love of Christ, which "compel[led]" him, left him no option (2 Corinthians 5:14). That was the love that had captured and broken his rebellious heart. Second was a sense of inescapable obligation. "I feel myself under a sort of universal obligation," he said. "I owe something to all men, from cultured Greek to ignorant savage" (Romans 1:14 PHILLIPS). Since all men were included in the scope of Christ's salvation, he felt equally indebted to all classes. Social status, poverty, illiteracy were alike irrelevant to him. His ambition was funneled into a single channel—"this one thing I do"—and it unified his whole life.

It is small wonder he succeeded in the face of daunting difficulties when he was so willing to pay the price of spiritual excellence. In his great poem "St. Paul," F. W. H. Myers highlights this:

How have I knelt with arms of my aspiring,
Lifted all night in irresponsive air,
Dazed and amazed with overmuch desiring,
Blank with the utter agony of prayer.

At the funeral of Dawson Trotman, founder of the wide-spreading Navigator movement, Billy Graham delivered the sermon. In the course of his address he made this revealing statement: "Here was a man who did not say, 'These forty things I dabble in,' but, 'This one thing I do.'" A master ambition such as that overcomes all obstacles and thrives on difficulties and discouragements.

Our Lord was gripped by a master ambition that integrated the whole of His life. It can be summarized in a single sentence: "I have come to do your will, O God" (Hebrews 10:7). When at life's end He offered His wonderful high-priestly prayer, He was able to report the complete achievement of this ambition: "I have brought you glory on earth by completing the work you gave me to do" (John 17:4).

CONTESTED AMBITION

As with the Master, so the ambition of the disciple will be challenged all along the way. There was so much to weaken His resolve and deflect Him from His purpose—the malignity of His enemies, the fickleness of His friends, and even the attempted dissuasion of His intimates.

Through years of mounting disappointments, Joseph maintained his integrity and loyalty to his God. One day in the course of his duties, the wife of Potiphar, his master, tried to seduce him. His godly purpose to keep himself pure stood him in good stead in the first shock of the unexpected temptation. But it was a constantly repeated assault: "Though she spoke to Joseph day after day, he refused to go to bed with her or even be with her" (Genesis 39:10). His purpose was challenged every day. The devil is a persistent tempter.

A study of the lives of men and women who have achieved great things for Christ and His church reveals that they have this in common: they cherished a master ambition.

Jonathan Edwards, noted revivalist and educator, declared: "I will live with all my life while I live."

The founder of the Salvation Army, William Booth, claimed: "So far as I know, God has had all there was of me."

With all the resources of God at our disposal, we need not plead our weakness or inadequacy as an excuse for poor performance. The least promising among us may yet be used greatly by God.

Thomas Scott, 1747–1821, was the dunce of his school. The teachers expected little of him, so why bother with him?

But his brain and heart only needed to be awakened. One day some statement of a teacher penetrated his deepest being.

Then and there he formed a resolute purpose, a master ambition. Although his progress was slow, the teachers noticed a difference. He grew to be a strong and worthy man and succeeded the noted former slave-trader John Newton, composer of the hymn "Amazing Grace," as rector of the church at Aston Sandford. He also wrote a large and valuable commentary on the whole Bible, which had a great influence on his generation. So valuable was the work of this erstwhile dunce that the commentary is still available in America today.

Other class members are all forgotten. The one of whom least was expected, and who labored under the greatest handicap, is the one whose name and influence endures. And all because he was gripped by a master ambition.

In an article in *Crusade* magazine, John R. W. Stott has this to say about the lack of worthy ambition in our day:

> The motto of our generation is, "Safety first." Many young men are looking for a safe job in which they can feather their nest, secure their future, insure their lives, reduce all risks, and retire on a fat pension.
>
> There is nothing wrong in providing for your future, but this spirit pervades our lives until life becomes soft and padded and all adventure is gone. We are so thickly wrapped in cotton wool that we can neither feel the pain of the world nor hear the Word of God. . . .
>
> Jesus did not remain in the social immunity of heaven, or hide away in the safety of the skies. He

> entered the zone of danger, risking contamination. . . .
> How can we make safety our ambition?

If we embrace Paul's ambition "to please Him," we will discover that at the same time we are pleasing everyone else who is worth pleasing.

CHAPTER 9

The Disciple's Love

An alabaster jar of very expensive perfume. . . .
"It could have been sold for more than a year's wages."
MARK 14:3, 5

The incident recounted in Mark 14:1–9, in which a woman broke a jar of expensive perfume and poured it on Jesus' head, is a glowing example of the extravagance of love. The context of the action highlighted the joy and comfort it must have brought to the Lord when the shadow of the cross loomed so near.

This lovely gesture was made when "the chief priests and the teachers of the law were looking for some sly way to arrest Jesus and kill him" (v. 1). The implacable hatred of religious man served as a dark backdrop to the devoted love of a disciple.

The scene closes on an equally somber note: "Then Judas Iscariot, one of the Twelve, went to the chief priests to betray Jesus to them. They were delighted to hear this and promised to give him money. So he watched for an opportunity to hand him over" (vv. 10–11).

Between those two sordid events, there was enacted one of the most moving scenes of the Lord's life.

The identity of the anonymous woman has been widely debated, but there are some grounds for thinking it may have been Mary of Bethany, and I will follow that idea.

In the Gospels, women often had a special ministry to the Lord, and this was one of those occasions. In the East it was a common practice to sprinkle a few drops of oil on the head of a guest. The oil would cost only a few cents.

A feast was being held in the Lord's honor in the home of Simon the Leper. Was he the father of Martha, Mary, and Lazarus? Did he, as a leper, live in a separate house? These are questions to which Scripture gives no answer.

While Jesus was reclining at the table, Mary "came with an alabaster jar of very expensive perfume, made of pure nard . . . and poured the perfume on his head" (v. 3).

This was the most costly of all fragrant oils in the world. Some ingredients came from the distant Himalayas, and it was reserved for the use of royalty and the very rich. Mark records that its value was more than one year's wages.

Stop and think of the average wage, and you will have an idea of the cost to Mary of her impulsive act of love. In a moment of time she had spent more than a year's wages, seemingly for no useful purpose. The significant thing was that she did not pour only a few drops on her Lord's head. She broke the neck of the beautiful jar and, with lavish hand, poured all the perfume on His head.

THE DISCIPLES' ASSESSMENT

"Why this waste of perfume?" (v. 4)

It Was Sheer Extravagance. Why should the woman be so lavish, when a few drops would have sufficed?

Prudence and parsimony, with cold calculation, would dictate how much (or how little) would be sufficient for the occasion. To them it was a matter of profit and loss. To Mary it was the supreme moment of her life, the moment when she avowed her pure love for her Lord.

Had Mary used only a few drops of perfume as they suggested,the story would never have been passed down through the centuries. Nor would other hearts be stimulated to a similar expression of the love that means so much to the Lord. Do we calculatingly reckon up our gifts to Him, carefully measuring out the expenditure of time and strength we devote to the interest of His kingdom? His heart aches for the abandon of love, and His work languishes when it is absent.

David set an example for us when he refused to accept the threshing floor of Araunah as a gift. "Shall I give to the Lord that which costs me nothing?" he protested (see 2 Samuel 24:24).

"Why this waste of perfume?"

It Was Waste. Why not do something useful with the money it would bring on the market? Why not be practical? "You serve God best by serving His creatures." Think of the number of poor people it would have fed! True, it would have fed many, but thank God it was not sold.

In His ministry, Jesus had demonstrated abundantly that He was not indifferent to the plight of the poor. He was constantly ministering to their physical as well as their spiritual needs. It must have hurt Mary deeply when they so harshly rebuked her.

There had been several options open to her: (1) she could have sold the perfume—and turned it into hard cash and done something "useful" with it; (2) she could have saved it as provision for her old age; (3) she could have used it on herself, to enhance her beauty in the Lord's eyes; (4) she might have left it until too late.

Are there not somewhat similar options open to us in our relationship to the Lord?

"What a waste!" they said when the brilliant young Cambridge scholar Henry Martyn—who at the age of twenty had gained the highest award in mathematics the world had to offer—threw away his prospects in exchange for seven years of missionary work. But in those seven years he gave the world the New Testament in three of the major languages of the East.

"What a waste," they said when William Borden, heir to the Borden millions, turned his back on his alluring business prospects to instead become a missionary to the Muslims and died before he reached the field. But that proved to be fruitful waste, for his biography, *Borden of Yale*, has influenced thousands toward the mission field.

Perhaps God is not so economical and utilitarian as we are. What waste and prodigality we see in His creation. But there are some things of the heart and the spirit that cannot be measured in cold cash.

How much do we know in practice of this seemingly wasteful and extravagant expenditure of ourselves in His service out of simple love for Him? Or are we stingy and calculating in our self-giving? "He who sows sparingly shall reap sparingly" (see 2 Corinthians 9:6).

HER OWN ASSESSMENT

The jar of perfume was her own prized possession. It may have been a family heirloom. She was under no necessity to expend it on the Lord. She might have used it to draw attention to herself, but she did not.

Are we using God's gifts to us for our own adornment, or are we pouring them out at His feet? Mary's was the spontaneous, uncalculating action of self-forgetful love. Her greatest delight was to bestow her choicest treasure on One she dearly loved.

One of the missionaries of the Overseas Missionary Fellowship lay dying of cancer. Her only daughter was about to sail for the mission field when the disease struck. Naturally, the daughter wanted to stay and nurse her mother in her hour of need. The mother could have kept her "jar of fragrance" for herself, yet its sweetness would have been spoiled for her. She would not let her daughter postpone her sailing. The people without Christ in that far-off land were in greater need than she was. To her, nothing was too precious for Jesus.

CHRIST'S ASSESSMENT

Jesus rebuked the disciples as sharply as they had rebuked Mary: "Leave her alone. . . . Why are you bothering her? She has done a beautiful thing to me. The poor you will always have with you, and you can help them any time you want. But you will not always have me" (vv. 6–7).

Of course we must care for the poor, but the Son of God, away from His home, longed for some personal expression of love; something done for Himself alone, out of pure, self-forgetful love. And Mary gave Him just that. Otherwise the pouring of the perfume would have been purposeless. It still means much to the Lord when He finds someone with a heart like Mary's.

"She did what she could," Jesus said of her action. There were many things that as a woman she could not do; but she did what she could. She poured her perfume on His head as an act of love while He was able to appreciate it.

Christ's prediction in verse 9 has been wonderfully fulfilled: "Wherever the gospel is preached *throughout the world,* what she has done will also be told, in memory of her." Implicit in this statement is the invincible confidence Jesus had that His disciples would carry His gospel into the whole world. And we are the beneficiaries of that promise. The fragrance from that broken jar has reached us two thousand years later.

Her act won no applause from her companions, but to her beloved Master it was a refreshing oasis in the midst of the desert of man's indifference and hatred.

Have we ever offered a gift, done an act, emptied our jar of perfume out of pure love for Him alone? This He treasures more than all our service, for it is the love behind the service that makes the fragrance.

CHAPTER 10

The Disciple's Maturity

Let us . . . go on to maturity.
HEBREWS 6:1

God's revealed purpose is to produce disciples who will reflect the perfect humanity of His Son in both personal life and Christian service. This is an alluring prospect; yet the example of our Lord's life is so far above the level of our attainment that it is not difficult to become discouraged at the slowness of our progress.

The maturity He has in view is not confined to the spiritual life, for it must be lived out in the context of the body. This means more than the popular motto *"Let go and let God,"* for moral effort on our part is involved—moral effort, but not purely self-effort.

Bishop Westcott, in his commentary on Hebrews, brings out that point. He suggests that "let us . . . go on to maturity" is capable of three translations, each of which is a warning against a peril:

We May Stop Too Soon. We may feel we have arrived. But the writer rules out complacency as Paul did—"Not that I have already obtained" (Philippians 3:12). No! "Let us go on." There are further heights to scale.

We May Succumb to Discouragement and drop our bundle as John Mark did. No! "Let us keep pressing on."

We May Feel We Have to Achieve It Alone. No! "Let us be borne on." In our pursuit of spiritual maturity, we have the cooperation of the triune God. We are not left to our paltry efforts but have the promised working of the Holy Spirit to enable us to do His good pleasure.

It takes all three meanings to convey the rich message of the text. Maturity in the spiritual realm is not attained overnight, any more than it is in the physical. It is a dynamic process that continues throughout life.

AIDS TO MATURITY

The aspiring disciple should, like a student, be prepared to work through his courses. There is no such thing as instant maturity. It will involve the same diligence and discipline as does a college course if we are to graduate in the school of God.

There are certain things we must do for ourselves; God will not do them for us. While the motto *"Let go and let God"* emphasizes one aspect of truth, it can be a dangerous half-truth and induce an unwholesome passivity. Self-discipline and perseverance are essential ingredients.

Excellence in the realm of the intellect or music or sport is not alone the work of the teacher; it involves the active cooperation of the student and cannot be achieved without strong motivation and deliberate self-denial.

No rapid growth in Christian maturity will be attained until the first indispensable step of *submission to the lordship* of Christ has been taken. The key question that determines whether or not He has been given that place of authority in the life is, "Who makes the decisions?"

What dynamics will bear us on to maturity? "We, who with unveiled faces all reflect [or behold] the Lord's glory, are being transformed into his likeness with ever-increasing glory, which comes from the Lord, who is the Spirit" (2 Corinthians 3:18).

The *objective* means, "beholding the glory of the Lord," produces a *subjective* result, transformation in the disciple who practices it. We tend to become like those we admire. Robert Murray McCheyne used to say, "A glance at Christ will save, but it is the gazing at Christ that sanctifies." This necessarily means that time will be set aside to enable the Spirit to effect the transformation.

While we spend time gazing at the Christ who is revealed in the Scriptures and long to be more like Him, the Holy Spirit silently effects the progressive change. He achieves that by increasing our aspiration, and revealing and imparting the graces and virtues of our Lord in response to our trust.

ACCEPTING EXTERNAL DISCIPLINES

Some experiences of life will greatly accelerate the maturing process. Although the three Hebrew youths (Daniel 3:16–29) must have been mystified by God's failure to intervene on their behalf, they matured rapidly in the fiery furnace experience. And so can we in our trials. Our attitude will determine whether God's disciplines are bane or blessing, whether they sweeten or sour.

Samuel Rutherford wrote, "O what I owe to the furnace,

fire and hammer of my Lord!" God orders the circumstances of our lives with meticulous care. He never makes a mistake.

The presence or absence of spiritual maturity is never more noticeable than in one's attitude to the changing circumstances of life. Too often they generate anxiety, anger, frustration, or bitterness, whereas God's design is always for our spiritual growth. "God disciplines us for our good" (Hebrews 12:10). Someone said, "There is something about maturity that comes through adversity. If you don't suffer a little, you will never stop being a kid!"

Paul's testimony to that truth was hammered out on the anvil of tough experience. Read the catalog of his trials in 2 Corinthians 11:23–28, and then hear him say,

> *I have learned* to be content whatever the circumstances. I know what it is to be in need, and I know what it is to have plenty. *I have learned the secret* of being content in any and every situation, whether well fed or hungry, whether living in plenty or in want. (Philippians 4:11–12)

That is spiritual maturity. Needless to say, Paul did not reach that victorious position overnight. It was a costly learning process, but through dependence on the Holy Spirit, he mastered that very difficult lesson. The same Spirit and the same grace are available to us.

At a gathering of aging Christians, the speaker startled them by saying, "It is not your arteries that are your problem, it is your attitudes." There is more than a grain of truth in his assertion. William Barclay tells of a woman who had recently lost her husband. A sympathetic friend, in trying to be comforting, said, "Sorrow does color life, doesn't it?"

"Yes, indeed it does," was the response, "but I intend to choose the colors!" She was well along the road to recovery from her grief. The colors she chose were neither black nor purple.

In the days of the early church, there were four attitudes that people adopted toward the trials and sufferings of life.

The *fatalist* regarded whatever happened as inevitable and unalterable, so why fight against it? Why not ignore it? The Muslim fatalist dismisses it with: "It is the will of Allah!"

The *Stoic's* outlook was, since you can do nothing about it, harden yourself, defy the circumstances, and let them do their worst.

The *Epicurian's* attitude was, "Let us eat, drink, and be merry, for tomorrow we die." Let us ameliorate our sufferings by indulging in the sensual pleasures of life.

The *mature disciple*, however, goes far beyond grimly submitting to the inevitable and unalterable will of God. He or she not only accepts the will of God but embraces it joyously, even though it be through tears.

Regarding Paul's mastery of his circumstances, note that it was a process, not a crisis. His mastery covered every type of circumstance from plenty to want. The secret of which he spoke is found in Philippians 4:13: "I can do everything through him who gives me strength." It was because of his vital union with Christ that he was able to triumph and be content. He did not run away from the difficult circumstance but embraced it and made it tributary to his spiritual growth.

Because he was so dependent on Christ, he could be independent of circumstances.

DEVELOPING RIGHT ATTITUDES TOWARD TEMPTATION

God uses even the temptations that come from Satan to produce strong and mature character. As used in the King James Version, the word *temptation* is applied to the activity of both God and Satan. In the original languages, two parallel Hebrew and Greek words are used, but each in a different sense. Their meaning is: (1) *to test*, as seen in the refining process that separates the dross and alloy from the pure gold. This testing is sent from God and is always employed in a good sense; (2) *to tempt* or probe, in order to find a weak spot that is open to attack. It is almost always used in a bad sense. Since God never tempts man to evil (James 1:13), this is the activity of Satan.

In the experience of Joseph, both aspects synchronized, and the two conflicting experiences can be traced. Joseph himself, in reviewing his past, was able to say to his brothers, "You intended to harm me, but God intended it for good" (Genesis 50:20).

Satan tempts and seduces the disciple to sin. God tests the disciple to produce the gold of proved character and lead him to greater spiritual maturity. James tells us the correct attitude to testing: "Consider it pure joy, my brothers, whenever you face trials of many kinds, because you know that the testing of your faith develops perseverance. . . . Blessed is the man who perseveres under trial" (James 1:2, 12).

The classic text on temptation is:

> God is faithful; he will not let you be tempted beyond what you can bear. But when you are tempted, he will also provide a way out so that you can stand up under it. (1 Corinthians 10:13)

That passage is full of comfort for the tempted soul. It tells us four things about God that will provide a mainstay in temptation's hour.

He Is Faithful. He will not abandon those who trustfully look to Him for help and keeping. He will be unfailingly true to His Word.

He Is Sovereign. He controls the circumstances of life and will limit the strength of the temptation, for He knows our individual "load limit." That gives us assurance that we will be able to stand the strain.

He Is Impartial. He allocates tests that are "common to man." In the heat of temptation, many feel that they are the only ones to experience such a trial, but it is not so. Although the exact temptation may be different, the same principles and escape hatches are open to all alike.

He Is Powerful. He has an escape route from every kind of temptation. The key to the door is hanging nearby. Defeat is avoidable. The word translated "stand up under it," or "endure," means "to pass through unscathed." We must, however, be watchful for the Enemy's snares and wiles, for he is subtle and underhanded in his methods.

Our Enemy chooses his timing shrewdly. The temptation to discouragement and flight came to Elijah when he was totally exhausted both physically and emotionally. Joseph was tempted by Potiphar's wife when there were no men in the house and nobody else would have known. Jonah found the ship to Tarshish ready and waiting when he was disobediently running away from the divine command. David was tempted when he was neglecting his kingly duties and indulging in illegitimate relaxation. Jesus was tempted by Satan when He had fasted for forty days and was under intolerable spiritual pressure.

Satan chose the occasion in each case with diabolical skill, so that it would come with maximum impact. How important, then, is Peter's warning: "Be self-controlled and alert. Your enemy the devil prowls around like a roaring lion looking for someone to devour" (1 Peter 5:8).

CULTIVATING RIGHT HABITS

In one sense, life consists largely of making habits and breaking habits, for we are all creatures of habit. We are unconsciously forming and fracturing habits all the time, and for that reason this area of life must be brought under Christ's control. It is an essential part of the soul's education.

It is helpful to remember that after conversion we are no longer unregenerate personalities. As Paul wrote, "If anyone is in Christ, he is a new creation; the old has gone, the new has come!" (2 Corinthians 5:17). We are now indwelt by the Holy Spirit, whose supreme desire is to make us like Christ. To that end, God has promised to supply both the impulse and the power.

"It is God who works in you to will and to act according to his good purpose" (Philippians 2:13). Our task is to relate these truths and promises to our making and breaking of habits.

We all have bad habits, some of which may be patently wrong. Others may not be inherently wrong but are unhelpful. Take, for example, the habit of not being punctual. Some people are always late. They seem to have no concern about the amount of other people's time they waste. It has become an ingrained habit. Such people should seriously face the consequences to others of their delinquency, for it is that. They should form an inflexible purpose to push their program ten minutes earlier, break the old habit, and form a new one. The aid of the Holy Spirit is always available in the forming of a new and good habit, but it is we who must do it. God does not act instead of us: it is a partnership.

God gives the soil, the seed, the rain. Man supplies the skill, the toil, the sweat. In other words, the disciple must work out what God works in (Philippians 2:12–13).

In the culture of the soul, no habit is more crucial and formative than maintaining a consistent devotional life—a regular time reserved for fellowship and communion with God. Not everyone finds that easy, but its importance and value cannot be exaggerated. Since that is the case, it is only reasonable to expect that the habit will be the focus of relentless attack from our adversary.

Although it may not always be possible, there is both logical and spiritual value in observing the first hour of the day.

Or e'er a word or action
Has stained its snowy scroll,
Bring the new day to Jesus
And consecrate the whole.

Then fear not for the record
He surely will indite,
Whatever Jesus doeth,
It shall be, must be, right.

Later hours of the day have routine duties that must be performed. Interruptions often break the routine, but in spite of these, it is most helpful to establish a regular routine that enables one to breathe the incense of heaven before inhaling the smog and fog of earth.

In the quiet hour the mind can be adjusted before meeting people or facing difficult problems. The day's duties and responsibilities can be committed to God. We can memorize a Scripture verse to chew on during the day. We should be alert to look for some special thought or message in our reading.

We can relate the principles of Scripture to the details of daily life, remembering that the Bible contains *principles* to guide, *commands* to obey, *warnings* to heed, *examples* to emulate, and *promises* to claim.

With regard to prayer in the quiet time, we should first seek to realize the presence of God. He encouraged us with the words "Draw near to God and He will draw near to you" (James 4:8 NASB). Communion has two sides, so silence is sometimes appropriate in order to hear the voice of God.

Pray audibly if that helps in concentration. If privacy is difficult to find, retire into the inner part of your being. In the evening, review the day with confession and thanksgiving, and let your last thoughts be of God.

CHAPTER 11

The Disciple's Olympics

Take time and trouble
to keep yourself spiritually fit.
1 TIMOTHY 4:7 PHILLIPS

The Olympic Games are not usually associated with anything of a religious nature, but those staged in Melbourne, Australia, in 1956 were a notable exception. A striking feature of the spectacular opening ceremony was the deeply impressive singing by massed choirs of the "Hallelujah Chorus" from Handel's *Messiah.*

Although they were pagan in origin, there is much for the disciple to learn from the Pan-Hellenic games, of which the Olympics are the most famous. The New Testament writers, Paul in particular, drew many parallels between the training and performance of the competing athlete and the duties and privileges of the Christian. It is most probable that Paul would have had in mind the Isthmian Games, which were hosted by Corinth every third year. He was familiar with the rivalries and ambitions inherent in the sport, to which there are more than fifty references in the New Testament.

Every serious entrant to the Games then, as now, was determined to excel and to defeat his rivals. His aim was nothing short of winning the prize in his particular event.

Recently, I saw a young New Zealand cyclist win a grueling race in which he broke the national record. In a subsequent interview by the TV sports commentator, he was asked the question, "And what do you aim at for the future?" With not a moment's hesitation the reply came back: "I aim to be one of the best cyclists in the world."

In order to realize his ambition, he was prepared to pay any price in training—grueling discipline, forfeiture of social life, self-denial in many areas—and all for a piece of gold, or even bronze. Why is it that so few disciples have a similar, fixed ambition to excel for Christ? Are we "taking time and trouble to keep spiritually fit," or have we grown soft and flabby?

Immediately before his death, Polycarp, the saintly bishop of Smyrna, prayed: "O God, make me a true athlete of Jesus Christ, to suffer and to conquer." His prayer was answered in his martyrdom. In our sports-conscious world the great majority are only TV athletes, and too few are participants. Unfortunately, in large measure the same is true in the church.

THE INDISPENSABLE TRAINING

> Take time and trouble to keep yourself spiritually fit. Bodily fitness has a limited value, but spiritual fitness is of unlimited value, for it holds promise both for this present life and for the life to come. (1 Timothy 4:7–8 PHILLIPS)

In writing to his Corinthian friends, Paul reminded them that "every competitor in athletic events goes into serious training. Athletes will take tremendous pains—for a fading crown of leaves" (1 Corinthians 9:25 PHILLIPS). It was an inflexible condition of entering the Olympic Games that the athlete undergo ten months of rigorous training. No exceptions were tolerated.

During those months, they had to live rigorously disciplined lives, bridling their normal desires and refraining from certain pastimes that might affect their fitness. They had to have a balanced diet and get rid of all superfluous fat. In our day the more popular outlook is: "Do your own thing. If it feels good, do it." This is not the way athletes for Christ are produced.

The actual rules of the contest were recorded by Horace. "There must be ordinary living, but spare food. Abstain from confections. Make a point of exercising at the appointed times in heat and cold. Drink neither cold water nor wine at random. Give yourself to the training master as to a physician, and then enter the contest."

What challenging words these are to the lax and undisciplined disciple.

In reality there should be no such thing as an undisciplined disciple. Both words come from the same root, yet discipline has become the ugly duckling in modern society.

A great deal of prominence is given to the Holy Spirit today, and rightly so. But little prominence is given to Galatians 5:22–23: "the fruit of the Spirit is . . . [discipline] self-control." One of the clearest evidences that the Holy Spirit is working in power in our lives is seen not merely in our emotional experience, but in an increasingly disciplined lifestyle.

The athlete who aspires to win the coveted prize does not indulge himself. He is prepared to take a stand against the spirit of this godless age. Is it not ironic that while people will applaud and admire the sacrifice, discipline, and self-control of the athlete, they are turned off when it is suggested that there should be a comparable dedication on the part of the disciple of the disciplined Christ?

The word Paul uses for "train" in 1 Timothy 4:7 is that from which we get our word *gymnasium*—the place where the athlete learns to harden his muscles, prolong his wind, and gain flexibility. The Holy Spirit urges each of us to do in the spiritual sphere what the athlete does in the gymnasium. It is commendable that so many are taking up aerobics today. It would be beneficial to the disciple to be equally zealous in spiritual aerobics.

A pampered body means a lost race. A flabby athlete gains no medals. Augustine knew this. He had a prayer that he often offered:

O God, that I might have towards my God,
a heart of flame;
Towards my fellow-men a heart of love;
Towards myself, a heart of steel.

OLYMPICS FOR THE AGING

It is encouraging for those of us who are older to realize that God is not exclusively youth-orientated. In thinking of the Olympic contests, we automatically associate them with virile youth. They are the athletes.

But in his reference to the Games, Paul viewed himself as nearing the end of the race—but still in training. Hear his words:

> Do you remember how, on a racing track, every competitor runs, but only one wins the prize? Well, you ought to run with your minds fixed on winning the prize! . . . *I run the race then with determination. I am no shadow boxer, I really fight!* I am my body's sternest master, for fear that when I have preached to others I should myself be disqualified. (1 Corinthians 9:24–27 PHILLIPS)

Thank God we older disciples are not out of the race! We entered the race at conversion. At first it may have seemed to be a 100-meter dash, but we have proved it to be a 26-mile marathon that has tested our perseverance and spiritual stamina. And now it is for us still to "run with perseverance the race marked out for us" (Hebrews 12:1) so that we might win the prize.

It is easy to grow lax and less disciplined as the years go by. Are we mentally lazy and undisciplined? Do we feel we have earned the right to drop out of the race? Not that way went the Crucified, and not that way went the men and women who have counted for God.

God, harden me against myself,
The coward with pathetic voice.

OLYMPIC RULES

"If anyone competes as an athlete, he does not receive the victor's crown unless he competes according to the rules."
(2 Timothy 2:5)

Mastery of the rules of the contest is a first priority for the athlete. Unless he conforms to them there will be no prize.

Enforcing this condition, Augustine challenged a runner: "You may be making great strides, but are you running outside the track?"

How diligently the aspiring driver studies the provisions of the *Rules of the Road*! Are we equally diligent in mastering and conforming to the rules governing the Christian race?

The Christian athlete's rule book is, of course, the New Testament. In it he will find all the guidance he needs for what is allowable and what is not. But this Book has an advantage over the Olympic book of rules; it promises adequate power to enable the runner to complete the race. Paul availed himself of that power, and on reaching the tape he was able to testify: "I have fought the good fight, I have finished the race" (2 Timothy 4:7).

OBSTACLES IN THE RACE

"You were running well. Who hindered you from obeying the truth?" (Paul in Galatians 5:7 NASB)

There are many influences to deflect us from reaching the goal. We have a wily adversary who will draw on his six millennia of nefarious experience to lure us from the track.

There is an interesting Greek story of Atalanta and Hippomenes. The fleet-footed Atalanta challenged any young man to a race. The reward of victory would be her hand in marriage. The penalty of defeat would be death. She must have been a very attractive girl, for a number of men accepted the challenge, only to lose the race and their lives as well.

Hippomenes, too, accepted her challenge, but before setting out on the race, he secreted on his person three golden apples. When the race began, Atalanta easily outstripped him. He took out a golden apple and rolled it in front of her. The glitter of the gold caught her eye, and as she stopped to pick it up, he shot past her. She quickly recovered and again outdistanced him. Another golden apple rolled across her track, and again she stopped to pick it up, allowing Hippomenes again to sweep past her. The goal was near and he was ahead, but once more she overtook him. Seizing his last chance, he rolled the third apple, and while Atalanta wavered, Hippomenes reached the tape. They were married and lived happily ever after!

Our wily adversary is adept in deploying his golden apples. He does not observe the rules of the game, and he will use every subtlety to prevent our winning the prize. But Paul had every reason to claim, "We are not unaware of his schemes" (2 Corinthians 2:11). Not all of us are able to make a similar assertion. Too many are spiritual illiterates when it comes to discerning and anticipating his subtleties.

The writer of the letter to the Hebrews was aware of the obstacles and hindrances the athlete would meet and urged his readers: "Therefore, since we are surrounded by such a great cloud of witnesses, let us throw off everything that hinders and the sin that so easily entangles, and let us run with perseverance the race marked out for us" (Hebrews 12:1).

It was customary for the Olympic athlete to discard his flowing robes—his track suit—before he went to the track. Those garments were cumbersome and would impede progress, so he threw them off and ran almost naked.

In our own race, have we thrown off every entangling and hindering thing—the besetting and upsetting sins that prevent progress toward spiritual maturity? That is not something God does, but something we must do with full purpose of will. Satan's lures come to us along the main avenues of appetite, avarice, and ambition. We should check to see whether any of Satan's golden apples operate in any of those areas of our lives.

FIXITY OF AIM

"Let us fix our eyes on Jesus, the author and perfector of our faith." (Hebrews 12:2)

The Greek foot race was regarded as the sharpest and most violent physical exercise then known. In one race, Addas, the victor, burst over the finishing line and then collapsed, a motionless heap of muscle—dead. The exertion had overextended his physical reserves. Winning a race makes great demands on the stamina and perseverance of the athlete.

Once the race has begun, the athlete cannot afford to look back. He must press on to the tape without distraction. His eyes must be fixed on the umpire's stand at the end of the track if he is to win the prize. That was the background of Paul's notable statement, "One thing I do: Forgetting what is behind and straining toward what is ahead, I press on toward the goal to win the prize for which God has called me heavenward in Christ Jesus" (Philippians 3:13–14).

So must the disciple run his race with eyes steadfastly fixed on his encouraging Lord, who is at once Judge, Umpire, and Awarder. He is not to look back either wistfully or hopelessly but to resolutely forget what is behind—failures and disappointments as well as successes and victories. He must strain forward to the tape with eyes fixed on his welcoming Lord. It was He who initiated our faith, and it is He who will strengthen us to complete the course.

After employing the figure of the runner in 1 Corinthians 9:25, Paul turns to the sport of boxing: "I do not run like a man running aimlessly; I do not fight like a man beating the air. No, I beat my body and make it my slave" (1 Corinthians 9:26–27).

Boxing was one of the sports in the Pentathlon at the Olympic Games, and Paul used it to illustrate his own attitude toward his body, which was so often the focus of temptation. He realized that his greatest foe lodged in his own breast: "I know that nothing good lives in me, that is, in my sinful nature" (Romans 7:18).

There is a man who often stands
'twixt me and Thy glory.
His name is Self, my carnal Self
stands 'twixt me and Thy glory.
O mortify him! mortify him!
Put him down, my Saviour;
Exalt Thyself alone,
Lift high the standard of the cross
and 'neath its folds
Conceal the standard-bearer.
—Anonymous

In some Eastern cities, as one walks along the street in the darkness of early morning, it is a common sight to see men with clenched fists, punching the empty air. But there is nothing to fear from them. They are only shadowboxers.

Paul disclaimed being a shadowboxer. "I land every blow," he claimed, "and the blows land on my own body. Thus I make it my slave and not my master."

THE PRIZE

"Run in such a way as to get the prize."
(1 Corinthians 9:24)

What moves the athlete to exercise such self-discipline and exhibit such feats of strength and endurance? Surely it will be a large purse or some trophy of great value. But no. "They do it to get a crown that will not last" (v. 25 NIV)—a mere chaplet of laurel leaves, of no intrinsic value at all. And yet it was the most coveted of all the honors the nation could confer. Cicero maintained that the Olympic victor received more honor than the returning conquering general. But it was a prize that did not last.

The gorgeous Olympic pageant reached its climax when the crown of victory was placed on the victor's head by the umpire of the Games. Flowers and gifts were showered on him by his admirers.

With that scene in his mind, Paul anticipated the day when he would be crowned by the Judge of all the earth: "Now there is in store for me the crown of righteousness, which the Lord, the righteous Judge, will award to me on that day—and not only to me, but also to all who have longed for his appearing" (2 Timothy 4:8).

Throughout the years that he had run the race, Paul kept his gaze fixed on Christ. To receive from His nail-pierced hands the crown would be abundant compensation for all his sufferings. To hear his Lord and Master say, "Well done!" would make the self-renunciations seem as nothing.

Paul finished his brief paragraph about the Games on a serious note. Despite the vast scope of his achievements, he still recognized the subtlety of his Enemy and the frailty of his own human nature. "I beat my body and make it my slave," he said, "so that after I have preached to others, I myself will not be disqualified for the prize" (1 Corinthians 9:27).

As he grew older, he found that the world was no less delusive, sin no less seductive, and the devil no less malicious than in his youth, and that caused him a wholesome fear.

The word *disqualified* had no reference to his salvation. He had no fear of losing that, but he did fear being disapproved or disqualified by the Judge, thus having run in vain. Let us entertain a similar, wholesome fear and run so as to win the prize.

Teach me Thy way, O Lord,
Teach me Thy way,
Thy gracious aid impart,
Teach me Thy way
Until my journey's done,
Until the race is run,
Until the crown is won,
Teach me Thy way.
—B. M. R.

CHAPTER 12

The Disciple's Compassion

When he saw the crowds,
he had compassion on them.
MATTHEW 9:36

Sit down, young man! When God purposes to save the heathen, He will do it without your help!" God could doubtless have done it without the help of the young cobbler, but He didn't. He took an obscure young disciple from an obscure town, called and equipped him, and used him to initiate the modern missionary era.

William Carey was innocent of systematic theology and missiology at that stage, but he had qualities that uniquely equipped him for that strategic task. He had a passionate love for Christ and a compassionate love for those in distant lands who did not know Him.

As he worked away at his cobbler's bench, with a globe of the world in front of him, God was laying on his heart a great burden for the lost. The compassion that moved the Lord when He saw the crowds "harassed and helpless, like sheep without a shepherd" (Matthew 9:36), was reborn in William Carey's heart.

Not all Christians, even in evangelical circles, believe that all men and women without Christ are lost. A creeping universalism is gaining ground. Many feel that, at the last, God's love will triumph over His wrath, and He will save all men. One does not impugn the motives of those who embrace this view, but the crucial question is, Is that what Christ and the apostles clearly taught in the Scriptures?

Scripture nowhere states or implies that pagan people will be lost simply because they have not heard the gospel. Multiplied millions have never had the opportunity. If pagan people are lost, it is for exactly the same reason as you and I were lost—because they, like us, are sinful by nature and by practice. Paul makes this crystal clear: "*There is no difference*, for all have sinned and fall short of the glory of God" (Romans 3:22–23).

THOSE WHO HAVE NEVER HEARD

Paul draws no distinction between those who have heard the gospel and those who have not. All are equally lost because all are equally sinful. God has "concluded all under sin" (Gal. 3:22 KJV), and this fact enables Him to offer mercy to all who will receive it.

This is not the place to enlarge upon this subject, the implications of which are so painful and on which there are conflicting views, but those who hold universalistic views have some questions to answer.

1. Was the Lord's statement, "I am the way. . . . No one comes to the Father except through me" (John 14:6), relative or absolute? Can men come to a Father of whom they have never heard?

2. When Jesus said, "No one can enter the kingdom of God unless he is born of water and the Spirit" (John 3:5), did He have unrevealed exceptions in mind? Are pagans automatically born again without their consent?
3. What did Paul mean when he reminded the Ephesian Christians of their condition as heathen and said, "Remember that . . . you were separate from Christ . . . *without hope and without God* in the world" (Ephesians 2:12)?
4. Is there scriptural warrant for saying that the names of the heathen are automatically inscribed in the Book of Life (Revelation 20:12)? If so, would not that rather argue for *not* giving them the gospel, lest they reject it as so many do?
5. Was John deluded when he wrote that the portion of those who practiced magic arts (witchcraft) and all idolaters will be in the fiery lake of burning sulphur (Revelation 21:8)?
6. What did Paul mean when he posed the four devastating questions of Romans 10:13–15?

"Everyone who calls on the name of the Lord will be saved," he announced.

"How, then, can they call on the one they have not believed in?

"And how can they believe in the one of whom they have not heard?

"And how shall they hear without someone preaching to them?

"And how can they preach unless they are sent?"

Was he just indulging in heartless casuistry, or is there an answer?

These Scriptures and others, on the face of them, seem to present a *prima facie* case for the lost state of unevangelized pagans. If the salvation of lost men and women is so serious that it demanded the sufferings of Christ on the cross, then how serious is their condition and how urgent should be our endeavor to relieve it?

Other Scriptures, of course, make clear that the responsibility of those who have not heard the gospel is immeasurably less than that of those who have heard and rejected it. In the light of Calvary, we can rest in the assurance that "the Judge of all the earth [will] do right" (Genesis 18:25).

HEATHEN IGNORANCE NOT TOTAL

In point of fact, the heathen are not so ignorant and their sin not so involuntary as some may think. A friend of mine who was a missionary in Zaire, when it was known as the Belgian Congo, wished to discover the degree of light enjoyed by a raw pagan who had had no contact with Europeans or Christians. He went with an interpreter to a village that had never been visited by a white man. After establishing rapport he asked, in terms the chief could understand, what things he considered to be sin. Without hesitation, the chief replied, "Murder, theft, adultery, witchcraft."

That meant that every time he indulged in any of those practices, he knew he was sinning against the light he had. Was this not what Paul said?

> Indeed, when Gentiles, who do not have the law, do by nature things required by the law, they are a law for themselves, even though they do not have the law, since *they show that the requirements of the law are written on their hearts,* their consciences also bearing witness, and their thoughts now accusing, now even defending them. (Romans 2:14–16)

Since that is the case, every disciple of the compassionate Christ will be concerned to see that the unevangelized millions will have an opportunity to hear the gospel.

It was when Jesus saw the crowds of people who thronged Him, "without hope and without God," that He had compassion on them.

THE THREE ESSENTIALS

John Ruskin, famous poet and art critic, once said that a good artist must possess three qualities: (1) *an eye to see* and appreciate the beauty of the scene he desires to catch on canvas; (2) *a heart to feel* and register the beauty and atmosphere of the scene; (3) *a hand to perform*—to transfer to canvas what the eye has seen and the heart has felt.

Are not they three of the qualities most essential to the disciple in his work for the Master?

We need an *eye to see* the spiritual need of the men and women around us. Physical need is much more readily discerned than is spiritual need because it makes a visual impression on us, whereas spiritual need is sensed only by those who are spiritual.

How did Jesus see His world? "When he saw the crowds, he had compassion on them." He saw a crowded world. It has been estimated that in our Lord's time, the population of the world was about 250 million. What kind of world do we see? Five thousand million—twenty times as many!

He saw a helpless world. How contemporary! With all our sophistication, we move helplessly from one crisis to another, with few solutions. Those people were bewildered, crushed by injustice and oppression. His heart ached for them in their inability to improve their spiritual condition.

He saw a *shepherdless* world. Sheep have no sense of direction, no weapon of offense or defense. Jesus saw them as lost, with no one to care for their spiritual destitution. And are there not still vast numbers in the less developed countries who are in the same condition?

When worldly men see a crowd, each sees something different. The educator sees potential students. The politician, potential voters. The merchant, potential customers. Each sees them with the thought of the way he can profit from them. Jesus never exploited any man for His own benefit. "When He saw [them], he had compassion on them." And soon that compassion would lead Him to the cross.

Eyes that look are common. Eyes that see are rare. Do we have eyes that see?

We need *a heart to feel* for the spiritual needs of men and women. Compassion is much more than pity. That kind of emotion by no means always leads to loving action. The word *compassion* means "to suffer together with." It is the Latin form of the Greek word that gives us *sympathy*, and it implies identification with its object.

A. W. Tozer once said that there was abroad an irresponsible pursuit of happiness and that most people would rather be happy than feel the wounds of other people's sorrows. That is borne out by the almost pathological pursuit of happiness by the crowds. But they miss the true Source of joy and satisfaction.

If we keep sensitively in touch with the Christ of the broken heart we will share His concern. Compassion is the language of the heart and is intelligible in any tongue. It is not difficult, however, to be so engrossed in our own lives that our hearts become calloused and insensitive to the needs of others.

Television has had a deleterious effect on the emotions of many of its devotees. Constant familiarity with scenes of tragedy, horror, violence, and simulated emotion has made their emotions so superficial that it is difficult for them to feel anything deeply. We see terrible scenes, are shocked for a few moments, and then turn to the next program. We have grown emotionally superficial, and that has spilled over into the spiritual life.

Luke tells us that when Jesus "approached Jerusalem and saw the city, he wept over it" (Luke 19:41). His compassion was not dry-eyed. How different from the Greek gods! They came to earth to enjoy and indulge themselves. The Son of God expressed His concern in salty tears. As He foresaw the future doom of the city when judgment would fall on it for its sin and impenitence, His heart overflowed its banks.

What a concept—a weeping God! Tears streamed down His face in compassion for the very men who shortly would crucify Him outside that city! Imagine the incredulity of the angels. They were not the synthetic tears of television but tears of genuine concern for lost men and women.

Paul's ministry was not dry-eyed. He shared the passion and compassion of his Lord. When he bade the Ephesian Christians farewell, he said to them, "Remember that for three years I never stopped warning each of you night and day *with tears*" (Acts 20:31).

Do we share our Lord's concern and compassion?

We need *a hand to perform*, to act out our compassion. Christ's compassion was not stillborn; He did something about it. Seeing and feeling are sterile unless we are moved to action.

In the parable of the Good Samaritan, Jesus taught His disciples a memorable lesson in compassion (Luke 10:29–37). The robbers saw in the wounded traveler a victim to exploit; the priest and Levite, a nuisance to ignore; the lawyer who sparked the story saw a problem to be solved; the innkeeper, a customer from whom he could profit. The hated Samaritan saw him as a neighbor he could help in his hour of need.

> "Which of these three do you think was a neighbor to the man who fell into the hands of robbers?"
>
> The expert in the law replied, "The one who had mercy on him."
>
> Jesus told him, "Go and do likewise."
>
> (Luke 10:36–37)

The highest expression of compassion is compassionate action; otherwise, it is only stillborn sentiment.

The caring disciple whose eyes have been opened to see the plight of this lost world, whose heart has been moved by men's tragic condition, must swing into action.

George R. Murray, general director of the Bible Christian Union Mission, tells that up to the time he fully dedicated his life to the Lord he had been sincerely including God in his plans, but God wanted him to be included in His plan.

At a missionary prayer meeting at Columbia Bible College, it became clear that God's plan for him was full-time missionary service, preaching Christ where He was not known. It was then that he saw the world as God must see it. Before that time, he was willing to go but planning to stay. However, from that time on, his attitude was that he was planning to go but willing to stay. He soon had his call from God.

CHAPTER 13

The Disciple's Prayer Life

The Spirit helps us in our weakness.
We do not know what we ought to pray for.

ROMANS 8:26

Our Lord set the disciples such a glowing example in prayer that they pled with Him, "Lord, teach us to pray, just as John taught his disciples" (Luke 11:1). As they had heard Him pray, a yearning had sprung up in their hearts to know a similar intimacy with the Father. We do well to echo their request.

Prayer is an amazing paradox. It is a blending of simplicity and profundity. It can be an agony or an ecstasy. It can focus on a single objective, or it can roam the world. It is "the simplest form of speech that infant lips can try," and yet at the same time is "the sublimest strains that reach the Majesty on high." Small wonder, then, that even Paul, spiritual giant though he was, had to confess: "We do not know what we ought to pray for."

GOD'S INTERESTS MUST COME FIRST

To the maturing disciple, God's interests will always be paramount. The prayers of the immature Christian usually revolve around self. In response to the disciples' plea to be taught to pray, Jesus said, "This, then, is how you should pray," and He gave them a pattern by which to model their prayers. It is noteworthy that in the prayer recorded in Matthew 6:9–13, the first half of the prayer is totally occupied with God and His interests. Only after that do personal petitions find a place. Worship, praise, and thanksgiving have first place. As would be expected, the prayers of Paul follow the Master's model.

THE DISCIPLE CAN PRAY WITH AUTHORITY

We are engaged in a relentless spiritual warfare that knows no truce. Our foes are unseen and intangible, but they are powerful. Against them only spiritual weapons will prevail. Paul wrote:

> We do not wage war as the world does. The weapons we fight with are not the weapons of the world. On the contrary, they have divine power to demolish strongholds. (2 Corinthians 10:3–4)

Of these weapons, prayer is the most formidable and potent in our conflict with "the spiritual forces of evil in the heavenly realms" (Ephesians 6:12).

Restraining prayer, we cease to fight,
Prayer makes the Christian's armour bright;
And Satan trembles when he sees
The weakest saint upon his knees.
—*William Cowper*

The fulcrum on which defeat or victory turns is our ability to pray aright and make intelligent use of our weapons.

Jesus nowhere envisages His church in retreat. To the seventy eager disciples who returned from an evangelistic foray elated with their success, He made this powerful statement: "I saw Satan fall like lightning from heaven. *I have given you authority* to trample on snakes and scorpions and *to overcome all the power of the enemy*" (Luke 10:18–19).

The unmistakable inference is that through the exercise of this delegated authority in their own sphere of service, the disciples, too, would see the overthrow of Satan. This promised authority was never withdrawn. But later, when the disciples lost faith in the promise, they were powerless to deliver a demon-possessed boy. They were paralyzed by their own unbelief. Jesus told them the remedy: "This kind can come out only by prayer" (Mark 9:29).

Restful and trustful prayer has an important place in the Christian life, but Paul taught and practiced a different kind of praying. Only strenuous and aggressive prayer that laid hold of the power released by the cross and the resurrection would dislodge the enemy from his agelong stronghold. It is that kind of praying that releases the power and resources of God and brings them into play in the field of battle.

Samuel Chadwick contended that Satan fears nothing from prayerless studies, teaching, and preaching. "He laughs at our toil, mocks at our wisdom, but trembles when we pray."

To the captious Pharisees, Jesus gave the illustration of a strong, well-armed man, feeling safe in his fortress: "How can anyone enter a strong man's house and carry off his possessions unless he first ties up the strong man? Then he can rob his house" (Matthew 12:29).

It is the responsibility of the disciple to exercise this delegated authority in prayer in his conflict with Satan and the power of darkness. In this way Christ's triumph becomes the triumph of His weakest follower.

THE DISCIPLE SHOULD PRAY AUDACIOUSLY

The mature disciple should be no stranger to this kind of praying. In the light of the wide-ranging promises to the intercessor, it is surprising that our prayers are so tepid. They seldom soar above past experience or natural thought. How seldom we pray for the unprecedented, let alone the impossible!

Thou art coming to a King!
Large petitions with thee bring,
For His grace and power are such,
None can ever ask too much.

Scripture bears witness to the fact that God delights to answer daring prayers that are based on His promises. Jesus encouraged His disciples to ask as freely for the impossible as the possible. He said to them, "If you have faith as small as a mustard seed, you can say to this mountain, 'Move from here to there' and it will move. Nothing will be impossible for you" (Matthew 17:20–21). All difficulties are the same size to God.

THE DISCIPLE WILL SOMETIMES WRESTLE IN PRAYER

"Epaphras, who is one of you and a servant of Christ Jesus, . . . is always wrestling in prayer for you."
(Colossians 4:12)

That type of prayer is the experience of the mature disciple. Epaphras was one of these. But how pale a reflection of the praying of Epaphras are our prayers.

It is from the Greek word for "wrestle" that we derive our word *agonize*. It is used in the New Testament of men toiling until they are weary; of the athlete on the track, straining every muscle and nerve; of the soldier battling for his very life. This kind of prayer has been termed "an athletic of the soul."

THE DISCIPLE SHOULD PRAY WITH IMPORTUNITY

Jesus enforced the necessity of importunity and persistence in prayer by telling two parables—the three friends and the unprincipled judge. In each He taught by contrast, for God is neither a lazy, selfish neighbor, nor is He an unprincipled judge.

The Three Friends. In the parable recorded in Luke 11:5–8, one friend found himself in the embarrassing position of having no bread to set before a visitor who had dropped in on him unexpectedly. He hurried to a friend and asked for the loan of three loaves. From behind closed doors the "friend" replied that he was in bed and couldn't be bothered getting up to oblige him. However, the embarrassed host persisted until at last his lazy friend, because of his importunity, rose and gave him what he needed.

In applying the parable, Jesus contrasted by implication the surly selfishness of the reluctant friend with the willing generosity of His Father. If even an utterly selfish man, the argument ran, to whom sleep was more important than a friend's need, will reluctantly get up at midnight to comply with his friend's request because of his unabashed persistence, how much more will God be moved by the importunate entreaty of His children (11:13)?

The Unprincipled Judge. In the second parable, recorded in Luke 18:1–8, a widow who had been swindled took her case to court. The presiding judge was a man who "neither feared God nor cared about men." Time after time he rebuffed heartlessly the woman's entreaties for justice to be done. At last, exasperated by her persistence and in order to rid himself of the nuisance, he dealt with her case, and justice was done.

The argument is that if a nagging widow by her shameless persistence can overcome the obstinacy of an unprincipled judge, how much more will God's children receive the answer to their urgent prayers, since they are appealing, not to an adversary, but to a caring Advocate whose attitude is the antithesis of that of the uncaring judge.

Thus, by luminous parables Jesus depicted by way of contrast a true delineation of the character and attitude of His Father. He is not like an unjust judge who dispenses reluctant justice to a defrauded widow only because her persistence creates a nuisance.

The lesson to be drawn is that it is "shameless persistence" that comes away with full hands; and the opposite is also true. Tepid praying does not move God's arm. In contrast, John Knox cried, "Give me Scotland or I die." If our desire is so feeble that we can do without what we are asking and it is not something we must have at all costs, why should our prayer be answered?

Adoniram Judson of Burma said,

> God loves an importunate prayer so much that He will not give us much blessing without it. He knows that it is a necessary preparation for our receiving the richest blessing He is longing to bestow.
>
> I never prayed sincerely and earnestly for anything but it came at some time, no matter how distant a day somehow, in some shape, probably the last I would have devised, it came.

That naturally raises the question: Why can God not simply answer the prayer without requiring us to importune Him for an answer?

Why is importunity necessary?

God has assured us that there is no reluctance on His part to bestow any good gift. It is not that He wants to be coaxed. The repeated "how much more" in the above parables assures us of that. So the answer must be looked for elsewhere.

The necessity of importunity lies in us, not in God. William E. Biederwolf suggests that importunity is one of the instructors in God's training school for Christian culture. Sometimes He delays the answer because the petitioner is not in a fit state to receive it. There is something God desires to do in him first.

THE PROBLEM OF UNANSWERED PRAYER

The mature disciple will not stumble because of apparently unanswered prayer. He will not, however, adopt a fatalistic attitude; he will examine his prayers and seek to discover the cause of failure.

The plain fact is that God does not always say yes to every prayer (though we usually expect Him to do so). Moses entreated the Lord earnestly that he might enter the Promised Land. But God answered no (Deuteronomy 34:4). Paul prayed repeatedly that his "thorn in [the] flesh" might be removed, but God said no (2 Corinthians 12:7–9). However, He promised compensating grace. God is sovereign and all-wise, and we should be sensible enough and humble enough to recognize His sovereignty in the realm of prayer.

Our Lord's brother gives one reason for unanswered prayer: "When you ask, you do not receive, *because you ask with wrong motives*" (James 4:3). God does not undertake to answer every self-centered petition, but He does promise to answer every prayer that is according to His good and perfect will.

It may be that our prayer was not the prayer of faith, but only the prayer of hope. Jesus said, "According to your faith will it be done to you" (Matthew 9:29), not according to your hope. Are many of your prayers only prayers of hope?

Or we may have been substituting faith in prayer for faith in God. We are not told anywhere to have faith in prayer but to "have faith in God," the One who answers the prayer. This is more than a matter of semantics. Sometimes we sigh, "Our prayers are so weak and ineffective!" or, "My faith is so small!"

Jesus anticipated this reaction when He said, "I tell you the truth, if you have faith as small as a mustard seed, you can say to this mountain, 'Move from here to there' and it will move. Nothing will be impossible for you" (Matthew 17:20).

The naked eye sees little difference between a grain of sand and a mustard seed, but there is a world of difference between the two. In one is the germ of life. It is not the size of our faith that is important, but is it a living faith in a living God?

The mature disciple will not become discouraged because of a delay in the answer to his prayer. He knows that a delayed answer is not necessarily a denied answer.

Unanswered yet? Nay, do not say, ungranted,
Perhaps your part is not yet fully done.
The work began when first your prayer was offered,
And God will finish what He has begun.
If you will keep the incense burning there,
You shall have your desire—
Sometime, somewhere!
—Ophelia R. Browning

God's timing is infallible. He takes every factor and contingency into account. We often want to pluck unripe fruit, but He will not be pressured into premature action.

If He in His wisdom delays the answer to our prayer, that delay will in the long run prove to be for our good (Hebrews 12:10). It will be either because He has some better thing for us, or because there is something He desires to achieve in our lives that can be effected in no other way.

As we mature spiritually and get to know our heavenly Father more intimately, we will be able to implicitly trust His love and wisdom, even when we cannot understand His actions. Jesus prepared His disciples for this experience when He said, "You do not realize now what I am doing, but later you will understand" (John 13:7).

CHAPTER 14

The Disciple's Rights

Don't we have the right . . . ?
I have not used any of these rights.
1 CORINTHIANS 9:4, 15

Few would question the assertion that we should renounce the wrong things in our lives. It is self-evident that such things mar our lives, spoil our enjoyment of life, and limit our usefulness to God and man. But not everyone is equally convinced that in the interest of the gospel the disciple of Christ may need to renounce some things that are perfectly right and legitimate.

I once heard an arresting message on this theme preached by Rowland V. Bingham, founder of the Sudan Interior Mission, whose sacrificial missionary career gave him the right to speak with authority. Although it was sixty years ago, much that he said is still clear in my memory and colors this study.

Four times in 1 Corinthians 9 Paul asserts his rights in the gospel. Three times he claims that he has refrained from exercising these rights in the higher interests of spreading the gospel. He affirms that he is ready to forgo any right he may have, and forsake any privilege, out of love for Christ and in the interests of the progress of the gospel. Listen to the lengths to which he is prepared to go: "*We did not use this right.* On the contrary, we put up with anything rather than hinder the gospel of Christ" (v. 12).

Oswald Chambers had some trenchant words to say in this connection:

> If we are willing to give up only wrong things for Jesus, never let us talk about being in love with Him. Anyone will give up wrong things if he knows how, but are we prepared to give up the best we have for Jesus Christ? The only right a Christian has is the right to give up his rights. If we are to be the best for God, there must be victory in the realm of legitimate desire as well as in the realm of unlawful indulgence.

Elsewhere the apostle insisted that everything that is legitimate is not necessarily helpful under all circumstances:

> "Everything is permissible for me"—but not everything is *beneficial.* (1 Corinthians 6:12)
> "Everything is permissible"—but not everything is *constructive.* (1 Corinthians 10:23)

He knew from experience that it was possible to indulge in permissible things to an inordinate degree and thus become a slave to them. So he adds yet another restraint:

> "Everything is permissible for me"—but I will not be *mastered* by anything. (1 Corinthians 6:12)

That means that the disciple must choose his priorities very carefully, even in things that are right in themselves. If we are aiming at the heights of Christian experience, there will always come the challenge to voluntary renunciation of some rights.

The Christian life is not the only realm in which this is the case. What renunciations the aspiring athlete is prepared to make in order to break a record or win a prize!

As in all else, our Lord set a shining example in His earthly life. As Son of God He was "heir of all things" and enjoyed rights and privileges beyond our dreaming. Yet for our sake He renounced them. Consider the stupendous surrender of rights involved in the Incarnation, when He "forsook the courts of everlasting day, and chose with us a darksome house of mortal clay."

A seventeenth-century poet depicts the scene when the Son of God renounced His rights to the enjoyment of the glories of His position as "heir of all things" in these vivid words:

Hast thou not heard what my Lord Jesus did?
Then let me tell you a strange storie.
The God of power, when He did ride
In His majestick robes of glorie,
Resolved to light; and so one day
He did descend, unrobing all the way.
The starres His tires of light and rings obtained,
The cloud His bow, the fire His spear,
The sky His azure mantle gained.
And when they asked what He would wear,

He smiled, and said as He did go,
He had new clothes amaking down below.
—George Herbert

On earth He surrendered His right to the comforts of home life, the right to the congenial company of heaven, and at the last, the right to life itself. The only rights He did not surrender were those essential to His role as Mediator between God and man. "I lay down my life for the sheep," Jesus claimed. "No one takes it from me, but I lay it down of my own accord" (John 10:15, 18). If sacrifice is "the ecstasy of giving the best we have to the one we love the most," it follows that at times there will be lower rights that must be renounced in favor of those who are higher.

Once a traveler has paid his fare, he is entitled to a seat on the bus. No one can legitimately take it from him. And when a mother with a baby in one arm and a bag of groceries in the other boards the crowded bus, he still has the right to keep his seat. But he also has the higher choice of giving it up to the lady. In the same way, at times the interests of the gospel—and that is Paul's preoccupation in this passage—requires the renunciation of some of our rights.

Paul practiced what he preached. "Though I am free and belong to no man, I make myself a slave to everyone, to win as many as possible" (1 Corinthians 9:19). He makes reference to his personal rights in four areas (vv. 4–6, 11), but he asserts that although he might have done so legitimately, he exploited none of them to the full (vv. 12, 15, 18).

THE RIGHT TO GRATIFY NORMAL APPETITE

"Don't we have the right to food and drink?" he asked (1 Corinthians 9:4). He may have been asserting his liberty to eat certain foods, for food offered to idols was a theme of the previous chapter. But the context would rather suggest that he is claiming the right to eat and drink at the expense of the church—the right of the Christian worker to be maintained on the material level by those whom he serves in spiritual things.

But his question could be expanded to include not only food and drink but also all his normal physical appetites. Because they are bestowed by God, they are not unholy. In themselves they are legitimate, but they can be indulged in to such a degree or in such a relationship as to render them sinful. Because they are legitimate, that does not mean that we should always use our right to the full, much less abuse it.

The joy of sharing the gospel was to Paul of far greater importance than food or drink. When the interests of the gospel demanded it, he gladly went hungry and thirsty. Hear his testimony: "I know what it is to be in need, and I know what it is to have plenty. I have learned the secret of being content in any and every situation, whether well fed or hungry, whether living in plenty or in want" (Philippians 4:12).

Do we share his outlook? Have we discovered for ourselves his secret?

It can rightly be argued that a missionary has just as valid a right to rich and attractive food as any of his fellow believers in the homeland. But there may be times when he may need to live at subsistence level if needy people are to be reached with the good news. His first priority must be the glory of God in the winning and discipling of souls.

John Wesley emulated the apostle Paul in his determination not to be enslaved by appetite. In order to gain this mastery, he lived solely on potatoes for two whole years. Apparently that did not affect his health adversely, for he lived to be eighty-nine years of age. He was no ascetic, but he would not tolerate being bossed by his appetite, especially if it would hinder the gospel of Christ (1 Corinthians 9:12).

THE RIGHT TO NORMAL MARITAL LIFE

"Don't we have the right to take a believing wife along with us," Paul asked, "as do the other apostles and the Lord's brothers and Cephas?" (1 Corinthians 9:5). This raises the much-debated question: Had Paul been married?

This is probably a question that cannot be answered decisively. But there is presumptive evidence that he may have been married. He stated that when Stephen was condemned, he had cast his vote against him. This would imply that he had been a member of the Sanhedrin, a qualification for which was that one had to be a married man. If that was indeed the case, his wife may have predeceased him or left him when he embraced Christianity. But whether married or not, Paul asserted his right to a normal marital life, having his wife accompany him; but he added, "We did not use this right" (v. 12).

Many married people who are called to the ministry of the Word, either at home or overseas, voluntarily release their partners for longer or shorter periods, in the interests of the gospel. Others voluntarily renounce the right to romance and marriage so that they can give themselves with greater abandon to the ministry entrusted to them. Such costly sacrifices are not forgotten by the Lord, and they will have their own reward.

In the realm of romance Paul had his priorities right. To him the will of God and the winning of souls were of greater importance. His paramount concern he stated in a single statement: "to win as many as possible" (v. 19). All else must take second place. Romance in the will of God is wonderful, but out of the will of God it is tragic. Experience proves that the crucial point of our surrender to Christ often lies just here.

When William Carey shared his missionary call and vision with his wife, she was totally unresponsive. He wept and pleaded with her in vain. At last he urged: "If I were called to government service in India, I would have to make arrangements for you and go. I am called by a higher One. I will make arrangements for you and go."

In the event, the captain of the ship refused to take him, and he had to wait for another ship. In the interval his wife changed her mind and decided to accompany him. Carey put God first in his marital relations, and God honored his faith and dedication.

Let it be said with all confidence that it is utterly safe to commit our plans for romance and marital life into the hands of the God who cares. For the single missionary this is often a recurring problem that needs sympathetic understanding. For a minority it will be God's will for them to remain single. Where that is the case only unhappiness will result from taking romance into one's own hands.

Here, as in all else, difficult though it may be, peace lies in the acceptance of the will of God. He never penalizes those who surrender their rights in this sphere.

THE RIGHT TO NORMAL REST AND RECREATION

"Is it only I and Barnabas who must work for a living?" (1 Corinthians 9:6). The question here is the disciple's right to refrain from manual labor and, instead, be supported by the church as were the other apostles. Once again he renounced this right. "If others have this right of support from you, shouldn't we have it all the more?" he asked. Then he adds: *"But we did not use this right"* (v. 12).

There were cogent reasons for his refusing support from them. He did not want to be classed with the greedy priests who exploited their office to their own advantage. Then, too, he desired to maintain his own independence. He could exercise his apostolic authority more freely when financial considerations were not involved. Too often those who give the money want to call the tune. If he took no money, they could not dictate to him on matters of policy, and he would be freer to act in matters of discipline.

The principle involved here could be widened to include the right of the disciple to normal rest and recreation or the missionary to normal furlough. In Old Testament times God made provision for regular rest and recreation in the various festivals of the Lord. They were occasions for physical as well as spiritual renewal.

There is a place for recreation in the life of the disciple. A good test of the validity of our recreation would be this:

Will it make me a better and healthier servant and a more effective winner of men?

Many Christian workers, including myself, have paid a heavy price for failing to allot adequate time for rest and recreation—as did the saintly young Scottish minister Robert Murray McCheyne. He lay on his deathbed when only twenty-nine, completely worn-out by his unremitting labors. To the friend sitting at his bedside, McCheyne said, "The Lord gave me a horse to ride and a message to deliver. Alas, I have killed the horse and I cannot deliver the message!"

It must be acknowledged, however, that in the course of our Christian work, whether at home or overseas, occasions will arise when, in the interests of the gospel and the ungathered harvest, recreation or furlough will need to be forgone for a period. The disciple must hold himself in readiness to have his rights set aside where needs of fellow men are involved.

THE RIGHT TO APPROPRIATE REMUNERATION

"If we have sown spiritual seed among you, is it too much if we reap a material harvest from you? If others have this right of support from you, shouldn't we have it all the more? *But we did not use this right*" (1 Corinthians 9:11–12).

In support of his contention, the apostle cites the generally accepted principle that the farmer who produces the crop has the right to a share of it, as also the vintner his share of the wine. In other words, there is nothing wrong in being a paid preacher. Even the ox is not muzzled when he is engaged in threshing the grain. "In the same way, the

Lord has commanded that those who preach the gospel should receive their living from the gospel" (v. 14).

Throughout his ministry Paul was meticulous in his financial dealings. He refused to allow monetary considerations to influence his decisions or actions. Money is an acid test of character. Our real riches are what go into our character, and these abide with us eternally. In his attitude toward money Paul was "clean"—something that cannot be said of all Christian workers. He had victory in the realm of finance, and he renounced his right to be supported by the church in order that he might win more souls to Christ (v. 12).

Whether we possess much money or little, it is our attitude toward it that is revealing. There is no moral quality in riches or poverty per se, but our attitude toward it is a test of true spirituality. In a world in which material and financial values are paramount, it is not easy to escape their taint.

Discover a person's attitude toward money, and you will learn a great deal about his or her character. Not every Christian worker has mastered the problem of financial stewardship, and as a result many have lost spiritual effectiveness. Paul did not fall into that trap.

THE MOTIVATION

The voluntary renunciation of our rights in the four sensitive areas discussed above will require more than ordinary motivation and dedication. Some may find the price too steep and draw back. We should be grateful that Paul not only set the standard but shared the motivation that enabled him to make such costly renunciations with joy.

First, the positive factors: "That in preaching the gospel I may offer it free of charge, and so not make use of my rights in preaching it" (1 Corinthians 9:18). "I have become all things to all men so that by all possible means I might save some" (v. 22). "I do all this for the sake of the gospel, that I may share in its blessings" (v. 23). "We do it to get a crown that will last forever" (v. 25).

He supports this positive motivation by strong, though negative, motives: "We did not use this right. On the contrary, we put up with anything rather than hinder the gospel of Christ" (v. 12). "I have not used any of these rights. . . . I would rather die than have anyone deprive me of this boast" (v. 15). "I beat my body and make it my slave so that . . . I myself will not be disqualified for the prize" (v. 27).

Taken together, these motives make a powerful appeal to the disciple who is zealous in the cause of Christ, prepared to pay the price of true discipleship, and has a passion for the spread of the gospel. In the history of Christian missions especially, we have not been without many whose renunciation of rights has paralleled that of Paul. Who will follow in their train?

CHAPTER 15

The Disciple's Example

Set an example for the believers in speech,
in life, in love, in faith and in purity.
1 TIMOTHY 4:12

Paul was anxious that his protégé should develop into "a good minister of Jesus Christ" (1 Timothy 4:6). In his two letters to Timothy he aimed to brace and encourage him in view of his ministry in the important church at Ephesus, which was the most mature church to which Paul wrote. It had enjoyed a galaxy of talent in its ministry, including Paul himself. One can well imagine that the young man would have felt very keenly his comparative youth and inexperience and would have viewed his responsibility with trepidation. So the aged and experienced apostle gave him advice and encouragement that would, if followed, develop his leadership potential and further equip him for his strategic ministry. This advice is as relevant in the world today as it was then.

THE SEARCH FOR MODELS

In everything set them an example by doing what is good.
(Titus 2:7)

In our times, when social structures are collapsing and home life deteriorating, there are a great number of confused young people who have no one to whom they can look as inspiring role models. They grow up with no father in the home, or no mother, and in a society that fosters sexual promiscuity, intemperance, and violence. As a consequence, they are unconsciously looking for models who will set an attractive example.

Recently I was startled while having a conversation with a friend.

"Do you remember when Hazel was in your office forty years ago?" she asked.

When I answered yes, my friend said, "Did you know that she was brought up in an orphanage? She did not know who her parents were, had never experienced love from anyone, and had never seen love between a husband and wife. So when she came to your office, she watched you and your wife closely to see if there really is such a thing as love."

Of course I knew her background, but never for a moment had I realized that all that time my wife and I had been under the microscope of a young woman desperately seeking a role model. I trembled to think what might have become of that young woman had we failed her.

How exhilarating it is to think that we can model the qualities of Christ to those who are searching for Him.

By an exemplary lifestyle, the disciple can make his or her Lord attractive to others. In his letter to Titus, Paul urged him to teach slaves to work to please their masters "so that in every way they will make the teaching about God our Savior attractive" (2:10). Obviously, our lives can make our teaching attractive to others. People should not only hear truth worth hearing but see lives worth emulating.

The word Paul uses in that verse is rendered *adorn* in the King James Version—in every way "adorn the doctrine." That word is used of arranging jewels in such a way as to show off their beauty to the best advantage. This is our privilege.

The private life of the disciple can neutralize the effectiveness of his or her public ministry. At a meeting I was addressing, a well-known archdeacon of a local church was present. At the close of the address he asked if he might speak.

"God has been speaking to me this evening," he said. "Most of you people know me, and I want to make a confession. When I am with you in public, I am always jovial and cheery and the life of the party, but at home I am a different person. I have been a street angel and a home devil. I have been bad-tempered and have given my wife and family a bad time. I have asked God to forgive me and to make me in private more like what I have tried to appear in public." His private life had been neutralizing his public ministry.

In his first letter to Timothy (especially in vv. 6–16 of chapter 4) Paul gave advice of timeless relevance to the younger man, and from it every disciple can profit today, whether in recognized ministry or in ordinary lay activity. "If you point these things out to the brothers, you will be a good minister of Christ Jesus," he wrote (v. 6). We will consider some of his injunctions:

TRAIN YOURSELF TO BE GODLY

We do not become more godly automatically. Becoming more godly rests in our own hands, and as Paul says, it involves training. As indicated before, the word *train* in the original text gives us our word *gymnasium*, and in this connection conveys the idea of "exercising the body or mind." J. B. Phillips renders verse 7: "Take time and trouble to keep yourself spiritually fit." The implication is that we are to be as eager to keep spiritually fit as the athlete is to win the Olympic gold.

Training involves regular strenuous effort, which will make demands on our time and activities. That is something we have to do. Above everything else, it will involve maintaining a consistent devotional life.

COMPENSATE FOR YOUR YOUTH

"Don't let anyone look down on you because you are young: see that they look up to you because you are an example to believers in your speech and behaviour, in your love and faith and sincerity [purity]." (v. 12 PHILLIPS)

Paul was saying that Timothy need not feel his comparative youthfulness to be a handicap to his leadership. In any case, time would take care of that. Meanwhile, he could compensate for his youth by the quality of his life, by the model he provided for the church.

The apostle specified five areas in which Timothy should be watchful. These are areas in which younger people are sometimes deficient—speech, lifestyle, love, faithfulness, purity.

Although Timothy was not a mere youth, many of the elders in the Ephesian church would have been older than he. Yet he was not to allow them to push him aside as a stripling. He was there in response to a divine call. The tense of the verb gives the meaning: "Stop allowing anyone to push you round. . . . Give no one any ground by any fault of character, for despising your youth" (Wuest).

DEVOTE YOURSELF TO THE PUBLIC READING OF SCRIPTURE

"Devote yourself to the public reading of Scripture, to preaching and to teaching." (v. 13)

Timothy was to give attention to seeing that the three elements in the ministry of the Word were given due prominence. It is through the public reading of Scripture that the voice of God is heard. It is regrettable that that injunction is not more faithfully observed. In liturgical churches several readings from different portions of Scripture are read, but that is rare in many other churches.

The second element is preaching. Preaching is the exhortation that follows the reading of Scripture. To be profitable, truth must be acted on. It is spiritually harmful to repeatedly hear truth without responding to it. The exhortation will include advice, encouragement, and warning against error. In our day preaching has been somewhat downgraded in favor of dialogue, discussion, and counseling, but the injunction stands: "Preach the Word."

The third element is teaching—delivering a systematized body of teaching on the great central truths of the Christian faith. We are surrounded by a plethora of cults, and, as Robert H. Mounce writes, "correct theology is the best antidote to error."

STOP NEGLECTING YOUR GIFT

Do not neglect your gift, which was given you. (v. 14)

This gift of grace was the special inward endowment that the Holy Spirit had bestowed upon Timothy to fit and equip him for his ministry. We are not told what the gift was. The tense of the verb rendered *neglect* would give the meaning "stop neglecting," or "do not grow careless" about the gift. It would seem that the diffident Timothy needed prodding on this point.

It should be noted that the impartation of the "charisma," the spiritual gift, was not bestowed by means of prophecy but to the accompaniment of prophecy. The laying on of hands is always symbolic and not efficacious. The gift had been bestowed for the benefit of others; therefore, he was to keep on exercising it. By doing so he would demonstrate the progress he had made since he received it (v. 15).

BE ABSORBED IN THE TASK

"Be diligent in these matters;
give yourself wholly to them." (v. 15)

He must throw himself into his ministry with abandon. A. T. Robertson says that "be diligent" here would be like our "up to the ears in work." No foot-dragging!

What end should Timothy have in view? "So that everyone may see your progress" (v. 15). His progress in holiness and likeness to Christ is to be so marked that it would be visible to everyone—to outsiders as well as to the church family. A convicting question to ask oneself is, "Is my progress in the spiritual life so obvious that it is clearly visible to those with whom I live and work or to whom I minister? Or is my spiritual life static?"

The disciple is exposed to two perils of which he should be aware. One is the danger of an unduly protracted spiritual infancy. Paul had in mind that possibility when writing to the richly gifted yet confused and spiritually immature church at Corinth: "I could not address you as spiritual but as worldly—*mere infants in Christ.* I gave you milk, not solid food, for you were not ready for it. Indeed you are still not ready" (1 Corinthians 3:1–2).

The second peril was spiritual senility. The writer of the letter to the Hebrew Christians was concerned that some of them had retrogressed into a spiritually senile state, so he gave this warning:

> Though by this time you *ought to be teachers*, you need someone to teach you the elementary truths of God's word all over again. You need milk, not solid food! Anyone who lives on milk, *being still an infant*, is not acquainted with the teaching about righteousness. But *solid food is for the mature*." (Hebrews 5:12–14)

Timothy had to be on his guard against those perils and make steady and visible progress toward maturity (Hebrews 6:1).

DISPLAY CONSISTENT PROGRESS

"So that everyone may see your progress."
(1 Timothy 4:15)

It is a salutary experience, as I know from personal experience, to take up this challenge and measure our degree of visible progress—or lack of it. One of the best measuring rods for this purpose is Paul's description of the fruit of the Spirit in Galatians 5:22–23. Let us embark on a voyage of discovery. Here is the standard: "The fruit of the Spirit is love, joy, peace, patience, kindness, goodness, faithfulness, gentleness and self-control."

Those delightful qualities, which flourished so luxuriantly in the life of our Lord, will provide us with a sure test of our spiritual caliber. Let us ask relevant questions such as: Am I a more loving person than I was three months ago? Has my progress in love been visible? Who has seen it?

It should be noted that the nine qualities are regarded as a unit, as, for example, a bunch of grapes. But love is the all-embracing quality. The succeeding eight are but different manifestations of love, which is the motivating principle of them all. Here is the checklist:

The first three qualities concern my private walk with God.

Love. There is no selfishness in love. The kind of love spoken of here is the unselfish side of life. It is more than mere human love. Rather it is the love of God poured into our hearts by the Holy Spirit (Romans 5:5). The Spirit produces both a sense of the divine love and the disposition to love God and others. It is an element that flowers even in the presence of the unlovely and hostile.

Can others discern progress in love in my life?

Joy. There is no depression in love, for joy is the natural outcome of love. Lovers are joyous people. *Joy* is more than vivacity and hilarity. It is the Christian equivalent of the world's "happiness, having a good time." But it transcends that by far, for it does not depend on *outside* happenings.

Christian joy is independent of circumstances and can cohabit with sorrow. Paul said he was "sorrowful, yet always rejoicing" (2 Corinthians 6:10). A heart filled with the love of God is filled with "joy in the Holy Spirit" (Romans 14:17).

Do others see me as a joyous person?

Peace. There is no anxiety in love. Instead there is an inner serenity and tranquility—no borrowing of tomorrow's troubles today. Peace is love in repose. It is not so much the absence of trouble as the presence of God. Like joy, it is part of the Lord's legacy to His disciples. "I have told you these things, so that in me you may have peace" (John 16:33). When the Holy Spirit is not grieved, the dove of peace is able to alight on the heart.

Am I making progress in the conquest of worry?

The next three qualities relate to my walk with my fellow men.

Patience. There is no impatience or irritability in love. Elsewhere Paul says "love suffers long" (1 Corinthians 13:4 NKJV). Patience is one of the outstanding attributes of God, one of which we have so often been the beneficiaries. It is not concerned so much with what we do as with what we can refrain from doing. "The strength of our love can be measured by the length of our patience." This desirable quality enables us to bear with the foibles and failures, the irritations and idiosyncrasies of others even when we are sorely tried.

Am I more patient than I was three months ago?

Kindness. There is no abrasiveness in love, for "love is kind." It is a reflection of God's attitude toward us (Ephesians 2:4). A kind person is sensitive to the feelings of others and is always looking for the opportunity to perform a kindly act, even for the unlovely and undeserving. Kindness mellows a word or action that might otherwise seem harsh or austere.

Am I developing a more kindly disposition?

Goodness. There is no depravity in love. Goodness tends to be a neglected waif in contemporary society. Goodness is not news. It is often snubbed and sneered at. If you want to insult a person, call him a goody-goody.

It is an arresting fact that when "God anointed Jesus of Nazareth with the Holy Spirit and power" (Acts 10:38), the outcome was said to be not ecstatic experience, spectacular miracles, or flamboyant sermons, but simply going about "doing good." Goodness is active benevolence.

Am I visibly a better person than I was?

The last three qualities have to do with my private walk with myself.

Faithfulness. There is no fickleness in love. This fruit is not so much "faith" in the sense of belief as "faithfulness" in the sense of dependability, reliability, trustworthiness—a quality that is highly esteemed. In a coming day the highest commendation of the exalted Lord will be, "Well done, good and *faithful* servant"—if we have indeed done well and been faithful in the discharge of our trust. Faithfulness has been described as the reliability that never gives up and never lets down.

Am I making strides in dependability?

Meekness. There is no retaliation in love. Meekness is not mere mildness of disposition. It is not a quality that is universally admired or desired, and yet the Master claimed, "I am meek and lowly in heart" (Matthew 11:29 KJV). Meekness is the antithesis of self-assertion. The meek person does not fight for his rights and prerogatives, unless a point of principle is involved or the interests of the kingdom are at stake. Jesus assured us that it is the meek, not the aggressive, who inherit the earth (Matthew 5:5).

Do I increasingly manifest a meek spirit?

Discipline. There is no laxness in love. Thayer-Grimm defines this quality as "a virtue which consists in mastery of the appetites and passions, especially the sensual ones." Paul employs the discipline exercised by competitors in the Olympic Games as an example of what the discipline of the disciple should be. Discipline is not the control of self by self! It is control by the Holy Spirit, who holds our appetites and passions in check as we yield ourselves to His control.

Do others see me as a graciously disciplined person?

PERSEVERE IN THESE THINGS

Perseverance. Paul's final exhortation was to perseverance: "Persevere in [these things]" (1 Timothy 4:16). That is, "Continue to focus your mind on holy living and unsleeping vigilance." If he perseveres in these things, the apostle says, he will "save both yourself and your hearers" (v. 16)—in the sense of helping them to be delivered from the "present evil age" (Galatians 1:4).

And what is the dynamic that will enable the disciple to continue making steady progress in the divine life? Paul gives us the cue when he attributes those qualities to the Holy Spirit. He produces the fruit in our lives as we live under the lordship of Christ. In 1 Corinthians 12:3 he says, "No one can say"—i.e., keep on saying—"'Jesus is Lord,' except by the Holy Spirit." If we are to make consistent progress in likeness to Christ, we need to be constantly filled with the Spirit, so that He can produce lovely fruit in our lives.

CHAPTER 16

The Disciple's Loneliness

You will leave me all alone.
Yet I am not alone, for my Father is with me.
JOHN 16:32

Some degree of loneliness is natural and normal in the human situation. It is part of the human predicament. It invades the lives of great and small, and shows neither fear nor favor. The fact that one is a disciple of Christ does not put one beyond the reach of its tentacles, for it is endemic in the world.

Jesus, the Son of Man, experienced loneliness during His life on earth, and therefore there is no sin in being lonely. It can be classed as one of the sinless infirmities of human nature. So there is no need for the lonely disciple to add a burden of guilt to his pain. But loneliness can easily breed sin.

Loneliness has become one of the most pervasive problems of society, and its ravages have been exacerbated by the widespread breakdown of moral and social standards.

Loneliness is defined as "the state of having no companionship, being solitary, feeling forlorn." The very word is onomatopoetic, carrying with it the echo of its own desolation. It is no recent problem, for it had its beginning in the Garden of Eden. It is striking that God's first recorded utterance was to the effect that loneliness is not a good thing: "The Lord God said, 'It is not good for the man to be alone. I will make a helper suitable for him'" (Genesis 2:18).

But later Adam experienced a different loneliness—the loneliness of sin. After he and Eve had fallen to the tempter's ploy, they were gripped by the icy hands of fear. Instead of enjoying uninhibited fellowship with God, they now knew the loneliness of alienation from Him, which is the most poignant of all forms of loneliness.

Loneliness comes in many guises. Sometimes it is like an inner vacuum, a sense of emptiness; or it is an acute sense of desolation; a deep craving for an ill-defined satisfaction. The loss of a close and precious relationship sparks one of its more distressing forms.

Contemporary social and environmental factors are one of the most fruitful causes. Chief among these is the loss of a life partner, especially if there has been a long relationship. Moving from the family home that is too large after the children leave can be a traumatic experience. Removal from familiar scenes and friends leaves gaps and scars.

Almost everyone who is involved in a divorce or a separation—whether adults or children—has to tread the path of loneliness. It leaves an aching void.

SOLITUDE NOT LONELINESS

It is wrong to equate loneliness with solitude. Solitude is something we choose, whereas loneliness comes unbidden and unwelcome. Solitude is physical, loneliness is psychological. Loneliness is negative and unproductive, but solitude can be constructive and fruitful.

It was when "Jacob was left alone" (solitude), awaiting in his tent with justified apprehension the approach of the brother he had defrauded, that he had his life-changing experience.

There are several levels on which loneliness attacks. The emotional level is perhaps the most distressing. The loss or absence of intimate relationships with other human beings creates a vacuum that is hard to fill. The only way it can be relieved is by establishing new in-depth relationships. To the person involved, that often seems to be impossible, but it is not. It will take a firm purpose, but it can be done.

On the social level, the victim may feel "left out" or "unwanted," with the consequence that he or she withdraws and loses touch with the community in which he lives. This is usually, though not always, a self-imposed isolation. That sense of social alienation or segregation is especially common among ethnic groups. Sad to say, it is not uncommon even in church groups, which should be leaders in manifesting the love of Christ and ministering to the lonely.

As has been already intimated, loneliness on the spiritual level is most desolating. It is isolation from God, who alone can fill and satisfy the human heart.

NO STAGE OF LIFE EXEMPT

This malady of the soul is not confined to any one stage of life. In one of his plays, Shakespeare describes *The Seven Ages of Man.* With his pungent pen he delineates the characteristics of each stage of life with more or less accuracy. But one thing is certain, there is no age at which man is immune to the onset of loneliness.

Surprisingly, researchers have discovered that loneliness is much more prevalent in its acute form among adolescents and young people than among the old. Youth feel a desperate need to be accepted, especially by their peers, and they will do almost anything to win their approval. They feel "in between"—neither young nor old—and find it difficult to identify with either. That, in turn, causes them to resort to drugs, alcohol, or other hurtful habits.

Loneliness takes young people by surprise, but older people, although not welcoming it, are somewhat conditioned to the idea that it will come to them in some form sooner or later. They are therefore not so surprised when they have to face the reality.

However, older people do feel desperately lonely when friends and loved ones are called home one by one, or when children are far away and failing strength makes life a burden. They feel that they are no longer needed or perhaps no longer wanted.

One group that is expanding at a frightening rate is composed of solo parents and singles, who by choice live alone or have opted out of marriage. Our society is still couples-oriented, and people in that category often find themselves excluded from the social life of the community.

Single women who yearn for home and motherhood, but to whom the opportunity does not come, are in the same category. They tend to feel that they are regarded as second-class citizens. The Bible, however, lends no countenance to this idea. In writing of the single state in 1 Corinthians 7, Paul three times says concerning singleness, "It is good." His whole emphasis is that the single lifestyle is honorable and good; but not all singles share Paul's opinion. There is something to be said, however, for the view that with so many marriages ending in divorce and so many battered wives, "single bliss is better than marital misery." It should not be forgotten that a large part of the missionary enterprise is carried on by single women.

Divorce is essentially and inevitably a lonely experience for those who are involved. The pain is not over when the decree is signed; indeed, it has just begun. The world is full of lonely divorcees. One tragic side effect is that the children lose one parent—sometimes two. Inevitably that creates loneliness for the innocent.

The lot of the widow or widower is not enviable. Even when the marriage had not been ideal, there was at least some companionship, and the meal table was not silent. In the early days of bereavement, there is usually a great deal of support from friends and loved ones, but then life just goes on for them. Visits and invitations inevitably grow fewer. In many cases the widower is more poorly equipped to handle the changed situation than is the widow.

Bereavement is a desolating experience, and in the earlier stages one feels that the sun will never shine again. It should be accepted that it is not wrong or weak to grieve. Grief should be unashamedly expressed. Tears are therapeutic. Bereavement must be accepted as part of the human situation.

Although time does not remove the sense of loss, it does blunt the sharp edge of the sorrow. But immeasurably more potent than time is the comfort of God. "Praise be to . . . the God of all comfort, who comforts us in all our troubles, so that we can comfort those in any trouble with the comfort we ourselves have received from God" (2 Corinthians 1:3–4).

Some people hug their sorrow and, like the psalmist, refuse to be comforted, thus cheating themselves of the very thing they most need—the comfort of God. Jesus appropriated Isaiah 61:1 to Himself: "He has sent me to bind up the brokenhearted." Let Him do it!

REMEDIAL ACTION

Having reviewed many of the causes of loneliness, we now suggest ways in which its pangs can be assuaged.

It should be clearly stated at once that there is no simple and single panacea. Recovery from the condition will require wholehearted cooperation. There can, however, be an optimistic prognosis if the victim is prepared to take steps himself. Willingness to face reality and adjust to it is imperative.

There is hope of change only when the one who is lonely recognizes that he is responsible for change. One man's testimony was, "I realized that the only way to escape loneliness was through my own initiative." That was facing reality. There are certain things only God can do, and other things that only we can do. We are not robots. The attitude of mind and heart is vitally important.

Many proposed remedies are only palliatives, not cures—a travel holiday, another career, and so on. Such suggestions may well prove helpful, but they do not touch the real problem, for we take our lonely selves with us wherever we go. Frenzied activities will never fill the vacuum. To drop out of circulation will only compound the problem. Those alternatives are only Band-Aids on a broken leg. They may afford temporary distraction, but they do not effect a cure.

Most of us have at times found the medicine prescribed by the physician very unpleasant to take. But no mature adult would refuse to take the remedy simply because it was unpalatable. Some of the following suggestions may not seem palatable, but if the loneliness is sufficiently acute, the wise person will at least give some of them a trial.

1. Believe that the Lord is with you in your loneliness. Here are some relevant promises awaiting claim:

   "My Presence will go with you, and I will give you rest." (Exodus 33:14)

   "Do not fear, for I am with you." (Isaiah 41:10)

   "They will call him Immanuel"—which means, "God with us." (Matthew 1:23)

   God has said, "Never will I leave you; never will I forsake you." So we say with confidence, "The Lord is my helper; I will not be afraid. What can man do to me?" (Hebrews 13:5–6)

2. Since there is no sin in being lonely, don't add false guilt to your problem.
3. If outward circumstances cannot be changed, inward attitudes can and should be adjusted.
4. Don't constantly depreciate yourself. If God has accepted you, you must be valuable in His sight. Accept His valuation of you.

5. Clear the ground spiritually. If there is unconfessed sin, confess it honestly and fully, forsake it, and appropriate the forgiveness and cleansing promised (1 John 1:9). In that way you will get it out of your system. It will have the same effect on your spiritual life as draining a suppurating sore would have on the physical life.
6. Share your feelings, your struggles, and yes, your failures, with your understanding Lord. "He knows how we are formed, he remembers that we are dust" (Psalm 103:14). Unburden yourself to your pastor or a trusted Christian friend and seek his counsel and prayers. A problem shared is often a problem halved.
7. Learn to live with some unsolved problems. Jesus told us to do this when He said, "You do not realize now what I am doing, but later you will understand" (John 13:7).
8. Abandon self-pity—"that dismal fungus." In many instances self-pity is the villain of the piece. To be sorry for oneself perpetually is a one-way ticket to loneliness. In one sense, self-pity is a denial of our personal responsibility to deal with the condition, and it frustrates the possibility of a cure.

If we persist in focusing our thoughts on ourselves, that will only serve to fuel the fires of loneliness. If, instead, we turn our thoughts outward and begin caring for others, then our condition can be reversed, and we will be able to break out of the shell of our own desolation.

9. If circumstances cannot be changed, accept them rather than fighting against them; then adapt yourself to them and seek to adorn them.

ESTABLISHING NEW RELATIONSHIPS

Establishing new relationships is the real cure for loneliness, yet it is the hardest thing to do. But it must be done, for the alternative is a continuation of the status quo. Here are some suggestions as to how new relationships can be formed.

1. Pray and look for opportunities to make friendly overtures to another Christian whom you think might become a friend.
2. In preparation for the approach, think of matters of mutual interest that could form topics of easy conversation.
3. Take the first step and make the approach. It will involve a definite act of the will.
4. Encourage the other person to talk about himself or herself. Show a genuine interest in the other person's concerns, and forget about yourself.
5. If you are shy and find it difficult to talk with others, think through opening and maintaining a conversation.
6. Remember that no single social contact will solve all your problems quickly. The fullest relief will be found in living fellowship with the living Christ.
7. Set your desires and ambitions on objectives outside yourself. Lose yourself in the interests of others.

8. Take the first step to break the pattern today. Don't wait for a more convenient time. It will never come.

In a meeting I conducted in Australia, a young man in obvious distress opened his heart to me. He had met with disappointments and had withdrawn into himself. He was desperately lonely.

I told him that he must take the first step and make the first approach if he wished for relief. I urged him to do it immediately. That evening he came with a beaming face.

"I've done it! I've approached my neighbor who has not been friendly, and he has promised to do Bible study with me." The Lord had answered his prayer.

CHAPTER 17

The Disciple's Second Chance

The pot he was shaping from the clay was marred in his hands; so the potter formed it into another pot, shaping it as seemed best to him.

JEREMIAH 18:4

The patriot-prophet Jeremiah was heartbroken. Despite his tears and entreaties, his beloved nation had proven intransigent and was drifting further and further from God. His earnest endeavors to avert catastrophe had proved unavailing. He had exhausted all his own resources, and there seemed no alternative to deserved judgment.

It was just when he had reached this crisis that God gave Jeremiah a vision of hope. "Go down to the potter's house," the Lord said, "and there I will give you my message" (Jeremiah 18:2). Although Israel had persistently thwarted the divine purpose of blessing, if the nation would repent and once again yield to His touch, the heavenly Potter would make it into a new nation and give it another chance even at this late hour.

Although the vision was a contemporary message to Israel, the application is timeless. Just as the elements of the potter's art are essentially the same as in Jeremiah's day, so are God's methods and dealings with His children in every age. The context and trappings may differ, but the underlying principles are unchanging.

When Jeremiah went obediently to the potter's house, he saw the revolving wheel controlled by the potter's foot; a pile of clay inert and unable to improve its condition, of no intrinsic value; a pot of water for use in softening the clay and rendering it malleable; a scrap heap on which the potter cast the pots that had failed to realize his design; and, of course, he saw the skillful and experienced potter himself. "Then the word of the LORD came to me," Jeremiah wrote. "'O house of Israel, can I not do with you as this potter does?' declares the LORD. 'Like clay in the hand of the potter, so are you in my hand'" (vv. 5–6).

That assertion of the absolute, sovereign power of God sounds rather harsh and forbidding. His power is so final, and we are so powerless. But Isaiah the prophet softens the picture: "O LORD, you are our Father. We are the clay, you are the potter; we are all the work of your hand" (Isaiah 64:8).

True, God is sovereign in His power, but He also has a Father's heart. We can be absolutely certain that His sovereignty will never clash with His paternity. All His dealings with His frail and failing children are dictated by unchanging love.

As Jeremiah watched the potter at work, he saw:

THE VESSEL SHAPED

"I saw him working at the wheel." (Jeremiah 18:3)

The potter took a lump of plastic clay and threw it into the very center of the revolving wheel. Had he placed it a little to one side, the vessel would have emerged eccentric, lopsided. The spiritual lesson needs no emphasis.

Then, as his skillful fingers molded and caressed the clay, the pattern conceived in the potter's mind began to emerge. He shaped it first from without and then from within until the shapeless clay began to be a thing of beauty.

The potter was an experienced and skillful man. God is supremely skillful in the molding of human lives. He is no experimenter. He makes no mistakes. He never spoils His own work. The tragedy is that sometimes we arrogantly assume the role of the potter and try to shape our own lives, with disastrous results.

The wheel on which the vessel is molded represents the circumstances of daily life that shape our characters. How varied they are! Heredity, temperament, and environment are largely beyond our control, but they have strong, formative influence. God's providential dealings also play their part—adversity and prosperity, sorrow and joy, bereavement and sometimes tragedy, trials, and temptations. All are factors that God uses to change us progressively into the likeness of Christ.

He placed thee 'mid this dance
Of plastic circumstance,
Machinery just meant
To give thy soul its bent,
Try thee, and turn thee forth,
Sufficiently impressed.
—Robert Browning

In the clay we can see our human nature. "You molded me like the clay," said Job (10:9). Clay is without value apart from the touch of the potter. Its paramount value lies in its capacity to receive and retain the pattern in the potter's mind. "It is the art which gives the value [to the clay], not the material" (Christopher Dresser).

On one occasion I attended an art auction at Sothebys, the well-known art auctioneers in London. A small, and to me quite unattractive, piece of pottery was held up by the auctioneer, and to my amazement bidding began at £25,000! Then it rose to £50,000, £70,000, £75,000, and £78,000 when bidding ceased. The clay in the vessel would be worth a few pennies! The amazing value of the vessel to the purchaser had all been imparted by the touch of the potter.

A human life, like clay, has almost limitless potential when yielded to the heavenly Potter's touch. Why are some lives radiant and others drab? They are made from the same material. The difference is in the degree to which the Potter is allowed to work out the beautiful design in His mind.

There are endless varieties of clay, and each requires individual treatment, adapted to its texture and other distinctive qualities. So is it with the life of each disciple. Accordingly, God's dealings with each of us are unique and exclusive. There is no mass production in God's pottery!

THE VESSEL MARRED

"The pot he was shaping from the clay
was marred in his hands." (Jeremiah 18:4)

As Jeremiah was admiring the emerging vessel, suddenly it collapsed into a shapeless lump of clay. All the potter's work had gone for nothing. The beautiful design of the potter was thwarted, and the prophet expected the potter to throw it on the scrap heap. We are not told the reason for the collapse, but it was doubtless due to some failure in the clay's response to the potter's touch.

Does this scene find correspondence in your life? The collapse was not due to any carelessness or lack of skill on the part of the potter. No artist spoils his own work. We set out on life with high hopes and ideals, but often we are worsted in the battle of life. The vessel is marred, but there is a bright ray of hope. The clay is still "in His hands." He has not thrown it on the scrap heap!

The heavenly Potter's design may be thwarted in a number of ways, the most common of which is the toleration of sin in the life. It may be open sin or sin cherished in the imagination. It may be sins of the spirit such as jealousy, pride, covetousness, or sins of speech. Those may seem more respectable than the grosser sins of the flesh, but they are no more acceptable to God. Sin of any kind will mar the vessel.

It may be resistance to the known will of God. The clay of our wills is too stiff to yield to the delicate touch of the Potter. A crucial battle often rages around one point of resistance—and that mars the vessel.

Or it might be some wrong or unhelpful relationship that is short-circuiting God's blessing.

These matters call for drastic action. They must be thoroughly thought through and ruthlessly dealt with if life is to get back on the right track.

THE VESSEL RESHAPED

"So the potter formed it into another pot,
shaping it as seemed best to him." (v. 4)

Here is God's message of hope. Jeremiah's potter did not throw the misshapen vessel on the scrap heap, but of the very same clay, perhaps softened with some water, he made it into another pot. Such a pot may not have been quite as beautiful as that originally intended, but it is still "fit for the Master's use."

It was foretold of our Lord, "He will not falter or be discouraged till he establishes justice on earth" (Isaiah 42:4). Nor did He. The Scriptures are replete with illustrations of marred vessels whom He has remade.

Who but He would have chosen Jacob to head up the holy nation through which the Messiah would come? Jacob's very name meant "cheater, supplanter." Someone has said that he was so crooked he could hide behind a corkscrew. Before the determining crisis of his life, he had spent twenty years cheating and being cheated by his uncle, Laban. Then God maneuvered him into a corner from which there was no escape.

> So Jacob was left alone, and a man wrestled with him till daybreak. . . . His hip was wrenched as he wrestled with the man. Then the man said, "Let me go, for it is daybreak." But Jacob replied, "I will not let you go unless you bless me."
>
> The man asked him, "What is your name?"
>
> "Jacob," he answered.

> Then the man said, "Your name will no longer be Jacob, but Israel, because you have struggled with God and with men and have overcome." (Genesis 32:24–28)

Up until that time Jacob had resisted the Potter at every turn and pursued his own devious way; but at last he was defeated. He laid down the sword of his rebellion. And God changed him from a cheat into a prince.

Simon Peter was not very promising material. After many failures, he reached the nadir of his experience when he denied his Lord with oaths and curses. When he went out from the Lord's presence and wept bitterly, he doubtless thought that was the end for him. It had been a lovely dream while it lasted, but now he had "blown it." He had better go back to fishing.

But the heavenly Potter was not discouraged. He did not throw Peter on the scrap heap. In fifty days' time that same Peter was preaching the flaming Pentecost sermon that swept three thousand into the kingdom of God. Jesus did not even put him on a period of probation! "He knew what was in man," and He saw the depth and reality of Peter's repentance. Not only did He reinstate him in the apostolate, but Peter became its leader; he was entrusted with the keys that opened the kingdom of heaven to both Jews and Gentiles.

John Mark was a promising young man who became a dropout. When Barnabas and Saul set out on their first missionary journey Mark accompanied them full of high hopes and honored to travel with such men. But as opposition increased and the travel grew more arduous and dangerous, his initial enthusiasm evaporated. He left them and went back home (Acts 13:13)—a dropout.

When Barnabas suggested that they take him with them on their next tour, Paul would not hear of it. Mark had let them down once—no second chance. But Barnabas and the heavenly Potter did not drop him; they gave him another chance, and he made good. The dropout became the biographer of the Son of God! Marvelous grace of the undiscourageable Potter.

THE VESSEL PERFECTED

In his art, the potter uses the fire as well as the wheel. Without the fire of the kiln, the vessel will not retain its shape. In the fire, moisture and unwanted elements are burned out. As the temperature rises, the clay becomes purer, and the beautiful colors of the potter's pattern are burned in.

What pattern does our Potter have in mind? It is no afterthought. Paul tells us what it is: "Those God foreknew *he also predestined to be conformed to the likeness of his Son,* that he might be the firstborn among many brothers" (Romans 8:29).

Every touch of the Potter on our lives has that desirable end in view. The touches we sometimes fear are designed only to remove the ugly things from our lives and to replace them with the graces and virtues of our Lord.

When through fiery trials thy pathway shall lie,
My grace all sufficient shall be thy supply;
The flame shall not hurt thee; I only design
Thy dross to consume, and thy gold to refine.
—Robert Keene

The fire makes the pattern permanent. While walking through a friend's pottery, we came to the kilns where the vessels were to be fired. My friend made a remark that sparked a comforting thought. "We never put an article into the fire unshielded," he said. "We always encase it in a stronger, fire-resisting material. Otherwise the fierce heat would spoil the article." My thoughts went to Isaiah's prophecy in which the Lord said: "Fear not, for I have redeemed you; I have summoned you by name; you are mine. When you pass through the waters, *I will be with you.* . . . When you walk through the fire, you will not be burned; the flames will not set you ablaze" (Isaiah 43:1–2). We are never left to pass through the fires of testing alone—but do we always believe and lay hold of that fact?

The three young men, despite their affirmation of faith in God's ability to deliver them, were not spared from the flames of the furnace, but they were "encased" and shielded from their destructive power and in addition had the unspeakable privilege of personal fellowship with the Son of God. We do not always realize what design the Potter is working out in our lives.

King George VI of Britain was inspecting a famous pottery. When they came to a room where afternoon tea sets were being made, the escorting potter said, "Your Majesty, there is the tea set you ordered for the palace," and pointed to a black tea set.

On seeing it, the king protested: "But we didn't order a black tea set!"

"Oh no," rejoined the potter. "You ordered a gold tea set. Underneath that black substance there is gold. But if we put the gold into the fire unprotected, the set would be spoiled, so we paint it over with the black substance. When that is burned off, only the burnished gold is left."

When we are passing through the dark and testing experiences of life, we tend to see only the black. We forget that there is, underneath, the gold of purified character—more likeness to Christ.

After the series of devastating reverses and sufferings that overtook Job, he bore this testimony, to which numberless saints in subsequent years have subscribed: "He knows the way that I take; when he has tested me, I will come forth as gold" (Job 23:10).

Judas persistently rebuffed the beneficent touch of the Potter on his life, with the result that there was no other place for him but on the scrap heap. Was it mere coincidence that the embezzler-suicide was buried in the potter's field that the priests had purchased with the thirty pieces of silver for which he betrayed Christ? His end is a solemn warning to any who, like him, are resisting the Potter's touch.

Lie still, and let Him mould thee!
O Lord, I would obey,
Be Thou the skillful Potter
And I the yielding clay.
Mould me, O mould me to Thy will,
While I am waiting, yielded and still.
—Author Unknown

CHAPTER 18

The Disciple's Renewed Commission

This is what the LORD Almighty says: "If you will walk in my ways and keep my requirements, then you will govern my house and have charge of my courts, and I will give you a place among these standing here."

ZECHARIAH 3:7

C. I. Scofield, editor of the annotated Bible that is associated with his name, used to tell of his resentment that every time he met with Dwight L. Moody, the noted American evangelist, he would pray that Scofield's commission might be renewed. He did not care for the implications of that prayer. But later he came to see that the clear-sighted Moody had discerned his Achilles' heel. Moody saw that with Scofield's intense preoccupation with the intellectual side of the Christian faith he was in danger of losing his zeal for God and love for his fellow men. Hence the evangelist's repeated petition for his friend.

Every disciple, especially those with a strongly intellectual bent, faces the same peril. We can learn valuable lessons in this connection from the manner in which the commission of Joshua, Israel's high priest, was renewed. Although the symbolic vision had primary application to the times in which Zechariah lived, it has a contemporary significance as well. Zechariah tells the story of the vision he saw:

> Now Joshua was dressed in filthy clothes as he stood before the angel. The angel said to those who were standing before him, "Take off his filthy clothes."
>
> Then he said to Joshua, "See, I have taken away your sin, and I will put rich garments on you."
>
> Then I said, "Put a clean turban on his head." So they put a clean turban on his head and clothed him, while the angel of the LORD stood by. (Zechariah 3:3–5)

THE DISQUALIFIED HIGH PRIEST

In vision, Zechariah was introduced to a scene in heaven. A trial was in process, with Joshua, the high priest and representative of his people, in the dock. Standing at his right hand was Satan, his adversary and accuser. To his dismay the prophet saw Joshua garbed in filthy clothes. According to the Mosaic law, that disqualified him from functioning as high priest.

The accusing counsel was not slow to make capital out of the situation and leveled his charges against Joshua. The accusations seemed only too well founded, for he offered no defense and stood self-accused.

Suddenly, to Zechariah's relief and delight, the suspense was broken by the Judge's spontaneously intervening and rebuking and refuting the charges made by the accuser. Then "the LORD said to Satan, 'The LORD rebuke you, Satan! The

LORD, who has chosen Jerusalem, rebuke you! Is not this man a burning stick snatched from the fire?'" (v. 2). So Joshua's accuser was rebuked and silenced.

Next, as tangible evidence that the accused was acquitted, his filthy clothes were removed, and in their place he was arrayed in rich, festal clothing. His priestly commission was renewed, and once again he was qualified to minister before the Lord as His representative to the nation. Joshua—and in him the whole nation—was forgiven, cleansed, and restored to fellowship with God.

Because Christ has constituted us "a kingdom and priests to serve his God and Father" (Revelation 1:6), it is the privilege and function of every disciple to minister before God. In discharging that office, we may expect, like Joshua, to attract the hostile attentions of our adversary in his role as "accuser of our brethren" (Revelation 12:10 NASB). Joshua was doubtless one of the holiest men of his day, and yet when he found himself in the blazing light of God's holiness, he realized his utter unfitness to act as priest of the living God.

As representative of the nation, he was identified with them in their sin and guilt, and Satan had much with which he could righteously accuse them. Malachi the prophet records the condition into which the nation had fallen. So corrupt and avaricious had they become that instead of offering unblemished animals for sacrifice to God, they brought the maimed and diseased to the altar. Even Joshua's own sons had married foreign wives. Instead of rebuking and restraining them and lifting the nation to the divine standards, he had accepted and condoned their evil practices. Small wonder he had no answer to Satan's accusations.

THE ACCUSING COUNSEL

It is not without good reason that Satan is designated "the accuser of our brethren" (Revelation 12:10 NASB), for that is his favorite role. The noted infidel Ernest Renan termed Satan "the malevolent critic of creation." He is "the father of lies" (John 8:44), but he can speak the truth when it suits his plan. Whether false or true, he spews out his accusations against the believer, generating a sense of condemnation and effectively discouraging and unfitting him for service.

The devil delights to see a Christian "clothed in filthy garments," and as he did with Joshua, he will do all in his power to prevent their removal. He knows that nothing can harm the cause of Christ more than a Christian who falls into sin. The whole evangelical cause around the world has been greatly harmed by the moral delinquency of some television evangelists, and Satan has gained a notable victory. But the final victory is not with him.

He is always on the alert to find something of which he can accuse us to God and discredit us before men. All too often we supply him with the ammunition. He is vastly experienced and knows how to exploit the weak spots in our characters, and he will stoop to any underhanded method to attain his end.

It is noteworthy that in Zechariah's vision the Judge did not deny the accusations brought by the accuser against Joshua and the nation, but He refused to entertain them. "The LORD rebuke you, Satan," was His rejoinder. "Is not this man a burning stick snatched from the fire?"

This latter is an interesting figure. Imagine an important document being inadvertently thrown into the fire. Just in time it is discovered and snatched out. The edges are charred, but the essential document is still intact. It is valuable though somewhat defaced. The fact that God troubled to snatch Joshua—and us—from the fire is our assurance that we are valuable in His sight and that He will perfect in us the work He has begun. "He who began a good work in you will carry it on to completion" (Philippians 1:6).

We should recognize that Satan has no right to level any charge against a believer. If you are troubled by his accusing voice, remember that the only One who has the right to prefer a charge against one of Christ's disciples is the One against whom he has sinned. That is implicit in the Lord's words to the penitent prostitute: "Neither do I condemn you. . . . Go now and leave your life of sin" (John 8:11).

Paul was reveling in a sense of complete spiritual absolution when he wrote the thrilling words: "Who will bring any charge against those whom God has chosen? It is God who justifies. Who is he that condemns? Christ Jesus, who died—more than that, who was raised to life—is at the right hand of God and is also interceding for us" (Romans 8:33–34).

When in a dream the accuser of the brethren confronted Martin Luther with a daunting list of his sins, he penitently owned them all as his. Then, turning to his accuser he said, "Yes, they are all mine, but write across them all 'The blood of Jesus, his Son, purifies us from all sin'" (1 John 1:7). That is the perfect and adequate answer to every accusation of Satan.

THE ACQUITTING JUDGE

When God chose Israel as the nation and Jerusalem as the city through which He would bring blessing to the whole world, He foreknew their whole tragic rebellious future. Their actions and reactions did not take Him by surprise, any more than do ours. It was as though He said, "I chose Israel and Jerusalem knowing all they would be and do. I did not choose them because they were greater or better than other nations, but because I set My love upon them. No accusation you can bring against them will cause My purposes of grace to fail. Is not this a burning stick snatched from the fire?"

That is a message of encouragement for the disciple who has lost touch with God. Even with the memory of our most recent failure before us, it is still true that knowing all, God chose us before the foundation of the world (Ephesians 1:4). Although they have not surprised Him, our sins have deeply grieved our loving Father. But His foreknowledge did not quench His love. Because all the charges that could be brought against us were answered at the cross, He is able to rebuke and silence the accuser. True, we are just burning sticks snatched from the fire, but the Lord still has a purpose for our lives, as He had for Joshua's.

There is boundless comfort in the fact that although Joshua had a malicious and vindictive accuser, he also had an almighty Advocate. It is to our own loss that we so often listen to the voice of the accuser but do not hear the reassuring voice of our Advocate.

I hear the Accuser roar
Of evils I have done.
I know them all, and thousands more,
Jehovah findeth none.

THE RECOMMISSIONING LORD

There were four steps in Joshua's recommissioning and reinstatement.

He Was Cleansed. "Take off his filthy clothes" (Zechariah 3:4).

The words were addressed to the bystanders. Clothes, of course, stand for the character with which we are clothed. Filthy clothes signify impurity and sin in character. God will not rest, will not cease disturbing our lives until they are removed, and we should be glad that that is the case.

Nothing unclean can enter in,
When God in glory reigns,
His eyes so pure cannot endure
The sight of spots and stains.
—J. Nicholson

It would not be sufficient for the old clothes to be covered with new, leaving the filthy ones beneath. Every sinful and disqualifying thing must be removed. Both Paul and Peter exhort us to "put off the old man" (KJV)—the man of old—the nature we inherited from the first Adam. Doing that involves an act of the will, an act of decisive renunciation. We do not grow out of dirty clothes; we put them off. It is not necessarily a long, drawn-out process. It can be done suddenly and permanently. We can say, "I am done with that sinful habit, that doubtful thing, that unlawful association." When we take that attitude, we will find the Holy Spirit there to strengthen us to maintain that stand.

He Was Clothed. "Then he said to Joshua, 'See, I have taken away your sin, and I will put rich garments on you'" (Zechariah 3:4).

Cleansing was the prelude to clothing. What balm those words must have brought to Joshua's troubled spirit, as every disqualification to further service for the Lord was removed.

The reference here is to the festal attire of the high priest. Removal of the filthy garments and cleansing from impurity were purely negative in significance. But God had something glorious with which to replace them—a wardrobe with rich attire suitable to fit and grace any figure and qualified to move in any company.

Augustine had lived his early years in sin and licentiousness, despite the prayers and tears of his godly mother, Monica, until one day he heard a voice say, "Take and read." He took up his Bible and read: "Let us behave decently . . . not in orgies and drunkenness, not in sexual immorality and debauchery, not in dissension and jealousy. Rather, *clothe yourselves with the Lord Jesus Christ,* and do not think about how to gratify the desires of the sinful nature" (Romans 13:13–14)

God spoke to him powerfully through those words. He said to himself, "I have spent all my time allowing the flesh to tyrannize over me, and now God has commanded me to put on the Lord Jesus Christ." By an act of his will he appropriated Christ as the complement of his every need, and from that very hour his life was completely transformed. The profligate became one of the greatest Christian leaders in antiquity.

God's wonderful wardrobe is at our disposal. It is for us, by a definite act of the will, to put off "the garments spotted by the flesh"—to renounce and have done with them. Christ waits to be appropriated to meet all our daily and hourly needs.

Every need so fully met in Jesus,
Not a longing that He will not fill,
Not a burden but His love will lighten,
Not a storm but His own peace will still.
—J. Stuart Holden

He Was Crowned. "Then I said, 'Put a clean turban on his head'" (Zechariah 3:5).

It would appear that up to this time Zechariah had been only an awestruck observer. But now, when he saw Joshua cleansed and clothed in rich garments, he interrupted excitedly and said, "Complete the restoration! Put a clean turban on his head!" He was referring to the turban of the high priest that bore the golden plate inscribed with the words "Holiness to the Lord." It was on this turban, too, that the fragrant anointing oil was poured. "So they put a clean turban on his head" (v. 5). The restoration was complete. His priestly authority could once again be exercised.

He Was Commissioned. "The angel of the LORD gave this charge to Joshua: 'This is what the LORD Almighty says: "If you will walk in my ways and keep my requirements, then you will govern my house and have charge of my courts, and I will give you a place among these standing here"'" (vv. 6–7).

The pardoning Lord had done His part magnanimously. It now remained only for Joshua to accept the charge, enjoy the privileges that were bestowed, and walk in His ways. In New Testament language, that would be the equivalent of "walking in the Spirit."

Joshua was not only recommissioned but was admitted to privileges he had never before enjoyed—the right of access to the immediate presence of God and admission into the very counsels of the Almighty.

CHAPTER 19

The Disciple's Dynamic

I am going to send you what my Father has promised; but stay in the city until you have been clothed with power from on high.

LUKE 24:49

You will receive power when the Holy Spirit comes on you; and you will be my witnesses.

ACTS 1:8

In these words, spoken before His ascension, Jesus urged His disciples not to embark on their public ministry until they were clothed—endued—with power from on high. He Himself had set the example. Despite His holy life, He did not embark on His public ministry until after "he saw the Spirit of God descending like a dove and lighting on him" (Matthew 3:16).

The disciples heeded His command, and on the day of Pentecost "all of them were filled with the Holy Spirit" (Acts 2:4). Until that time they had caused little stir, but before long they were being called "these men who have turned the world upside down." The dynamic power of the Holy Spirit transformed their ministry and made it mightily effective.

In these days when there is a good deal of confusion about the ministry and operations of the Holy Spirit, it is easy for zeal for opposing views to breed intolerance and to negate the spirit of love that Jesus said was the evidence of true discipleship. We should by all means speak the truth as we see it, but it must be spoken in love (Ephesians 4:15).

The Holy Spirit is not to be conceived in terms of an emotional experience. He is not a mysterious, mystical influence that pervades one's being; nor is He a power, like electricity, which we can use for our purposes. He is a divine Person, equal with the Father and the Son in power and dignity; and He is equally to be loved, worshiped, and obeyed.

There is a line of teaching that leaves the impression that the Holy Spirit is a luxury for a spiritually elite group of advanced Christians and that those who do not have certain experiences are second-class citizens. But that is a misconception. Indeed, Jesus taught exactly the opposite. Hear His words:

> Which of you fathers, if your son asks for a fish, will give him a snake instead? Or if he asks for an egg, will give him a scorpion? If you then, though you are evil, know how to give good gifts to your children, *how much more* will your Father in heaven give the Holy Spirit to those who ask him! (Luke 11:11–13)

In a parallel passage, Jesus adds, "Which of you, if his son asks for bread, will give him a stone?" (Matthew 7:9).

Thus, in illustrating the nature and work of the Holy Spirit, the Lord does not compare Him with the luxuries of Eastern life but with the staple food in the everyday Eastern home—bread, fish, eggs. Meat was too expensive for the average home and was regarded as a luxury.

So the point Jesus was making was that the Holy Spirit is not to be regarded as a special luxury for the spiritual elite, but like bread, fish, and eggs, His ministry is indispensable for normal Christian living.

The same truth emerges in Paul's conversation with the Ephesian elders. He apparently detected a missing note in their experience so he asked them, 'Did you receive the Holy Spirit when you believed?' They answered 'No, we have not even heard that there is a Holy Spirit'" (Acts 19:2).

After instructing them in areas where their knowledge was deficient, Paul laid his hands on them and "the Holy Spirit came on them" (v. 6). The Holy Spirit had already been given on the day of Pentecost to the whole church, but the Ephesian elders had to believe that and appropriate the divine gift. That acknowledged lack accounted for their apparently anemic witness.

BE FILLED WITH THE SPIRIT

The command to be filled with the Spirit (Ephesians 5:18) is not directed to especially holy people, or to an advanced stage of the Christian life, any more than bread, fish, and eggs are reserved for adults and kept from children. The Holy Spirit's gracious ministry is an indispensable and universal need at every stage of the disciple's life. Being filled with the Spirit is the indispensable minimum for a full Christian life. God does not hold His children to the bare essentials of life, but He opens to us an inexhaustible reservoir of blessing.

The tense of the verb in Ephesians 5:18 gives the sense "Let the Holy Spirit keep on filling you"—a continuing action, as foretold by the Lord: "'If anyone is thirsty, let him come to me and drink. Whoever believes in me, as the Scripture has said, streams of living water will flow from within him.' *By this he meant the Spirit,* whom those who believed in him were later to receive" (John 7:37–39).

What does it mean to be "filled" in this passage? We are not passive receptacles waiting for something to be poured into us. We are vibrant personalities, capable of being controlled and guided by the Holy Spirit—and that is what the word means. In Ephesians 5:18, "Do not get drunk on wine" is set in opposition to "be filled with the Spirit." In other words, "Don't be controlled by the spirit of wine, which produces disorder, but be controlled by the Holy Spirit"—bring your life under His control.

The same word, *filled,* is used elsewhere of being filled with sorrow or with fear—emotions that can powerfully control our actions and reactions. So when I am filled with the Spirit, my personality is voluntarily and cooperatively surrendered to His control.

It seems strange that although the twelve apostles had enjoyed three years of concentrated individual instruction under the peerless Teacher, their lives were characterized more by weakness and failure than by power and success. Pentecost changed all that; they were filled with the Spirit. After His resurrection, Jesus assured them that that defect would be remedied.

THE PROMISE OF POWER

"*But you will receive power* when the Holy Spirit comes on you; and you will be my witnesses in Jerusalem, and in all Judea and Samaria, and to the ends of the earth." (Acts 1:8)

A craving for power of various kinds seems to be innate in human nature. That craving is not necessarily wrong, but its motivation must be carefully monitored. Power is not always a blessing. Hitler had power, but because it was not matched by purity, and its motivation was terribly wrong, it plunged the whole world into chaos. The devil has power—"his power and craft are great"—but he uses it for destruction.

Two words are used for power: *exousia*, meaning "authority," and *dunamis*, meaning "ability, power, energy." It was *dunamis* that the Lord promised His disciples. He spoke of no mere intellectual or political or oratorical power, but power that comes directly from God through the Holy Spirit—power that revolutionizes life and energizes for effective spiritual service.

Note the change in the disciples after they were filled with the Spirit and received the promised power. It is recorded that earlier, in the hour of their Master's greatest need, "they all forsook him and fled." But now "they were full of power." "They preached the word with boldness."

In nature the laws of power are fixed, as for example in electricity. Obey the law, and it will serve you. Disobey it, and it will destroy you.

The Holy Spirit is the greatest of all powers, and He acts according to the laws governing His power. Obey those laws, and He serves you. Transgress them, and power is short-circuited. Peter underlined one of those laws when he wrote of "the Holy Spirit, whom God has given to those who obey him" (Acts 5:32).

Before Pentecost, the apostles' witness had made a minimal impact; but after that transforming experience, their words had singular power.

In his Pentecost sermon, Peter spoke with such power that "they were cut to the heart and said, 'Brothers, what shall we do?'"

Words differ in their penetrating and convicting power. The words spoken by a man controlled by the Holy Spirit will produce conviction in his hearers, whereas the same words spoken by another not so endued will leave them unmoved. The difference is the presence or absence of "unction," the anointing of the Spirit.

In the experience of the disciples on and after the day of Pentecost, we are given a prototype of the essentials of the filling of the Spirit. From that time on they had:

A New Consciousness of Christ's Abiding Presence. In all their utterances and preaching, one gets the impression that Christ was just at their elbow. They were not reciting a piece, they were presenting a Person.

A New Likeness to Christ's Character. Through the now unhindered work of the Holy Spirit, they were being "transformed into his likeness" (2 Corinthians 3:18).

A New Experience of Christ's Power. When they conformed to the law of the power they craved but did not have, it was bestowed. Contrast "Why could not we cast [the demon] out?" (Matthew 17:19 KJV) with "These that have turned the world upside down are come hither also" (Acts 17:6 KJV).

One writer made the interesting observation that after

the Pentecost effusion, the apostles did not rent the upper room for holiness meetings: instead they went out into the street and witnessed to Christ.

Just as there is diversity in spiritual gifts, so there is diversity in the manner in which the Spirit works in different lives at different times. In one person, the result is seen in a passion for souls; in another, an unusually voracious appetite for the Word of God; in another, a great social concern. But it is "one and the selfsame Spirit" who is at work in each.

SOCIAL CONCERN

There is a tendency to think of the ministry of the Spirit only in connection with spiritual activities. But a study of the book of Acts reveals that He was involved in the social and racial problems His disciples faced, as well as in their ecclesiastical and economic concerns.

Jesus required the anointing of the Spirit and power, not only for vocal ministry but also for going about doing good (Acts 10:38). The power of the Spirit is needed as much for service in home, business, and community as in pulpit and church. Many of the 120 at Pentecost are never heard of again. Doubtless many went back home to live normal, godly lives. God sees and promises to reward the unrecognized workers.

Stephen was one of the seven chosen by the apostles to oversee the distribution of relief to the poor Hellenistic widows in the Jerusalem church. The apostles recognized that that was a right and necessary service, and they delegated the responsibility to other capable men. That was not because they themselves were above such menial service but because they had a primary responsibility that they were not prepared to neglect—the ministry of the Word and prayer. Others could minister to the needy—God had given them that gift—but they had their apostolic responsibility, which no one else could discharge.

One of the qualifications for this social ministry was that the men chosen should be "known to be full of the Spirit and wisdom" (Acts 6:3). Stephen's faithful discharge of this hidden social ministry later opened the way for the powerful preaching ministry that culminated in his martyrdom. One of the important ministries of the Spirit is to equip the disciple for effective service in the body of Christ.

There is one verse that holds great promise, but which, to me, appeared to be redundant. It is: "If you then, though you are evil, know how to give good gifts to your children, how much more will your Father in heaven give the Holy Spirit to those who ask him!" (Luke 11:13).

H. B. Swete points out that where "*the* Holy Spirit" occurs in the Greek, the reference is to the Holy Spirit as a *Person*. Where there is no definite article, just "Holy Spirit," the reference is to His operations and manifestations.

Thus in that verse Jesus was not encouraging them to ask for the Person of the Holy Spirit but for the operation of the Spirit they needed to effectively fulfill their ministry and do the will of God.

What a wonderful area of possibility this opens up to the disciple who is conscious of his own inadequacy.

Which operation of the Spirit do we need? Is it wisdom, power, love, purity, patience, discipline? *How much more* will your Father in heaven give that operation of the Spirit that is needed.

CHAPTER 20

The Disciple's Hope

The grace of God . . . teaches us to say "No" to ungodliness and worldly passions . . . while we wait for the blessed hope—the glorious appearing of our great God and Savior, Jesus Christ.
TITUS 2:11–13

Few intelligent disciples will challenge the contention that we are rapidly approaching the consummation of the age. Not the *end* of the age merely, for a campaign can come to an end with nothing achieved. *Consummation* means that the goal in view has been attained.

The New Testament constantly envisages the final triumph of Christ in time and within history. We are nowhere told to expect a cosmic Dunkirk, a rescue operation for a privileged generation. But we are encouraged to believe that there will be a complete world conquest for our glorious Lord and Savior.

The "blessed hope" of the disciple of Christ is not the rapture of the church, certain though that is, but "the glorious appearing of our great God and Savior, Jesus Christ." We humans are so self-centered that we tend to think of that glorious event in terms of what it will mean to us rather than what it will mean to Him. Even our hymns tend to be self-centered:

O that will be, glory for me,
Glory for me, glory for me.

The consummation of the age will be attained when Christ is crowned King of kings and Lord of lords and is acknowledged as such by the whole creation. It is toward this glorious event that the disciple's gaze should be directed.

SIGNS OF CHRIST'S RETURN

To a unique degree this generation has witnessed the universal and dramatic fulfillment of prophecy. Many of the signs Jesus said would herald His return have developed before our eyes.

The Evangelistic Sign. "This gospel of the kingdom will be preached in the whole world as a testimony to all nations, and then the end will come" (Matthew 24:14).

The Religious Sign. This prophecy has been fulfilled in our generation to a degree that has never before been the case. There is now no major nation in which there is no Christian witness. But as Christ has not yet returned, it is obvious that our task has not been fully completed.

"That day will not come until the rebellion occurs and the man of lawlessness is revealed" (2 Thessalonians 2:3).

Unfortunately, we can see this sign being fulfilled all around us. As Jesus foretold, the love of the many is growing cold (Matthew 24:12). But also in many parts of the world there is an unprecedented gathering of the harvest, so we do not need to be discouraged.

The Political Sign. Could prevailing world conditions have been more accurately and comprehensively described than in our Lord's words in Luke 21:25–26? "There will be signs . . . . On the earth, nations will be in anguish and perplexity . . . . Men will faint from terror, apprehensive of what is coming on the world."

The Jewish Sign. "Jerusalem will be trampled on by the Gentiles until the times of the Gentiles are fulfilled" (Luke 21:24).

There are broad and general signs that Jesus gave to His disciples as precursors of His return. These and many other signs have been intensified and have come to fulfillment in our day. For the first time in 2,500 years, Jerusalem is not dominated by Gentiles.

Jesus reserved one of His sharpest satires for the Pharisees who demanded a sign from heaven to prove that He had divine approval:

> When evening comes, you say, "It will be fair weather, for the sky is red," and in the morning, "Today it will be stormy, for the sky is red and overcast." You know how to interpret the appearance of the sky, but you cannot interpret the signs of the times. (Matthew 16:2–3)

Whatever view we hold regarding the details surrounding the second coming of Christ, if we fail to discern in these broad signs an intimation of the imminence of His return, we should warrant a similar rebuke. History is moving rapidly—not to cataclysm merely, but to consummation.

CHRIST'S RETURN CONTINGENT

The fact that our Lord has not yet returned is a clear indication that the task committed to the church, to make disciples of all nations, has yet to be completed. The uncertainty of the time of His return, rather than discouraging us, should spur us to more urgent endeavor. For His own wise purposes, God has chosen to make Himself dependent on the cooperation of His people.

Since, as we have seen, Jesus made His return contingent on our preaching the gospel as a testimony to all nations (Matthew 24:14), the responsibility of each and every disciple is clear. Peter spells it out for us:

> The day of the Lord will come like a thief. The heavens will disappear with a roar; the elements will be destroyed by fire . . . . Since everything will be destroyed in this way, what kind of people ought you to be? You ought to live holy and godly lives as you look forward to the day of God **and speed its coming**. (2 Peter 3:10–12)

The clause "speed its coming" is rendered "work to hasten it on" in some translations. Any seeming delay in Christ's return is not of His making. "The Lord is not slow in keeping his promise," Peter assures us (2 Peter 3:9). The delay, therefore, must be due to the disobedience of the church, which has been slack in its response to the Great Commission.

The above statement of Scripture could imply that the date of Christ's return is not so inexorably fixed that its timing could not be accelerated by the more rapid response of the church to His command. If that is the case, then the converse also is true—we can delay it by our disobedience.

Scripture appears to teach that three things are involved in the timing of Christ's return:

The Bride Must Be Ready in Some Degree. "Let us rejoice and be glad and give him glory! For the wedding of the Lamb has come, and *his bride has made herself ready.* Fine linen, bright and clean, was given her to wear. (Fine linen stands for the righteous acts of the saints.)" (Revelation 19:7–8).

It should be noted that this is something the bride does in anticipation of the return of the Bridegroom. The apostle John says the same thing in other words in his first letter: "Everyone who has this hope in him purifies himself, just as he is pure" (1 John 3:3).

Whatever else these verses may mean, a purging and purifying of the church is in view. Who will deny that the trauma and suffering of the last thirty years have not resulted in the emergence of a purer and more mature church in China? It is almost the antithesis of more affluent and indulgent churches in Western lands.

The Bride Must Be Complete Before He Comes. The apostle John's description of the multitude assembled in heaven is the picture of a group that is fully representative of humanity:

> After this I looked and there before me was a great multitude that no one could count, *from every nation, tribe, people and language*, standing before the throne and in front of the Lamb. They were wearing white robes and were holding palm branches in their hands. (Revelation 7:9)

Ever since the ascension of the Lord, the Holy Spirit has been busily at work finding a bride for Christ, and He has co-opted us for that privileged task. Not until the bride is complete—that is to say, until the last person has been won—will the Bridegroom come. The last stone has yet to be laid in the building, the last soul has yet to be won—and then He will come.

The Church Must Have Finished Its Task. This is more nearly the case than ever before in history. It can now be said for the first time that Christianity is known worldwide. But it is relevant here to ask the question: *Is the task of world-wide evangelism possible to complete in this generation,* thus to clear the way for Christ's return? No previous generation has achieved it, so should ours be the exception? I believe the answer is an unqualified yes. On the first recorded occasion when Jesus made mention of His church, He made a positive commitment: "On this rock I will build my church, and the gates of Hades will not overcome it" (Matthew 16:18).

God does not tantalize His children by requiring of them something that is impossible to achieve. John Wesley said in this connection, "I do not ask if the task is compassable—I ask only, Is it commanded?" Because Jesus commanded it, it is possible. Some generation, either now or in the future, will launch the final assault on the strongholds of Satan and will achieve final victory. Why should it not be ours?

If we listen to the voice of history, the task of completing world evangelization (not world conversion) does not seem so impossible.

In 500 B.C. Mordecai the Jew succeeded in distributing the decree of King Ahasuerus, granting the Jews the right of self-defense to all 127 provinces of the vast Persian Empire. It was a prodigious task. The royal secretaries

> wrote out all Mordecai's orders to the Jews, and to the satraps, governors and nobles of the 127 provinces stretching from India to Cush. These orders were written in the script of each province and the language of each people and also to the Jews in their own script and language. (Esther 8:9)

But note the urgency with which the couriers executed the king's command. "The couriers, riding the royal horses, raced out, spurred on by the king's command" (8:14). When one compares this zeal and haste to obey the king with the lethargy shown by the church to obey the orders of the King of kings, it puts us to shame. They had none of our modern inventions—no cars or airplanes, no printing presses, no postal service, and yet they achieved this prodigious task in nine months! That helps to put the possibility of achieving our task into perspective.

When revival came to the little colony founded by Count Nikolaus Zinzendorf at Herrnhut, Germany, there were only three hundred members. And yet, when the count died, in a day when foreign missions were almost unheard of, the Moravian church had sent out 296 missionaries to all Europe, North and South America, Africa, Greenland, and the West Indies. In twenty years, they sent out more missionaries than the evangelical churches had sent out in two centuries up to that time. For one hundred years the Moravian church conducted an unbroken chain of prayer, day and night.

THE MODERN CHALLENGE

Why has God reserved most of the great inventions for this generation, if not to facilitate and accelerate the spread of the gospel? Think of the advantages we enjoy compared with all previous generations:

- We have almost total mobility. With the advent of the airplane, the world has become a global village.
- Radio, television, and other electronic media have brought the whole world within range of the gospel.
- Improved linguistic techniques have greatly reduced the drudgery of language study.
- Ill health, which decimated the ranks of the early missionaries, is no longer as serious a menace.
- The church has abundant finance if members release it.
- There is an unparalleled reservoir of trained men and women.

Carl F. H. Henry, a well-informed Christian leader, maintains that seldom in history has the evangelical movement had such potential for world impact.

The task committed to us by our Lord is compassable. The motto that moved a previous generation of InterVarsity Christian Fellowship students to more urgent missionary endeavor—Evangelize to bring back the King—could well be revived.

Our generation will be without excuse if we fail our Lord. We must mobilize all our forces and resources and quicken the pace of missionary endeavor. The same Holy Spirit who empowered the early disciples to "turn the world upside down" (Acts 17:6 KJV) is at work in the world today.

Ralph D. Winter, one of the best-informed missiologists of our day, is not pessimistic about the future of missions, although he is well aware of the adverse factors. He writes: "The world is about to see the most concentrated [missionary] effort in history. It will be the final assault by the most potent missionary force ever gathered. The modern-day battalions of William Careys will be made up mostly of young people."

Is the bride keeping the Bridegroom waiting because she is not making herself ready? Because she has not completed her assignment?